THE AMERICAN SONNET

THE AMERICAN SONNET

An Anthology of Poems and Essays

EDITED BY
DORA MALECH AND
LAURA T. SMITH

University of Iowa Press   *Iowa City*

University of Iowa Press, Iowa City 52242
Copyright © 2022 by Dora Malech and Laura T. Smith
uipress.uiowa.edu
Printed in the United States of America

Design by Nola Burger

No part of this book may be reproduced or used in any form or by any means without permission in writing from the publisher. All reasonable steps have been taken to contact copyright holders of material used in this book. The publisher would be pleased to make suitable arrangements with any whom it has not been possible to reach.

Printed on acid-free paper

Library of Congress Cataloging-in-Publication Data
Names: Malech, Dora, editor. | Smith, Laura T., 1975– editor.
Title: The American Sonnet : An Anthology of Poems and Essays / edited by Dora Malech & Laura T. Smith.
Identifiers: LCCN 2022017117 (print) | LCCN 2022017118 (ebook) | ISBN 9781609388713 (paperback) | ISBN 9781609388720 (ebook)
Subjects: LCSH: Sonnets, American. | Sonnets, American—History and criticism.
Classification: LCC PS593.S6 A44 2022 (print) | LCC PS593.S6 (ebook) | DDC 811/.04209—dc23/eng/20220708
LC record available at https://lccn.loc.gov/2022017117
LC ebook record available at https://lccn.loc.gov/2022017118

"'This resonant, strange, vaulting roof': Contemporary Sonnets beyond Iambic Pentameter" by Anna Lena Phillips Bell previously appeared in April 2021 in *Annulet: A Journal of Poetics*.

Additional resources, references, and commentary appears at this book's companion website, www.theamericansonnet.com.

Introduction   1

POEMS

David Humphreys (1752–1818)
Sonnet III. On the Prospect of Peace, in 1783   9

Phillis Wheatley (1753–1784)
To the King's Most Excellent Majesty. 1768.   10

William Cullen Bryant (1794–1878)
Sonnet—To an American Painter Departing for Europe   11

Ralph Waldo Emerson (1803–1882)
Woods: A Prose Sonnet   12

Walt Whitman (1819–1892)
I Saw in Louisiana a Live-Oak Growing   13

Frederick Goddard Tuckerman (1821–1873)
That boy, the farmer said, with hazel wand   14
Sometimes I walk where the deep water dips   14

Helen Hunt Jackson (1831–1885)
Her Eyes   16

Emma Lazarus (1849–1887)
The New Colossus   17
Assurance   17

Lizette Woodworth Reese (1856–1935)
One Night   19

George Marion McClellan (1860–1934)
A January Dandelion   20

James Weldon Johnson (1871–1938)
Plácido's Farewell to His Mother   21

Paul Laurence Dunbar (1872–1906)
Slow through the Dark   22

Alexander Posey (1873–1908)
On the Capture and Imprisonment of Crazy Snake,
    January, 1900   23

Lola Ridge (1873–1941)
Electrocution   24

Amy Lowell (1874–1925)
The Matrix   25

Gertrude Stein (1874–1946)
Sonnets That Please   26

Robert Frost (1874–1963)
Hyla Brook   28

Alice Moore Dunbar-Nelson (1875–1935)
To Madame Curie   29

Lucian B. Watkins (1878–1920)
The New Negro   30

Leslie Pinckney Hill (1880–1960)
"So Quietly"   31

Mani Leyb (1883–1953)
A Plum   32

Elinor Wylie (1885–1928)
Sonnet   33

Fradel Shtok (1888–1952)
Sonnet   34

Claude McKay (1889–1948)
If We Must Die   35
America   35

Edna St. Vincent Millay (1892–1950)
from "Sonnets from an Ungrafted Tree"   37
Sonnet I   37

E. E. Cummings (1894–1962)
next to of course god america i   39

Ruth Muskrat Bronson (1897–1982)
from "Sonnets from the Cherokee"   40

Louise Bogan (1897–1970)
Roman Fountain ... 41

John Wheelwright (1897–1940)
Phallus ... 42

Langston Hughes (1902–1967)
from "Seven Moments of Love: An un-sonnet
   sequence in Blues" ... 43
Two Weeks ... 43

Countee Cullen (1903–1946)
From the Dark Tower ... 45

Helene Johnson (1906–1995)
A Missionary Brings a Young Native to America ... 46
Sonnet to a Negro in Harlem ... 46

Elizabeth Bishop (1911–1979)
Sonnet ... 48
Sonnet of Intimacy ... 48

Muriel Rukeyser (1913–1980)
Sonnet ... 50

Robert Hayden (1913–1980)
Frederick Douglass ... 51

Margaret Walker (1915–1998)
The Struggle Staggers Us ... 52

Robert Lowell (1917–1977)
History ... 53

Gwendolyn Brooks (1917–2000)
kitchenette building ... 54
the rites for Cousin Vit ... 54
A Lovely Love ... 55

Dunstan Thompson (1918–1975)
This Tall Horseman, My Young Man of Mars ... 56

Mary Ellen Solt (1920–2007)
moonshot sonnet ... 57

Mona Van Duyn (1921–2004)
The Beginning ... 58

Anthony Hecht (1923–2004)
The Feast of Stephen — 59

James Merrill (1926–1995)
The Broken Home — 62

James Wright (1927–1980)
May Morning — 66

Adrienne Rich (1929–2012)
from "Twenty-One Love Poems" — 67

Rhina P. Espaillat (b. 1932)
Butchering — 68

Sylvia Plath (1932–1963)
Sonnet: To Eva — 69

Ted Berrigan (1934–1983)
Sonnet XXXIV — 70

June Jordan (1936–2002)
Sunflower Sonnet Number Two — 71

Lucille Clifton (1936–2010)
the death of fred clifton — 72

Joan Larkin (b. 1939)
"Vagina" Sonnet — 73

Lyn Hejinian (b. 1941)
The Eye of the Storm — 74

Marilyn Hacker (b. 1942)
I want this love to be resilient — 76

Ellen Bryant Voigt (b. 1943)
The bride is in the parlor, dear confection — 77

Lorenzo Thomas (1944–2005)
MMDCCXIII½ — 78

Bernadette Mayer (b. 1945)
Sonnet (You jerk you didn't call me up) — 79

Kay Ryan (b. 1945)
New Rooms — 80
Say Uncle — 80

Wanda Coleman (1947–2013)
American Sonnet 18 — 82
American Sonnet 79 — 83

Marilyn Nelson (b. 1946)
Tears, through the patchwork drapery of dream — 84

Aaron Shurin (b. 1947)
I come to cafe, I sit, I bear — 85

Maggie Anderson (b. 1948)
Sonnet for Her Labor — 86

Richard Kenney (b. 1948)
Glass Is Not Crystalline — 87

Agha Shahid Ali (1949–2001)
Postcard from Kashmir — 88

Julia Alvarez (b. 1950)
from "33" — 89

Charles Bernstein (b. 1950)
Questionnaire — 90

Patricia Smith (b. 1955)
from "Salutations in Search Of" — 92

Diane Seuss (b. 1956)
The sonnet, like poverty, teaches you what you can do — 94

Henri Cole (b. 1956)
Arte Povera — 95

Carl Phillips (b. 1959)
Givingly — 96

Simone Muench (b.1969) and Jackie K. White (b. 1961)
Against Teleology — 97

Elizabeth Alexander (b. 1962)
When — 98

Tyehimba Jess (b. 1965)
Millie and Christine McKoy — 99

Natasha Trethewey (b. 1966)
Graveyard Blues — 100

Adrienne Su (b. 1967)
from "Four Sonnets about Food" — 101

Anna Maria Hong
Nude Palette — 102

giovanni singleton
from "The Black and White Sonnet Series" — 103

Philip Metres (b. 1970)
Ismail & Abla to Ahmed, Their Son — 104

Terrance Hayes (b. 1971)
American Sonnet for My Past and Future Assassin
   (The song must be cultural, confessional, clear) — 105
American Sonnet for My Past and Future Assassin
   (I lock you in an American sonnet that is part prison) — 105

Jen Bervin (b. 1972)
from "Nets" — 107

Nathan Spoon (b. 1972)
Kiddo — 109

Douglas Kearney (b. 1974)
Sonnet Done Red — 110

Joyelle McSweeney (b. 1976)
from "Toxic Sonnets" — 111

Jericho Brown (b. 1976)
Duplex — 112
The Tradition — 113

Brandy Nālani McDougall (b. 1976)
from "Ka ʻŌlelo: ʻelima" — 114

Natalie Diaz (b. 1978)
My American Crown — 115

Tarfia Faizullah (b. 1980)
Reading Celan at the Liberation War Museum — 117

Craig Santos Perez (b. 1980)
Love in a Time of Climate Change — 122

Tacey M. Atsitty (b. 1982)
Lacing: XII — 123

Meg Day (b. 1984)
from "Boy Corona": Crucifying — 124

Lo Kwa Mei-en (b. 1987)
The Alien Crown (The conquerers came and wrote the
conquered into being) — 126

Nate Marshall (b. 1989)
African american literature — 127

torrin a. greathouse (b. 1994)
Ars Poetica *or* Sonnet to Be Written across My Chest & Read
in a Mirror, Beginning with a Line from Kimiko Hahn — 128

ESSAYS

THE NATIONAL AND GLOBAL SONNET

Jahan Ramazani
Self-Metaphorizing "American" Sonnets — 133

Benjamin Crawford
The Rising Poems of America: Nationalistic Origins
of the American Sonnet — 146

John James
Origins of Rupture: Emerson, Wheatley, and the Early
American Sonnet — 153

Gillian Huang-Tiller
E. E. Cummings: The Iconic Metasonnet and the Cultural
Emblem of the American "i/Eye" — 161

Timo Müller
Sonnets into the American: Translation and Transnation
in the Harlem Renaissance — 170

Walt Hunter
Claude McKay's Lonely Planet: The Sonnet Sequence
    and the Global City   177

Matthew Kilbane
John Wheelwright, Sound Engineer   182

Donna Denizé
The Resonances of McKay's Sonnet Voice, Then and Now   191

WHOSE SONNET?

Carl Phillips
Whose Sonnet? (A Transgression)   201

Nathan Spoon
The Sonnet As: Neuroqueerness in the American Sonnet   207

Ariel Martino
"From the you to me": Interpersonal Exchange in
    Margaret Walker's *For My People* Sonnet Sequence   214

Lisa L. Moore
The Sonnet Is Not a Luxury   221

Jodie Childers
Mapping Radical Poetic Geographies: The Sonnets of
    Frank X Walker and Maggie Anderson   229

Michael Dumanis
Subverting the Tradition in *The Tradition*: Jericho Brown's
    Reconceptualization of the Sonnet   235

Meg Day
Deafing the Sonnet   242

WRESTLING WITH THE LANGUAGE AND TRADITION

Hollis Robbins
Wrestling with the Language: Dialect and Form in
    Paul Laurence Dunbar   249

Zoë Pollak
Sensuous Waste in the Sonnets of
    Frederick Goddard Tuckerman   255

Jonathan F. S. Post
Frost in the Company of Shakespeare and Wordsworth   260

Michael Theune
Strange Voltas   267

Lesley Wheeler
Partial Visibility: Short-Lined Sonnets   273

Nate Mickelson
Sonnets and/as Boxes: Ken Taylor, Joseph Cornell,
    and the New Lyric Studies   278

Rebecca Morgan Frank
Standing in One Place to Move: The Repeated-Line Sonnet   285

Anna Lena Phillips Bell
"This resonant, strange, vaulting roof":
    Contemporary Sonnets beyond Iambic Pentameter   291

Diana Leca
Kay Ryan's Miniature Sonnets   296

Marlo Starr
Restaging the American "Freakshow" in *Olio:*
    Tyehimba Jess's Syncopated Sonnets   304

HOME, INTERIORITY, INTIMACY

Stephen Regan
Broken Hearts and Broken Homes: The Desolation
    of the American Sonnet   313

Eleanor Wakefield
Helene Johnson's "Barbaric Songs," "Choked"   319

Tess Taylor
But Could a Dream: Form and Freedom in
    Gwendolyn Brooks's Domestic Sonnets   326

Jon Woodson
Gwendolyn Brooks's Esoteric Sonnet "A Lovely Love"
   as an Alchemical Metatext   333

Anna Maria Hong
Three Mothers, Two Eves: Female Virtuosity and
   Outrage in the American Sonnet   340

Jordan Finkin
A Plummy Sonnet by Mani Leyb   345

Abdul Ali
Eulogizing a Generation in Elizabeth Alexander's "When"   350

Yuki Tanaka
Animals and the Self in Henri Cole's *Middle Earth*   355

Acknowledgments   361
Index   362

THE AMERICAN SONNET

Introduction

DORA MALECH AND LAURA T. SMITH

Nearly eight hundred years since its invention, the sonnet is in a period of extraordinary production and development, taken up by poets of every aesthetic persuasion. In American poetry, some two dozen collections have centered on the sonnet in the past few years alone, often in book-length sequences. *The American Sonnet* celebrates the multiplicity of the contemporary sonnet while widening the historical lens to contextualize this flourishing in light of its deep roots—a centuries-long, ongoing, and varied tradition of reckoning with the sonnet. But more, as this volume shows, the American sonnet's story hinges on the work of historically marginalized poets, even as, or perhaps because, the sonnet has long functioned as a poetic bellwether, as poets seek to engage with forebears and tradition as they negotiate public and private questions of nation, race, class, gender, sexuality, and diaspora within the form's peculiar confines.

American sonneteers early and late often write as if they are asserting the right to belong—or aren't sure they want to belong—to the history of the sonnet, explicitly weaving their own landscape, politics, and interiority into the tradition, sometimes showing the seams, and sometimes not. And while some in each generation have held the sonnet up as either the crowning jewel or an irrelevant relic of a poetic past, others have continued to plumb and sound its ongoing present. Despite a litany of challenges to the sonnet's relevance, from early American suspicion of poetry in favor of the intellectual and moral rigors of prose to the modernist imperative to "make it new" to feminist concerns that fixed forms don't allow for "authentic experience or individual speech" (Keller 261), 250 years of American writers have claimed the form as theirs to use and shape.

The American Sonnet traces this tradition of a socially and politically engaged—even radical—American sonnet to the present day and makes these lineages visible in their multiplicity. The poems and essays in this volume also illustrate the aesthetic debates that have accompanied the American sonnet as generations of marginalized writers—Indigenous, Black, feminist, Jewish, queer—questioned the politics and value of the sonnet form for literary representation, reshaping this prestige form to their needs. The American sonnet has long been used by marginalized writers as a shape through which to claim literary and social space and voice as their negotiations with prosodic and thematic conventions form a transhistorical discourse and a transformative literary tradition.

American negotiation with the sonnet form is not new. In 1849, the same year that *The North American Review* featured William Cullen Bryant's translation of Afro-Cuban poet Plácido, a roundup of "The Female Poets of America" praised the poems of writer and women's rights activist Elizabeth Oakes Smith, while noting that she "has shown a partiality for the form of verse generally called a sonnet, but which is not entitled to be so called" (430). Holding the form to the conventions of the Italian sonnet—particularly the limit of two rhymes in the sestet, disqualifying Shakespeare and even Petrarch at times—the reviewer insists: "Those who wish to have a perfect idea of the sonnet, so as to fully appreciate its harmony and grace, are recommended not to take as a model any English [language] writer. In this country, the rules seem to be set at defiance, only that of the number of lines being regarded" ("Female Poets" 431–32). While it is interesting to note that our contemporary conversation about what "counts" and doesn't "count" as a sonnet is far from new—and this collection's wide embrace is more interested in the conversation enacted *in* form than in any critical attempt to shut the sonnet's gates—it helps to have a sense of the form's history and the historical contexts in which it has persisted. For example, Lucian B. Watkins's 1923 "The New Negro" (*p. 30*) articulates a vision of the new Black man who "thinks in black," as it eschews the English and finds form in the "perfection" of the traditional Italian sonnet, down to the two rhymes of the sestet. That its octave only has two rhymes as well gives the sense, perhaps, of the repetitions of a tolling bell—the hour of a reckoning long overdue, culminating (in rhyme and life), with a call to Black power. Yes, the American sonnet often "seems to be set at defiance," but as in Watkins's "The New Negro," that defiance can take many forms—including the most prosodically traditional.

The sonnets collected in this volume, comprising a selection of the poems and poets discussed in the essays, are representative of a broad and eclectic range of eras and aesthetics but are hardly exhaustive. We have complemented (and perhaps complicated) them with a few personal choices as well that engage the essays in interesting ways or more fully articulate the diversity of the sonnet in America. The flourishing of the contemporary American sonnet in the past few decades is part of the inspiration for this collection, and a sampling of that output is represented in these pages, but in balancing the contemporary with the historical, we make the case that the cultural and aesthetic diversity and the topical, often subversive discourse in American sonnets is no new phenomenon, but a long-standing tradition in and of itself. We have often made the choice to represent underanthologized writers and poems that tell that story.

Following a historical selection of sonnets, organized chronologically by poet, we have grouped the selected essays around four areas of shared concern. These groupings build discourse, not borders, between essays, and we hope readers will take note of the ways in which the essays—like the poems they discuss—defy or bridge classification. As each essay section follows a rough chronology, it also emphasizes connections across literary periods and movements within the American sonnet tradition and represents a range of critical voices, genres, and methodologies that present the burgeoning field of American sonnet studies.

"The National and Global Sonnet" positions the tradition in light of both national belonging and international exchange. While "Americanness" is a concept that inspires pride for some, for many it has long been experienced instead as a political cudgel, a purity test, or a broken promise. Why mention America at all? The poets and scholars collected in *The American Sonnet* address that question in myriad ways, often shaped by the interplay between American mythologies and American realities. From Louis Untermeyer's acknowledgment of "hybrid, idiomatic, or 'American' sonnets" (58) in 1935 to Wanda Coleman's description of her "American Sonnet" as a "jazz sonnet"—improvisational, free but formal, uniquely American in its lineage—Americanness in the sonnet has long been formulated as an aesthetic and thematic departure from European tradition. The essays in this section, however, also articulate the oppositional potential of the American sonnet *intra*nationally, questioning America itself, and further reveal political and cultural solidarity across borders through translation networks and political communities of exchange, articulating multicultural, multilingual, and transnational identities that complicate easy categories of national belonging.

"Whose Sonnet?" continues to press the question of belonging for female, Black, queer, trans, neurodiverse, working class, Appalachian, and Deaf poets writing the sonnet, historical and contemporary. The essays and poems featured recover histories, construct and reclaim lineages, illustrate modes of access, and show the sonnet as a ready site of resistance. Through craft essays, close readings, and scholarly analyses, this section argues that questions of form, identity, access, and power are germane to the sonnet, to what Carl Phillips calls its "inherent sonic restlessness." And it's true, while the sonnet's proportions can conjure a sense of mathematical balance (at times evoking aesthetic ideals such as the golden ratio or rule of thirds), its relationship with *im*balance is perhaps what's most striking. Just to scratch the surface of the sonnet's enduring thematic association with love has always been to reveal its equally enduring relationship with power.

While essays throughout the volume engage form, the third section, "Wrestling with the Language and Tradition" brings these questions to the fore, highlighting formal and aesthetic negotiations from Frederick Goddard Tuckerman and Paul Laurence Dunbar to the present. Poets and scholars together explicate poets' engagements with metrical variation, lineation, stanzaic structure, volta, rhyme, repetition, the visuality of the sonnet, and the conceptual sonnet tradition.

The final section, "Home, Interiority, Intimacy" examines the sonnet as an ongoing space for domestic and intimate negotiation in the contexts of public and private living and loss that span this collection. As they focus on such spaces of affect, these essays acknowledge that engagement not only with love but also with trauma is central to the tradition of the American sonnet.

This volume builds on readings and talks presented at the Sonnets from the American virtual symposium in October 2020, an event that itself became a kind of metaphor for the life of the sonnet as participants in a constellation of private rooms connected in lively discourse across time zones and oceans through screens' small boxes—a confined space capable of global intimacies. In keeping with these origins, this volume extends beyond these pages and back into virtual space as the collection expands on this project's website, theamericansonnet.com. We encourage you to continue your reading there.

Works Cited

Coleman, Wanda. Email to Paul E. Nelson. 23 Nov. 2008; paulenelson.com/workshops/wanda-coleman-american-sonnets/.

Griswold, Rufus Wilmot. "The Female Poets of America." *North American Review*, vol. 68, no. 143. Boston, MA, Little and Brown, April 1849, pp. 413–36.

Keller, Lynn. "Measured Feet in 'Gender-Bender Shoes.'" *Feminist Measures: Soundings in Poetry and Theory*, edited by Lynn Keller and Cristanne Miller, U of Michigan P, 1994, pp. 260–86.

Untermeyer, Louis. "Merrill Moore: Comment on His 'American Sonnet.'" *The Sewanee Review*, vol. 43, no. 1, Jan.–Mar. 1935, pp. 58–61.

POEMS

David Humphreys (1752–1818)

Sonnet III. On the Prospect of Peace, in 1783

From worlds of bliss, above the solar bounds,
Thou, Peace! descending in these skirts of day,
Bring heav'nly balm to heal my country's wounds,
Joy to my soul, and transport to my lay!

   Too long the cannon, 'mid the grim array
Of charging hosts, insufferably roar'd;
When rose th' Almighty pow'r, with sovereign sway,
To end the battle mutual inroads gor'd,
Spare squander'd blood, and sheath the wearied sword.

   Now bids that voice divine th' invaders yield,
From glooms of midnight morn's gay prospects rise:
There, see the dawn of heav'n's great day reveal'd,
Where new auroras dim our dazzled eyes,
Flash o'er th' Atlantic waves, and fire the western skies!

David Humphreys, who served as a Revolutionary War colonel, is distinguished both as America's earliest sonneteer and as progenitor of a sonnet that takes nation as theme in the American context. See Benjamin Crawford's essay (*pp. 146–52*).

SOURCE: David Humphreys, "Sonnet III. On the Prospect of Peace, in 1783," *The Miscellaneous Works* (New York: T. and J. Swords, 1804), p. 233.

Phillis Wheatley (1753–1784)

To the King's Most Excellent Majesty. 1768.

Your subjects hope, dread Sire—
The crown upon your brows may flourish long,
And that your arm may in your God be strong!
O may your sceptre num'rous nations sway,
And all with love and readiness obey!

But how shall we the *British* king reward!
Rule thou in peace, our father, and our lord!
Midst the remembrance of thy favours past,
The meanest peasants most admire the last.
May *George*, beloved by all the nations round,
Live with heav'n's choicest constant blessings crown'd!

Great God, direct, and guard him from on high,
And from his head let ev'ry evil fly!
And may each clime with equal gladness see
A monarch's smile can set his subjects free!

In this highly formal fifteen-line poem to England's King George III, and throughout her oeuvre, *Phillis Wheatley* writes in dialogue with European and American poetic conventions, including the sonnet. One might read the unrhymed, short-footed first line as an address leading into the sonnet-shaped fourteen lines that follow, the echo of a sonnet's turn at the beginning of the second stanza, and the sonnet's closure in the final couplet, with its freedom call. See John James's essay (*pp. 153–60*).

SOURCE: Phillis Wheatley, "To the King's Most Excellent Majesty. 1768," *Poems on Various Subjects, Religious and Moral*, reprinted from the London edition. (London: A. Bell; Boston: Cox and Berry, 1773), p. 17.

William Cullen Bryant (1794–1878)

Sonnet—To an American Painter Departing for Europe

Thine eyes shall see the light of distant skies:
    Yet, Cole! thy heart shall bear to Europe's strand
    A living image of thy native land,
Such as on thy own glorious canvass lies.
Lone lakes—savannahs where the bison roves—
    Rocks rich with summer garlands—solemn streams—
    Skies, where the desert eagle wheels and screams—
Spring bloom and autumn blaze of boundless groves.
Fair scenes shall greet thee where thou goest—fair,
    But different—every where the trace of men,
    Paths, homes, graves, ruins, from the lowest glen
To where life shrinks from the fierce Alpine air.
    Gaze on them, till the tears shall dim thy sight,
    But keep that earlier, wilder image bright.

William Cullen Bryant, an early champion of a distinctively American literature, draws on devotional and Romantic sonnet traditions to paint an idealized continent infused with strains of transcendentalism and nationalism.

SOURCE: William Cullen Bryant, "Sonnet—To an American Painter Departing for Europe," *Poems* (New York: E. Bliss, 1832), p. 184.

Ralph Waldo Emerson (1803–1882)

Woods: A Prose Sonnet

Wise are ye, O ancient woods! wiser than man. Whoso goeth in your paths or into your thickets where no paths are, readeth the same cheerful lesson whether he be a young child or a hundred years old. Comes he in good fortune or bad, ye say the same things, & from age to age. Ever the needles of the pine grow & fall, the acorns on the oak, the maples redden in autumn, & at all times of the year the ground pine & the pyrola bud & root under foot. What is called fortune & what is called Time by men— ye know them not. Men have not language to describe one moment of your eternal life. This I would ask of you, o sacred Woods, when ye shall next give me somewhat to say, give me also the tune wherein to say it. Give me a tune of your own like your winds or rain or brooks or birds; for the songs of men grow old when they have been often repeated, but yours, though a man have heard them for seventy years, are never the same, but always new, like time itself, or like love.

Ralph Waldo Emerson makes an argument for a transcendentalist-inflected, organic form sonnet: "like the spirit of a plant or an animal, it has architecture of its own, and adorns nature with a new thing." See John James's essay (*pp. 153–60*).

SOURCE: Ralph Waldo Emerson, "Woods: A Prose Sonnet," Entry [365], Journal D, *The Journals and Miscellaneous Notebooks of Ralph Waldo Emerson*, vol. 7, 1838–1842, edited by A. W. Plumstead and Harrison Hayford (Cambridge, MA: The Belknap Press of Harvard University Press), p. 248. Copyright © 1969 by the President and Fellows of Harvard College. Used by permission. All rights reserved.

Walt Whitman (1819-1892)

I Saw in Louisiana a Live-Oak Growing

I saw in Louisiana a live-oak growing,
All alone stood it, and the moss hung down from the branches;
Without any companion it grew there, uttering joyous leaves of dark green,
And its look, rude, unbending, lusty, made me think of myself;
But I wonder'd how it could utter joyous leaves, standing alone there without its friend, its lover near—for I knew I could not;
And I broke off a twig with a certain number of leaves upon it, and twined around it a little moss,
And brought it away—and I have placed it in sight in my room;
It is not needed to remind me as of my own dear friends,
(For I believe lately I think of little else than of them;)
Yet it remains to me a curious token—it makes me think of manly love;
—For all that, and though the live-oak glistens there in Louisiana, solitary, in a wide flat space,
Uttering joyous leaves all its life without a friend, a lover, near,
I know very well I could not.

While *Walt Whitman*'s expansive poetics might seem at odds with the sonnet's structural confinement, Whitman greatly admired Shakespeare's sonnets ("For superb finish, style, beauty, I know of nothing in all literature to come up to these sonnets") and, in an early manuscript, described the sequence of which "I saw in Louisiana a Live-Oak Growing" is the second as "A Cluster of Poems, Sonnets expressing the thoughts, pictures, aspirations." Robert Hass has called this thirteen-line poem "perhaps the first free verse sonnet."

SOURCE: Walt Whitman, "I Saw in Louisiana a Live-Oak Growing," *Leaves of Grass* (New York: W. E. Chapin & Co., Printers, 1867), p. 135.

Frederick Goddard Tuckerman (1821–1873)

That boy, the farmer said, with hazel wand

That boy, the farmer said, with hazel wand
Pointing him out, half by the haycock hid,
Though bare sixteen, can work at what he's bid
From sun till set, to cradle, reap, or band.
I heard the words, but scarce could understand
Whether they claimed a smile or gave me pain:
Or was it aught to me, in that green lane,
That all day yesterday, the briars amid,
He held the plough against the jarring land
Steady, or kept his place among the mowers
Whilst other fingers, sweeping for the flowers,
Brought from the forest back a crimson stain?
Was it a thorn that touched the flesh, or did
The pokeberry spit purple on my hand?

Sometimes I walk where the deep water dips

Sometimes I walk where the deep water dips
Against the land. Or on where fancy drives
I walk and muse aloud, like one who strives
To tell his half-shaped thought with stumbling lips,
And view the ocean sea, the ocean ships,
With joyless heart: still but myself I find
And restless phantoms of my restless mind:
Only the moaning of my wandering words,
Only the wailing of the wheeling plover,
And this high rock beneath whose base the sea
Has wormed long caverns, like my tears in me:
And hard like this I stand, and beaten and blind,
This desolate rock with lichens rusted over,
Hoar with salt-sleet and chalkings of the birds.

Frederick Goddard Tuckerman's sonnets meditate on decomposition in delayed and extended rhymes, evading prosodic and thematic closure. As Zoë Pollak writes (*pp. 255–59*), they "force us to sit with these raw subjects and struggle over how to (re)digest them."

SOURCE: Frederick Goddard Tuckerman, "That boy, the farmer said, with hazel wand," *Poems* (Boston: Ticknor and Fields, 1864), II:I, p. 199; "Sometimes I walk where the deep water dips," *The Sonnets of Frederick Goddard Tuckerman*, edited by Witter Bynner (London: Knopf, 1931), III:X, p. 122.

Helen Hunt Jackson (1831–1885)

Her Eyes

That they are brown, no man will dare to say
He knows. And yet I think that no man's look
Ever those depths of light and shade forsook,
Until their gentle pain warned him away.
Of all sweet things I know but one which may
Be likened to her eyes.   When, in deep nook
Of some green field, the water of a brook
Makes lingering, whirling eddy in its way,
Round soft drowned leaves; and in a flash of sun
They turn to gold, until the ripples run
Now brown, now yellow, changing as by some
Swift spell.   I know not with what body come
The saints. But this I know, my Paradise
Will mean the resurrection of her eyes.

Best remembered for her later prose writings protesting the United States government's treatment of Native Americans, *Helen Hunt Jackson*'s poetry also circulated widely. She was a lifelong, famous friend to the then obscure Emily Dickinson.

SOURCE: Helen Hunt Jackson, "Her Eyes," *Poems by Helen Jackson* (Boston: Roberts Brothers, 1893), p. 115.

Emma Lazarus (1849–1887)

The New Colossus

Not like the brazen giant of Greek fame,
With conquering limbs astride from land to land;
Here at our sea-washed, sunset gates shall stand
A mighty woman with a torch, whose flame
Is the imprisoned lightning, and her name
Mother of Exiles. From her beacon-hand
Glows world-wide welcome; her mild eyes command
The air-bridged harbor that twin cities frame.
"Keep, ancient lands, your storied pomp!" cries she
With silent lips. "Give me your tired, your poor,
Your huddled masses yearning to breathe free,
The wretched refuse of your teeming shore.
Send these, the homeless, tempest-tost to me,
I lift my lamp beside the golden door!"

Assurance

Last night I slept, and when I woke her kiss
Still floated on my lips. For we had strayed
Together in my dream, through some dim glade,
Where the shy moonbeams scarce dared light our bliss.
The air was dank with dew, between the trees,
The hidden glow-worms kindled and were spent.
Cheek pressed to cheek, the cool, the hot night-breeze
Mingled our hair, our breath, and went,
As sporting with our passion. Low and deep
Spake in mine ear her voice: "And didst thou dream,
This could be buried? This could be sleep?
And love be thralled to death! Nay whatso seem,
Have faith, dear heart; this is the thing that is!"
Thereon I woke and on my lips her kiss.

Emma Lazarus's "The New Colossus" is an aspirational American call of welcome by a woman born to a family of Jewish immigrants. Critic Zohar Weiman-Kelman situates "Assurance," unpublished until 1980, within the long genealogy of the lesbian sonnet. In a single body of work, these two poems represent the full spectrum of public and private modes available to the American sonnet.

SOURCES: Emma Lazarus, "Assurance," in "Manuscript notebook from the Emma Lazarus collection, 1877–1987," Center for Jewish History, 19. Included by permission of The American Jewish Historical Society. "The New Colossus," *The Poems of Emma Lazarus, vol 1* (Boston and New York: Houghton, Mifflin, and Company, 1889), pp. 202–3.

Lizette Woodworth Reese (1856–1935)

One Night

One lily scented all the dark. It grew
Down the drenched walk a spike of ghostly white.
Fine, sweet, sad noises thrilled the tender night,
From insects couched on blades that dripped with dew.
The road beyond, cleaving the great fields through,
Echoed no footstep; like a streak of light,
The gaunt and blossoming elder gleamed in sight.
The boughs began to quake, and warm winds blew,
And whirled a myriad petals down the air.
An instant, peaked and black the old house stood;
The next, its gables showed a tremulous gray,
Then deepening gold; the next, the world lay bare!
The moon slipped out the leash of the tall wood,
And through the heavenly meadows fled away.

A lifelong resident of Baltimore, *Lizette Woodworth Reese* was named Poet Laureate of Maryland in 1931. She identified strongly as a working woman and taught English in Baltimore schools for nearly fifty years, from 1873–1921. Her poems, including many sonnets, often documented everyday sights. She was well regarded in her lifetime but largely overlooked in the century that followed.

SOURCE: Lizette Woodworth Reese, "One Night," *A Handful of Lavender* (Boston and New York: Houghton, Mifflin, and Company, 1891), p. 73.

George Marion McClellan (1860–1934)

A January Dandelion

All Nashville is a chill. And everywhere
Like desert sand, when the winds blow,
There is each moment sifted through the air,
A powdered blast of January snow.
O! thoughtless Dandelion, to be misled
By a few warm days to leave thy natural bed,
Was folly growth and blooming over soon.
And yet, thou blasted yellow-coated gem,
Full many a heart has but a common boon
With thee, now freezing on thy slender stem.
When the heart has bloomed by the touch of love's warm breath
Then left and chilling snow is sifted in,
It still may beat but there is blast and death
To all that blooming life that might have been.

———

A teacher, principal, and Congregational minister in Nashville, as well as a poet and fiction writer, *George Marion McClellan* uses prosodic and imagistic strategies to convey racial discrimination as violence in nature. His sonnet places the sestet in the poem's center, creating a halting, unsettled quality that doesn't conform to a sonnet's expected trajectory.

SOURCE: George Marion McClellan, "A January Dandelion," *Poems* (Nashville: Publishing House A. M. E. Church Sunday School Union, 1895), p. 60.

James Weldon Johnson (1871–1938)

Plácido's Farewell to His Mother

> (*Written in the Chapel of the Hospital de Santa Cristina
> on the Night Before His Execution*)

If the unfortunate fate engulfing me,
The ending of my history of grief,
The closing of my span of years so brief,
Mother, should wake a single pang in thee,
Weep not. No saddening thought to me devote;
I calmly go to a death that is glory-filled,
My lyre before it is forever stilled
Breathes out to thee its last and dying note.

A note scarce more than a burden-easing sigh,
Tender and sacred, innocent, sincere—
Spontaneous and instinctive as the cry
I gave at birth—And now the hour is here—
O God, thy mantle of mercy o'er my sins!
Mother, farewell! The pilgrimage begins.

*Translation of "Despedida a Mi Madre" by Plácido
(Gabriel de la Concepción Valdés), 1809–1844*

Timo Müller's essay (*pp. 170–76*) attends to transnational affinities in translation of the African diaspora, including *James Weldon Johnson*'s translation of the outspoken anticolonial Afro-Cuban poet Plácido, situating the sonnet as an apt site not only for national politics but for border-crossing Black solidarity.

SOURCE: James Weldon Johnson, "Plácido's Farewell to His Mother," in appendix to *The Book of American Negro Poetry*, edited by James Weldon Johnson (New York: Harcourt, Brace, and Company, 1922), p. 207.

Paul Laurence Dunbar (1872–1906)

Slow through the Dark

Slow moves the pageant of a climbing race;
Their footsteps drag far, far below the height,
And, unprevailing by their utmost might,
Seem faltering downward from each hard won place.
No strange, swift-sprung exception we; we trace
A devious way thro' dim, uncertain light,—
Our hope, through the long vistaed years, a sight
Of that our Captain's soul sees face to face.
Who, faithless, faltering that the road is steep,
Now raiseth up his drear insistent cry?
Who stoppeth here to spend a while in sleep
Or curseth that the storm obscures the sky?
Heed not the darkness round you, dull and deep;
The clouds grow thickest when the summit's nigh.

———

One of the first Black authors to achieve widespread recognition in America, *Paul Laurence Dunbar* used the gravity of the traditional sonnet form (as in this Petrarchan sonnet's call to fortitude) to intentionally "balance" his famous dialect poems. See Hollis Robbins's essay (*pp. 249–54*).

SOURCE: Paul Laurence Dunbar, "Slow through the Dark," *Lyrics of Love and Laughter* (New York: Dodd, Mead and Company, 1903), pp. 135–36.

Alexander Posey (1873–1908)

On the Capture and Imprisonment of Crazy Snake, January, 1900

Down with him! chain him! bind him fast!
Slam to the iron door and turn the key!
The one true Creek, perhaps the last
To dare declare, "You have wronged me!"
Defiant, stoical, silent,
Suffers imprisonment!

Such coarse black hair! such eagle eye!
Such stately mien!—how arrow-straight!
Such will! such courage to defy
The powerful makers of his fate!
A traitor, outlaw,—what you will,
He is the noble red man still.

Condemn him and his kind to shame!
I bow to him, exalt his name!

Muskogee Creek writer and politician *Alexander Posey* uses a short-lined, couplet-heavy sonnet variation to honor Creek leader Chitto Harjo, an outspoken opponent of US allotment of tribal land. The final couplet allows for stark perspectival juxtaposition, drawing from European form while resisting the assumption of American allegiance or assimilation.

SOURCE: Alexander Lawrence Posey, "On the Capture and Imprisonment of Crazy Snake, January, 1900," *The Poems of Alexander Lawrence Posey*, edited by Minnie H. Posey (Topeka, KS: Crane, 1910), p. 88.

Lola Ridge (1873–1941)

Electrocution

He shudders... feeling on the shaven spot
The probing wind, that stabs him to a thought
Of storm-drenched fields in a white foam of light,
And roads of his hill-town that leap to sight
Like threads of tortured silver...while the guards—
Monstrous deft dolls that move as on a string,
In wonted haste to finish with this thing,
Turn faces blanker than asphalted yards.

They heard the shriek that tore out of its sheath
But as a feeble moan...yet dared not breathe,
Who stared there at him, arching—like a tree
When the winds wrench it and the earth holds tight—
Whose soul, expanding in white agony,
Had fused in flaming circuit with the night.

Born in Ireland, raised in New Zealand, and educated in Australia, *Lola Ridge* moved to America in 1907. A politically radical advocate of the proletariat, she wrote "Electrocution" before the execution of Sacco and Vanzetti, using the sonnet to architect a visceral indictment of state violence and its proxies.

SOURCE: Lola Ridge, "Electrocution," *Red Flag* (New York: The Viking Press, 1927), p. 65.

Amy Lowell (1874–1925)

The Matrix

Goaded and harassed in the factory
That tears our life up into bits of days
Ticked off upon a clock which never stays,
Shredding our portion of Eternity,
We break away at last, and steal the key
Which hides a world empty of hours; ways
Of space unroll, and Heaven overlays
The leafy, sun-lit earth of Fantasy.
Beyond the ilex shadow glares the sun,
Scorching against the blue flame of the sky.
Brown lily-pads lie heavy and supine
Within a granite basin, under one
The bronze-gold glimmer of a carp; and I
Reach out my hand and pluck a nectarine.

In "The Matrix," imagist *Amy Lowell* uses the duality of a Petrarchan sonnet to critique a fragmented and frenetic modern industrial conception of time, contrasting it with the timeless singularity afforded by imagination and the fantasy of a natural world untouched by industry.

SOURCE: Amy Lowell, "The Matrix," *A Dome of Many-Coloured Glass* (Boston and New York: Houghton, Mifflin, and Company, 1912), p. 85.

Gertrude Stein (1874–1946)

Sonnets That Please

I see the luck
And the luck sees me I see the lucky one be lucky.
I see the love
And the love sees me
I see the lovely love be lovely.
I see the bystander stand by me. I see the bystander stand by inside me.
I see.

Another Sonnet That Pleases

Please be pleased with me.
Please be.
Please be all to me please please be.
Please be pleased with me. Please please me. Please please please with me please please be.

Sonnets That Please

How pleased are the sonnets that please.
How very pleased to please.
They please.

Sonnets That Please

I please the ribbon the leather and all. I please the Christian world. I please the window the door and the bird. I please the Hindoos a third. And Elsie Janis.
I follow the sonnets that please with ease.
If we must part let us go together.
I miss a trick. I sit up quick, quickly.
Eddying

How often do I mention that I am not interested. She is so loyal so easily moved so quickly roman catholic so entrancing. And how plainly we speak. How caressingly, all nature eats every day.

I am persuaded still.

He was deceived by the color.

And now for Sunday.

A Sunday is measured by sawing.

Upright stands and swinging. We never sing.

Why not.

Because voices are so useful to me.

The sound of them. No the color of vegetables. Vegetables are flat and have no color.

Flowers are irregular and have a variety of color.

And rubbish. Rubbish lies in heaps when it is not a birthday. How sweetly birthdays bear their fruit. And trees, trees the leaves of trees are transparent, because they have been eaten.

I can make a description.

I am excessively sleepy.

Every day will be Sunday by and by.

And now we dream of ribbons and skies.

We will win prizes.

We will announce pleasures.

We will resume dresses.

How pleasantly we stutter.

Of the avant-garde *Gertrude Stein*'s posthumously published subversion of the sonnet sequence, Virgil Thompson wrote: "'Sonnets That Please' are exactly what the title says. They read like sonnets, feel like sonnets, sum up the sonnet by avoidance of all of its conventions save that of being expressions in the first person."

SOURCE: Gertrude Stein, "Sonnets That Please," *Bee Time Vine and Other Pieces, 1913–1927* (New Haven, CT, Yale University Press, 1969), pp. 220–21. Reprinted by permission of David Higham Associates.

Robert Frost (1874–1963)

Hyla Brook

By June our brook's run out of song and speed.
Sought for much after that, it will be found
Either to have gone groping underground
(And taken with it all the Hyla breed
That shouted in the mist a month ago,
Like ghost of sleigh-bells in a ghost of snow)—
Or flourished and come up in jewel-weed,
Weak foliage that is blown upon and bent
Even against the way its waters went.
Its bed is left a faded paper sheet
Of dead leaves stuck together by the heat—
A brook to none but who remember long.
This as it will be seen is other far
Than with brooks taken otherwise in song.
We love the things we love for what they are.

Robert Frost's innovations within and influence on the American sonnet, traced throughout this volume, include nonce and terza rima sonnets and the fifteen-line sonnet above. Jonathan Post writes that Frost's sonnets reflect the long tradition of "reshaping the courtly into the vernacular" (*pp. 260–66*).

SOURCE: Robert Frost, "Hyla Brook," *Mountain Interval* (New York: Henry Holt, 1916), p. 34.

Alice Moore Dunbar-Nelson (1875–1935)

To Madame Curie

Oft have I thrilled at deeds of high emprise,
And yearned to venture into realms unknown,
Thrice blessed she, I deemed, whom God had shown
How to achieve great deeds in woman's guise.
Yet what discov'ry by expectant eyes
Of foreign shores, could vision half the throne
Full gained by her, whose power fully grown
Exceeds the conquerors of th' uncharted skies?
So would I be this woman whom the world
Avows its benefactor; nobler far,
Than Sybil, Joan, Sappho, or Egypt's queen.
In the alembic forged her shafts and hurled
At pain, diseases, waging a humane war;
Greater than this achievement, none, I ween.

An early twentieth-century writer of poems, short stories, essays, and journals, *Alice Moore Dunbar-Nelson* was an advocate of African American and women's rights. In "To Madame Curie," Dunbar-Nelson writes into gendered affinity and admiration across race and nationality. One might place this poem in a sonnet-ode tradition, with Alexander Posey's sonnet for Crazy Snake (*p. 23*) and Robert Hayden's "Frederick Douglass" (*p. 51*).

SOURCE: Alice Moore Dunbar-Nelson, "To Madame Curie," *The Philadelphia Public Ledger*, August 21, 1921.

Lucian B. Watkins (1878–1920)

The New Negro

He thinks in black. His God is but the same
John saw—with hair "like wool" and eyes "as fire"—
Who makes the vision for which men aspire.
His kin is Jesus and the Christ who came
Humbly to earth and wrought His hallowed aim
'Midst human scorn. Pure is his heart's desire;
His life's religion lifts; his faith leads higher.
Love is his Church, and Union is its name.

Lo, he has learned his own immortal role
In this momentous drama of the hour;
Has read aright the heaven's Scriptural scroll
'Bove ancient wrong—long boasting in its tower.
Ah, he has sensed the truth. Deep in his soul
He feels the manly majesty of power.

A United States Army sergeant, poet, teacher, and native of Chesterfield County, Virginia, *Lucian B. Watkins* heralds the coming of the New Negro as a cultural and spiritual harbinger in this Petrarchan sonnet bookended by Black power.

SOURCE: Lucian B. Watkins, "The New Negro," *Negro Poets and Their Poems*, edited by Robert T. Kerlin (Washington, DC: Associated Publishers, 1923), p. 238.

Leslie Pinckney Hill (1880–1960)

"So Quietly"

News item from the *New York Times* on the lynching of a Negro at Smithville, Ga., December 21, 1919.

"The train was boarded so quietly... that members of the train crew did not know that the mob had seized the Negro until informed by the prisoner's guard after the train had left the town.... A coroner's inquest held immediately returned the verdict that West came to his death at the hands of unidentified men."

So quietly they stole upon their prey
And dragged him out to death, so without flaw
Their black design, that they to whom the law
Gave him in keeping, in the broad, bright day,
Were not aware when he was snatched away;
And when the people, with a shrinking awe,
The horror of that mangled body saw,
"By unknown hands!" was all that they could say.

So, too, my country, stealeth on apace
The soul-blight of a nation. Not with drums
Or trumpet blare is that corruption sown,

But quietly—now in the open face
Of day, now in the dark—and when it comes,
Stern truth will never write, "By hands unknown."

A Harvard graduate and lifelong educator, *Leslie Pinckney Hill*, whose father had been enslaved, served as president of what is now Cheyney University of Pennsylvania for nearly forty years. This Petrarchan sonnet documents a 1919 lynching and the lack of justice that followed.

SOURCE: Leslie Pinckney Hill, "So Quietly," *The Wings of Oppression* (Boston: The Stratford Co., 1921), pp. 17–18.

Mani Leyb (1883–1953)

A Plum

In the cool evening, the husband
plucked from the tree a ripe plum
together with its leaf, and bit into
its dewy blue skin. Then, set free,

the slumbering sap sprayed out
with cool foam. And so as to capture
all its juice—not losing a drop—
he walked slowly, as one carries a glass

of wine, with both hands full of plum,
bringing it to his wife and gently raising it
to her lips. Then she, with a charming

"Thank you," began gnawing the plum
from out of his hands. Till all that was left
were the skin, stone, and abounding foam.

Translated by Jordan Finkin

Like many of the sonnet writers in this collection who challenge (or reject) an "American" identity, Yiddish-language writers such as *Mani Leyb* complicate the assumption that an American sonnet is an English-language sonnet. For an in-depth look at Leyb's sonnet, see Jordan Finkin's essay (*pp. 345–49*); for a radically different Yiddish-language sonnet, see Fradel Shtok (*p. 34*).

SOURCE: Jordan Finkin, "A Plum," translation of Mani Leyb's "A Floym." Reprinted courtesy of author.

Elinor Wylie (1885–1928)

Sonnet

You are the faintest freckles on the hide
Of fawns; the hoofprint stamped into the slope
Of slithering glaciers by the antelope;
The silk upon the mushroom's under side
Constricts you, and your eyelashes are wide
In pools uptilted on the hills; you grope
For swings of water twisted to a rope
Over a ledge where amber pebbles glide.

Shelley perceived you on the Caucasus;
Blake imprisoned you in glassy grains of sand;
And Keats in goblin jars from Samarcand;
Poor Coleridge found you in a poppy-seed;
But you escaped the clutching most of us,
Shaped like a ghost, and imminent with speed.

Elinor Wylie (1885–1928) claims a lineage with the British Romantics in describing her sonnet's mysterious and sought-after subject. Popular in her own lifetime, feminist critics and scholars have once again recognized the value and distinction of Wylie's poetic work in recent decades.

SOURCE: Elinor Wylie, "Sonnet," *The Houston Post*, Sunday, July 30, 1922, p. 7.

Fradel Shtok (1888–1952)

Sonnet

My friend, my terrible friend, how you are evil,
And proudly chaste as any saintly John
who made the nights of the king's daughter sleepless.
And as she hated him, I hate you now.

Your face is not as pale and cool as ivory,
Your hair does not curl, writhing like young snakes,
Your youth's heart is not as pure as any other's—
So why am I engulfed by burning hate?

I hate you. I reiterate it now:
And as I dance the sinful dance once more,
I gesture at the bidding of the devil.

And for my dance he'll show his gratitude
With pay well-worthy of a sinful heart:
He'll give me what I crave—your lilac tongue.

Translated by Kathryn Hellerstein

Fradel Shtok's brief career belies the power of her sensual Yiddish-language poetry. This Salome-inspired poem reinvigorates the sonnet as space not only for declarations of love but for explorations of hate, violence, carnality, and power.

SOURCE: Kathryn Hellerstein, translation of Fradel Shtok, "Sonnet," *Jewish American Literature: A Norton Anthology*, edited by Jules Chametzky, John Felstiner, Hilene Flanzbaum, and Kathryn Hellerstein (New York: Norton, 2001), p. 294. Reprinted by permission of author.

Claude McKay (1889–1948)

If We Must Die

If we must die—let it not be like hogs
Hunted and penned in an inglorious spot.
While round us bark the mad and hungry dogs,
Making their mock at our accursèd lot.
If we must die—oh, let us nobly die,
So that our precious blood may not be shed
In vain; then even the monsters we defy
Shall be constrained to honor us though dead!

Oh, kinsmen! We must meet the common foe;
Though far outnumbered, let us still be brave,
And for their thousand blows deal one death-blow!
What though before us lies the open grave?
Like men we'll face the murderous, cowardly pack,
Pressed to the wall, dying, but—fighting back!

America

Although she feeds me bread of bitterness,
And sinks into my throat her tiger's tooth,
Stealing my breath of life, I will confess
I love this cultured hell that tests my youth!
Her vigor flows like tides into my blood,
Giving me strength erect against her hate.
Her bigness sweeps my being like a flood.
Yet, as a rebel fronts a king in state,
I stand within her walls with not a shred
Of terror, malice, not a word of jeer.
Darkly I gaze into the days ahead,
And see her might and granite wonders there,
Beneath the touch of Time's unerring hand,
Like priceless treasures sinking in the sand.

Jamaican-born *Claude McKay* emerges in this collection and beyond as a touchstone figure in the history and creation of the Black American sonnet as a form for racial pride, sociopolitical critique, and transnational engagement. Jahan Ramazani discusses "America" (*pp. 133–45*), and both Walt Hunter (*pp. 177–81*) and Donna Denizé (*pp. 191–99*) focus exclusively on McKay's sonnets.

SOURCES: Claude McKay, "America," *Harlem Shadows* (New York: Harcourt, Brace, 1922), p. 6; "If We Must Die," *The Liberator*, July 1919, p. 21.

Edna St. Vincent Millay (1892–1950)

from "Sonnets from an Ungrafted Tree"

I.

So she came back into his house again
And watched beside his bed until he died,
Loving him not all. The winter rain
Splashed in the painted butter-tub outside,
Where once her red geraniums had stood,
Where still their rotted stalks were to be seen;
The thin log snapped; and she went out for wood,
Bareheaded, running the few steps between
The house and shed; there, from the sodden eaves
Blown back and forth on ragged ends of twine,
Saw the dejected creeping-jinny vine,
(And one, big aproned, blithe, with stiff blue sleeves
Rolled to the shoulder that warm day in spring,
Who planted seeds, musing ahead to their far blossoming).

Sonnet I

Thou art not lovelier than lilacs,—no,
Nor honeysuckle; thou art not more fair
Than small white single poppies,—I can bear
Thy beauty; though I bend before thee, though
From left to right, not knowing where to go,
I turn my troubled eyes, nor here nor there
Find any refuge from thee, yet I swear
So it has been with mist,—with moonlight so.

Like him who day by day unto his draught
Of delicate poison adds him one drop more
Till he may drink unharmed the death of ten,
Even so, inured to beauty, who have quaffed
Each hour more deeply than the hour before,
I drink—and live—what has destroyed some men.

Edna St. Vincent Millay's (1892–1950) sustained engagement with the sonnet and its capacities influenced many writers, including Louise Bogan (*p. 41*) and Adrienne Rich (*p. 67*). Audre Lorde (whose heirs preferred not to reprint her early sonnet "Spring" in this volume without Lorde's own blessing) and Lucille Clifton (*p. 72*) both credited her sonnets as early inspirations (see Lisa L. Moore's essay, *pp. 221–28*). Millay's sonnet "rooms" reveal domestic unrest and disappointment, as Stephen Regan argues (*pp. 313–18*).

SOURCES: Edna St. Vincent Millay, "Sonnet I," *Renascence and Other Poems* (New York: Harper, 1917), p. 68; "Sonnets from an Ungrafted Tree: I," *The Harp-Weaver and Other Poems* (New York: Harper, 1923), p. 77.

E. E. Cummings (1894–1962)

next to of course god america i

"next to of course god america i
love you land of the pilgrims' and so forth oh
say can you see by the dawn's early my
country 'tis of centuries come and go
and are no more what of it we should worry
in every language even deafanddumb
thy sons acclaim your glorious name by gorry
by jingo by gee by gosh by gum
why talk of beauty what could be more beaut-
iful than these heroic happy dead
who rushed like lions to the roaring slaughter
they did not stop to think they died instead
then shall the voice of liberty be mute?"

He spoke. And drank rapidly a glass of water

One of more than two hundred iconoclastic sonnets he wrote, *E. E. Cummings*'s "next to of course god america i" falls in the tradition of the portrait sonnet, though not a flattering one. As Gillian Huang-Tiller argues (*pp. 161–69*), Cummings's popular association with experimental typography and free verse elides his lifelong interest in the forms of structural and visual play afforded by the sonnet.

SOURCE: E. E. Cummings, "next to god of course america i," *is 5* (New York: Liveright, 1926, p. 62). Copyright 1926, 1954, © 1991 by the Trustees for the E. E. Cummings Trust. Copyright © 1985 by George James Firmage. From *Complete Poems: 1904–1962* by E. E. Cummings, edited by George J. Firmage. Used by permission of Liveright Publishing Corporation.

Ruth Muskrat Bronson (1897–1982)

from "Sonnets from the Cherokee"

II.

A Thousand, thousand years ago I lived
And waited for your coming then, as now,
Before the wailing waters taught me how
To weep; nor never knew how sad I grieved,
Nor with what empty pain my soul, bereaved
Through need of you, lifted its throbbing brow;
Until the softly whispered plighted vow,
Of sighing trees, from branches silver-leaved
Swept through my soul and waked me from my sleep.
Since then I've roamed a thousand worlds, I think
Seeking your face, too hungry souled to wait
For you to come to me; too sad to weep:
While chains of ages pass me, link by link;
Knowing that I shall find you soon or late.

———

A Cherokee writer and Native American rights activist, *Ruth Muskrat Bronson* was born on the Delaware Nation Reservation and held leadership positions at the Bureau of Indian Affairs and the National Congress of American Indians. Her sonnet sequence nods to Elizabeth Barrett Browning's *Sonnets from the Portuguese* and was published in the *University of Oklahoma Magazine* in 1922 with the parenthetical "(May Mrs. Browning Pardon Me)."

SOURCE: Ruth Margaret Muskrat (Bronson), "Sonnets from the Cherokee: II." *University of Oklahoma Magazine* vol. 10, January 1922, p. 11.

Louise Bogan (1897–1970)

Roman Fountain

Up from the bronze, I saw
Water without a flaw
Rush to its rest in air,
Reach to its rest, and fall.

Bronze of the blackest shade,
An element man-made,
Shaping upright the bare
Clear gouts of water in air.

O, as with arm and hammer,
Still it is good to strive
To beat out the image whole,
To echo the shout and stammer
When full-gushed waters, alive,
Strike on the fountain's bowl
After the air of summer.

Poet and critic *Louise Bogan* was poetry editor of *The New Yorker* from 1931 to 1969 and the first female poet laureate of the United States. Her sonnet reflects both minimalist and metrically variant sonnet lineages. See the essays by Lesley Wheeler (*pp. 273–77*), Anna Lena Phillips Bell (*pp. 291–95*), and Diana Leca (*pp. 296–303*) on these traditions.

SOURCE: Louise Bogan, "Roman Fountain," *The Blue Estuaries* by Louise Bogan (New York: Farrar, Straus and Giroux, 1995), p. 80. Copyright © 1968 by Louise Bogan. Copyright renewed 1996 by Ruth Limmer. Reprinted by permission of Farrar, Straus and Giroux. All rights reserved.

John Wheelwright (1897–1940)

Phallus

Friends need not guard each other as a jealous
Moslem must segregate his odalisque,
no more than one need see the symbolled phallus
while meditating at an obelisk.
    If we could be together day after day,
    companionship, pointed with entering wedge
    compact, whittled by common task and play
    inevitable and slow, would split the pledge
    which kisses tallied once in valediction:
    that our hidden selves in separation meet.
    The corollary's simple contradiction
    may render yet the contract obsolete.
Habit is evil,—all habit, even speech;
and promises prefigure their own breach.

Matthew Kilbane (*pp. 182–90*) links *John Wheelwright*'s interest in both the radio and the sonnet as "sonorous technologies," while also highlighting Wheelwright's use of the sonnet to articulate "the erotics of same-sex friendship." This Shakespearean sonnet brings with it an era's distasteful Orientalist stereotype, but it also carries a playfully frank homoeroticism ahead of its time in American poetry.

SOURCE: John Wheelwright, "Phallus," *Collected Poems of John Wheelwright* (New York: New Directions, 1983), p. 94. Copyright ©1971 by Louise Wheelwright Damon. Reprinted by permission of New Directions Publishing Corp.

Langston Hughes (1902–1967)

from "Seven Moments of Love: An un-sonnet sequence in Blues"

3. Bed Time

If this radio was good I'd get KDQ
And see what Count Basie's playing new.
If I had some money I'd stroll down the street
And jive some old broad I might meet.
Or if I wasn't so drowsy I'd look up Joe
And start a skin game with some chumps I know.
Or if it wasn't so late I might take a walk
And find somebody to kid and talk.
But since I got to get up at day,
I might as well put it on in the hay.
I can sleep *so* good with you away!
House is *so* quiet!... Listen at them mice.
Do I see a couple? Or did I count twice?
Dog-gone little mouses! I wish I was you!
A human gets lonesome if there ain't two.

Two Weeks

She was a little girl who smelled
Of nice cologne and castille soap.
I loved her with a simple passion
That some love poems and a look had given hope.

I remember when I told her that I loved her
A blush made red each pallid little cheek.
She put her stubby hands upon a chair back,
Looked at her shoes, and did not speak.

That useless little girl could tell me
Nothing new, so I began to see
Her love as quite too young for lovers' ways.

Facts are, scarcely did we smile or pine—
We spoke five times and looked nine—
And it lasted only fourteen days.

Translation of "2 semanas" by Nicolás Guillén

———

Titan of the Harlem Renaissance, *Langston Hughes* is better known for his work with the blues than the sonnet, but engagements with the form like the tetrameter couplets from his "un-sonnet sequence" and his translation of Afro-Cuban poet Nicolás Guillén (1902–1989), with whom Hughes shared Communist politics, show Hughes making the sonnet his own through his characteristic embrace of vernacular and persona. See Natasha Trethewey (*p. 100*) for a contemporary example of the blues sonnet, and Timo Müller (*pp. 170–76*) on Harlem Renaissance sonnet translation.

SOURCES: Langston Hughes, "3. Bed Time," from "Seven Moments of Love: An un-sonnet sequence in Blues," *The Collected Poems of Langston Hughes*, edited by Arnold Rampersad with David Roessel, associate editor (New York: Vintage, 1995), p. 218. Copyright © 1994 by the Estate of Langston Hughes. Used by permission of Alfred A. Knopf, an imprint of the Knopf Doubleday Publishing Group, a division of Penguin Random House LLC. All rights reserved. Reprinted by permission of Harold Ober Associates. Copyright 1951 by the Langston Hughes Estate. "Two Weeks," translation of "2 semanas" by Nicolás Guillén, *Opportunity* 11 (March 1933), p. 88. Reprinted by permission of Harold Ober Associates. Copyright 1951 by the Langston Hughes Estate.

Countee Cullen (1903–1946)

From the Dark Tower

We shall not always plant while others reap
The golden increment of bursting fruit,
Not always countenance, abject and mute,
That lesser men should hold their brothers cheap;
Not everlastingly while others sleep
Shall we beguile their limbs with mellow flute,
Not always bend to some more subtle brute;
We were not made to eternally weep.

The night whose sable breast relieves the stark,
White stars is no less lovely being dark,
And there are buds that cannot bloom at all
In light, but crumple, piteous, and fall;
So in the dark we hide the heart that bleeds,
And wait, and tend our agonizing seeds.

———

Harlem Renaissance poet *Countee Cullen* repurposes elements of the English canon (the sonnet form itself and a title that alludes to Shakespeare by way of Robert Browning) to create a hybrid Petrarchan-Shakespearean sonnet of Black pride and survival despite current subjugation, with a sestet composed of three couplets ringing the way forward.

SOURCE: Countee Cullen, "From the Dark Tower," *Copper Sun* (New York: Harper, 1927). Copyright owned by the Amistad Research Center, New Orleans, LA. Licensing administered by Thompson and Thompson.

Helene Johnson (1906-1995)

A Missionary Brings a Young Native to America

All day she heard the mad stampede of feet
Push by her in a thick unbroken haste.
A thousand unknown terrors of the street
Caught at her timid heart, and she could taste
The city grit upon her tongue. She felt
A steel-spiked wave of brick and light submerge
Her mind in cold immensity. A belt
Of alien tenets choked the songs that surged
Within her when alone each night she knelt
At prayer. And as the moon grew large and white
Above the roof, afraid that she would scream
Aloud her young abandon to the night,
She mumbled Latin litanies and dreamed
Unholy dreams while waiting for the light.

Sonnet to a Negro in Harlem

You are disdainful and magnificent—
Your perfect body and your pompous gait,
Your dark eyes flashing solemnly with hate,
Small wonder that you are incompetent
To imitate those whom you so despise—
Your shoulders towering high above the throng,
Your head thrown back in rich, barbaric song,
Palm trees and mangoes stretched before your eyes.
Let others toil and sweat for labor's sake
And wring from grasping hands their meed of gold.
Why urge ahead your supercilious feet?
Scorn will efface each footprint that you make.
I love your laughter arrogant and bold.
You are too splendid for this city street!

Eleanor Wakefield's essay asks the reader to consider how *Helene Johnson*'s sonnets offer "complex... portrayals of Black women's interiority" and "embody and critique the American sonnet tradition" (*pp. 319–25*). In doing so, she also makes a case for a renewed appreciation of the significance of Johnson's work.

SOURCE: Helene Johnson, "A Missionary Brings a Young Native to America" and "Sonnet to a Negro in Harlem." Reprinted from *This Waiting for Love: Helene Johnson, Poet of the Harlem Renaissance* (Amherst: University of Massachusetts Press, 2000), pp. 40 and 43. Copyright © 2000 by the University of Massachusetts Press.

Elizabeth Bishop (1911–1979)

Sonnet

Caught—the bubble
in the spirit-level,
a creature divided;
and the compass needle
wobbling and wavering,
undecided.
Freed—the broken
thermometer's mercury
running away;
and the rainbow-bird
from the narrow bevel
of the empty mirror,
flying wherever
it feels like, gay!

Sonnet of Intimacy

Farm afternoons, there's much too much blue air.
I go out sometimes, follow the pasture track,
Chewing a blade of sticky grass, chest bare,
In threadbare pajamas of three summers back,

To the little rivulets in the river-bed
For a drink of water, cold and musical,
And if I spot in the brush a glow of red,
A raspberry, spit its blood at the corral.

The smell of cow manure is delicious.
The cattle look at me unenviously
And when there comes a sudden stream and hiss

Accompanied by a look not unmalicious,
All of us, animals, unemotionally
Partake together of a pleasant piss.

Translation of "Sonêto de intimidade" by Vinícius de Moraes

The formal care and ingenuity of *Elizabeth Bishop*'s widely anthologized forms such as the sestina and villanelle invite the reader to consider the rhetoric of her short-lined "Sonnet," as Lesley Wheeler's essay does (*pp. 273–77*). Elizabeth Bishop spent much of her adult life living abroad, including fifteen years in Brazil, and "Sonnet of Intimacy" (which, unlike Elizabeth Barrett Browning's *Sonnets from the Portuguese,* is a sonnet actually translated from the Portuguese) reminds readers that the "American" sonnet is not a closed circuit but a transnational engagement.

SOURCES: Elizabeth Bishop, "Sonnet," *Poems* by Elizabeth Bishop (New York: Farrar, Straus and Giroux, 2011), p. 192. Copyright © 2011 by The Alice H. Methfessel Trust. Publisher's Note and compilation copyright © 2011 by Farrar, Straus and Giroux. Reprinted by permission of Farrar, Straus and Giroux. All rights reserved. From *Poems* by Elizabeth Bishop published by Chatto & Windus. Reprinted by permission of The Random House Group Limited. "Sonnet of Intimacy," translation of "Sonêto de intimidade" by Vinícius de Moraes, from *Poems: The Centenary Edition* by Elizabeth Bishop, edited by Saskia Hamilton (London: Chatto & Windus, 2011), p. 192. Copyright © 2011 Alice H. Methfessel Trust. Reprinted by permission of The Random House Group Limited. Publisher's Note and compilation copyright © 2011 by Farrar, Straus and Giroux. Reprinted by permission of Farrar, Straus and Giroux. All rights reserved.

Muriel Rukeyser (1913–1980)

Sonnet

My thoughts through yours refracted into speech
transmute this room musically tonight,
the notes of contact flowing, rhythmic, bright
with an informal art beyond my single reach.
Outside, dark birds fly in a greening time   :
wings of our sistered wishes beat these walls   :
and words afflict our minds in near footfalls
approaching with latening hour's chime.

And if an essential thing has flown between us,
rare intellectual bird of communication,
let us seize it quickly   :   let our preference
choose it instead of softer things to screen us
each from the other's self   :   muteness or hesitation,
nor petrify live miracle by our indifference.

Feminist and progressive activist *Muriel Rukeyser*'s "Sonnet" is a call to connection. As in many sonnets, one might also read in its lines an oblique interrogation of the purpose and possibilities of the sonnet itself.

SOURCE: Muriel Rukeyser, "Sonnet," *The Collected Poems of Muriel Rukeyser* (Pittsburgh: University of Pittsburgh Press, 2005), pp. 13–14. Copyright © 2005 by Muriel Rukeyser. Reprinted by permission of ICM Partners.

Robert Hayden (1913-1980)

Frederick Douglass

When it is finally ours, this freedom, this liberty, this beautiful
and terrible thing, needful to man as air,
usable as earth; when it belongs at last to all,
when it is truly instinct, brain matter, diastole, systole,
reflex action; when it is finally won; when it is more
than the gaudy mumbo jumbo of politicians:
this man, this Douglass, this former slave, this Negro
beaten to his knees, exiled, visioning a world
where none is lonely, none hunted, alien,
this man, superb in love and logic, this man
shall be remembered. Oh, not with statues' rhetoric,
not with legends and poems and wreaths of bronze alone,
but with the lives grown out of his life, the lives
fleshing his dream of the beautiful, needful thing.

Jon Woodson (*pp. 333–39*) argues that many irregular African American sonnets, including *Robert Hayden*'s "Frederick Douglass," can be best understood when situated within the African American esoteric tradition; one might read this poem both within the tradition of the sonnet-ode and as a statement of spiritual worldview inspired by Hayden's Bahá'í faith.

SOURCE: Robert Hayden, "Frederick Douglass." Copyright © 1966 by Robert Hayden, *Collected Poems of Robert Hayden* by Robert Hayden, edited by Frederick Glaysher (New York: Liveright, 2013), p. 62. Used by permission of Liveright Publishing Corporation.

Margaret Walker (1915–1998)

The Struggle Staggers Us

Our birth and death are easy hours, like sleep
and food and drink. The struggle staggers us
for bread, for pride, for simple dignity.
And this is more than fighting to exist;
more than revolt and war and human odds.
There is a journey from the me to you.
There is a journey from the you to me.
A union of the two strange worlds must be.

Ours is a struggle from a too-warm bed;
too cluttered with a patience full of sleep.
Out of this blackness we must struggle forth;
from want of bread, of pride, of dignity.
Struggle between the morning and the night.
This marks our years; this settles, too, our plight.

As Ariel Martino (*pp. 214–20*) argues, *Margaret Walker*'s use of the sonnet functions as a "mask" to slip political content "past the literary tastemakers, both Black and white." Winner of the 1942 Yale Younger Poets Prize, Walker was part of the African American movement that claimed and transformed the sonnet in the twentieth century.

SOURCE: Margaret Walker, "The Struggle Staggers Us." Reprinted with permission from *This Is My Century: New and Collected Poems* by Margaret Walker (Athens: University of Georgia Press, 1989), p. 51.

Robert Lowell (1917–1977)

History

History has to live with what was here,
clutching and close to fumbling all we had—
it is so dull and gruesome how we die,
unlike writing, life never finishes.
Abel was finished; death is not remote,
a flash-in-the-pan electrifies the skeptic,
his cows crowding like skulls against high-voltage wire,
his baby crying all night like a new machine.
As in our Bibles, white-faced, predatory,
the beautiful, mist-drunken hunter's moon ascends—
a child could give it a face: two holes, two holes,
my eyes, my mouth, between them a skull's no-nose—
O there's a terrifying innocence in my face
drenched with the silver salvage of the mornfrost.

Robert Lowell's influential blank-verse sonnets reflect the duality of his legacy as both the "confessional" poet for whom M. L. Rosenthal first coined the term and a "poet-historian," whom his biographer Paul Mariani singled out as the last in an American tradition of "influential public poets."

SOURCE: Robert Lowell, "History," *Collected Poems* by Robert Lowell, edited by David Gerwanter and Frank Bidart (New York: Farrar, Straus and Giroux, 2003), p. 199. Copyright © 2003 by Harriet Lowell and Sheridan Lowell. Reprinted by permission of Farrar, Straus and Giroux. All Rights Reserved.

Gwendolyn Brooks (1917–2000)

kitchenette building

We are things of dry hours and the involuntary plan,
Grayed in, and gray. "Dream" makes a giddy sound, not strong
Like "rent," "feeding a wife," "satisfying a man."

But could a dream send up through onion fumes
Its white and violet, fight with fried potatoes
And yesterday's garbage ripening in the hall,
Flutter, or sing an aria down these rooms

Even if we were willing to let it in,
Had time to warm it, keep it very clean,
Anticipate a message, let it begin?

We wonder. But not well! not for a minute!
Since Number Five is out of the bathroom now,
We think of lukewarm water, hope to get in it.

the rites for Cousin Vit

Carried her unprotesting out the door.
Kicked back the casket-stand. But it can't hold her,
That stuff and satin aiming to enfold her,
The lid's contrition nor the bolts before.
Oh oh. Too much. Too much. Even now, surmise,
She rises in the sunshine. There she goes,
Back to the bars she knew and the repose
In love-rooms and the things in people's eyes.
Too vital and too squeaking. Must emerge.
Even now she does the snake-hips with a hiss,
Slops the bad wine across her shantung, talks
Of pregnancy, guitars and bridgework, walks
In parks or alleys, comes haply on the verge
Of happiness, haply hysterics. Is.

A Lovely Love

Lillian's

Let it be alleys. Let it be a hall
Whose janitor javelins epithet and thought
To cheapen hyacinth darkness that we sought
And played we found, rot, make the petals fall.
Let it be stairways, and a splintery box
Where you have thrown me, scraped me with your kiss,
Have honed me, have released me after this
Cavern kindness, smiled away our shocks.
That is the birthright of our lovely love
In swaddling clothes. Not like that Other one.
Not lit by any fondling star above.
Not found by any wise men, either. Run.
People are coming. They must not catch us here
Definitionless in this strict atmosphere.

The first African American to win the Pulitzer Prize, *Gwendolyn Brooks* eventually distanced her poetics from European prosody and cut ties with white establishment publishers, but her sonnets depicting unvarnished lives in the "Black Metropolis" of Chicago's Bronzeville remain influential and beloved. See the essays by Tess Taylor (*pp. 326–32*) and Jon Woodson (*pp. 333–39*) for two very different takes on Brooks's work.

SOURCES: Gwendolyn Brooks, "kitchenette building," "A Lovely Love" and "the rites for Cousin Vit" *Blacks* (Chicago: Third World Press, 1987), pp. 20, 363, and 125. Reprinted by Consent of Brooks Permissions.

Dunstan Thompson (1918–1975)

This Tall Horseman, My Young Man of Mars

This tall horseman, my young man of Mars
Scatters the gold dust from his hair, and takes
Me to pieces like a gun. The myth forsakes
Him slowly. Almost mortal, he shows the scars
Where medals of honor, cut-steel stars,
Pin death above the heart. But bends, but breaks
In his hand, my love, whose wretched machinery makes
Time, the inventor, weep through a world of wars.
Guilt like a rust enamels me. I breed
A poison not this murdering youth may dare
In one drop of blood to battle. No delight
Is possible. Only at parting do we need
Each other; together, we are not there
At all. Love, I farewell you out of sight.

Martial imagery from *Dunstan Thompson*'s experiences in the US Army in World War II appears in this sonnet, which taps into the form's long engagement with erotic power dynamics. Thompson's poems openly reflect his life as a gay man, decades before same-sex love was "legalized" in either the United States or Britain, where Thompson lived as an adult. The heavily enjambed lines (just three end-stopped) reinforce the poem's urgency.

SOURCE: Dunstan Thompson, "This Tall Horseman, My Young Man of Mars," *Here at Last Is Love: Selected Poems*, edited by Gregory Wolfe (Eugene, OR: Wipf and Stock, 2015), p. 29. Used by permission of Wipf and Stock Publishers, www.wipfandstock.com.

Mary Ellen Solt (1920-2007)

moonshot sonnet

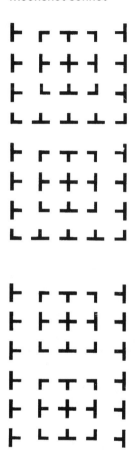

An influential figure in the concrete poetry movement, *Mary Ellen Solt* appropriates NASA symbols used on lunar photographs in her "moonshot sonnet." Solt's conceptual send-up of the sonnet critiques its contemporary relevance ("We have not been able to address the moon in a sonnet successfully since the Renaissance"), but she notes that "the sonnet was a supranational, supralingual form as the concrete poem is."

SOURCE: Mary Ellen Solt, "moonshot sonnet" (1964), *An Anthology of Concrete Poetry*, edited by Emmett Williams (New York: Something Else Press, 1967). Courtesy of the Estate of Mary Ellen Solt.

Mona Van Duyn (1921–2004)

The Beginning

The end
of passion
may refashion
a friend.

Eyes meet
in fear
of such dear
defeat.

The heart's core,
unbroken,
cringes.

The soul's door
swings open
on its hinges.

Mona Van Duyn's "minimalist sonnets" share common ground with those discussed by Lesley Wheeler (*pp. 273–77*) and Diana Leca (*pp. 296–303*). In "The Beginning," Van Duyn expands the sonnet's traditional thematic connections with love to include the "dear defeat" of eros cooled to friendship.

SOURCE: Mona Van Duyn, "The Beginning," *Firefall* by Mona Van Duyn (New York: Knopf, 1993), p. 15. Copyright © 1992 by Mona Van Duyn. Used by permission of Alfred A. Knopf, an imprint of the Knopf Doubleday Publishing Group, a division of Penguin Random House LLC. All rights reserved.

Anthony Hecht (1923–2004)

The Feast of Stephen

I

The coltish horseplay of the locker room,
Moist with the steam of the tiled shower stalls,
With shameless blends of civet, musk and sweat,
Loud with the cap-gun snapping of wet towels
Under the steel-ribbed cages of bare bulbs,
In some such setting of thick basement pipes
And janitorial realities
Boys for the first time frankly eye each other,
Inspect each others' bodies at close range,
And what they see is not so much another
As a strange, possible version of themselves,
And all the sparring dance, adrenal life,
Tense, jubilant nimbleness, is but a vague,
Busy, unfocused ballet of self-love.

II

If the heart has its reasons, perhaps the body
Has its own lumbering sort of carnal spirit,
Felt in the tingling bruises of collision,
And known to captains as *esprit de corps*.
What is this brisk fraternity of timing,
Pivot and lobbing arc, or indirection,
Mens sana in men's sauna, in the flush
Of health and toilets, private and corporal glee,
These fleet caroms, *pliés* and genuflections
Before the salmon-leap, the leaping fountain
All sheathed in glistening light, flexed and alert?
From the vast echo-chamber of the gym,
Among the scumbled shouts and shrill of whistles,
The bounced basketball sound of a leather whip.

III

Think of those barren places where men gather
To act in the terrible name of rectitude,
Of acned shame, punk's pride, muscle or turf,
The bully's thin superiority.
Think of the *Sturm-Abteilungs Kommandant*
Who loves Beethoven and collects Degas,
Or the blond boys in jeans whose narrowed eyes
Are focussed by some hard and smothered lust,
Who lounge in a studied mimicry of ease,
Flick their live butts into the standing weeds,
And comb their hair in the mirror of cracked windows
Of an abandoned warehouse where they keep
In darkened readiness for their occasion
The rope, the chains, handcuffs and gasoline.

IV

Out in the rippled heat of a neighbor's field,
In the kilowatts of noon, they've got one cornered.
The bugs are jumping, and the burly youths
Strip to the waist for the hot work ahead.
They go to arm themselves at the dry-stone wall,
Having flung down their wet and salty garments
At the feet of a young man whose name is Saul.
He watches sharply these superbly tanned
Figures with a swimmer's chest and shoulders,
A miler's thighs, with their self-conscious grace,
And in between their sleek, converging bodies,
Brilliantly oiled and burnished by the sun,
He catches a brief glimpse of bloodied hair
And hears an unintelligible prayer.

Anthony Hecht's sonnet sequence calls to mind the tradition of homosociality in the sonnet in Elizabethan courts and beyond while drawing into relief the process by which fraternity permits or becomes violence. As a soldier, Hecht was present at the liberation of the Flossenburg Concentration Camp and served as interpreter for those imprisoned there.

SOURCE: Anthony Hecht, "The Feast of Stephen," *Collected Earlier Poems* by Anthony Hecht (New York: Knopf, 1990), pp. 150–51. Copyright ©1990 by Anthony E. Hecht. Used by permission of Alfred A. Knopf, an imprint of the Knopf Doubleday Publishing Group, a division of Penguin Random House LLC. All rights reserved.

James Merrill (1926–1995)

The Broken Home

Crossing the street,
I saw the parents and the child
At their window, gleaming like fruit
With evening's mild gold leaf.

In a room on the floor below,
Sunless, cooler—a brimming
Saucer of wax, marbly and dim—
I have lit what's left of my life.

I have thrown out yesterday's milk
And opened a book of maxims.
The flame quickens. The word stirs.

Tell me, tongue of fire,
That you and I are as real
At least as the people upstairs.

My father, who had flown in World War I,
Might have continued to invest his life
In cloud banks well above Wall Street and wife.
But the race was run below, and the point was to win.

Too late now, I make out in his blue gaze
(Through the smoked glass of being thirty-six)
The soul eclipsed by twin black pupils, sex
And business; time was money in those days.

Each thirteenth year he married. When he died
There were already several chilled wives
In sable orbit—rings, cars, permanent waves.
We'd felt him warming up for a green bride.

He could afford it. He was "in his prime"
At three score ten. But money was not time.

When my parents were younger this was a popular act:
A veiled woman would leap from an electric, wine-dark car
To the steps of no matter what—the Senate or the Ritz Bar—
And bodily, at newsreel speed, attack

No matter whom—Al Smith or José María Sert
Or Clemenceau—veins standing out on her throat
As she yelled *War mongerer! Pig! Give us the vote!*,
And would have to be hauled away in her hobble skirt.

What had the man done? Oh, made history.
Her business (he had implied) was giving birth,
Tending the house, mending the socks.

Always that same old story—
Father Time and Mother Earth,
A marriage on the rocks.

One afternoon, red, satyr-thighed
Michael, the Irish setter, head
Passionately lowered, led
The child I was to a shut door. Inside,

Blinds beat sun from the bed.
The green-gold room throbbed like a bruise.
Under a sheet, clad in taboos
Lay whom we sought, her hair undone, outspread,

And of a blackness found, if ever now, in old
Engravings where the acid bit.
I must have needed to touch it
Or the whiteness—was she dead?
Her eyes flew open, startled strange and cold.
The dog slumped to the floor. She reached for me. I fled.

Tonight they have stepped out onto the gravel.
The party is over. It's the fall
Of 1931. They love each other still.
She: Charlie, I can't stand the pace.
He: Come on, honey—why, you'll bury us all!

A lead soldier guards my windowsill:
Khaki rifle, uniform, and face.
Something in me grows heavy, silvery, pliable.

How intensely people used to feel!
Like metal poured at the close of a proletarian novel,
Refined and glowing from the crucible,
I see those two hearts, I'm afraid,
Still. Cool here in the graveyard of good and evil,
They are even so to be honored and obeyed.

…Obeyed, at least, inversely. Thus
I rarely buy a newspaper, or vote.
To do so, I have learned, is to invite
The tread of a stone guest within my house.

Shooting this rusted bolt, though, against him,
I trust I am no less time's child than some
Who on the heath impersonate Poor Tom
Or on the barricades risk life and limb.

Nor do I try to keep a garden, only
An avocado in a glass of water—
Roots pallid, gemmed with air. And later,

When the small gilt leaves have grown
Fleshy and green, I let them die, yes, yes,
And start another. I am earth's no less.

A child, a red dog roam the corridors,
Still, of the broken home. No sound. The brilliant
Rag runners halt before wide-open doors.
My old room! Its wallpaper—cream, medallioned
With pink and brown—brings back the first nightmares,
Long summer colds and Emma, sepia-faced,
Perspiring over broth carried upstairs
Aswim with golden fats I could not taste.

The real house became a boarding school.
Under the ballroom ceiling's allegory
Someone at last may actually be allowed
To learn something; or, from my window, cool
With the unstiflement of the entire story,
Watch a red setter stretch and sink in cloud.

Stephen Regan observes that "each of Merrill's seven sonnets tries out a different formal arrangement at the level of line and meter, as if trying to repair the broken home" (*pp. 313–18*). Despite the sonnet's long association with resolution and structural unity, *James Merrill*'s sonnets employ the form to explore disintegrative personal narratives.

SOURCE: James Merrill, "The Broken Home," *Collected Poems* by James Merrill, edited by J. D. McClatchy and Stephen Yenser (New York: Knopf, 2002), pp. 197–200. Copyright © 2001 by the Literary Estate of James Merrill at Washington University. Used by permission of Alfred A. Knopf, an imprint of the Knopf Doubleday Publishing Group, a division of Penguin Random House LLC. All rights reserved.

James Wright (1927–1980)

May Morning

    Deep into spring, winter is hanging on. Bitter and skillful in his hopelessness, he stays alive in every shady place, starving along the Mediterranean: angry to see the glittering sea-pale boulder alive with lizards green as Judas leaves. Winter is hanging on. He still believes. He tries to catch a lizard by the shoulder. One olive tree below Grottaghlie welcomes the winter into noontime shade, and talks as softly as Pythagoras. Be still, be patient, I can hear him say, cradling in his arms the wounded head, letting the sunlight touch the savage face.

"May Morning," one of *James Wright*'s final poems, is a prose poem hiding a Petrarchan sonnet in its lines, combining slant and full rhymes and complete stretches of iambic pentameter. As his biographer Jonathan Blunk notes, we see in this poem Wright's form-finding guided by his precise ear.

SOURCE: James Wright, "May Morning," *Above the River: The Complete Poems* by James Wright, introduction by Donald Hall (New York: Farrar, Straus and Giroux, 1990), p. 333–34. Copyright © 1990 by Anne Wright, introduction © 1990 by Donald Hall. Reprinted by permission of Farrar, Straus and Giroux. All rights reserved.

Adrienne Rich (1929-2012)

from "Twenty-One Love Poems"

    XIII

The rules break like a thermometer,
quicksilver spills across the charted systems,
we're out in a country that has no language
no laws, we're chasing the raven and the wren
through gorges unexplored since dawn
whatever we do together is pure invention
the maps they gave us were out of date
by years... we're driving through the desert
wondering if the water will hold out
the hallucinations turn to simple villages
the music on the radio comes clear—
neither *Rosenkavalier* nor *Götterdämmerung*
but a woman's voice singing old songs
with new words, with a quiet bass, a flute
plucked and fingered by women outside the law.

Published in 1976, *Adrienne Rich*'s "Twenty-One Love Poems" imagine, with their "we," a lesbian sonnet of presence, mutuality, and touch, countering a heterosexual tradition of separation and solitary meditation. Carl Phillips (*pp. 201–6*) and Lisa L. Moore (*pp. 221–28*) trace the influence of Rich's sonnet as it spills over its own structures and points toward new possibilities.

SOURCE: Adrienne Rich, "Twenty-One Love Poems," XIII, *Collected Poems: 1950–2012* by Adrienne Rich (New York: Norton, 2016), p. 471–72. Copyright © 2016 by the Adrienne Rich Literary Trust. Copyright © 1978 by W. W. Norton & Company, Inc. Used by permission of W. W. Norton & Company, Inc.

Rhina P. Espaillat (b. 1932)

Butchering

My mother's mother, toughened by the farm,
hardened by infants' burials, used a knife
and swung an axe as if her woman's arm
wielded a man's hard will. Inured to life
and death alike, "What ails you now?" she'd say
ungently to the sick. She fed them too,
roughly but well, and took the blood away—
and washed the dead, if there was that to do.
She told us children how the cows could sense
when their own calves were marked for butchering,
and how they lowed, their wordless eloquence
impossible to still with anything—
sweet clover, or her unremitting care.
She told it simply, but she faltered there.

Born in the Dominican Republic in the Trujillo era, *Rhina P. Espaillat*'s family was granted political asylum in the United States and immigrated to New York. She is associated with New Formalism, to which she brings her lifelong commitment to bilingualism and the exploration of the everyday domestic through the lenses of gender, sexuality, ethnicity, and ancestry.

SOURCE: Rhina P. Espaillat, "Butchering," *And After All* (San Jose, CA: Able Muse, 2018), p. 7. © Rhina P. Espaillat, 2019. Used by permission of Able Muse Press.

Sylvia Plath (1932–1963)

Sonnet: To Eva

All right, let's say you could take a skull and break it
The way you'd crack a clock; you'd crush the bone
Between steel palms of inclination, take it,
Observing the wreck of metal and rare stone.

This was a woman: her loves and stratagems
Betrayed in mute geometry of broken
Cogs and disks, inane mechanic whims,
And idle coils of jargon yet unspoken.

Not man nor demigod could put together
The scraps of rusted reverie, the wheels
Of notched tin platitudes concerning weather,
Perfume, politics, and fixed ideals.

The idiot bird leaps up and drunken leans
To chirp the hour in lunatic thirteens.

With its lengthy lines and feminine rhymes, *Sylvia Plath*'s "Sonnet: To Eva," written during her college years, presses against form while keeping its boundaries, heightening our experience of constriction. Anna Maria Hong, analyzing its feminist poetics of virtuosity and outrage, writes: "This poem inhabits the sonnet as a kind of corset" (*pp. 340–44*).

SOURCE: Sylvia Plath, "Sonnet: To Eva," *The Collected Poems* by Sylvia Plath (New York: HarperCollins, 1992), pp. 304–5. Copyright © 1960, 1965, 1971, 1981 by the Estate of Sylvia Plath. Used by permission of HarperCollins Publishers and Faber and Faber Ltd.

Ted Berrigan (1934–1983)

Sonnet XXXIV

Time flies by like a great whale
And I find my hand grows stale at the throttle
Of my many faceted and fake appearance
Who bucks and spouts by detour under the sheets
Hollow portals of solid appearance
Movies are poems, a holy bible, the great mother to us
People go by in the fragrant day
Accelerate softly my blood
But blood is still blood and tall as a mountain blood
Behind me green rubber grows, feet walk
In wet water, and dusty heads grow wide
Padré, Father, or fat old man, as you will,
I am afraid to succeed, afraid to fail,
Tell me now, again, who I am

———

In his sonnet workshop at the Poetry Project, *Ted Berrigan* said, "I discovered that the basic unit of the sonnet was the line, the single line…. And I was going to make [the lines] like a ladder, a ladder with the sides taken away." Berrigan's 1964 *The Sonnets* invigorated interest in the sonnet's experimental and serial capacities.

SOURCE: Ted Berrigan, "Sonnet XXXIV," *The Sonnets* by Ted Berrigan, edited by Alice Notley (New York: Penguin, 2000), p. 31. Copyright © 2000 by Alice Notley, Literary Executrix of the Estate of Ted Berrigan. Used by permission of Viking Books, an imprint of Penguin Publishing Group, a division of Penguin Random House LLC. All rights reserved.

June Jordan (1936–2002)

Sunflower Sonnet Number Two

Supposing we could just go on and on as two
voracious in the days apart as well as when
we side by side (the many ways we do
that) well! I would consider then
perfection possible, or else worthwhile
to think about. Which is to say
I guess the costs of long term tend to pile
up, block and complicate, erase away
the accidental, temporary, near
thing/pulsebeat promises one makes
because the chance, the easy new, is there
in front of you. But still, perfection takes
some sacrifice of falling stars for rare.
And there are stars, but none of you, to spare.

Dated 1975, *June Jordan*'s "Sunflower Sonnet Number Two" shares similarities in style, theme, and diction with Rich's "Twenty-One Love Poems" (*p. 67*). See also John James's reference to Jordan's "The Difficult Miracle of Black Poetry in America, or Something Like a Sonnet for Phillis Wheatley" (*pp. 153–60*).

SOURCE: June Jordan, "Sunflower Sonnet Number Two," *The Essential June Jordan*, edited by Jan Heller Levi and Christoph Keller (Port Townsend, WA: Copper Canyon Press, 2021), p. 207. © June M. Jordan Literary Estate Trust. Used by permission. www.junejordan.com.

Lucille Clifton (1936–2010)

the death of fred clifton

11/10/84

age 49

i seemed to be drawn
to the center of myself
leaving the edges of me
in the hands of my wife
and i saw with the most amazing
clarity
so that i had not eyes but
sight,
and, rising and turning,
through my skin,
there was all around not the
shapes of things
but oh, at last, the things
themselves.

Recent critical attention has turned increasingly to the ways craftedness makes possible the immediate, vatic qualities of *Lucille Clifton*'s poems. As Jahan Ramazani (*pp. 133–45*) and Lisa L. Moore (*pp. 221–28*) note, Clifton's spare sonnet, "the death of fred clifton," like other short-lined sonnets in this collection, takes advantage of and revises the shape and potentiality of the sonnet form. Like Audre Lorde (see Moore's essay), Clifton cited the sonnets of Edna St. Vincent Millay as an early influence.

SOURCE: Lucille Clifton, "the death of fred clifton," *The Collected Poems of Lucille Clifton*, edited by Kevin Young and Michael S. Glaser (Rochester, NY: BOA Editions, 2012), p. 307. Copyright © 1987 by Lucille Clifton. Reprinted with the permission of The Permissions Company, Inc., on behalf of BOA Editions, Ltd., www.boaeditions.org.

Joan Larkin (b. 1939)

"Vagina" Sonnet

Is "vagina" suitable for use
in a sonnet? I don't suppose so.
A famous poet told me, "Vagina's ugly."
Meaning, of course, the *sound* of it. In poems.
Meanwhile he inserts his penis frequently
into his verse, calling it seriously, "My
Penis." It *is* short, I know, and dignified.
I mean of course the sound of it. In poems.
This whole thing is unfortunate, but petty,
like my hangup concerning English Dept. memos
headed "Mr./Mrs./Miss"—only a fishbone
In the throat of the revolution—
a waste of brains—to be concerned about
this minor issue of my cunt's good name.

Included in *Joan Larkin*'s first collection, *Housework*, and in the 1975 anthology *Amazon Poetry*, one of the first anthologies of lesbian poetry (both from Out & Out Books, a lesbian feminist collective), "'Vagina' Sonnet" uses humor to question what and who "belongs" in the canon exemplified by the sonnet tradition. Larkin has continued her exploration of the unrhymed sonnet for nearly half a century.

SOURCE: Joan Larkin, "'Vagina' Sonnet," *Housework* (Brooklyn: Out & Out Books, 1975), p. 70, reprinted in *My Body: New and Selected Poems* (Brooklyn: Hanging Loose Press, 2007), p. 142. Copyright © 1975 and 2007 by Joan Larkin.

Lyn Hejinian (b. 1941)

The Eye of the Storm

There are many weathers, some that shrink as the day goes by, some predatory, some like feathers randomly falling on distant interesting lands

The young win a game against far older rivals and people step out of shops, houses, apartment buildings, banks—they converge on the sidewalks and overflow onto the street, just becoming aware of the rioting that's about to break out: two excitements

Along come the tall young woman with the small yellow dog and her "come on, follow me" with the darker other woman in a red coat with her "different materials are differently affected by the sun" and the man with the cell phone in a pouch hooked on his belt, along comes the child with her "that's so cool" and camera

And the dead?—they eat peas and dandelions from the roots up, they eat the roots of daffodils, redwoods, and roses

Our investigation now stumbles on and fearfully, clumsily, entirely, we follow, groping, greeting, grinding

There once was a young woman who late in life grew a second, small, superfluous tongue under the first, but she could find no purpose for it and from lack of use it soon withered away

The chair is red—the red of a pudding, a camel, and a cartoon

One in daisy white, the other in dairy white—twice the same girl with black shoes in two different dresses and a girl in mushroom white

The silent ceramic poet glazed by rising fire roars "Love" and at that inevitable note of hopelessness the silent ceramic cracks

I will not be cruel, said Cruelty, but that is a given, said the girl with a grin who was not *a* girl but *the* girl, ferocious and uncruel

But let us celebrate what was as that which is and the very very slow violence of forests, the gentle violence of the trees

Let us take our surrogate selves out and leave them like guinea pigs to sniff and browse on swirls while we sit cross-legged in a sun-swept amphitheater

O child, be contemporary, your soul an ornament of consciousness

In the statue's rock is insouciant life, respite, lingering, hard

For Susan Bee
In memory of Emma Bee Bernstein

Associated with the innovative strategies of Language Poetry, *Lyn Hejinian*'s expansive antisonnets from *The Unfollowing* explore the disordered movement of grief through non sequitur. Carl Phillips discusses the role of resistance to the sonnet within the sonnet tradition (*pp. 201–6*).

SOURCE: Lyn Hejinian, "The Eye of the Storm," *The Unfollowing* (Oakland, CA: Omnidawn, 2016), 35, p. 47. © 2016 by Lyn Hejinian. The poem appears with the permission of Omnidawn Publishing. All rights reserved.

Marilyn Hacker (b. 1942)

I want this love to be resilient

I want this love to be resilient
as crabgrass cracking the interstices
of paving stones until the sidewalks burst. Its ease
is difficulty, rough when crossed, ebullient
in adversity, still new, unruly, int-
ermittently stormy, rolling with June thunder.
We're getting over, rootlings pushing under
ramshackle walls, knocking them down. A brilliant
midsummer sky, cleaner than metaphors,
blazes above the river. We are three
months old since midnight, appropriately
cheered on a French map, then under the sheet.
I lie beside you now, absorbing heat,
light, currents of cold air, the season's, yours.

Marilyn Hacker's book-length sonnet sequence, *Love, Death, and the Changing of the Seasons* (1995), builds on the lesbian sonnet lineage of Adrienne Rich (*p. 67*), June Jordan (*p. 71*), and others. Critic Lynn Keller argues that Hacker's sonnets highlight the artificiality of the form and thus gender itself, again avoiding the oppositionality of the I/you relationship. Hacker has sustained her engagement with the traditional sonnet sequence to the present day, throughout a lifetime's oeuvre.

SOURCE: Marilyn Hacker, "I want this love to be resilient," *Love, Death, and the Changing of the Seasons* by Marilyn Hacker (New York: Norton, 1995), p. 132. Copyright © 1986 by Marilyn Hacker. Used by permission.

Ellen Bryant Voigt (b. 1943)

The bride is in the parlor, dear confection

The bride is in the parlor, dear confection.
Down on his knee at the edge of all that white,
her father puts a penny in her shoe.

Under the stiff organza and the sash,
the first cell of her first child slips
into the chamber with a little click.

The family next door was never struck
but we lost three—was that God's will? And which
were chosen for its purpose, us or them?

The Gospel says there is no us and them.
Science says there is no moral lesson.
The photo album says, who are these people?

After the paw withdraws, the world
hums again, making its golden honey.

From her 1995 collection, *Kyrie*, imagining the influenza epidemic of 1918–19 in the wake of World War I, *Ellen Bryant Voigt*'s sonnet sequence takes elements from the portrait sonnet and the reflective, Romantic mode, as well as the elegiac sonnet, through which she personalizes collective tragedy as Elizabeth Alexander does in memorializing those lost to the HIV-AIDS epidemic (*p. 98*). The poem's discomfort comes through in unrhymed, end-stopped lines, questions, and a diction that favors the grotesque.

SOURCE: Ellen Bryant Voigt, "The bride is in the parlor, dear confection," *Kyrie* by Ellen Bryant Voigt (New York: Norton, 1995), p. 49. Copyright © 1995 by Ellen Bryant Voigt. Used by permission of W. W. Norton & Company, Inc.

Lorenzo Thomas (1944-2005)

MMDCCXIII ½

The cruelty of ages past affects us now
Whoever it was who lived here lived a mean life
Each door has locks designed for keys unknown

Our living room was once somebody's home
Our bedroom, someone's only room
Our kitchen had a hasp upon its door.

Door to a kitchen?

And our lives are hasped and boundaried
Because of ancient locks and madnesses
Of slumlord greed and desperate privacies

Which one is madness? Depends on who you are.
We find we cannot stay, the both of us, in the same room
Dance, like electrons, out of each other's way.

The cruelties of ages past affect us now

Born in Panama and raised in New York City, *Lorenzo Thomas* was a member of the Umbra Workshop, which preceded the Black Arts Movement. Thomas brings Black musicality to the sonnet, his own, creating repeat openings and closures in the rhyme and meter. See Rebecca Morgan Frank's essay for further discussion of repeated-line sonnets (*pp. 285–90*).

SOURCE: Lorenzo Thomas, "MMDCCXIII½," *The Collected Poems of Lorenzo Thomas* (Middletown, CT: Wesleyan University Press, 2019), p. 267. © 2019 The Estate of Lorenzo Thomas. Published by Wesleyan University Press. Used by permission.

Bernadette Mayer (b. 1945)

Sonnet (You jerk you didn't call me up)

You jerk you didn't call me up
I haven't seen you in so long
You probably have a fucking tan
& besides that instead of making love tonight
You're drinking your parents to the airport
I'm through with you bourgeois boys
All you ever do is go back to ancestral comforts
Only money can get—even Catullus was rich but

Nowadays you guys settle for a couch
By a soporific color cable t.v. set
Instead of any arc of love, no wonder
The G.I. Joe team blows it every other time

Wake up! It's the middle of the night
You can either make love or die at the hands of
the Cobra Commander

To make love, turn to page 121.
To die, turn to page 172.

—

An influential figure in the literary circle associated with the Poetry Project at St. Mark's Church in Manhattan during the 1960s and 1970s, *Bernadette Mayer*'s experiments with the sonnet form, collected in *Sonnets* (1989), endure as central to her body of work and to the lineage of the experimental sonnet.

SOURCE: Bernadette Mayer, "Sonnet (You jerk you didn't call me up)" by Bernadette Mayer, *A Bernadette Mayer Reader* (New York: New Directions, 1992), p. 93. Copyright © 1968 by Bernadette Mayer. Reprinted by permission of New Directions Publishing Corp.

Kay Ryan (b. 1945)

New Rooms

The mind must
set itself up
wherever it goes
and it would be
most convenient
to impose its
old rooms—just
tack them up
like an interior
tent. Oh but
the new holes
aren't where
the windows
went.

Say Uncle

Every day
you say,
*Just one
more try*.
Then another
irrecoverable
day slips by.
You will
say *ankle*,
you will
say *knuckle*;
why won't
you why
won't you
say *uncle*?

Former US Poet Laureate *Kay Ryan*'s poetry is characterized by its compression, its wit, and what Ryan herself has called "recombinant" rhyme. See Diana Leca's essay on Ryan's "miniature" sonnets (*pp. 296–303*).

SOURCES: Kay Ryan, "New Rooms," *Erratic Facts* (New York: Grove, 2015), p. 1. Copyright © 2015 by Kay Ryan. "Say Uncle," *The Best of It* (New York: Grove, 2010), p. 149. Copyright © 2010 by Kay Ryan. Used by permission of Grove/Atlantic, Inc. Any third party use of this material, outside of this publication, is prohibited.

Wanda Coleman (1947–2013)

American Sonnet 18

—after June Jordan

this is the place where all the lives
are planted in my eyes. black things writhe
on the ground. red things gush from
volcanic gaseous tremblings/become blood and light
mountains of flesh raging toward rapturous seas
where crowns of trees inspired by flame extol the night

(my abysmal hear compels the moon compels
wave upon wave. compels reason)

the tombs are fertile with sacred
rememberings. the ancient rhymes. the
disaster of couplings. the turbulent blaze of
greed's agonies. shadows reaching for time and time
unraveling and undone.

sky river mother—your tongue plunders my mouth

American Sonnet 79

—after Melville

blue blooms on ridges, pale lips and nails
   son o son
hard's the harp in my soul's wailing
boy turned man turned ravaged babe in fate's maw
lightsome slim and sinking as implacable dream
serene sounds the precipice above, below
white fevers tear the reason from his brain
   nurse o nurse o nurse
and morphine brings on icy slumber

till on a sigh he slips away

the horror of sheer impotence strands us
in nameless chill
and we are dumbed.
mother father brother—all dumbed

after. i take cuttings of his hair and kiss the air

Wanda Coleman began developing her "American Sonnet" series in the early 1980s and published the poems in multiple collections over the next decade. Defining the American Sonnet as a "jazz sonnet," she wrote that it "would be as open as possible, adhering only to the loosely followed dictate of number of lines. I decided on 14 to 16 and to not exceed that, but to go absolutely bonkers within that constraint. I also give the sonnets a jazzified rhythm structure, akin to platter patter and/or scat and tones like certain Beat writers.... I decided to have fun—to blow my soul."

SOURCES: Wanda Coleman, "American Sonnet 18" and "American Sonnet 79," *Wicked Enchantment: Selected Poems*, edited by Terrance Hayes (Boston, MA, Black Sparrow Press, 2020), pp. 131 and 156. Copyright © 1998 by Wanda Coleman. Reprinted with the permission of The Permissions Company, LLC on behalf of Black Sparrow / David R. Godine Publisher, Inc., www.godine.com.

Marilyn Nelson (b. 1946)

Tears, through the patchwork drapery of dream

Tears, through the patchwork drapery of dream,
for the hanging bodies, the men on flaming pyres,
the crowds standing around like devil choirs,
the children's eyes lit by the fire's gleams
filled with the delight of licking ice cream,
men who hear hog screams as a man expires,
watch-fob good-luck charms teeth pulled out with pliers,
sinner I can't believe Christ's death redeems,
your ash hair, Shulamith—Emmett, your eye,
machetes, piles of shoes, bulldozed mass graves,
the broken towers, the air filled with last breaths,
the blasphemies pronounced to justify
the profane, obscene theft of human lives.
Let me gather spring flowers for a wreath.

Drawn from *Marilyn Nelson*'s narrative sonnet crown, *A Wreath for Emmett Till*, this single sonnet calls on the sonnet and crown forms to anchor and guide the ritual work of witnessing and mourning the atrocity of Till's lynching. The sonnet crown recurs in poems by Meg Day (*pp. 124–25*), Tarfia Faizullah (*pp. 117–21*), Lo Kwa Mei-en (*p. 126*), and Joyelle McSweeney (*p. 111*).

SOURCE: Marilyn Nelson, "Tears, through the patchwork drapery of dream," A Wreath for Emmett Till (Boston: Houghton Mifflin, 2005). Text copyright © 2005 by Marilyn Nelson. Reprinted by permission of Mariner Books, an imprint of HarperCollins Publishers.

Aaron Shurin (b. 1947)

I come to cafe, I sit, I bear

I come to cafe, I sit, I bear
my part in the general cruise. One, sadly
won't look at me, another
won't look away; ridiculous assumption and snarled consumer joy
in abeyance, ordering
quotidian life according to compulsions or ordered *by*, focus shifting
       but always aligned. Well, gladly
I'd mother
that guy with stubble but he wants a father. I won't annoy
his diligent linearity. Man I just yesterday had sex with in a park
    —sing
muse—said "Yum" and somehow knew to pull my head on his
       shoulder, little bleating sounds.
One heart, one mind, once chance but right now one
second's second chance he just walked by this cafe walkman in ear
real time I could've run and, what, left the poem? Composition
       deems none
such interruption permissible; shit, the sheer complexity confounds.

As Jen Bervin reworks Shakespeare's sonnets through erasure in *Nets* (*pp. 107–8*), *Aaron Shurin* draws on their final rhymes throughout *Involuntary Lyrics*, layering his own erotics onto the originals. In this sonnet, the rhymes of Shakespeare's Sonnet VIII ("sadly," "joy," "gladly," "annoy") appear in the context of highly colloquial and contemporary diction. Shurin describes his procedure as "combining the right-brain and the left-brain emphases ... where one is fixed (the seen word) and the other is mutable (the rest of the line)." See also Meg Day's essay on using Donne's end rhymes as an adaptive device (*pp. 242–46*).

SOURCE: Aaron Shurin, "I come to cafe, I sit, I bear," *Involuntary Lyrics* © 2005 by Aaron Shurin (Oakland, CA: Omnidawn Press, 2005), VIII, p. 19. The poem appears with the permission of Omnidawn Publishing. All rights reserved.

Maggie Anderson (b. 1948)

Sonnet for Her Labor

My Aunt Nita's kitchen was immaculate and dark,
and she was always bending to the sink
below the window where the shadows off the bulk
of Laurel Mountain rose up to the brink
of all the sky she saw from there. She clattered
pots on countertops wiped clean of coal dust,
fixed three meals a day, fried meat, mixed batter
for buckwheat cakes, hauled water, in what seemed lust
for labor. One March evening, after cleaning,
she lay down to rest and died. I can see Uncle Ed,
his fingers twined at his plate for the blessing;
my Uncle Craig leaning back, silent in red
galluses. No one said a word to her. All that food
and cleanliness. No one ever told her it was good.

Using the prestigious sonnet form to portray a "feminist family lineage of labor in the West Virginia coalfields," *Maggie Anderson* counters "stereotypical and superficial depictions of contemporary Appalachia," writes Jodie Childers (*pp. 229–34*).

SOURCE: Maggie Anderson, "Sonnet for Her Labor," *Windfall: New and Selected Poems* by Maggie Anderson (Pittsburgh: University of Pittsburgh Press, 2000), p. 55. © 2000. Reprinted by permission of the University of Pittsburgh Press.

Richard Kenney (b. 1948)

from "The Hours of the Day"

Glass Is Not Crystalline

Molten glass was blown to a bubble, then twirled
until it flattened, cooled, and cut in squares....
Not crystalline, but technically amorphous.... Physics
demonstrates that glass is an exceptionally viscous
liquid, rather than a solid. That would seem a hard
reach for our minds, accustomed to this world
once spun four billion years ago from matter
that resolved itself in three states, each distinct:
intelligence is latticed like a quartz;
although I think we mimic the amorphous skirls
of weather in our music— *Bagpipes, bubbles, bladders*
sewn around a mystery, and daggered with the syrinx
in a nomad's hand... enormous dead hearts
that squeeze and squeeze and drown us in dark ink—

In a 2019 interview, *Richard Kenney* states in regard to poetic form: "The forms can take care of themselves. They're not at root quaint cultural artifacts, they're Darwinian solutions to questions posed by human neurology. The elements or affordances of the art never change; their local iterations respond to history."

SOURCE: Richard Kenney, "The Hours of the Day: Glass Is Not Crystalline," *The Evolution of the Flightless Bird* (New Haven, CT: Yale University Press, 1984). Reprinted by permission of author.

Agha Shahid Ali (1949-2001)

Postcard from Kashmir

Kashmir shrinks into my mailbox,
my home a neat four by six inches.

I always loved neatness. Now I hold
the half-inch Himalayas in my hand.

This is home. And this the closest
I'll ever be to home. When I return,
the colors won't be so brilliant,
the Jhelum's waters so clean,
so ultramarine. My love
so overexposed.

And my memory will be a little
out of focus, in it
a giant negative, black
and white, still undeveloped.

As Jahan Ramazani notes (*pp. 133–45*), the sonnet, sometimes seen as a box, a room, a prison cell, becomes, in "Postcard from Kashmir," a familiar object that compresses vast geographies and histories. Born in New Delhi, *Agha Shahid Ali*, a Kashmiri American Muslim poet, published primarily in English but drew on global literary forms and traditions, including the sonnet and the ghazal.

SOURCE: Agha Shahid Ali, "Postcard from Kashmir," *The Half-Inch Himalayas* (Middletown, CT: Wesleyan University Press, 1987), p. 1. © by Agha Shahid Ali. Reprinted by permission of Wesleyan University Press.

Julia Alvarez (b. 1950)

from "33"

Mami asks what I'm up to, that means men
in any declension except sex; it
means do I realize I am thirty-
three without a husband, house, or children
and going on thirty-four? Papi extends
an invitation to come live with them,
there are two empty bedrooms I can write
in and handouts until I make it big
which means men at publication parties
asking me what mentors shaped my style
and has anyone ever told me how beautiful
I am having written something worthwhile?
Their drinks tinkle in their hands like keys
to doors closed at the closing of stories.

Julia Alvarez's sequence of thirty-three sonnets was written in 1984 for her thirty-third birthday, when Latinx literature was still an emerging stream in American literature. Alvarez, who moved between New York City and the Dominican Republic as a young person, joins Emma Lazarus (*pp. 17–18*), Rhina P. Espaillat (*p. 68*), and others in this volume who employ the sonnet form to write about the particular labor of being an immigrant, a woman, and a bridger of cultures.

SOURCE: Julia Alvarez, "Mami asks what I'm up to, that means men," in "33," *Homecoming* (New York: Penguin, 1996), p. 59. Copyright © 1984, 1996 by Julia Alvarez. Published by Plume, an imprint of Penguin Random House; originally published by Grove Press. By permission of Susan Bergholz Literary Services, New York, NY, and Lamy, NM. All rights reserved.

Charles Bernstein (b. 1950)

Questionnaire

DIRECTIONS: For each pair of sentences, circle the letter, a or b, that best expresses your viewpoint. Make a selection from each pair. Do not omit any items.

1. a) The body and the material things of the world are the key to any knowledge we can possess.
   b) Knowledge is only possible by means of the mind or psyche.

2. a) My life is largely controlled by luck and chance.
   b) I can determine the basic course of my life.

3. a) Nature is indifferent to human needs.
   b) Nature has some purpose, even if obscure.

4. a) I can understand the world to a sufficient extent.
   b) The world is basically baffling.

5. a) Love is the greatest happiness.
   b) Love is illusory and its pleasures transient.

6. a) Political and social action can improve the state of the world.
   b) Political and social action are fundamentally futile.

7. a) I cannot fully express my most private feelings.
   b) I have no feelings I cannot fully express.

8. a) Virtue is its own reward.
   b) Virtue is not a matter of rewards.

9. a) It is possible to tell if someone is trustworthy.
   b) People turn on you in unpredictable ways.

10. a) Ideally, it would be most desirable to live in a rural area.
    b) Ideally, it would be most desirable to live in an urban area.

11. a) Economic and social inequality is the greatest social evil.
    b) Totalitarianism is the greatest social evil.

12. a) Overall, technology has been beneficial to human beings.
    b) Overall, technology has been harmful to human beings.

13. a) Work is the potential source of the greatest human fulfillment.
    b) Liberation from work should be the goal of any movement for social improvement.

14. a) Art is at heart political in that it can change our perception of reality.
    b) Art is at heart not political because it can change only consciousness and not events.

Charles Bernstein, like Lyn Hejinian (*pp. 74–75*), is associated with the avant-garde disjunctions of Language Poetry. His sonnet, "Questionnaire," takes an unconventional structure while engaging with classic sonnet themes such as self, meaning-making, and the role of nature and art. Essayist Nathan Spoon places Bernstein's poem in the context of neuroqueer poetics and dyslexia specifically, observing that it "allows for the creation of an individualized text" (*pp. 207–13*).

SOURCE: Charles Bernstein, "Questionnaire," *Girly Man* (Chicago: University of Chicago Press, 2006), pp. 67–68. Reprinted by permission of author.

Patricia Smith (b. 1955)

from "Salutations in Search Of"

1.

Dear floaters, bloated kin. Dear flooded necks
and reckless leapers manic for the flow.
Though you are elegant in flight, your wrecks
distress the ocean's floor—the stark tableaus
of sliding skin and swarms of slither set
to drumbeat in your hollows. This is free
proclaimed by slaver's scourge—do you regret
rebutting scar with water? Dear debris,
that ocean mothers all your rampant funk
and spurts her undulating arms for you.
She likes to think that you are simply drunk
with purpose. Dear the voyage never knew
your name. You rise in pieces, loved to death,
at last unshackled. Time will hold your breath.

2.

Dear wild tumultuous, your mouth. *Dear God.*
Your mouth, in fevered skirmish with the tongue,
denying sound for *rope* or *goldenrod*.
Dear mouth, still bulging with Atlantic, wrung
into its new. Your tangled words are lash
into the back, intending to explain
the gritted teeth inspected for a flash
of rot, the hefted cock or breast, a chain
that's wrenched away with clinging shreds of skin.
Dear going to market, beauty on the block,
seed driven deep. Dear chartered womb, within
you squirms a tendency. A paradox.
You trusted voyage, trussed to kin, and found
the tongue through tumult. Now you need a sound.

3.

Dear mute contrivance, graceless drudge. Dear hexed,
Dear wily roots and conjures, Dear persist
with your existence—flaunting all that flexed
and bumptious brawn. Dear flagrantly dismissed,
the writhing in the cottonwood. Dear flail
and drip. Dear runaway who runs the hell
away. Dear prey for drooling cur. Dear veil
of Judas moon, its murmured decibel
of light. Dear cautious measurer of splay
and fury in a heedless star. (Dear we.)
Dear woman, who must now learn to unsay
her purpose as a mute machine. Dear be
that soft alive. Dear man, whose beating drum
was lost at sea. What nouns will you become?

Patricia Smith has found new ways to write the radical Black sonnet throughout her career. Of working with traditional prosody, she says, "It would be overwrought if you did it all with the content, but you can do something that the reader can't point to right away, and they can leave the poem with the feeling you want them to leave with, without knowing how they got it."

SOURCE: Patricia Smith, "Salutations in Search Of," *Literary Hub*, July 16, 2020. Reprinted by permission of author.

Diane Seuss (b. 1956)

The sonnet, like poverty, teaches you what you can do

The sonnet, like poverty, teaches you what you can do
without. To have, as my mother says, a wish in one hand
and shit in another. That was in answer to I wish I had
an Instamatic camera and a father. Wish in one hand, she
said, shit in another. She still says it. When she tells me
she wishes I were there to have some of her bean soup
she answers herself. Wish in one hand, she says, shit in another.
Poverty, like a sonnet, is a good teacher. The kind that raps your
knuckles with a ruler but not the kind that throws a dictionary
across the room and hits you in the brain with all the words
that ever were. Boxed fathers buried deep are still fathers,
teacher says. Do without *the*. Without *and*. Without hot
dogs in your baked beans. A sonnet is a mother. Every word
a silver dollar. Shit in one hand, she says. Wish in another.

Diane Seuss was raised in rural, working-class Michigan. Her massive sonnets clock in at fourteen long lines, overflowing with syllables and rhymes that multiply, imagining new ways the sonnet can hold everything despite limited resources. Her expanded sonnet reinvents sprung rhythm in a meter spring-loaded with trochaic rhythms and trade-offs, playing on the sonnet's traditional push-pull.

SOURCE: Diane Seuss, "The sonnet, like poverty, teaches you what you can do," *frank: sonnets* (Minneapolis: Graywolf Press, 2021), p. 117. Copyright © 2015 by Diane Seuss. Reprinted with the permission of The Permissions Company, LLC on behalf of Graywolf Press, Minneapolis, Minnesota, www.graywolfpress.org.

Henri Cole (b. 1956)

Arte Povera

In the little garden of Villa Sciarra,
I found a decade of poetry dead.
In the limestone fountain lay lizards
and Fanta cans, where Truth once splashed from The Source.

How pleased I was and defiant because
a dry basin meant the end of description & rhyme,
which had nursed and embalmed me at once.
Language was more than a baroque wall-fountain.

Nearby, a gas-light shone its white-hot tongue,
a baby spat up—the stomach's truth-telling—
a mad boy made a scene worthy of Stalin.
Ah, to see the beast shitting in its cage!

Then the lying—"Yes sir, Daddy"—which changes nothing.
My soul-animal prefers the choke-chain.

Henri Cole has been engaged with the free-verse sonnet for decades. "Arte Povera," like other sonnets in this collection, pushes against what content and language befits the form. Yuki Tanaka writes about Cole's relationships with nonhuman and animal others: "Cole presents himself not in isolation but in relation to others, creating a less solipsistic kind of lyric" (*pp. 355–58*).

SOURCE: Henri Cole, "Arte Povera," *The Visible Man* by Henri Cole (New York: Farrar, Straus and Giroux, 2005), p. 3. Copyright © 1998 by Henri Cole. Reprinted by permission of Farrar, Straus and Giroux. All rights reserved.

Carl Phillips (b. 1959)

Givingly

—So here we are again, one-handedly fingering
the puckered edges of the exit wounds
memory leaves behind, he said, and he tossed
his leash made of stars, then tightened it,

around the antlers it seems I forget, always,
about having. Smell of nightfall when it
hasn't settled yet. Insatiability and
whatever else hidden behind the parts

that hide it. Surely any victim—sacrificial
or not—deserves better, I thought, him leading me
meanwhile toward the usual place, the branches
grow more givingly apart there, as if to say

Let pass. The wind was clean. The wind
was a good thing, in his hair, and across our faces.

Sonnet and sonnet-like works occur throughout *Carl Phillips*'s oeuvre in poems that highlight the erotics of form. Phillips emphasizes the sonnet's "inherent sonic restlessness," that imbalance that motivates its internal push and pull (*pp. 201–6*).

SOURCE: Carl Phillips, "Givingly," *Wild Is the Wind* by Carl Phillips (New York: Farrar, Straus and Giroux, 2018), p. 10. Copyright © 2018 by Carl Phillips. Reprinted by permission of Farrar, Straus and Giroux. All rights reserved.

Simone Muench (b. 1969) and Jackie K. White (b. 1961)

Against Teleology

They made Eve an event, a teleology
we've teethed too many mouths upon, jawing
uneven through supposed apple skin. We've
seeded and ceded enough. Enough gnawing

on our bones by canonized men. Let fang
become fallout, reverse this ache, this *sorry*.
Let bees shimmer inside our eyes instead
of men's glory. Let's mouth a modern story,

revise every exodus, each line of dread
they put upon us in sackcloth or satin.
We took the garden with us, now the gavel

is our godhead. We'll not be suckled or bled
to ghosts again. We're the heart's rattle,
razored at our core. Full of sharp. Full of sheen.

Through collaborative authorship, *Simone Muench* and *Jackie K. White*'s sonnets highlight the dialogism of the form, and not only imagine but guarantee a listener. Anna Maria Hong's essay emphasizes the importance of "female virtuosity and expression of attendant outrage...being heard" (*pp. 340–44*). While this collaboration feels highly contemporary, the tradition of sonnets-as-dialogue (*tenzone*) is as old as the sonnet form itself.

SOURCE: Simone Muench and Jackie K. White. "Against Teleology," *Hex & Howl* (Black Lawrence Press, 2021), p. 7. First appeared in *The Journal*. Reprinted by permission of the authors.

Elizabeth Alexander (b. 1962)

When

In the early 1980s, the black men
were divine, spoke French, had read everything,
made filet mignon with green peppercorn sauce,
listened artfully to boyfriend troubles,
operatically declaimed boyfriend troubles,
had been to Bamako and Bahia,
knew how to clear bad humours from a house,
had been to Baldwin's villa in Saint-Paul,
drank espresso with Soyinka and Senghor,
kissed hello on both cheeks, quoted Baraka's
"Black Art": "Fuck poems/and they are useful,"
tore up the disco dance floor, were gold-lit,
photographed well, did not smoke, said "Ciao,"

then all the men's faces were spotted.

―

As Abdul Ali notes in his essay, *Elizabeth Alexander* turns the sonnet's traditional blazon into a catalog of praise of Black men, celebrating an "expansion of black male identity that is capacious and translocating," while also remembering those lost to and the silence surrounding HIV-AIDS (*pp. 350–54*).

SOURCE: Elizabeth Alexander, "When." © Elizabeth Alexander 2005, is used with the permission of the author and was first published by Graywolf Press and subsequently published by Graywolf Press in *Crave Radiance: New and Selected Poems 1990–2010*, by Elizabeth Alexander (Minneapolis: Graywolf Press), 2010, p. 160. © Elizabeth Alexander 2010.

Tyehimba Jess (b. 1965)

Millie and Christine McCoy

We've mended two songs into one dark skin	*We ride the wake of each other's rhythm*
bleeding soprano into contralto	*beating our hearts' syncopated tempo*
—we're fused in blood and body—from one thrummed stem	
budding twin blooms of song. We're a doubled rose	
descended from raw carnage of the South	*with a music all our own. With our mouths*
bursting open our freedom. We sing past rage	*seeped in the glow of hand-me-down courage*
grown from hard labor that made our mother shout,	
spent with awe. We hymn to pay soft homage	
to the worksong's aria. It leaves us	*drenched in spiritual a cappellas,*
soaked in history like our father's sweat	*flowing soul from bone through skin. We pay debts*
borne of and beyond the flesh: we are just	
two women singing truths we can't forget	
from plantation to grave. Lord, here we are,	*from broken chattel to circus stars,*
freed twin sisters who've hauled our voices far . . .	*we sing straight from this nation's barbwired heart . . .*

To the tradition of the innovative Black sonnet, *Tyehimba Jess* brings his own syncopated sonnet, drawing on archival sources to reanimate the multiple voices of America's history of minstrelsy. Marlo Starr writes, "Through syncopation, Jess multiplies the Shakespearean sonnet form to create multi-voiced poems that can be recited like hymns sung in round, duets, or simultaneous voices singing in competing lyrics" (*pp. 304–9*).

SOURCE: Tyehimba Jess, "Millie and Christine McKoy," *Olio* (Seattle: Wave Books, 2006), p. 41. Copyright 2016 by Tyehimba Jess. Reprinted with permission of the author and Wave Books.

Natasha Trethewey (b. 1966)

Graveyard Blues

It rained the whole time we were laying her down;
Rained from church to grave when we put her down.
The suck of mud at our feet was a hollow sound.

When the preacher called out I held up my hand;
When he called for a witness I raised my hand—
Death stops the body's work, the soul's a journeyman.

The sun came out when I turned to walk away,
Glared down on me as I turned and walked away—
My back to my mother, leaving her where she lay.

The road going home was pocked with holes,
That home-going road's always full of holes;
Though we slow down, time's wheel still rolls.

> I wander now among names of the dead:
> My mother's name, stone pillow for my head.

Former US Poet Laureate *Natasha Trethewey*'s "Graveyard Blues" engages with both personal loss and shared forms, fusing sonnet and blues traditions in an elegy for her mother.

SOURCE: Natasha Trethewey, "Graveyard Blues," *Native Guard: Poems by Natasha Trethewey* (New York: Houghton Mifflin, 2007), p. 8. Copyright © 2006 by Natasha Trethewey. Reprinted by permission of Mariner Books, an imprint of HarperCollins Publishers.

Adrienne Su (b. 1967)

from "Four Sonnets about Food"

1

Words can't do
what bird bones
can: stew
to the stony
essence
of one
small soul, the spent
sacrifice boiled down
to the hard white
matter that nourishes
the mighty
predator, who flourishes
on the slaughtered
animal and water.

Lesley Wheeler's essay attends to *Adrienne Su*'s short-lined sonnet sequence (*pp. 273–77*). Su's first sonnet from "Four Sonnets about Food" engages in the sonnet's long tradition of self-interrogation, questioning its materials and capabilities.

SOURCE: Adrienne Su, "Four Sonnets about Food," *Middle Kingdom* (Farmington, ME: Alice James Books, 1997), pp. 65–68. Reprinted by permission of the author.

Anna Maria Hong

Nude Palette

What a muse, what a mess, this state of undress
descending the spiral stare—to look back is
to profess, resume the harness, and lose
the myth of progress—save us and tear us

apart to finesse this duress, stress by mis-
step. Give me access or emptiness—
the world is my terrace—
an embarrassment of purchase, promise—

Hello, virtuoso! You had me at emo.
I was dead as a dodo, a solo
soprano with a face for radio
and a case of mono, working *pro*

bono for the *ecce homo*. Show me the jello
en masse, in toto. Oh, no. Say yes.

In *Anna Maria Hong*'s "Nude Palette," strategies of sound and wordplay simultaneously amuse and destabilize, spinning feminist commentary from insistent rhyming and absurd associative echoes. See Anna Lena Phillips Bell's essay for an analysis of Hong's formal moves (*pp. 291–95*) and Hong's own essay for an exploration of the contemporary feminist sonnet (*pp. 340–44*).

SOURCE: Anna Maria Hong, "Nude Palette," previously appeared as "Klepto Cathexis" in the chapbook *Hello, virtuoso!* (Brooklyn: Belladonna* Collaborative, 2014), p. 16, and in *Fablesque* (North Adams, MA: Tupelo Press, 2020), p. 52. Reprinted by permission of author.

giovanni singleton

from "The Black and White Sonnet Series"

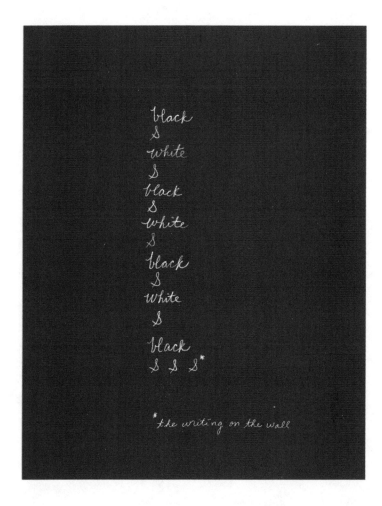

---

giovanni singleton's visual poems explore the intersection of image and language. "The Black and White Sonnet Series" draws on the reader-viewer's likely familiarity with and potential assumptions about the sonnet in its experimentation.

SOURCE: giovanni singleton, "The Black and White Sonnet Series," *Obsidian*, vol. 45 no. 9, 2019, p. 282. Reprinted by permission of author.

Philip Metres (b. 1970)

Ismail & Abla to Ahmed, Their Son

your body full / of fragments / harrowed was thy brain
spilled over your clothes / you / already not

of this world / in the shadow of our difficult / we plant
your heart inside / a teenaged girl you will

never touch / liver we bury / in a baby you will
never raise / elderly you'll never be / kidneys

we resettle in alien skin / your lungs now breathe
for two who could not breathe without you

we know your toy gun looked / death
in the eye but why / did they have to shoot you

twice / & now inside "the enemy" you rise
behind the lines of inside / you live

& see for yourself what none of us can see
ourselves / ourselves from the outside

Philip Metres's sonnets in *Shrapnel Maps* are monologues featuring Palestinian and Israeli voices. Stripped of many of the sonnet's recognizable prosodic elements, the personal and political engagement of Metres's contemporary sonnet, "Ismail & Abla to Ahmed, Their Son," might still be read in the *tenzone* tradition of sonnet sequence as poetic exchange.

SOURCE: Philip Metres, "Ismail & Abla to Ahmed, Their Son," *Shrapnel Maps* (Port Townsend, WA, Copper Canyon Press, 2020), p. 69. Copyright © 2020 by Philip Metres. Reprinted with the permission of The Permissions Company, LLC on behalf of Copper Canyon Press, www.coppercanyonpress.org.

Terrance Hayes (b. 1971)

American Sonnet for My Past and Future Assassin

The song must be cultural, confessional, clear
But not obvious. It must be full of compassion
And crows bowing in a vulture's shadow.
The song must have six sides to it & a clamor
Of voltas. The song must turn on the compass
Of language like a tangle of wire endowed
With feeling. The notes must tear & tear,
There must be a love for the minute & minute,
There must be a record of witness & daydream.
Where the heart is torn or feathered & tarred,
Where death is undone, time diminished,
The song must hold its own storm & drum,
And shed a noise so lovely it is sung at sunset
Weddings, baptisms, & beheadings henceforth.

American Sonnet for My Past and Future Assassin

I lock you in an American sonnet that is part prison,
Part panic closet, a little room in a house set aflame.
I lock you in a form that is part music box, part meat
Grinder to separate the song of the bird from the bone.
I lock your persona in a dream-inducing sleeper hold
While your better selves watch from the bleachers.
I make you both gym & crow here. As the crow
You undergo a beautiful catharsis trapped one night
In the shadows of the gym. As the gym, the feel of crow-
Shit dropping to your floors is not unlike the stars
Falling from the pep rally posters on your walls.
I make you a box of darkness with a bird in its heart.
Voltas of acoustics, instinct & metaphor. It is not enough
To love you. It is not enough to want you destroyed.

Terrance Hayes has returned to iterations of the sonnet form throughout his body of work. The sonnets collected in book form in *American Sonnets for My Past and Future Assassin* are explicitly indebted to Wanda Coleman's "American Sonnet" series *(pp. 82–83)*. Like Coleman's, Hayes's *American Sonnets* are dense and capacious, playful and political. See Ramazani's essay on the self-metaphorizing American sonnet *(pp. 133–45)*.

SOURCE: Terrance Hayes, "I lock you in an American sonnet that is part prison" and "The song must be cultural, confessional, clear," *American Sonnets for My Past and Future Assassin* by Terrance Hayes (New York: Penguin, 2018), pp. 46 and 11. Copyright 2018 by Terrance Hayes. Used by permission of Penguin Books, an imprint of Penguin Publishing Group, a division of Penguin Random House LLC. All rights reserved.

Jen Bervin (b. 1972)

from "Nets"

                              22

         My glass shall not persuade me **I am** old
         So long as youth and thou are **of one date**,
         But when **in** thee **time's furrows** I behold,
    4   Then look I death my days should expire.
         For all that beauty that doth cover thee
         Is but the seemly raiment of my heart,
         Which in thy breast doth live, as thine in me:
    8   How can I then be elder than thou art?
         O, therefore, love, be of thyself so wary
         As I, not for myself, but for thee will,
         Bearing thy heart, which I will keep so chary
   12   As tender nurse her babe from faring ill.
              Presume not on thy heart when mine is slain;
              Thou gav'st me thine, not to give back again.

68

>   This is his book the **map** of days outworn,
>   When beauty lived and died as flowers do now,
>   Before the bastard signs of fair were born,
> 4 Or durst inhabit on a living brow;
>   Before the golden tresses of **the** dead,
>   The right of sepulchres, were **shorn away**,
>   To live a second life on second head—
> 8 Ere beauty's dead fleece made another gay:
>   In him those holy antique hours are seen,
>   Without all ornament, itself and true,
>   Making no summer of another's green,
> 12 Robbing no old to dress his beauty new;
>   And him as for a **map** doth Nature store,
>   To show false Art **what beauty was** of yore.

Jen Bervin is one of a number of American writers who use innovative formal techniques to engage with the canonical sonnets of William Shakespeare (see Aaron Shurin's poem, *p. 85*). In *Nets*, Bervin uses erasure to paradoxically reveal new texts in the familiar works.

SOURCE: Jen Bervin, "Sonnet 22" and "Sonnet 68," *Nets* (Brooklyn: Ugly Duckling Presse, 2003), © Jen Bervin.

Nathan Spoon (b.1972)

Kiddo

What was it that slid through the field of my hand?
A mountain. I will say it was a mountain, although
it is no longer here for any other to see. It is elsewhere
and doubtless sitting like a toad whose voraciousness
desires to be appeased. At a key moment any hand may
grow warm and as sustaining as a grove of pawpaw
or sassafras trees. I will negotiate moving forward from

here, forward into the thickness that buries all
but the most willful homing. The seat is leather-like
and brown and the back is mint green. What kind
of sense does that make? Who knows? But at least
people needing to sit have somewhere to do that. There
are always turns as entirely unexpected as this. Often
a bright pair of shoelaces appears as if out of nowhere.

In his essay in this collection (*pp. 207–13*), *Nathan Spoon* illuminates qualities such as playfulness, self-distraction, mutuality, and self-assertion to begin a transhistorical conversation, exploring and making visible a neuroqueer sonnet tradition.

SOURCE: Nathan Spoon, "Kiddo." First published in *Gulf Coast*, Winter/Spring 2021. Reprinted by permission of author.

Douglas Kearney (b. 1974)

SONNET DONE RED

I love your body.
I love your body.
I **HATE** body.
I love your body.
IT
I love your body.
I love your body.

o,

I love your body.
I hate it.

o,

~~I hate~~
LOVE
~~your body.~~

even so

I love/hate your body/it?

Douglas Kearney's transmedial poetics fuse oral and visual traditions. "Sonnet Done Red," a visual poem from *Patter*, plays on the sonnet's troubadour-inflected tradition of contradictory or painful love in exploring the shared but isolating experience of miscarriage and infertility.

SOURCE: Douglas Kearney, "Sonnet Done Red," *Patter* (Pasadena, CA: Red Hen Press, 2014), 31. Courtesy of Douglas Kearney.

Joyelle McSweeney (b. 1976)

from "Toxic Sonnets"

4.

Death-fletched, alive, immune to all elixirs,
I sit like a drone pilot at a dock of screens.
My attention is a fang that sinks through plasma
like a toxic arrow or a tooth in Coke. I'm fine.
I'm sick. I grip a joy-stick. Outside, a pink
crust announces evening, buzzards ride
heat signatures at dusk. Inside, plasmodium
reshapes itself, now a slipper, now a gauntlet
tossed down in the gut, and now a Glock, a mouse,
a Mauser, the lucky cloud that mounts the hill
to breaks its blessing on the forehead of the bride
or the wedding guest who's dead
yet cocks his eye
at any light now breaking in the sky

Form is a kind of contagion in *Joyelle McSweeney*'s Necropastoral sonnet crown, "Toxic Sonnets: A Crown for John Keats." McSweeney describes the "Necropastoral" as "a political-aesthetic zone in which the fact of mankind's depredations cannot be separated from an experience of 'nature' which is poisoned, mutated, aberrant, spectacular, full of ill effects and affects. The Necropastoral is a nonrational zone, anachronistic, it often looks backwards."

SOURCE: Joyelle McSweeney, "Toxic Sonnets: 4." *Toxicon and Arachne* (Brooklyn: Nightboat Books, 2020), p. 32. Reprinted by permission of author.

Jericho Brown (b. 1976)

Duplex

The opposite of rape is understanding
A field of flowers called paintbrushes—

> A field of flowers called paintbrushes,
> Though the spring be less than actual.

Though the spring be less than actual,
Men roam shirtless as if none ever hurt me.

> Men roam that myth. In truth, one hurt me.
> I want to obliterate the flowered field,

To obliterate my need for the field
And raise a building above the grasses,

> A building of prayer against the grasses,
> My body a temple in disrepair.

My body is a temple in disrepair.
The opposite of rape is understanding.

The Tradition

Aster. Nasturtium. Delphinium. We thought
Fingers in dirt meant it was our dirt, learning
Names in heat, in elements classical
Philosophers said could change us. *Stargazer.*
Foxglove. Summer seemed to bloom against the will
Of the sun, which news reports claimed flamed hotter
On this planet than when our dead fathers
Wiped sweat from their necks. *Cosmos. Baby's Breath.*
Men like me and my brothers filmed what we
Planted for proof we existed before
Too late, sped the video to see blossoms
Brought in seconds, colors you expect in poems
Where the world ends, everything cut down.
John Crawford. Eric Garner. Mike Brown.

—

Jericho Brown's Pulitzer Prize–winning collection *The Tradition* includes variations on the sonnet form, such as its title poem, and also introduces his innovative "duplex," inspired by sonnet, ghazal, and blues forms. See Michael Dumanis's essay (*pp. 235–41*).

SOURCE: Jericho Brown, "Duplex" and "The Tradition," *The Tradition* (Port Townsend, WA: Copper Canyon Press, 2019), pp. 27 and 10. Copyright © 2019 by Jericho Brown. Reprinted with the permission of The Permissions Company, LLC on behalf of Copper Canyon Press, coppercanyonpress.org and Picador UK.

Brandy Nālani McDougall (b. 1976)

from "Ka ʻŌlelo

ʻelima

As the ʻape shoot, whose delicate shoots
shoot forth their young sprouts, and spread, and bring forth
in their birth, many branches find their roots
in the dark, wet ʻōlelo the earth bore.
My unripe tongue taps my palate, my teeth
like a blind koʻe that must feel its way
through the liquids, mutes and aspirates of speech,
the threading of breath and blood into lei:
"E aloha. ʻO wai kou inoa?"
I ask, after the language CD's voice.
"ʻO Kekauoha koʻo inoa,"
my grandfather answers, "Pehea ʻoe?"
So, we slowly begin, with what ʻōlelo
we know; E hoʻoulu ana kakou.

Brandy Nālani McDougall is a Kānaka Maoli writer, scholar, and literary activist, whose sonnet series "Ka ʻŌlelo" (of which "ʻelima" is the fifth sonnet) describes speaker and grandfather relearning their Hawaiian language. Her author's note emphasizes the limits of anthologizing categorization and the impulse to nationalize poetics.

AUTHOR'S NOTE: I do not identify as American. It's true that I am a U.S. citizen, but as an Indigenous person from an occupied place, I did not choose to be one and my ancestors were forced to be Americans. The circumstances that have made me "American" come from the U.S.'s illegal annexation of Hawaiʻi in 1898 and the accompanying violence of suppressing Hawaiian culture, language and knowledge systems, as well as the ongoing dispossession of our lands (and with that, the suppression of ways we would feed our bodies and spirits) for generations. —*Brandy Nālani McDougall*

SOURCE: Brandy Nālani McDougall, "'elima," from "Ka ʻŌlelo," *The Salt-Wind, Ka Makani Paʻakai* (Honolulu: Kuleana ʻŌiwi Press, 2008), p. 69. Reprinted by permission of author.

Natalie Diaz (b. 1978)

My American Crown

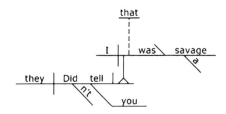

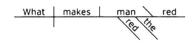

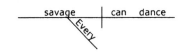

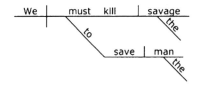

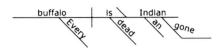

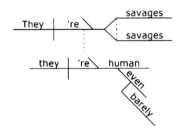

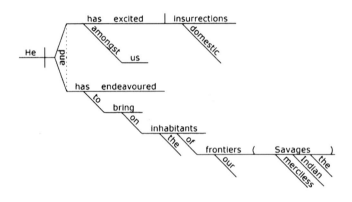

Natalie Diaz is a Pulitzer Prize–winning poet and Mojave language activist. Enrolled in the Gila River Indian Community, she identifies as Akimel O'odham (River People, also known as the Pima). Of "My American Crown," Diaz says: "Whereas in a sonnet crown the last line is repeated in the first line, in this series of diagrams I simply pressed into the iterated wound of a word: savages. I treated it as its own line, its own everything.... When I look at this sonnet crown, it feels like my experience of sonnet language."

SOURCE: Natalie Diaz, "My American Crown," in "Sonnet Crown Feature," *IthacaLit*, Summer 2018. Reprinted by permission of author.

Tarfia Faizullah (b. 1980)

Reading Celan at the Liberation War Museum

—*Independence Day Celebration 2011, Dhaka*

    i.

In a courtyard, in these stacks of chairs
    before the empty stage—*near are*
we Lord, near and graspable. Lord,
    accept these humble offerings:

stacks of biscuits wrapped in cellophane,
    stacks of bone in glass: thighbone,
spine. Stacks of white saucers, porcelain
    circles into which stacks of lip-worn

cups slide neat. Jawbone, Lord. Galleries
    of laminated clippings declaring war.
Hands unstack chairs into rows. *The dead:*
    they still go begging. What for, Lord?

Blunt bayonets, once sharp as wind?
    Moon-pale stacks of clavicle? A hand—

    ii.

Moon-pale stacks of clavicle a hand
    brushes dust from. *I lost a word*

that was left to me: sister. The wind
    severs through us—we sit, wait

for songs of nation and loss in neat
    long rows below this leaf-green

flag—its red-stitched circle stains
    us blood-bright blossom, stains

us river-silk—*I saw you, sister, standing*
    in this brilliance—I saw light sawing

through a broken car window, thistling
     us pink—I saw, sister, your bleeding

head, an unfurling shapla flower
     petaling slow across mute water—

    iii.

Petaling slow
         across mute water,
bows of trawlers
          skimming nets
of silver fish that ripple
           through open
hands that will carve them
          skin-

less. *We were hands,*
         we scooped
the darkness empty. We
         are rooted
bodies in rows silent before
          the sparked
blue limbs of dancers
         leafing the dark

light indigo, then
         jasmine alighting
into a cup, then
         hands overturning
postcards bearing flag
          and flower, hands
cradling the replica of a boat,
         hands

thrust there and into
         nothingness. You,
a corpse, sister, bathed
         jasmine, blue—

iv.

A corpse: sister, bathed jasmine. Blue,
                the light leading me from this gift shop into
a gallery of gray stones: *Heartgray puddles,*
                two mouthfuls of silence: the shadow

        cast by the portrait of a raped woman trapped
in a frame, face hidden behind her own black
            river of hair: photo that a solemn girl
your corpse's age stands still and small

        before. She asks, *Did someone hurt her?*
Did she do something bad? Her mother
            does not reply. Her father turns, shudders,
as the light drinks our silences, parched—

        as I too turn in light, spine-scraped—
you teach you teach your hands to sleep

v.

you teach you teach your hands to sleep
because her hands can't hold the shape
of a shapla flower cut from its green leaf
because her hands can't hold grief
nor light nor sister   in her hands fistfuls
of her own hair   on her wrists glass bangles
like the one you struggled over your hand
the same hand that slapped a sister's wan
face   look   the young girl stands before
the photo of the young woman who swore
she would not become the old woman

crouched low on a jute mat holding

out to you a bangle   *a strange lostness was*

bodily present   you came near to living

vi.

Bodily present, you came near to living,
    Poet, in this small blue dress still stained,

the placard states, with the blood of the child
    crushed dead by a soldier's boot. Who failed

and fails?—nights you couldn't bear the threshed
    sounds of your heart's hard beating. I press

a button: 1971 springs forth: black and white
    bodies marching in pixelated rows. Nights

you resuscitated *the Word, sea-overflowed,*
    star-overflown. A pixelated woman tied

with a white rope to a black pole, her white
    sari embroidered with mud or blood. Nights

you were the *wax to seal what's unwritten*—
    the screen goes white in downdrifting light.

vii.

The screen goes white. In downdrifting light,
    the stairwell is a charred tunnel. We walk out
of it into the courtyard—my skirt flares a rent
    into the burnt evening. *Something was silent,*

something went its way—something gnashes
    inside me, sister—along the yellow gashes
of paint guiding me through these rooms lined
    with glass cases, past machine gun chains

shaped into the word *Bangla*. Here, on this
    stage, a dancer bows low her limbs
once more before us. The stage goes silent.
    We gather ourselves: souvenirs of bone.

Pray, Lord. We are near. Near are we, Lord—
    in a courtyard, in these stacks of chairs.

Tarfia Faizullah's sonnet crown reckons with both personal and national trauma. A Bangladeshi American poet raised in Texas, her interviews with *birangona*—survivors of rape by Pakistani soldiers during the 1971 Liberation War—became part of her debut collection, *Seam*. In "Reading Celan at the Liberation War Museum," Faizullah both engages and interrogates the artifices of sonnet, exhibit, and performance while adding to the traditions of the elegiac and transnational sonnet.

SOURCE: Tarfia Faizullah, "Reading Celan at the Liberation War Museum," *Seam*, in the Crab Orchard Series in Poetry (Carbondale, IL: Crab Orchard Review & Southern Illinois University Press, 2014), pp. 51–57. Copyright © 2014 by Tarfia Faizullah.

Craig Santos Perez (b. 1980)

Love in a Time of Climate Change

recycling Pablo Neruda's "Sonnet XVII"

I don't love you as if you were rare earth metals,
conflict diamonds, or reserves of crude oil that cause
war. I love you as one loves the most vulnerable
species: urgently, between the habitat and its loss.

I love you as one loves the last seed saved
within a vault, gestating the heritage of our roots,
and thanks to your body, the taste that ripens
from its fruit still lives sweetly on my tongue.

I love you without knowing how or when this world
will end. I love you organically, without pesticides.
I love you like this because we'll only survive

in the nitrogen rich compost of our embrace,
so close that your emissions of carbon are mine,
so close that your sea rises with my heat.

Craig Santos Perez is an Indigenous Chamoru (Chamorro) from the Pacific island of Guåhan (Guam). His sonnets often engage with an ecopoetic tradition, as in the "recycling" of Neruda in "Love in a Time of Climate Change," which is both love poem and social critique.

SOURCE: Craig Santos Perez, "Love in a Time of Climate Change," *Habitat Threshold* (Oakland, CA: Omnidawn, 2020), p. 26. © 2020. The poem appears with the permission of Omnidawn Publishing and the author. All rights reserved.

Tacey M. Atsitty (b. 1982)

Lacing: XII

The lace hem of my skirt has become worn.
Or maybe it's always been this way: like wind,
we never felt the cracks of morn

that summer. I told him I'd turn them, wind
them even, if he wanted me to, until he'd think
I was making music—sometimes when I bind

them, they can be tuned beautiful still. Just a wink,
and I'll come wearing mountains over my shoulders,
come bearing lakes about my legs. Then in a blink

we'll tune ourselves to a field of lace, our shoulder
blades thrusting into the white, and our wrists—
they'll finish going round, ready to shoulder

the day we yellow together into old lace, old wrists.
Our lives rounded out like arcs of our wrists.

Tacey M. Atsitty, Diné (Navajo), is Tsénahabiłnii (Sleep Rock People) and born for Ta'neeszahnii (Tangle People). Her ongoing relationship with the sonnet form often engages with the sonnet's sensual and erotic traditions, while also "grounding" themselves in a sense of place.

SOURCE: Tacey M. Atsitty, "Lacing: XII," *Dispatches Journal* (April 30, 2020). Reprinted by permission of author.

Meg Day (b. 1984)

from "Boy Corona"

Crucifying

Don't leave? Brother, I'll be. Twinned half, you are a man
with a body like a cross you can't put down & whose weight might begat
your end even if they do not nail you to it. Ah, ambitious hate:
to desire the life that might take it from you. Once our reflections ran
flat hands down ace bandages in a pledge to a new promised land & can
you believe our ribs stayed put when the men kicked through them?
    Immaculate
ensemble, we bled our own flag. We hung it in strips from the shower bar,
    a fate
divined in dinnertime tickertape. What version of exodus can span
this wilderness: I remember the man who threw lot & leather, but it was
    she
I could not hear or see who cast the first vote & meant to kill me. By & by
we're gone before we can warn the next: two bodies diverge at a fist &
    both die
by metaphor. I salute your *I am*, Brother, neither of us similes. I sign
    T-H-E-E
as if English doesn't make my hand, too, a weapon. What is there to
    condole
but a wrong that's all my own? Isn't **me-WRONG** a kiss to the cheek &
    not the soul?

Meg Day's essay describes the experience of "Deafing" the sonnet, using John Donne's rhymes as an "auditory prosthetic" (*pp. 242–46*). Day's essay pushes back at ableist assumptions, asking "what might be possible when Deaf and disabled poets are not regulated by the limitations of the nondisabled imagination and allowed, without having to reiterate our existence, to freely make." In "Boy Corona," transness and Deafness inform the sonnet form. See torrin a. greathouse's "Ars Poetica" for another example of embodied intersectionality shaping the sonnet form (*p. 128*).

SOURCE: Meg Day, "Crucifying." This poem is a part of the "Boy Corona" crown of sonnets as it originally appeared in *The Nation* (February 3, 2021). Reprinted by permission of author.

Lo Kwa Mei-en (b. 1987)

The Alien Crown
(The conquerers came and wrote the conquered into being)

The conquerers came and wrote the conquered into being
guilt-making, but pretty good in retro, plus, gosh, pretty to boot.
Um—so, "like" but "not": a citizen has a soul in his face of
fair; it's why *they* don't all look the same. Toddlers fumble thru
veni / vidi / verify but can recite my *name / number / allegiance*
except on multi-colonial awareness day, a false password we live.
Without anger, they beg, *poems work—don't you want to arrive?* God,
do I? When a conqueror sleeps in the collar of his hand, how
xenophobic pencils might shudder on a page of the domestic:
come be historic and sample a vowel: then write an index
yes is said to. Amen. But come the future. But say we climb
back on the boat. Say we pack the hull with work with angry
zephyrs—to, say it, their hell—and over it heave the extra
anchor, aim it to a future minus a canon the color of quartz—

—

Lo Kwa Mei-en is from Singapore and Ohio. Her sonnet sequence "The Alien Crown"—dispersed throughout her collection *The Bees Make Money in the Lion*—explores migration, colonization, and belonging through a speculative lens. Eschewing rhyme and meter for variations on the abecedarian (in this case, a kind of double reverse abecedarian), Mei-en draws on a multitude of linguistic registers while reinvigorating the sonnet's complicated relationship with power and (as in its final line) looking beyond an all-white canon.

SOURCE: Lo Kwa Mei-en, "The Alien Crown (The conquerers came and wrote the conquered into being)." *The Bees Make Money in the Lion* (Cleveland, OH: Cleveland State University Poetry Center, 2016), p. 18. Reprinted by permission of author.

Nate Marshall (b. 1989)

African american literature

i like your poems because they seem so real.
i like your poems because they seem so real.
i like your poems because they seem so real.
i like your poems because they seem so real.

i like your poems because they seem so real.
i like your poems because they seem so real.
i like your poems because they seem so real.
i like your poems because they seem so real.

i like your poems because they seem so real.
i like your poems because they seem so real.
i like your poems because they seem so real.
i like your poems because they seem so real.

i like your poems because they seem so real.
f'sho, good look, this also a sonnet.

Nate Marshall's "African american literature" uses the sonnet's relationship with formal artifice to explore questions of race, expectation, and "authenticity" in relation to African American poetry. See Rebecca Morgan Frank's essay on the repeated-line sonnet (*pp. 285–90*), Michael Theune's essay on the sonnet's turn (*pp. 267–72*), and Michael Dumanis's essay on Jericho Brown (*pp. 235–41*).

SOURCE: Nate Marshall, "African american literature," *Finna: Poems* by Nate Marshall (New York: One World, 2020), p. 81. Copyright © 2020 by Nathaniel A. Marshall. Used by permission of One World, an imprint of Random House, a division of Penguin Random House LLC. All rights reserved.

torrin a. greathouse (b. 1994)

Ars Poetica
or
Sonnet to Be Written Across My Chest & Read in a Mirror,
Beginning with a Line from Kimiko Hahn

                        I could not return to the body that
                        contained only the literal world: here,

                        where I cannot say reflect & not suggest
                        a bending back. Where back does not suggest

                        the fractured glass of me. I am told to
                        sever, with a pencil's blade, the word body.

                        Taught that it does not belong, taught to cut
                        it away. But look, here it is, real

                        & irrefutable. Beneath the sonnet's
                        dark calligraphy, what cannot be spoken

                        with a psalm-less tongue, music unhinged
                        from inside a gaping mouth, a body—mine.

                        & at last a poem that can't be read without
                        it: crippled, trans, woman, & still   alive.

Nathan Spoon's essay situates *torrin a. greathouse*'s work in the tradition of the neuroqueer sonnet (*pp. 207–13*). In "Ars Poetica," a mirror-image sonnet, greathouse creates a ritual of poetic embodiment and an affirmation of intersectionality and survival.

SOURCE: torrin a. greathouse, "Ars Poetica *or* Sonnet to Be Written across My Chest & Read in a Mirror, Beginning with a Line from Kimiko Hahn," *Wound from the Mouth of a Wound* by torrin a. greathouse (Minneapolis: Milkweed Editions, 2020), p. 61. Copyright © by torrin a. greathouse. Reprinted with permission from Milkweed Editions. milkweed.org.

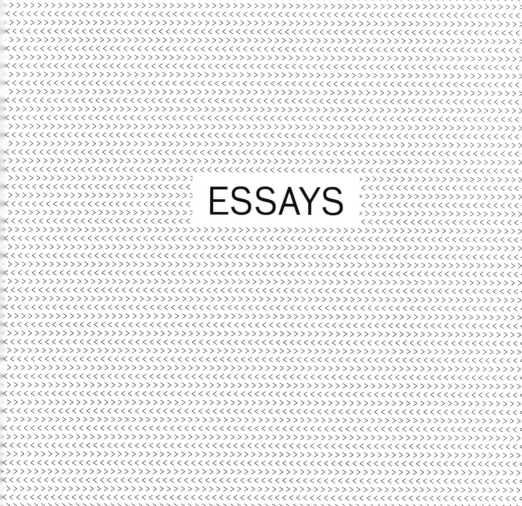

ESSAYS

THE NATIONAL AND GLOBAL SONNET

Self-Metaphorizing "American" Sonnets

JAHAN RAMAZANI

What is an American sonnet? Is it a box, a prison, or other enclosed space, as Terrance Hayes and other contemporary poets have suggested, developing the genre's long tradition of self-metaphorization? As such, can the sonnet function as a space of both involuntary confinement and welcome refuge within the larger enclosure of a nation beset by racist violence—"part prison, / Part panic closet, a little room in a house set aflame" (*p. 105*)? Or is it, as Hayes goes on to suggest, a boxlike mechanism for the production of sound and substance—"a form that is part music box, part meat / Grinder," the sonnet's machinery imagined as forcefully liberating "the song of the bird from the bone" (11)? Or, as this mention of song suggests, building on another durable cluster of self-figurations, is the sonnet a performance practice, also akin to instrumental music, ritual, and prayer?[1]

And what of the interlinked sonnet "crown"? Is it, in one of numerous botanical metaphors with long histories, a wildflower-woven garland, as in Marilyn Nelson's *A Wreath for Emmett Till* (*p. 84*), or is it, like the poet herself in Kiki Petrosino's "Happinefs," a twisting vine or "sedge grass / spiraling from the root / blade upon blade upon blade"—a metaphor for the poet's growth and racialization that evokes the sequence's spiral of repeat lines while alluding to the UVA Cavaliers' saber blades and Adrienne Rich's helicopter-like new woman's "fine blades" (Petrosino 20)?[2] What about revivified geographical tropes? Could the sonnet resemble, as in Lucille Clifton's "the mississippi river empties into the gulf," rivers and their "great circulation / of the earth's body, like the blood / of the gods" (37)? Or maybe, as in Agha Shahid Ali's "Postcard from Kashmir" (*p. 88*), is it a postcard that "shrinks" such vast geography into a charming "neatness" (1), years before Billy Collins figured thus the sonnet's "of what we feel" in his "American Sonnet" (329)?[3] As this very incomplete but sonnet-like enumeration is meant to suggest, there may be no genre that's more relentlessly and heterogeneously self-metaphorizing than the sonnet. In an effort to examine both the power and the limits of the sonnet's intrinsic models, or, if you will, its self-theorizations, let's see what we learn by testing them and our critical paradigms against one another and against the sonnets themselves.[4]

Although literary self-reflexivity is often associated with the postmodern novel, poetry's traditions of self-mirroring and self-metaphorizing go back to antiquity, prospering in sonnets on sonnets from the early modern period to today. Hayes's sonnets help revitalize the subgenre of the metasonnet for our time. In other sonnets and sonnet sequences, the self-referentiality is often more oblique. The genre's memory of its history, conventions, structures, and tropes is so rich, its tradition of self-metaphorization so strong, its self-awareness so intensified by its compression, that sonnets often talk about themselves when talking about love, race, nationality, the natural environment, or another subject

Think of Claude McKay's "America" (*p. 35*), which rapidly proliferates figures for the United States that also suggest the Shakespearean poetic form that, at once stultifying and enabling, the Jamaican immigrant remakes. This "analogy between the sonnet and th e nation" was, as Timo Müller notes, important for Black poets—a resemblance built, as with many such metaphors, around the mutually illuminating restrictions and affordances of each form (6). In McKay's first few metaphors, the poet's organs of speech and inspiration are impeded: the nation (or sonnet) is a bad mother ("she feeds me bread of bitterness"), a tiger ("And sinks into my throat her tiger's tooth"), and a thief ("Stealing my breath of life") (153). Phrasing in quasi-erotic terms his ambivalence toward both the political and the poetic form, the poet declares—his deictic "this" ambiguously pointing both ways—"I will confess / I love this cultured hell that tests my youth! / Her vigor flows like tides into my blood, / Giving me strength erect against her hate."[5] At the volta, the double gender switch emphasizes these figural metamorphoses, the "she" becoming "a king in state" confronted by a rebel, before swiftly morphing into a queen with a castle ("I stand within her walls"—a fortified enclosure that evokes the boundaries of both the state and the sonnet). Finally, in an allusion to Shelley's sonnet on Ozymandias,

America is a form destined for ruin, "her might and granite wonders /... sinking in the sand." Leaping from trope to trope, the poet indicates that none is sufficient by itself for the cruel mistress of the nation or of the sonnet. But if the nation's imperial future looks grim, McKay demonstrates the bright promise of the poetic form, showing off an imaginative inventiveness undefeated and indeed invigorated by "this cultured hell."

A century later, Joyelle McSweeney, revivifying the sonnet's oblique but metaphorically fecund self-figurations, reimagines in her sonnet crown "Toxic Sonnets" (*p. 111*) the tuberculosis bacterium that killed John Keats:

> Inside, plasmodium
> reshapes itself, now a slipper, now a gauntlet
> tossed down in the gut, and now a Glock, a mouse,
> a Mauser, the lucky cloud that mounts the hill
> to break its blessing on the forehead of the bride
> or the wedding guest who's dead
> yet cocks his eye
> at any light now breaking in the sky. (32)

Echoing the rapid-fire figurative mutations of earlier sonneteers, McSweeney metaphorizes a shape—pathogenic or poetic—as morphing from slipper to gun, mouse (technological or mammalian), and cloud. Infected by Keats's sonnet rhyme of "sky" with "eye" ("On First Looking into Chapman's Homer"), as well as his Shakespearean couplets, the poem glances at the contagion that gives rise to these very sonnets—compact, yet mercurial and self-reshaping.

Little, airborne, prolifically self-replicating, spreading easily and quickly, adaptable to new environments across the world, mutating as it develops—am I describing the sonnet or a pathogen? Not that they're the same. Keats's sonnets may have in some sense "infected" both McKay's and McSweeney's, but unless we wanted to go all in on Bloomian struggle-to-the-death anxiety, this strangely vitalizing contagion likely hasn't risked these poets' lives, any more than Shakespeare did Keats's or McKay's. Still, whereas the theory of the novel from Mikhail Bakhtin to Franco Moretti may suggest that the discursive and formal openness, looseness, and largeness of the novel help explain its transnational diffusion, the pathogenic analogy highlights how a form's compactness and tightness can, conversely, enable its speedy and successful transmission across the globe. It's paradoxically by virtue of being what's figured as a "closed" or "fixed" form that the sonnet, like the ballad, ghazal, haiku, pantoum, and villanelle, opens to the world.

Which brings us to the other part of my initial question: what is the *American* sonnet? After all, the sonneteer Karl Shapiro is hardly alone in worrying that the sonnet may be "un-American." But if it were ever true that the "packaging" of the sonnet and other closed forms seemed "pretty" and "polite," poets from at least McKay to Hayes have disproved the idea. It's a commonplace that the American sonnet often tends to violate the traditional norms of the sonnet. Still, the American sonnet's intrinsic container models as room or box and performance models as song or ritual can't be contained by Americanness. When we track how the sonnet has been locally transplanted or indigenized, Americanized, Arabized, or Russified, our points of reference are inevitably in part extralocal—fourteen lines, Petrarchan or Shakespearean, volta, octave, sestet, quatrain, couplet, iambic pentameter, enjambment, blazon, conceit, etc. And when poets struggle against the form's global inheritances, their sonnets invoke what they domesticate or even reject. Moreover, like prison or pathogen, the nationality of a sonnet is, strictly speaking, a trope, however naturalized. Even if a sonnet metaphorizes itself as "American" and displays what we think of as American traits, many of its formal and linguistic ingredients come from afar, and no sonnet can literally be "a citizen or subject of a particular state," in the words of the *OED* ("Nationality").

Consider Rita Dove's *Mother Love*, a book of sonnets that never loses sight of the tightly wound global form it repurposes. True, these sonnets translocate (one translation of *metapherein*) that global inheritance. Like many others, they exemplify what she refers to offhandedly as "ways to 'violate' the sonnet in the service of American speech or modern love or whatever" (Dove xii). They're largely unrhymed and unmetered, break and scatter lines across the page, and code switch between African American vernacular ("ain't nothing we can do") and formal Standard English ("Tonight men stride like elegant scissors across the lawn") (15, 8). But the cosmopolitan range of reference is already evident in the first few sentences of "An Intact World," the book's foreword that Müller calls "the most prominent discussion of the sonnet in the African American context" (8):[6]

> "Sonnet" literally means "little song." The sonnet is a *heile Welt*, an intact world where everything is in sync, from the stars down to the tiniest mite on a blade of grass. And if the "true" sonnet reflects the music of the spheres, it then follows that any variation from the strictly Petrarchan or Shakespearean forms represents a world gone awry.
>
> Or does it? Can't form also be a talisman against disintegration? (Dove xi)

Even before getting to Demeter and Persephone's "violated world," Dove hops from medieval Italy ("little song," "Petrarchan") to postwar Germany ("*heile Welt*," from the title poem of Werner Bergengruen's 1950 collection) and Renaissance England ("Shakespearean") via Pythagorean Greece ("the music of the spheres"). To adapt Wallace Stevens, the sonnet's "fire-fangled feathers dangle down" into literary history, while also spreading across the world. It's all the more ironic that Dove published her conspicuously transnational sonnet book while holding the nationally delimited office of US poet laureate.

In the sonnet crown "Her Island" that concludes her book, Dove writes of a journey to Sicily, site of origins not only of her book's mythical subtext—where Persephone was abducted—but also, in the thirteenth century, of the sonnet's courtly form. Once again, the sonnet's window onto the world is also a mirror. She begins and ends the crown with an evocative self-referential figure, "blazed stones, closed ground" (cf. the blazon and Wordsworth's "scanty plot of ground") (67).[7] Toward the end of the sequence she counterbalances this figure of spatial fixity with one of velocity. Dove and her husband arrive at the abduction site, Lake Pergusa, only to find that "around this perfect ellipse / they've built… a racetrack" (an ellipsis that conveys astonishment and puns on its doublet "ellipse") (75):

> To make a sport of death
> it must be endless: round and round
> till you feel everything you've trained for—
> precision, speed, endurance—reduced to this
> godawful roar, this vale of sound. (76)

Round and round goes this sonnet sound. The return of (occasional) rhyme, image, length, the final line of each sonnet at the start of the next, and the first line varied as last in the sequence—the poet races around the ellipse of the sonnet, or what she calls in her foreword "its prim borders" and "stultifying" yet comforting assertion of "Order" (xii), a circuit that demands "precision, speed, endurance" (76) that takes her to Sicily, to England, to Germany. At the book's end she hurtles toward a finish line that is at the same time a point of return: "Aim for the tape, aim *through* it. / Then rip the helmet off and poke your head / through sunlight, into flowers" (76). The sonnet champion is a triumphant Persephone, to recall a myth of perpetual return, akin to the form that bespeaks it. If the sonnet's transnationalism may be self-evident, it's worth reiterating that even a thoroughly Americanized sonnet like this one can never be, to adapt a phrase from a US poet who was against the sonnet before he was for it, a pure product of America. The value of poetry, as emphasized by works written in long-lived, world-traversing forms, is in part its polytemporality and polyspatiality, its long memory of itself and its radial enmeshment with global spaces.[8]

When Dove took over as poetry editor of the *New York Times Magazine* in 2018, she introduced a sonnet by her predecessor, Terrance Hayes, and reworked the nation-sonnet analogy by comparing his *American Sonnets for My Past and Future Assassin* to the United States—"multifarious and contradictory and complicated."[9] While Hayes's sequence thematizes the nation—in part as a space of racial terror—this sonnet redeploys a metaphor for itself that is *trans*national, namely, "song":

> The song must be cultural, confessional, clear
> But not obvious. It must be full of compassion
> And crows bowing in a vulture's shadow.
> The song must have six sides to it & a clamor
> Of voltas. (46)

Why "*American* sonnet," a phrase drawn from Wanda Coleman?[10] Obvious Americanizations in this example might include the use of ampersands in poetry and of the label "confessional" for poetry, the image of vulture-haunted crows and, in another hint at racial menace, of the heart "feathered & tarred," the audacious domesticating of Sturm und Drang, and the flouting of regular rhyme and meter. At the same time, neither the trope of sonnet as "song" nor an elevated, alliterative line such as "Where death is undone, time diminished" would be out of place in a Shakespeare sonnet (for "song," see Sonnets 8 and 102); nor would the clamorous punning (think of Shakespeare's "will"), on heteronyms such as "bowing" (down) and "bowing" (a violin), "tear" (drop) and "tear" (a heart), and "minute" (details) and the "minute" (hand)—examples of the multisidedness the poem declares ("six sides" glancing at the box metaphor).

Like many global examples before it, this metasonnet is, as Dove notes in her headnote to it, in the mode of an ars poetica. Making use of the prototypical sonnet tools of balance and antithesis, tension and paradox, it announces its aspiration to be both communal ("cultural") yet individual ("confessional"), "clear" yet indirect ("not obvious"), social ("witness") yet inward ("daydream"), affective ("love") yet impersonal ("record"). It even points to its variation on a specific technique, its "clamor / Of voltas," the most violent of which arrives in the last half line, and it nearly defines the volta—"The song must turn on the compass / Of language like a tangle of wire endowed / With feeling"—even as it makes a turn in another sense by signifying on metaphors in Renaissance poems: the Dark Lady's hair of "black wire" in Shakespeare's Sonnet 130 and Donne's twin compasses in "A Valediction: Forbidding Mourning." An imperative repeated and varied throughout, "The song must be" echoes the refrain "A poem should be" in Archibald MacLeish's "Ars poetica," itself an oblique double sonnet, its incantation famously culminating in the New Critical dictum "A poem should not mean / But be" (106). But by the poem's end, Hayes has interjected a note of self-doubt into these imperatives:

> The song must hold its own storm & drum,
> And shed a noise so lovely it is sung at sunset
> Weddings, baptisms & beheadings henceforth. (46)

If the sonnet must oxymoronically "shed a noise so lovely" that it would be sung at ritual events, including beheadings, would not such a "song" have turned monstrous? Unless he wishes his sonnet ritually sung at killings, including perhaps racial lynchings, the poem's tongue "must be" at least partly in its cheek.

Because the central metaphor the poem repeatedly invokes for itself is tied to the very name of the form, song from *sonetto* ("little song"), we might not notice its figurative force. Yet sonnets, though rooted in one or more oral forms, are for the most part unsung lyrics. Surely, they have some of the musical qualities of song (in Hayes's sonnet suggested by alliteration, lexical repetition, consonance, rhythmic pulse), and Wordsworth and other poets have long played on musical analogies—a lute's soothing melodies, a trumpet's stirring blast ("Scorn not the Sonnet"). But other qualities, such as the form's compression, complexity, tension, paradox, wit, and layering—intensified more than in song and prominent in Hayes—impede the performance-bound assimilability that Mark W. Booth attributes to song (7–13). Literary historians and poet-critics agree that, as Paul Oppenheimer and Phillis Levin state, the sonnet, though adapting song form, was from the start "a lyric meant to be read (to oneself or to others) instead of sung," "an instrument of self-reflection" (Levin xli, Oppenheimer 27–31); that, as Stephanie Burt and David Mikics assert, "It was asymmetrical, suited to meditative logic rather than music,... composed... for private enjoyment" (7); that, as Meg Tyler writes, "it is less a song than a space for meditation" (232); and that, as Stephen Regan states, by combining octave, sestet, and volta, it "creates a form more akin to speech than song, a discursive structure encouraging the progression of thought in meditation, reflection, and intellectual debate" (5). With his "clamor / Of voltas," his rapid-fire puns, syntactic contortions, structural asymmetries, and witty allusions, Hayes amplifies qualities of the sonnet that extend beyond song. Also hinting at the sonnet's difference from song, Dove refers to her sonnet speakers as "struggling to sing in their chains" (Dove xii), a figure of bondage that has an extended history in the African American sonnet, as Hollis Robbins shows, and that also echoes Dylan Thomas's "I sang in my chains like the sea" (172) and Keats's metasonnet's "our English must be chain'd... like Andromeda."[11] Despite being etymologically hitched to its sister genre, a sonnet is less a "little song" than it is a chained song, an impeded song, a writerly song.

By suggesting that sonnets are and are not songs, by metaphorizing sonnets and reining in their metaphors, Hayes and Dove might help us rethink a core tenet of a recent influential theorization of lyric poetry and may in turn help refine our understanding of the sonnet's metaphors for itself. In the capacious and important *Theory of the Lyric*, Jonathan Culler relies heavily on metaphors for lyric as song and ritual—overlapping metaphors that usefully highlight lyric's performativity, repetition, play, and sonic echoes, and that have the advantage of cutting across national and cultural borders. Since I parse the vexed entanglements of poetry and song in *Poetry and Its Others* (184–238), the sonnet gives me a chance to bear down instead on the related question of ritual, which sonnets sometimes also invoke, if less frequently, in metaphors for themselves (cf. Shakespeare's Sonnet 23 and Dante Gabriel Rosetti's "The Sonnet"). To what extent should we think of sonnets as ritualistic? Culler draws on Roland Greene's mapping of the ritual and fictional poles of sonnet sequences, such as Petrarch's *Canzoniere*, in a discussion that cites Denise Levertov's conception of the poet as priest and C. S. Lewis's view that a "good sonnet" is "like a good public prayer," which "a congregation can join in on," or like an "Elizabethan song" and "liturgies" that work "as collective score" (Greene 6). Embracing but swerving from Greene's two-pronged analysis in championing ritualism and not fictionality as key to "the distinctiveness of lyric," Culler states in a recent article that the "concept of ritual encourages concentration on the formal properties of lyric utterance, from rhythm and rhyme to other sorts of linguistic patterning" and performativity, and on "the principle of iterability (lyrics are constructed for repetition), along with a certain ceremoniousness" (24, 23).

With the question of self-metaphorization in mind, let's test the ritual model against a final example, Gwendolyn Brooks's "the rites for Cousin

Vit" (*p. 54*). Appearing in "The Womanhood," the final sequence of her Pulitzer Prize–winning *Annie Allen* (1949), the sonnet plays a "fictional" role in demonstrating Annie's development of skills of sharp social observation; but Culler is right that we often encounter such lyrics "in isolation" ("Poetics, Fictionality," 24). Is this elegiac sonnet "the rites" for the deceased, as the title and ritual model might suggest, or is it about or perhaps even in tension with such rites?

> Carried her unprotesting out the door.
> Kicked back the casket-stand. But it can't hold her,
> That stuff and satin aiming to enfold her,
> The lid's contrition nor the bolts before.
> Oh oh. Too much. Too much. Even now, surmise,
> She rises in the sunshine. There she goes (58)

This lyric doesn't resemble funeral rites or other rituals in the usual sense—"communal ceremonies closely connected to formally institutionalized religions or clearly invoking divine beings," in the words of anthropologist Catherine Bell (164). But might it exhibit the six characteristics that Bell, drawing on a range of anthropological theories, attributes to "ritual-like" (akin to Culler's "ritualistic") activities, such as sports, national anthems, or political rallies: "formalism, traditionalism, disciplined invariance, rule-governance, sacral symbolism, and performance" (138)?

Perhaps. But the commonalities also reveal differences. If ritual-like formalism involves "the use of a more limited and rigidly organized set of expressions," which are "more conventional and less idiosyncratic and personally expressive" (139), and if ritual-like traditionalism makes activities seem identical or consistent with older precedents, Brooks's waywardly antiformalist formalism, her antitraditionalist traditionalism, like the irrepressibly irreverent person she elegizes, showcases lyric idiosyncrasy and unconventionality. Yes, Brooks embraces the sonic returns that Greene and Culler identify with ritualism—iambic pentameter, internal rhyme, assonance, alliteration, and the Petrarchan sonnet's envelope rhymes, slightly varied. But she also distributes the volta, code-mixes elevated speech ("casket," "contrition," "surmise") with conversational ("Oh. Too much. Too much"), overruns line boundaries with enjambed verbs ("talks," "walks"), and fragments sentences, culminating in a final two-letter sentence to suggest the aptly named Vit's postmortem vitality: "Is." So too, at the diegetic level, the casket, perhaps recalling Shakespeare's sonnet tombs, is meant to ritually contain the "unprotesting" corpse of Cousin Vit, "But it can't hold her"—a woman who seems to defy casket and "contrition," sexual and social propriety and gender norms. Similarly, if ritualistic invariance and rule-governance prescribe "a disciplined set of actions marked by precise repetition and physical control," suppressing the "significance of the personal and particular moment in favor of the timeless authority of the group, its doctrines, or its practices" (150), Brooks's sonnet flaunts its ordering but also its variance and rule twisting: its first two iambic lines open with trochees consistent with African American syncopation ("Carried her," "Kicked back"), its jazzlike syntax, jaggedly runs, stops, and jolts, and its perfect rhymes conclude on a slightly dissonant variant (hiss/Is), just as the protagonist, albeit literally contained by a casket, bursts out of disciplinary and physical limits, even overpowering the boundary between death and life. Neither she nor the sonneteer suppresses the personal in favor of the collective. Although Brooks, like poets from Dante and Herbert to Henri Cole, may hint at ritualistic sacral symbolism (155–59) in the "stuff and satin," the "lid's contrition," and the rising in the sunshine, she limits and desacralizes the sacred by interweaving it with the mundane ("Slops," "bridgework," "alleys") and the erotic ("love-rooms," "snake-hips"). Finally, if in ritual-like performance, as Talal Asad states, "rites are to be performed" in "prescribed ways… according to rules that are sanctioned by those in authority" (58, 62), it's true that Brooks, despite a long history of racist discrimination, won over the Pulitzer judges in part because *Annie Allen* met the then regnant New Critical norms of wit, compression, and unity. But far from enacting "a stereotyped sequence of activities," as Victor Turner says ritual must (1100), her wayward poetic rites twist and creolize a number of sonnet protocols, as we've seen. Moreover, despite some resemblances between poet and the deceased, Brooks also defies the elegiac norm of an idealizing portrait. With a tonally complex wryness, she gently ironizes Cousin Vit as "Too vital and too squeaking," playfully suggesting that even in surmise, Vit may come "haply / On the verge of happiness, haply hysterics"—uncontrollable laughter or crying.

In short, if this and other sonnets are ritualistic, we should also account for countervailing features that also make them non-, anti-, or metaritualistic. Sonnets may participate in a large, transnational tradition's collectivity and rule-governance, but that ritualism also makes all the more visible their antiritualistic deviance and individuality. Ritual is akin to other intrinsic and critical metaphors for sonnets—enclosed spaces such as a coffin, box, prison, closet, music box, room in a house, postcard, racetrack, and nation; largely natural entities such as a river, garland, grass, and pathogen; and practices such as song, musical performance, prayer, and even meat grinding: like them, it illuminates some of the poetry's features but obscures others. The reach of the sonnet exceeds the grasp of even its most evocative, self-encapsulating metaphors.

Although I began with the power of sonnets' self-metaphorizations, I'm concluding with a suggestion that even as we learn from their illuminating force, we should also scrutinize them and our critical models. Like sonnets that multiply them (McKay and McSweeney), juxtapose them (Dove), or subtly ironize them (Hayes and Brooks), perhaps criticism could more often pluralize and compare such critical metaphors, play with and against them, though it would be folly to try to spring free of them. That said, I realize my proposed model of antiritualistic ritualism is at risk of ritually repeating an old paradox: that a sonnet must conform and yet also, if it's to count, demonstrate formal ingenuity and imaginative independence. One way to revitalize that chestnut might be to position the sonnet between two contrasting, if potentially complementary, theories of lyric: Culler's ritual model and Theodor Adorno's notion of the idiosyncratic individuality of lyric, which was for him a counterforce to the reifying forces of society (40). Indebted to Adorno, Edward Said hints at a dialectical approach when he writes that poets such as the Palestinian Mahmoud Darwish "possess that irresistibly rare combination of incantatory public style with deep and often hermetic personal sentiments," or what we might call a combination of Culler's ritualism with Adorno's idiosyncratic individuality—"a harassing amalgam of poetry and collective memory, each pressing on the other" (114, 115). As it happens, Darwish is one of the foremost contemporary poets to have adapted the sonnet into Arabic. But perhaps the metaphor of "adaptation" isn't adequate to the voltas of literary history, if the Arabist scholar Kamal Abu-Deeb is right to speculate that the famed thirteenth-century originator of the sonnet, Giacomo da Lentini (or Lentino), participating in the cross-cultural, polyglot Sicilian court of Frederick II, may have been influenced by the Arabic poetic form of the *muwashshah* (135–36). If so, we come full circle to the irrepressible globality and translocality of the sonnet. However much we may nationalize, ritualize, and metaphorize it, the seemingly container-like genre of the sonnet proves as uncontainable as Brooks's Cousin Vit: "There she goes," "Must emerge," "Is."

Notes

1. For a thoughtfully critical view of the prayer-sonnet equation, see Regan 390–91.

2. See the final section of Adrienne Rich's "Snapshots of a Daughter-in Law" (21), which draws on Simone de Beauvoir's helicopter metaphor.

3. I refer to the sonnet as a form insofar as it can be thought of as a set of shaping but changing aesthetic patterns, structures, configurations, and as a genre insofar as it can be thought of as a literary kind that bears with it certain evolving schemas, conventions, and assumptions.

4. Brief engagements with the sonnet's self-metaphorization/self-theorization have a long history; see, e.g., "Sonnets about Sonnets."

5. The *OED* cites examples of "erection" in a sexual sense going back to 1594; q.v. *erection, N.* 4, *OED Online*, www.oed.com.

6. Müller's introduction helpfully teases out the nineteenth-century transnational roots of the African American sonnet.

7. On this sonnet crown, including the "ellipse" pun, see Müller 121–25.

8. See the introduction to Ramazani, *Poetry in a Global Age* 1–24.

9. Rita Dove, headnote to "The song must be cultural, confessional, clear," *New York Times Magazine* (June 28, 2018), www.nytimes.com/2018/06/28/magazine/poem-american-sonnet-for-my-past-and-future-assassin.html.

10. See Malech, "American Sonnets." In her headnote, Dove says Hayes's "word plays" are "wry descriptions of an Anglo-America that has taken the historical discourse of Western civilization down to its own brash level."

11. On Black poets' adaptation of traditional tropes of bondage, enslavement, and the caged bird, see Robbins 44–61.

Works Cited

Abu-Deeb, Kamal. "The Quest for the Sonnet: The Origins of the Sonnet in Arabic Poetry." *Arab Shakespeares*," special issue of *Critical Survey*, vol. 28, no. 3, 2016, pp. 133–57.

Ali, Agha Shahid. "Postcard from Kashmir." *The Half-Inch Himalayas*. Wesleyan UP, 1987, p. 1.

Asad, Talal. *Genealogies of Religion: Discipline and Reasons of Power in Christianity and Islam*. Johns Hopkins UP, 1993.

Bell, Catherine. *Ritual: Perspectives and Dimensions*. Oxford UP, 1997.

Booth, Mark W. *The Experience of Songs*. Yale UP, 1981.

Brooks, Gwendolyn. *Selected Poems*. Harper and Row, 1963.

Burt, Stephanie, and David Mikics. Introduction. *The Art of the Sonnet*. Belknap Press of Harvard UP, 2010, pp. 5–25.

Clifton, Lucille. "the mississippi empties into the gulf." *The Terrible Stories*. BOA Editions, 1996, p. 37.

Collins, Billy. "American Sonnet." *Poetry*, March 1989, p. 329, www.poetryfoundation.org/poetrymagazine/browse?contentId=37394.

Culler, Jonathan. "Poetics, Fictionality, and the Lyric." *Dibur Literary Journal*, issue 2, 2016, pp. 19–25.

———. *Theory of the Lyric*. Harvard UP, 2017.

Dove, Rita. *Mother Love*. W. W. Norton, 1995.

Greene, Roland. *Post-Petrarchism: Toward a Poetics of Lyric and the Lyric Sequence*. Princeton UP, 1991.

Hayes, Terrance. *American Sonnets for My Past and Future Assassin*. Penguin Books, 2018.

Levin, Phillis. Introduction. *The Penguin Book of the Sonnet*. Penguin Books, 2001, pp. xxxvii–lxxiv.

MacLeish, Archibald. "Ars poetica." *Collected Poems, 1917—1982*. Houghton Mifflin, 1985, p. 106.

Malech, Dora. "American Sonnets (Part IV: As American As…)." *Kenyon Review*, November 27, 2017, kenyonreview.org/2017/11/american-sonnets-part-iv-american/.

McKay, Claude. "America." *Collected Poems*, edited by William J. Maxwell. U of Illinois P, 2004, p. 153.

McSweeney, Joyelle. "Toxic Sonnets." *Toxicon and Arachne*. Nightboat Books, 2020, pp. 27–42.

Müller, Timo. *The African American Sonnet: A Literary History*. UP of Mississippi, 2018.

"Nationality, *N*. 3a." *Oxford English Dictionary Online*, www.oed.com.

Oppenheimer, Paul. *The Birth of the Modern Mind: Self, Consciousness, and the Invention of the Sonnet*. Oxford UP, 1989.

Petrosino, Kiki. "Happinefs." *White Blood: A Lyric of Virginia*. Sarabande Books, 2020, pp. 17–33.

Ramazani, Jahan. *Poetry and Its Others: News, Prayer, Song, and the Dialogue of Genres*. U of Chicago P, 2014.

———. *Poetry in a Global Age*. U of Chicago P, 2020.

Regan, Stephen. *The Sonnet*. Oxford UP, 2019.

Rich, Adrienne. "Snapshots of a Daughter-in-Law." *The Fact of a Doorframe: Selected Poems, 1950–2001*. W. W. Norton, 2002, pp. 17–21.

Said, Edward W. "On Mahmoud Darwish." *Grand Street*, vol. 12, no. 48, 1993, pp. 112–15.

Shapiro, Karl. *The Bourgeois Poet*. Random House, 1964.

"Sonnets about Sonnets." *The Irish Monthly*, vol. 15, no. 172, 1887, pp. 568–77.

Thomas, Dylan. "Fern Hill." *Collected Poems*. New Directions, 2010, pp. 178–80.

Turner, Victor W. "Symbols in African Ritual." *Science* 179, no. 4078, 1973, pp. 1100–05.

Tyler, Meg. "'Named Airs': American Sonnets (Stevens to Bidart)." *A Companion to Poetic Genre*, edited by Erik Martiny, Wiley-Blackwell, 2012, pp. 220–33.

The Rising Poems of America
Nationalistic Origins of the American Sonnet

BENJAMIN CRAWFORD

The sonnet's historical roots in European poetic tradition could have been a harbinger against its adaptation by poets in the early American republic. Yet some poets used the form, engaging with it by crafting the beginning of a long tradition in American letters that embraced the sonnet in the expansion of a developing American literature. As Lewis G. Sterner notes, Colonel David Humphreys is considered America's first sonneteer with his "Addressed to my friends at Yale College, on Leaving them to Join the Army" (Sterner xi, 2), which was apparently composed in 1776 but was published as late as 1804 in Humphreys's *Miscellaneous Works*. While most American sonnet writers of the eighteenth and nineteenth centuries focused on traditional sonnet themes, including the metaphysical and nature, other poets used the form to express American nationalism in the nascent nation. This essay argues that the roots of the American sonnet tradition lie in the sonnets of Colonel David Humphreys not simply because he has been identified as America's first sonneteer historically but rather because his sonnets focus predominantly on nationalistic themes, something that curiously did not take hold in the majority of sonnets by other American poets from the nineteenth century onward.

While this essay focuses on Humphreys's sonnets, it is surprising, as Sterner notes, that the prolific "Poet of the American Revolution," Philip Freneau, does not appear to have written any sonnets himself (xi), but perhaps this was out of disdain for European poetic tradition or because his talents were simply not up to the challenge. Other early American sonnet writers include Henry Wadsworth Longfellow and William Cullen Bryant (who wrote only a few sonnets) (xvii), among many other minor poets who also engaged with the form. More recent scholars, such as Stephen Regan, tend to focus on later American sonnets, from Longfellow and onward rather than on earlier productions. The sonnet's form, with its concentrated meter and focused rhyme schemes, even in variance, along with its more limiting function of only fourteen lines, makes it a truly difficult form to master with the refinement that merits perpetuation across time. Sonnets that remain popular are difficult to write, and early American poets struggled to use the form effectively at first. According to Sterner, it was not until Longfellow began writing sonnets "that the American sonnet entered upon a distinguished career" (xii), and accordingly, in his recent study Stephan Regan begins his coverage of the American sonnet with Longfellow (220). This essay's focus on Humphreys rather than on the later iterations of the American sonnet that typically garner attention is therefore at odds with the general focus of academic narratives on the American sonnet.

Humphreys's connection with other early American poets is notable. He was a good friend of Timothy Dwight (Frank Landon Humphreys 29), who wrote America's first epic poem, *The Conquest of Canaan* (1787). Additionally, Humphreys was associated with the minor Connecticut Wits, along with Joel Barlow, Lemuel Hopkins, and John Trumbull, all of whom collaborated on the political mock epic *The Anarchiad* in 1786–87, mirroring the political interest that Humphreys demonstrated in his sonnets. Humphreys's poems are no longer commonly read or studied in undergraduate courses and often only acquire scholarly attention in regard to *The Anarchiad*. Nonetheless, his work was popular enough in his own lifetime to merit publication in a collected edition.

Appearing in 1804, Humphreys's *Miscellaneous Works* offered a retrospective of his poetic accomplishments. The collection includes a dozen sonnets, many of which are nationalistic in theme. According to his headnote (dated 1802) to the sonnets section, Humphreys had rediscovered them: "Upon lately looking over my papers, I found a few Sonnets which recalled to recollection some of the feelings with which they were written." He notes that these sonnets are reminiscences of "remarkable periods and events, which may serve to guide the memory in retracing our wanderings through this world of vicissitude and care" (232). Referring to his life's story, Humphreys's sonnets call to mind a host of his experiences in the Revolutionary War while also touching on other topics.

While Humphreys included twelve sonnets in the 1804 volume of his works, not all of the sonnets directly engage with nationalistic themes. "Sonnet I. Addressed to my Friends at Yale College, on my leaving them to join the Army," represents a hopeful attitude toward the impending war, an attitude that is tempered with more direct and bloody descriptions of warfare in later sonnets, reflecting his personal experience of war. Patriotic and hopeful, Humphreys approaches the volta with optimism: "Quick throbs my breast at war's untried alarms, / Unknown pulsations stirr'd by glory's charms" (lines 8–9). Humphreys concludes the poem by asking "Can death subdue th' unconquerable mind? / Or adamantine chains ethereal substance bind?" (lines 13–14). This poem demonstrates what one biographer has remarked on concerning Humphreys's oeuvre, that his "poems glow with patriotic impulse" (Frank Landon Humphreys 54). With hopefulness for eventual victory despite the physical tolls of war, Humphreys's celebratory sonnet aspires to the abstract, the "ethereal substance" of the ideals of the Revolutionary War, with its associated discourses on liberty and freedom invoked as "ethereal" and "unconquerable" even by death.

In "Sonnet II. On the Revolutionary War in America" Humphreys addresses the bloodshed of the war in apocalyptic terms. Describing the conflict as a "civil war" (line 1), a common perspective of the Revolutionary War when the outcome was not yet evident, Humphreys describes seeing "devastation crimson'd on my eye" (line 5), and he quickly moves to echo the apocalypse: "So broods, in upper skies, that tempest dire, / When fiercer heat these elements shall warm" (lines 10–11), referring to 2 Peter 3:12: "Looking for and hasting unto the coming of the day of God, wherein the heavens being on fire shall be dissolved, and the elements shall melt with fervent heat?" (KJV). Humphreys then directs his reference specifically to the Book of Revelation, writing: "What time, in robes of blood and locks of fire, / Th' exterminating angel's awful form / Blows the grave-rending blast, and guides the redd'ning storm" (lines 12–14), echoing Revelation 8:7: "The first angel sounded, and there followed hail and fire mingled with blood, and they were cast upon the earth: and the third part of trees was burnt up, and all green grass was burnt up" (KJV). While invoking images of nature, Humphreys's focus on the supernatural and the natural working in confluence in light of the Revolutionary War demonstrates that while he is drawing on traditional sonnet themes of the metaphysical and the spiritual, his understanding of these themes is influenced by the death and destruction of the war. By making the Revolutionary War the focus of the poem, Humphreys effectively transitions the sonnet form by applying political content, bringing to mind the use of the sonnet for political purposes since at least the sixteenth century, such as Milton's political sonnets (see Mueller). Additionally, Humphreys's use of apocalyptic imagery is not unique within the sonnet tradition. That too echoes back, perhaps unknowingly for Humphreys, to the sonnets of sixteenth-century Dutch poet Jan van der Noot and his French contemporary Joachim du Bellay (Norbrook 40–41, du Bellay xiii). What is important and unique, however, is that Humphreys is using these political and apocalyptic themes for the first time in American sonnets, specifically within an American nationalistic context that references the Revolutionary War.

In "Sonnet III. On the Prospect of Peace, in 1783" (*p. 9*), Humphreys celebrates the dawning of peace while mourning the cost of life from the war. Humphreys views the American victory as ordained by Divine Intervention: "Thou Peace... descending in these skirts of day / Bring heav'nly balm to heal my country's wounds" (2–3). While military prowess brought martial victory, Humphreys's deference to Providence as the source of peace draws from his upbringing in the home of a minister, the Reverend Daniel Humphreys (Frank Landon Humphreys 3). Like many of the founding fathers and mothers of the early republic, Humphreys maintained a strong religious faith that informed his poetic perspective—perhaps another reason why he and Timothy Dwight, who was a minister, maintained such a strong friendship throughout their lives. Writing in a publicly printed letter in 1803, Humphreys remarks: "I am afraid we have not been grateful enough to that *Almighty Protector* who has caused us to dwell in tranquility, while so many nations have been grievously afflicted with the calamities of war. A nation without religion and morals, is always ripening fast for that state of corruption which often precedes decay, and terminates in ruin" (372, italics in the original). Humphreys's religiosity denotes a strong sense of reliance on the blessings of divinity for both the country's peace and its success, first in the sonnet from 1783 and then in this letter from 1803 addressed to the contemporary governor of Connecticut, Jonathan Trumbull Jr., the son of a previous Connecticut governor, Jonathan Trumbull (Humphreys, "Considerations" 372, Warren 135). In both instances, as in Sonnet II, Humphreys conflates the political and religious in his writings.

Sonnet III reflects on the bloodshed of the Revolutionary War and suggests that, as in the second sonnet, it is God himself who has ended the conflict: "When rose th' Almighty pow'r, with sovereign sway, / To end the battle mutual" (lines 7–8). By bringing Providence to the side of America in this poem, Humphreys enacts a long political tradition that conflates religious and political ideologies. This allows him to move toward making this poem part of the "Rising Glory of America" genre that became popular in the early Republic: "Now bids that voice divine th' invaders yield, / From glooms of midnight morn's gay prospects rise" (lines 10–11). With divine order, the war ends and the promise of a new day takes hold; out of the "glooms of midnight" arises a new, hopeful future. In that future, according to Humphreys, the nation will continue to expand: "There, see the dawn of heav'n's great day reveal'd, / Where new auroras dim our dazzled eyes, / Flash o'er th' Atlantic waves, and fire the western skies!" (lines 12–14). The "Prospect of Peace" has brought "the dawn of heav'n's great day" with the advent of peace, and this peace has now provided America with new opportunities that inspire fellow citizens. This "dawn" (line 13) overtakes "th' Atlantic waves," arriving from Europe where the Treaty of Paris was signed in 1783, and "fire[s] the western skies!" (line 14). These "western skies" would quickly expand with the growing borders of the country through purchase and remorseless expansion at the expense of Native American homelands. This destruction is something that Humphreys ignores in the brevity of this sonnet, though he does briefly mention Native Americans in "Sonnet IX. On the Death of Major John Pallsgrave Wyllys." The future of America is apparently glorious, with the prescient echo of Manifest Destiny in the final lines of the poem, promising the possibility of expansion in the light of peace. Maintaining a hopeful tone in spite of the disorder and death of the war, Humphreys's Sonnet III celebrates both the end of the war and the birth of the nation.

While Sonnet III is concerned with celebrating the arrival of peace, "Sonnet IV. On Disbanding the Army" celebrates the dissolving of the Continental Army, no longer considered necessary with the cessation of war. In a sense, Sonnet IV serves as a bookend to a series of sonnets focused primarily on Revolutionary War experiences, beginning with Sonnet I, when Humphreys youthfully celebrates joining the Continental Army. Much like Sonnet I, Humphreys appeals to ideals of freedom (line 2) and the perspective of history (line 4) for those who served, while also acknowledging the role of death in the war, glossed over in Sonnet I when Humphreys takes leave of his friends to join the army. Humphreys reflects on the cost of fighting in the war and its benefit of guaranteeing eternal remembrance for the sacrifice of fighting: "Well have ye fought for freedom... / And time's last records shall your triumphs tell" (2, 4). Yet he also acknowledges and mourns those who lost their lives: "Ye, too, farewell, who fell in fields of gore, / And chang'd tempestuous toil for rest serene" (9–10). Though the war brought toil, those who have died are now at rest, as too are the soldiers now left to return to their farms, occupations, and families despite the bittersweet leaving of their comrades. Humphreys also commemorated the death of George Washington, engaging with the contemporary movement to memorialize the first president. In "Sonnet XII. On receiving the News of the Death of General Washington," Humphreys describes Washington as "our living light" whose "bright example still illumes our way" (lines 5, 6), glorifying him with typical hagiographic descriptions. By mourning Washington in a sonnet, Humphreys again uses the form for nationalistic purposes while also touching on a popular sonnet theme through his memorializing.

Humphreys's focus on nationalistic themes throughout his sonnets is historically and culturally important. As many authors of the late eighteenth and early nineteenth centuries tried to develop a distinctly American literature, oftentimes the primary focus of texts that were made "American" was either the landscape or nationalistic themes. Humphreys's focus on nationalistic themes in his sonnets demonstrates that despite its origins as a European form, the sonnet could be readily appropriated to American themes. Yet many early American authors who used the sonnet form did not actively use it for nationalistic purposes, leaving Humphreys's patriotic sonnets both unique in their status as the first American sonnets but also as among the minority of American sonnets that engaged with nationalistic themes. Perhaps the origins of the form and its typical focus on less political themes, such as nature, love, and religion, prompted the form in American literature toward those classic themes, despite the sonnet's historical uses politically. Humphreys did not, however, focus his sonnets exclusively on nationalistic themes; for example, "Sonnet VI. On a Night-Storm at Sea" and "Sonnet VIII. On the Immortality of the Soul," turn to nature and the spiritual respectively.

Some early American sonnets are tangentially nationalistic through brief references to the American landscape or other aspects of America that are not then treated as the primary focus of the poem. For example, John Quincy Adams's "To the Sun-Dial" is ostensibly concerned with the metaphysical aspects of time as represented in a sundial. Yet the poem's subtitle is "Under the Window of the Hall of the House of Representatives of the United States," thus positioning the poem within a particularly American and specifically governmental context. While the rest of poem seems unconcerned with politics, the subtitle nonetheless remains to remind readers of the sonnet's place within American culture. Similarly, William Cullen Bryant's "Sonnet—To an American Painter Departing for Europe" (*p. 11*) is not primarily focused on nationalistic themes but is nonetheless instilled with a sense of nationalism in the second and third lines: "Yet, Cole! thy heart shall bear to Europe's strand / A living image of thy native land." Both Adams's and Bryant's sonnets engage with a subdued nationalistic theme, in contrast to the direct patriotism of several of Humphreys's sonnets, ensuring that his role as America's first sonneteer would be solidified not only historically but culturally as well. By focusing on peculiarly American themes related especially to the Revolutionary War, David Humphreys used the perpetually popular form of the sonnet to capture the spirit of the early American Republic.

Works Cited

Adams, John Quincy. "To the Sun-Dial." *American Sonnets: An Anthology*, edited by David Bromwich, Library of America, 2007, p. 1.

Bryant, William Cullen. "Sonnet—To an American Painter Departing for Europe." *American Sonnets: An Anthology*, edited by David Bromwich, Library of America, 2007, p. 4.

Du Bellay, Joachim, and Richard Helgerson. *The Regrets: With, the Antiquities of Rome, Three Latin Elegies, and the Defense and Enrichment of the French Language; a Bilingual Edition*. U of Pennsylvania P, 2006.

Dwight, Timothy. *Conquest of Canäan—A Poem in Eleven Books*. Hartford: Elisha Babcock, 1785.

Holy Bible: Containing the Old and New Testaments in the King James Version. Thomas Nelson, 1990.

Humphreys, David. *The Anarchiad: A New England Poem; 1786–1787*. Gainesville, FL: Scholars' Facsimiles and Reprints, 1967.

———. "Considerations on the Means of Improving the Public Defence: In a Letter to His Excellency Governor Trumbull." *The Miscellaneous Works*. New York, 1804.

———. *The Miscellaneous Works*. New York, 1804.

Humphreys, Frank Landon. *Life and Times of David Humphreys*. Vol. 1. G. P. Putnam's Sons, 1917.

Mueller, Janel. "The Mastery of Decorum: Politics as Poetry in Milton's Sonnets." *Critical Inquiry*, vol. 13, no. 3, spring 1987, pp. 475–508.

Norbrook, David. *Poetry and Politics in the English Renaissance*. Oxford UP, 2009.

Regan, Stephen. *The Sonnet*. Oxford UP, 2019.

Sterner, Lewis G. *The Sonnet in American Literature: An Anthology of Representative American Sonnets*. U of Pennsylvania, PhD thesis, 1930.

Warren, Kenneth F. *Encyclopedia of U.S. Campaigns, Elections, and Electoral Behavior*. Sage, 2008.

Origins of Rupture

Emerson, Wheatley, and the Early American Sonnet

JOHN JAMES

Composed in 1839, nearly half a century before aestheticism introduced vers libre, and almost a full one before American free verse would emerge, Emerson's "Woods: A Prose Sonnet" (*p. 12*) appears to disregard nearly every convention familiar to the sonnet form, as well as most customs endemic to poetry as such. It contains no meter or rhyme scheme, nor is it broken into lines. While the logical turn toward its end ("This I would ask of you, o sacred Woods") might constitute a volta, even its subject—the wisdom imparted by nature—departs from the topic of romantic courtship, which many readers associate with the sonnet from Petrarch onward.[1] But as Paul Oppenheimer argues, the sonnet is, first and foremost, a "lyric of self-consciousness, or of the self in conflict" (3); and indeed, such tension governs the content of the piece, if not the strictly formal conventions in which it rather deliberately refuses to participate. The poem opens with an apostrophe, invoking the "ancient woods," whose wisdom, though concealed, extends beyond the knowledge immediately available to the decidedly anthropocentric consciousness from which the poet speaks. Yet the "needles," "acorns," and "redden[ing]" maples that constitute the woods maintain a semiotic function (27). The poet "readeth" in them a "cheerful lesson": that unlike the human individual, the natural world continually revives itself, rendering its youth "always new." Despite the note of praise that characterizes the speaker's tone throughout the poem, Emerson offers the somber reflection that "men have not language to describe one moment of your eternal life." The speaker's inability to articulate the temporal scale of natural cycles forges a conflict between the speaker's capacities for literacy and self-expression, and ultimately, between himself and the woods he so admires; he apprehends natural beauty by "reading" the woods, but his limited capacity for speech—and for creativity more generally—renders him impotent to converse with the woods or to recreate the sublimity he identifies therein.

Inasmuch as it comprises a mind-event in which an embattled consciousness seeks to resolve a psychically bound antagonism, Emerson's "sonnet" not only satisfies the form's most crucial criterion, it recalibrates what readers might expect from the form more generally. In that sense, the piece lives up to Emerson's own somewhat fraught aesthetic standard, established in his now famous ars poetica, 1844's "The Poet": "it is not metres, but a metre-making argument, that makes a poem,—a thought so passionate and alive, that, like the spirit of a plant or an animal, it has *architecture of its own*, and adorns nature with a new thing" (1641, emphasis mine). If content is meant to govern form, even in a sonnet, then Emerson seems to have constituted this "new thing" in the mold of his own thought—that is to say, in a formal logic that defies the "metres" of the sonnet while nonetheless engaging many of the form's argumentative conventions. In so doing, his prose sonnet resists the ossification Emerson later in the essay attributes to language itself: "Language is fossil poetry" (1645). In this poem, Emerson not only exemplifies the "genius" endemic to original thought but marks this idiosyncratic version of the sonnet as uniquely American. Framing the analogy in agricultural terms, he states: "This atom of seed [i.e., poetic genius] is thrown into a new place, not subject to the accidents which destroyed its parent two rods off." In other words, "when the soul of the poet has come to ripeness of thought, she detaches and sends away from it its poems or songs,—a fearless, sleepless, deathless progeny, which is not exposed to the accidents of the weary kingdom of time" ("The Poet" 1646). While, most directly, Emerson insists that the "seed" of poetic genius must fall away from the poet him- or herself and thus fashions an argument about aesthetic autonomy, the rhetoric of this "weary kingdom" rings clear: creative genius liberates the new American thought from the intellectual strictures of its European antecedents, a shift that also precipitates—or at least opens the possibility for—new verse forms.

For this reason, it can be tempting to read Emerson's prose sonnet in conjunction with his poetics, not only as representing a distinct break from European aesthetic models, but as foundational to an American tradition of formal radicalism that continues through the twentieth century and into contemporaneity. Some more heavily canonical narratives might bear this out.[2] Emerson grants license to poets as stylistically wide-ranging as John Ashbery, Gerald Stern, and Robert Hass to label as "sonnet" just about any short poem with a rhetorical "turn."[3] Today, it is something of a poetic commonplace for American poets to resist, in Billy Collins's words, "sing[ing] our songs in little rooms" or "pour[ing] our sentiments into measuring cups" ("American Sonnet" 5–6). Emerson himself echoes this sentiment in "The American Scholar" (1837/1849), where "rhyme" comes to stand synecdochically for complacency in thought: "It is a shame to him"—the scholar, the iconoclast, the original thinker—"if his tranquility, amid dangerous times, arise from the presumption, that, like children and women, his is a protected class; or if he seek a temporary peace by the diversion of his thoughts from politics or vexed questions, hiding his head like an ostrich in the flowering bushes, peeping into microscopes, and *turning rhymes*, as a boy whistles to keep his courage up" (1617, emphasis mine). Otherwise put, it is a dishonor to the American scholar—or to anyone who pretends to original thinking—to insulate his or her thought in decorative verse. "Rhyme" becomes "protective" inasmuch as it rehearses entrenched dogma, distracting readers from a real engagement with complex thought and with the political nuances of the present moment—which, presumably, prose permits. This has not been the legacy of the American free-verse sonnet, which has tackled such a range of themes as to render the form not *anti-* but perhaps *a*political. Certainly, the American "self-in-conflict" at play in the "little room" does little to further the liberatory "genius" so ardently imagined in Emerson's turn away from verse form.

More important, this narrative of the American sonnet's evolution willfully ignores what until recently might have been termed "marginal" movements operating outside the canon's "center." While such terms are always already problematic since they assume the presence of an imaginary "center" rather than clusters of distinct communities, a nuanced history of the American sonnet must not only account for but underscore the efforts of poets of color to work within the sonnet form, weaponizing its unique conventions. Poets such as Claude McKay, Gwendolyn Brooks, Wanda Coleman, and more recently, Terrance Hayes and Jericho Brown, have used the sonnet or variations of it both to carve out a space for themselves within an otherwise homogenous canon and to reimagine the aesthetic and political possibilities inherent to the form. McKay's "America" (1921) (*p. 35*), for instance, reinscribes the form and imagery of Percy Bysshe Shelley's "Ozymandias" (1818) to critique the racialized oppression of American empire. But this countercultural practice begins well before Emerson, evidenced earliest in the work of Phillis Wheatley, whose *Poems on Various Subjects, Religious and Moral* (1773) not only constitutes the first volume of verse published by a Black American but whose relationship to poetic convention evinces a similar reinscription and subversion as that seen in McKay. Though she wrote no stand-alone sonnets, and even those stanzas of hers that might be considered sonnets remain highly unconventional,[4] Wheatley is a highly formal poet, one whose careful manipulation of received forms produces a rhetorical subtlety that permits her to speak simultaneously to divergent readers (see *p. 10* for a related poem by Wheatley). In "On Being Brought from Africa to America," probably her most well-known poem, Wheatley uses commas to facilitate an ambiguity of address, undermining the long-standing color motif that associates whiteness with moral good. Wheatley writes, "Remember, Christian, Negroes, black as Cain, / May be refin'd, and join th' angelic train" (lines 7–8). Read one way, Wheatley might be thought to address the largely white audience of literate Boston Christians, urging them to realize that the Black population maintains the potential for perfectibility—to be "refin'd"—and implicitly urging them, on those grounds, to acknowledge the humanity of that community. The more subversive reading, onto which more recent scholarship has seized, is directed at the "Negro" reader, who in light of the moral abomination of slavery must be reminded that white Christians, sinful as they are, might still be redeemed.

While this piece is probably the most straightforward example of Wheatley's characteristically subversive ambiguity, much of her poetry demonstrates a similar capacity for play. This potential is often mediated through her use of verse form, which—unlike Emerson's—rigidly adheres to eighteenth-century British conventions. Indeed, Wheatley maintained a complex relationship with the European poetic canon, whose most central figures often served as her models.[5] Her most highly favored form, the heroic couplet, is one employed not only in the satirical mock epics of Alexander Pope but—and more significantly—by English laboring-class poets, among them Stephen Duck and Mary Collier, who used the form's close association with the Augustan verse master as an authorizing strategy, lending the formal trappings of canonicity to poems whose subjects and authors diverged radically from the aristocratic associations then tied to poetic production. Though it is unclear whether Wheatley had read Duck, Collier, or their contemporaries, she uses Pope's couplets to similar effect. In "To Maecenas," for instance, she combines the couplets with brief reflections on her classical forebears, whose heroic verse not only "quakes" the heavens and "trembles" the earth (line 10) but serves to please the titular patron.[6] Despite their heroic form, the speaker's verses seem to founder: "But I less happy, cannot raise the song, / The fault'ring music dies upon my tongue" (lines 35–36). The speaker attributes this failure, first, to a "grov'ling mind" (line 29), which might suggest an internalized racism common to the narratives of enslaved people. But the speaker defiantly exerts her agency, identifying a predecessor in the Afro-Roman playwright Terence—the "one alone of Afric's sable race" (line 40) to receive canonical recognition—and seizing the laurel from Maecenas's head, designates herself as a symbolic patron of the arts and revisionary gatekeeper of the canon.

Not only is this subversion represented symbolically in the "snatching" of the laurel, it is also marked by a deviation from the couplet form, whose dissonant extension of rhymed pairs signals both Wheatley's mastery of convention and her departure—one might argue, her escape—from it. The penultimate stanza reads:

> Thy virtues, great Maecenas! shall be sung
> In praise of him, from whom those virtues sprung:
> While blooming wreaths around thy temples spread,
> I'll snatch a laurel from thine honour'd head,
> While you indulgent smile upon the deed. (lines 43–47)

The extension of the final couplet into a third rhyming line facilitates a sense of addition. Wheatley builds on the poetic tradition of Homer, Virgil, and, yes, Terence, a contribution felt in the poem's refusal to shift into a novel rhyme. This lingering sensation is complicated by a deviation in sound: "deed" marks a sight rhyme, but sonically, it diverges from the assonantal regularity established in "spread" and "head." Rhetorically speaking, this change suggests that while the speaker might have established a place for herself in the Western literary tradition, that position remains culturally dissonant, marked not only by the racializing attitudes that insist on the creative inferiority of Black Americans[7] but by a ruptural identity forged by the Middle Passage. In fact, although Maecenas "smile[s]" upon the speaker's seizure of the laurel, and the "deed" is framed in playful terms, such "snatch[ing]" recalls the language employed in Wheatley's "To the Right Honourable William, Earl of Dartmouth," which narrates Wheatley's experience of being "snatch'd from Afric's fancy'd happy seat" (line 25). Wheatley mobilizes the experience of her own kidnapping, personalizing the sympathetic appeal endemic more generally to abolitionist rhetoric: "Steel'd was that soul and by no misery mov'd / That from a father seiz'd his babe belov'd: / Such, such was *my* case" (lines 29-31, my emphasis). The echo suggests that if a modern stand-in for Maecenas[8] extends patronage to this poet—as, from a moral standpoint, he must—that patron acknowledges both the value of a diasporic poetics forged by the act of seizure and the mastery, formal and cultural, of the poet seeking such acknowledgment.

Considering Wheatley's rigidly formal manipulation of convention and Emerson's radical break from it, this essay seeks to lodge a twofold critique against the canonical narrative of the American sonnet, and perhaps of American poetry more generally. First, I mean to destabilize the notion that American poetry begins in formal stricture and moves toward formal experimentation. While there are some American poets writing sonnets before Emerson, the nineteenth-century emergence of a distinctly American (as opposed to British) literature begins in the reduction of form and redefinition of poetry itself as quintessentially *other* than the formal conventions to which it has historically been tied. A poem is an original thought, and form is secondary, at least for the transcendentalists. By no means then does the American sonnet begin in formal convention. But second, the trajectory not only of the American sonnet but of American verse more broadly does not end in formal radicalism—in the dissipation of rhymed verse into free verse or some other prosodic formation. As I've demonstrated, formal strictures have been—and continue to be—a generative tool for serious political thought, and the sonnet is one of many forms that enable such thinking. Moreover, while American poets are unlikely to employ rhymed couplets today, poets and scholars alike continue to find Wheatley's use of form compelling and generative, in ways that continue to expand the possibilities of the sonnet per se.[9] I want to conclude, then, by suggesting that the American sonnet's evolution has signaled less a march toward or from formal radicalism but more a dialectic between various aesthetic commitments, whose tradition neither begins in rupture nor moves toward it. Often these commitments are political, and adherence to and manipulation of verse form often (but not always) reflects the broader social limitations under which such verse is written. Ultimately, though, the reinstantiation of radical thought that inheres specifically in the sonnet stems from the ongoing reinvention of this remarkably enduring, if compact poetic form, whose history has witnessed ruptures of various sorts but whose conventions and subject matter perpetually adapt to the dynamic world in which it continues to be produced.

Notes

1. Emerson follows the Romantic sonnet revival initiated by Charlotte Smith, William Wordsworth, John Keats, John Clare, and others, which shifted the form's subject of inquiry from Romantic love to, among other topics, the power of natural forces. Emerson's adoption of nature as a subject for the sonnet form is not, historically, new. Though the poem is now printed in myriad anthologies, during Emerson's life, it remained in manuscript form.

2. If, for instance, we view twentieth-century poetry as descending from Eliot and Pound into the New York School, Language Poetry, and other such experimental movements, then such a narrative might seem true.

3. See, for example, Ashbery's "Sonnet," from his first collection, *Some Trees* (Yale UP, 1956), winner of the Yale Younger Poets Prize.

4. Full stanzas of Wheatley's poems might resemble sonnets, but despite their fourteen-line structure and iambic meter, their rhymes are either inconsistent or organized into couplets. Because they are parts of longer poems, their content does not model the self-containment often ascribed to sonnets.

5. Aside from classical models, among them Horace, Ovid, Virgil, and Homer, Wheatley's poems and letters—Vincent Carretta has shown—demonstrate her close familiarity with Alexander Pope (her "principal poetic model"), John Milton (her "most admired modern poet"), and William Shenstone (xiv).

6. A friend and advisor to Caesar Augustus, Maecenas served as patron to a generation of Roman poets, most significantly, Virgil.

7. In his *Notes on the State of Virginia*, Thomas Jefferson contends that Wheatley's poetry "kindles the senses only, not the imagination," arguing that "religion indeed has produced a Phillis Whatley; but it could not produce a poet" (140).

8. The poem most likely appeals to Selina Hastings, Countess of Huntingdon, who funded the publication of various works comprising what we now recognize as the British Black canon, among them Wheatley's *Poems on Various Subjects*, which is dedicated to Hastings.

9. See June Jordan's "The Difficult Miracle of Black Poetry in America, or Something Like a Sonnet for Phillis Wheatley," *Some of Us Did Not Die: New and Selected Essays* (Perseus Books, 2002), pp. 174–86.

Works Cited

Carretta, Vincent. Introduction. *Phillis Wheatley: Complete Writings*. Penguin, 2001, pp. xiii–xxxvii.

Collins, Billy. "American Sonnet." *Poetry*, March 1989, p. 328.

Emerson, Ralph Waldo. "The American Scholar." *The Heath Anthology of American Literature*. Vol. B: *Early Nineteenth Century, 1800–1865*. Fifth edition. Edited by Paul Lauter, Houghton Mifflin, 2006, pp. 1609–21.

———. "The Poet." *The Heath Anthology of American Literature*. Vol. B: *Early Nineteenth Century, 1800–1865*. Fifth edition. Edited by Paul Lauter, Houghton Mifflin, 2006, 1638–53.

———. "Woods: A Prose Sonnet." *Great American Prose Poems: From Poe to the Present.* Edited by David Lehman. Scribner, 2003, p. 27.

Jefferson, Thomas. *Notes on the State of Virginia.* U of North Carolina P, 2011.

Oppenheimer, Paul. *The Birth of the Modern Mind: Self Consciousness, and the Invention of the Sonnet.* Oxford UP, 1989.

Wheatley, Phillis. *Complete Writings.* Edited by Vincent Carretta, Penguin, 2001.

E. E. Cummings

The Iconic Metasonnet and the Cultural Emblem
of the American "i/Eye"

GILLIAN HUANG-TILLER

In one of his final notes, E. E. Cummings jotted down:

—that my only salvation is to abandon wholly all previous schemes & systems (Groddeck, Jung, les Symbolistes, etc) & watch out for the dear, distinct uniqueness (the turn of the Spring worm in the earth) who's DIFFERENT: individual, here&now...

that I *must* take *wholly* seriously, as a symbol of My LIVING Self, the 'little church (no great cathedral)' with her

standing erect in the deathless truth of His presence

(welcoming humbly His light and proudly His darkness) as against any Goethean superman figure of a stuffedshirt colossus

—that my *only social* thesis must = each individual being for him-or herself ALONE: a Whole—vs *all* (conforming)

(MS Am 1923.7 (54), f. 1, s. 3; quoted in Kennedy 482)

This note not only summarizes poet-painter Cummings's modernist iconoclastic aesthetics but also encapsulates his poetic stance as a modern individual, imbued with a social consciousness that rejected all forms of conformity and collectivity. This stance, which Cummings developed throughout his adult life, also guided his poetry and poetic vision.

Cummings's avant-gardist aesthetics and cultural awareness, including his resistance to indoctrination and to formal constraints, are evident in his experimental poems. His language and formal distortion, familiar to readers of "Buffalo Bill 's," "in Just-," and "anyone lived in a pretty how town," has led to the critical impression of Cummings as a popular and radical poet whose earnest poetic vision was typography and free verse (Friedman 3–18). This view of Cummings's poetry would seem to exclude any structural play with the established form of the sonnet. Contrary to this persistent perception, Cummings published well over two hundred nonconventional sonnets, ranging from such themes as the demimonde and the erotic, the idea of a three-dimensional human, to nature and God. Using sonnets as structural devices for his collections (or "booksofpoems," as he called them), Cummings continually confronts the genre's set rules and generic expectations. Few people, however, realize how important Cummings's lifelong experimentation with the sonnet and its formal restrictions was to his poetic modernism.[1]

David Morton describes the sonnet literature at the turn of the twentieth century in *Sonnets of Yesterday and Today* (1926) as refined and restrictive: "the character of the grand body of sonnet literature remained—to the end of the century—'grand' and formal" (41). Morton notably demonstrates how the genre holds its place in the new movement in poetry not just as an icon of culture but also as an emblem of cultural change: "all of this has a peculiar interest in the case of a form on which tradition had placed a special emphasis of exclusiveness of theme and formal majesty of manner. There has been some surprise that the sonnet has survived, at all, in the late passion for 'free and full expression,' beyond all imposed restriction" (46–47).

Responding to the "free and full expression" of the new poetry, modernist Cummings strongly reacted to the imposition of thematic exclusiveness and fixed form on poetry. In his hands, the "grand and formal" sonnet became a genre uniquely capable of critiquing the society that had created and crystalized it. With "the Cambridge ladies" in mind, Cummings inverted the expectations of the established form, breaking its visual and verbal confines to reflect on the restrictiveness of culture, genre, and the self from within. In past studies of Cummings's modernist sonnets, I have shown how he took his sonnetry to the level of metasonnetry.[2] Unlike other modernists, Cummings, by rejecting traditional poetic forms for vers libre, did not follow the "make it new" tenet of modernism; he believed that the established forms, such as the orthodox sonnet upheld by the genteel tradition, could be remade and provide the basis for poetic renewal. In juxtaposition to the set tradition, these traditional forms could, in other words, be transformed from formulae into potentially liberating genres.

Morton's study of modern sonnets of the midtwenties highlights "peculiar" qualities of sonnetry, "that of character portraiture, and that of singing lyricism," indicating the genre's potential for renewal:

> I would not insist further upon peculiar qualities of the Twentieth Century sonnet, but I would mention, in passing, two uses made of the sonnet form today so extensive as to suggest two distinctive literatures within the sonnet field—that of character portraiture, and that of singing lyricism. Sonnets celebrative of great men have been, of course, common in English literature. Wordsworth's sonnet on Milton is in a well-known tradition. But we have something different in the meticulously etched-in portraits of Edwin Arlington Robinson's sonnets, where temperament and character, and career and destiny, are put together in a unified and revealing portrait. (48)

Morton's interest is in the change of subject matter, the Victorian genteel figures now becoming "portrait" sonnets of common men and women in realistic settings, such as Robinson's "Leffingwell" (Morton 49). Nonetheless, he does not mention Cummings, even though Cummings had won the *Dial* award in 1925 and had published some widely noted, provocative sonnets, such as "the Cambridge ladies" and "kitty" in his first "bookofpoems," *Tulips and Chimneys* (1923). Morton was not alone in overlooking Cummings's radical or ultramodern fourteenliners (Sterner 81), perhaps because they break the "grand" form in stanzaic groupings, line breaks, rhythmic and sound arrangements, and intense sensual images and move beyond what was recognizable at the time as a sonnet. This dismissal has had a lasting effect, in which Cummings is identified exclusively as an experimental modernist poet, but not as a "make it new" sonneteer. In terms of subject matter, however, Cummings's "portraiture" sonnets fall nothing short of Morton's notion of the "peculiar" qualities of the modern sonnet.

This essay highlights one of Cummings's frequently anthologized "i/eye portrait" sonnets, "next to of course god america i," from *is 5* (*Complete* 284) (*p. 39*), and shows how this post–World War I poem rejects a formulaic identification with New England Petrarchism (Huang-Tiller, "Modernism" 158)—what Cummings perceives as "sonnets—unrealities"—and simultaneously frustrates the expected Shakespearean ending for his stance, "my specialty is living said" (*Complete* 504).[3] Perhaps Cummings's structuring of his "i/eye" sonnet as a cultural emblem is even more peculiar than Morton would have recognized.

Departing from the highly stylized lyric form, Cummings applies the sonnet form's bipartite or tripartite rhetorical structure to the pictorial, rendering the poem a poetic and cultural witness to the speaking individual. In "next to of course god america i," the visual shape of the sonnet, stands forth like a verbal portrait, emblematic of pictorial composition in three parts (Welsh 49–50; Daly 141). The first thirteen lines form a visual block of direct speech with a "motto-like" opening line, followed by a series of rushed patriotic jingles in mixed trochaic-iambic lines that turn sounds into cacophony: "love you land of the pilgrims' and so forth oh / say can you see by the dawn's early my / country 'tis of centuries come and go" (lines 2–4).

A fast-talking speaker, heard from a compressed space, reveals no inner feeling, while gestures and body movements present a formulaic speech on patriotism: "by jingo by gee by gosh by gum / why talk of beauty what could be more beaut- / iful than these heroic happy dead" (lines 8–10). Visually, the politician, or demagogue, takes the entire space of the sonnet, except for the blank space between the thirteenth and fourteenth lines, drawing attention to the figure as disproportionately enlarged. The volume of the speaker's body is visually dramatized in a double pun on the volume of his voice: "'then shall the voice of liberty be mute?' // He spoke. And drank rapidly a glass of water" (lines 13–14). The image of drinking a glass of water further highlights the demagogue's gesture that is ubiquitous to all politicians. The separated line can also be seen as a visual inscription, revealing dryness in his platitudes and his propagandistic language.

The sonnet "rules" are mocked by Cummings's disregard for the expected volta, allowing the logorrheic speech to run on for thirteen lines, devoid of both punctuation and substance. The pace of reading and lack of syntactic breaks disrupt the expected dialogic movement of the Petrarchan form or the harmonized ending of a Shakespearean couplet. Instead, Cummings defers the turn until the thirteenth line, when the demagogue simply runs out of air and pauses, prompting the poet's prosaic observation about drinking a glass of water. In the sonnet space, no argument develops, and there is no prospect for reflection.

The recognizable regular sonnet rhyme scheme of the first two Shakespearean quatrains and the Petrarchan sestet contrasts with the lack of punctuation and the sonorous repetitions, transforming the parodic sonnet into an emblem for the meaningless political discourse that lacks, in this instance, even emotional appeal. Cummings's careful attention to rhyme establishes an ironic tension between regularity of the form and the emptiness and formlessness of the actual words. Cummings shows how the sonnet, as cultural emblem, voices its own decline into platitude, reflecting how the genteel sonnet had become trite, form without substance, just as the words of the politician are a string of clichés.

Most sonnet readers will find Cummings's use of a mixed Shakespearean and Petrarchan form (*ababcdcdefgfeg*) not necessarily rebellious. The hybrid form itself is not unfamiliar to Elizabethan sonneteers (Philip Sidney's

Astrophel and Stella comes to mind), but such sonnets would be considered "illegitimate" by the genteel sonneteers and critics in Cummings's time (Alden 267). Although the political hypocrisy in this sonnet is not disputed, I believe the poem also has much to say about the ideology of form in relation to genre, culture, and self. To begin, by splicing the Shakespearean and Petrarchan forms into one, Cummings turns the mixed sonnet form from a structural device to a subtle metaphor for self-reflexive "illegitimacy." Visually fragmenting the sestet into a one-line stanza at the end, in juxtaposition to the pastiche of patriotic bromides and song lines (a collage of nationalist emblems), Cummings provokes an examination of and second look into both the form and content of the "illegitimate" sonnet. As if using the "illegitimate" form to cast doubt on the concept of "legitimate" speech, Cummings adroitly challenges the assumptions of formal legitimacy, as well as expressions of nationalism as discourse. Concurrently, his fusion of the two sonnet forms, along with his consistent use of ungrammatical language in the sonnet, frees the genre from the limitations imposed on it.

Beyond mocking political rhetoric, Cummings also uses the sonnet form to verbally paint a naturalistic figure of a politician, (un)self here and now, turning the sonnet into a testing ground to reconsider what makes an individual. In the last line, Cummings reminds his readers (and himself) of their shared humanity with the speaker. The speaker, however, reveals a misguided sense of self. Like his rapid talk and rapid drink, the American "i" is missing individuality. As the speaker rushes the sentiment of patriotism, the lionized American "*i*fuls" (or "the heroic happy dead") rush mindlessly toward their "glorious" deaths: "who rushed like lions to the roaring slaughter / they did not stop to think they died instead" (lines 11–12). The "i" outside this sonnet intersects the speaker's "i" at the moment of the water break; the "eye" sees but stops, thinks, and suspends his/her identification. The sudden pause or an unexpected turn, characteristic of neither the Petrarchan sestet nor the Shakespearean couplet, compels this American moment to stop, look, and listen again. The American "i" in Cummings's portrait sonnets often provokes such an encounter with both the familiar and defamiliarized form for the other "i/eye." Through the reader's gazing, the politician is transformed into an artistic construct, set up as a catalyst for self-reflection. To look at and recognize the object moves the reader into the realm of a knowing experience; that is, to see and to know the difference between false and authentic self, and thus to his/her own transformation.

In the blank space after thirteen lines of rote phrases without a pause, Cummings presents the American "i" confronting the inauthenticity of his own discourse. In that moment of pause or intersection, the unexpected blank line opens the form for reassessment and compels the reader to examine him/herself to see if (s)he can go beyond these rhetorical trappings. The politician influences only those who are incapable of living on their own terms. Once subsumed into the rhetoric of form or formula, the individual ceases to be an individual. The demagogue or the politician—"that lying thieving cowardly treacherous unanimal called a politician," Cummings remarks in one of his unpublished notes ("A Politician")—is captured in this rapid and rattled speech. What readers "make of it" is left to them. Cummings's cultural consciousness of what makes an American un-American often gets transferred into his poetry. His typographical metasonnets prompt us to see ourselves as reading a cultural emblem rather than expecting the abstracted personage of conventional portraiture sonnets such as Wordsworth's Milton sonnet, "London, 1802."

In "next to god of course America i," Cummings seizes the "voice of liberty" to problematize the formalized rules and the formulaic talk that have conditioned our knowledge of "freedom of form" (Kennedy 318). In reimagining the sonnet, Cummings foregrounds his American "i" sonnet by presenting an open-ended living form, a speaking persona, performing, gesturing and alive, rendering the "i" within the form as the "i" who is seen and the "eye" that sees. Character portraiture sonnets are not uncommon in American literature, as the sonnets of Robinson and Edgar Lee Masters evidence. Cummings's iconoclastic portrait sonnets, however, stand out in form and content, intersecting with the culture of their time. More of a cultural modernist than a formalist of modern abstract aestheticism (Levenson 4; Altieri 383), Cummings creates "poempictures" (Cohen 16) that are communal, impersonal, and dramatic, as well as personal. His iconoclastic sonnets are life pieces of modern individuals in motion, often overlooked in sonnet literature. They include prostitutes, demagogues, drunks, lovers, and lives on the city streets (Dickey 215–16) in addition to tributes to friends and memorials. Through this gallery of portraits, Cummings underscores the quality of animated portraitures in a set of defamiliarized fourteenliners as encounters and emblems of modern American reality.

To enter Cummings's portrait sonnets is to enter a visual experience, intersecting and crossing consciousnesses with the "i" speaker. Reading Cummings's "live-portrait" sonnets is like reading an American emblem as well as reading the self, not just a persona or a parody of such a persona (Holden 22), but an American "i/eye" intersecting each other.[4] With a painter's eye, Cummings turns the American sonnet into a verbal portrait, alive with the transformative potential of the American i/eye for a renewed selfhood (a Verb, an Is, wholeness in Cummings's lexicon).[5] Seeing oneself through an iconic politician or emblematic American patriotism, for example, the American "i/eye" must make an individual decision whether or not to affiliate.

I conclude with Cummings's wedge-shaped yet sonnet-like poem, "i" (*Complete* 873) in his posthumous collection *73 Poems*, for his vision of the sonnet as an "i/eye" encounter. The syllabic arrangement of the first three lines, "i / never / guessed any" (lines 1–3), is mirrored in the final lines, "who's ama / zingly / Eye" (lines 13–15). With the speaker "i" perceiving a small, perfect universe, "almost invisible" to our human eye, the i/Eye is then arrested in the pivotal, interfaced eighth line, which embeds a mirrored vowel pattern, *ao-iii-e* to *eoa-eoa-eoa*, with three "invisible" -i's: "(*almost invisible* where *of a* there *of a*)here *of a*." The visual poem in its incremental line extension and subsequent contraction after the central eighth line is revealed to be a ruby-throated hummingbird's nest: "rubythroat's home with its still / ness which really's herself" (lines 9–10). The nest, whether seen from above, below, or from the side, is transformed into the mother bird and her eggs: "(and to think that she's / warming three worlds)" (lines 11–12). The sight of her "warming three worlds" signals a transcendent moment when "i/Eye" enter each other's consciousness. At the moment of gazing, the "i" meets her "Eye." In this mirrored form, seven lines above and seven lines below the eighth line form a visual conceit for the new volta (where two octets intersect, while also balanced with a syllabic pattern of 1-2-3-4-5-6-7-15-7-6-5-4-3-2-1). With this interlocking "i/Eye" turn from the set form, Cummings finds his own transcendent vision "to warm three worlds"[6] through the art of his iconic metasonnets.

Notes

1. Cummings himself declared, "as for the unconventionality of my writing:if you can count the sonnets in *Poems 1923–1950*, you have a lot more patience than the man who wrote them" ("Q&A.").

2. See my "Modernism, Cummings' Meta-Sonnets," "The Modernist Sonnet," *The Power of the Meta-Genre*, and "Reflecting 'EIMI'."

3. On the Shakespearean couplet, Cummings would concur with Carl Phillips on the form's "rebellious" potential ("Whose Sonnet? A Transgression," Keynote Address, *Sonnets from the American: A Virtual Symposium*, Oct. 3, 2020).

4. I appreciate a similar experience in the sessions and poetry readings presented at *Sonnets from the American: A Virtual Symposium*, Oct. 1–3, 2020. It was an i/Eye-opening

encounter with Jahan Ramazani's introduction to the American sonnet through Terrance Hayes's *My Past and Future Assassin* (2018) ("Self-Metaphorizing 'American' Sonnets," Keynote Address, *Sonnets from the American: A Virtual Symposium*, Oct. 2, 2020).

5. "For "a Verb, an Is, wholeness," see Cummings's note, quoted on the opening page of this essay. Kennedy, *Dreams in the Mirror*, p. 217. Huang-Tiller, "Definition of Is as an Intransitive Verb, to Feel," www.eecsocietyblog.org/?p=1259.

6. Etienne Terblanche connects the image of "warming three worlds" (line 12) to Cummings's typographical osmosis (16); Michael Webster in "Magic Iconism" suggests a range of readings of the third "world," from the mother bird warming herself, to hatching one extra egg, to the nest itself, and to the "identity of poet and nature" (107).

Works Cited

Alden, Raymond M. "The Sonnet." *The English Verse*. Henry Holt, 1903, pp. 267–97.

Altieri, Charles. *Painterly Abstraction in Modernist American Poetry: The Contemporaneity of Modernism*. Cambridge UP, 1989.

Cohen, Milton A. *Poet and Painter: The Aesthetics of E. E. Cummings's Early Work*. Wayne State UP, 1987.

Cummings, E. E. *Complete Poems 1904–1962*. Edited by George J. Firmage, W. W. Norton, 2016.

———. "A Politician." MS. notes. MS Am 1892.7(90), f. 5, s. 68. Harvard University, Houghton Library, Cambridge, MA.

———. "Q&A." MS. notes. MS Am 1823.7 (104), 3, s. 52. Houghton Library, Harvard University, Cambridge, MA.

Daly, Peter M. "Emblematic Poetry." *Literature in the Light of the Emblem: Structural Parallels between the Emblem and Literature in the Sixteenth and Seventeenth Centuries*. 2nd ed. U of Toronto P, 1998, pp. 122–52.

Dickey, Frances. *The Modern Portrait Poem: From Dante Gabriel Rossetti to Ezra Pound*. U of Virginia P, 2012.

Friedman, Norman. *(Re)Valuing Cummings: Further Essays on the Poet, 1962–1993*. U of Florida P, 1996.

Huang-Tiller, Gillian. "Modernism, Cummings' Meta-Sonnets, and *Chimneys*." *Spring: The Journal of the E. E. Cummings Society* 10, 2001, pp. 155–72.

———. "The Modernist Sonnet and the Pre-Postmodern Consciousness: The Question of Meta-Genre in E. E. Cummings' *W[ViVa]* (1931)." *Spring: The Journal of the E. E. Cummings Society*, 14–15, 2005–2006, pp. 156–77.

———. *The Power of the Meta-Genre: Cultural, Sexual, and Racial Politics of the American Modernist Sonnet*. U of Notre Dame, 2000, PhD dissertation.

———. "Reflecting 'EIMI' (1933): The Iconic Meta-Sonnet, Manhood, and Cultural Crisis in E. E. Cummings' 'No Thanks' (1935)." *Words into Pictures: E. E. Cummings' Art across Borders*, edited by Jioí Flajsar and Zénó Vernyik, Cambridge Scholars Press, 2007, pp. 27–57.

Holden, Jonathan. "Postmodern Poetic Form: A Theory." *New England Review and Bread Loaf Quarterly*, 6, no. 1, Autumn 1983, pp. 1–22.

Kennedy, Richard. *Dreams in the Mirror: A Biography of E. E. Cummings.* Liveright, 1980.

Levenson, Michael, editor. Introduction. *The Cambridge Companion to Modernism.* Cambridge UP, 1999.

Morton, David. *The Sonnet Today and Yesterday.* G. P. Putnam's Sons, 1926.

Santayana, George. "The Genteel Tradition in American Philosophy, 1911." *Selected Critical Writings of George Santayana,* edited by Norman Henfrey, vol. 2, Cambridge UP, 1968, pp. 85–107.

Sterner, Lewis G. *The Sonnet in American Literature: An Anthology of Representative American Sonnets.* U of Pennsylvania, PhD thesis, 1930.

Terblanche, Etienne. "The Osmotic Mandala: on the Nature of Boundaries in E. E. Cummings' Poetry." *Spring: The Journal of the E. E. Cummings Society* 10, 2001, pp. 9–22.

Webster, Michael. "Magic Iconism: Defamiliarization, Sympathetic Magic, and Visual Poetry (Guillaume Apollinaire and E. E. Cummings)." *European Journal of English Studies,* 2001, 5, no. 1, pp. 97–113.

Welsh, Andres. "Emblem." *Roots of Lyric: Primitive Poetry and Modern Poetics.* Princeton UP, 1978, pp. 47–66.

Sonnets into the American
Translation and Transnation in the Harlem Renaissance

TIMO MÜLLER

Now that the transnational range of African American literature is widely acknowledged, the sonnet, once an oddity in the Black canon, is increasingly recognized as one of its paradigmatic manifestations. Recent scholarship has shown that poets from Claude McKay to Rita Dove and beyond have used the sonnet to negotiate experiences of migration and transnational identity formation (Müller; Robbins)—not least because such experiences resonate with the form itself. The sonnet emerged at the multicultural court of Frederick II of Sicily and soon began to migrate across Europe and the world, undergoing manifold transformations in the process. These transformations become particularly visible in translations of sonnets from one language into another. The unusually stable form of the sonnet requires translators either to modify the form to suit the exigencies of the target language or to modify the content to suit the exigencies of the form. Either way, translated sonnets make readers and writers aware that the same form can carry different connotations in each culture. The sonnet form thus amplifies the negotiation of cultural difference that occurs in all translations (Gentzler; Regan).

For African American poets, the most momentous category of cultural difference has been race. Used to a culture that construed blackness as essential and absolute, even the earliest African American poets seized on transnational comparison to highlight the arbitrariness of such essentialism, bolster the case against white supremacy, and articulate Afro-diasporic identities. The Harlem Renaissance marked an epochal shift in the history of African American literature not least because it enabled a broad conversation around these goals (Edwards). It may not be accidental that the first sonnet translations by African American poets appeared in key publications of the Harlem Renaissance: *The Crisis, Opportunity, The Book of American Negro Poetry*. A close reading of these translations—by James Weldon Johnson, Countee Cullen, and Langston Hughes—reveals how the leading poets of the period focused a politics of Black transnationality through the combined affordances of translation and the sonnet form.

They deployed these affordances on several levels of poetic communication. On the semantic level, translation allowed them to control and modify the message of the original sonnet. Since the originals were usually by internationally renowned poets, the translators effectively appropriated these poets' cultural and political authority for messages of their own making. On a paratextual level, the translators signaled to a prejudiced American audience their exceptional knowledge of the original language, of the sonnet genre, and of the current state of world literature. By associating themselves with highly regarded literary traditions—usually French or Spanish—they challenged the widespread notion that Black literature was a matter of simple entertainment. On a cultural level, translation put these poets in a position to explain other cultures to Americans and, conversely, to establish a critical outside perspective on American culture. The illustrious genre history of the sonnet reinforced this multilevel communication by associating the translators with a transnational literary elite from whose point of view American racial prejudices could be dismissed as backward and embarrassing.

Perhaps most appealingly, the translation of sonnets allowed poets like Johnson, Cullen, and Hughes to negotiate the politics of blackness without making it the explicit subject of their work. Since the writers they translated were not themselves Black, their sonnets sidestepped the expectation that African American poets write about "their" people. They redirected attention to the poetic composition of the sonnets and thus to craftsmanship that could be evaluated independently of racial categories. Poets could use this attention to claim the universality of the sonnet for their own work but also to challenge this supposed universality and expose the racial presuppositions associated with the form. Either option promised a way out of the double bind of race that dominated debates around Black writing. By translating sonnets, the poets of the Harlem Renaissance could address race without explicitly writing about it; conversely, they could expand their writing beyond racial boundaries without denying that these boundaries existed.

Their awareness of these possibilities manifested in the January 1922 issue of *The Crisis*, which carried a two-page article on the Cuban poet and antislavery activist Plácido, excerpted from Johnson's preface to *The Book of American Negro Poetry*. Johnson points out that many leading Latin American poets have "Negro blood" but nevertheless "rank as great in the literatures of their respective countries without any qualifications whatever" (109). Plácido is his main example, and most of the article discusses a sonnet the poet wrote to his mother before his execution. Somewhat surprisingly, the discussion soon focuses on William Cullen Bryant's translation of that sonnet into English. "It is curious," Johnson notes, "how Bryant's translation totally misses the intimate sense of the delicate subtility of the poem" (110). The crucial mistake, Johnson argues, is Bryant's disregard of the introductory word *Si* ("If"): abandoned by his mother at an early age, Plácido did not even know if she would read his farewell or be affected by it, so that he chose the conditional mode for his sonnet. The proper tone for a translation, Johnson concludes, is therefore one of "nobility and dignity" instead of the personal affection Bryant's version conveys (110). Appended to the article are the original poem, Bryant's version, and a new translation made by Johnson himself (*p. 21*). Arranging them in parallel columns, Johnson projects confidence that readers will recognize his superior familiarity with the language, the poet, and the intricacies of poetic form. By pointing out the historical circumstances of the poem's composition, moreover, Johnson shifts the attention from Bryant's abstract romanticism to Plácido's abolitionist activities, thus enlisting the admired Cuban poet in the struggle against racism in the United States.

Both messages are articulated indirectly, through the translation of a widely respected poetic form. Johnson's appropriation of the sonnet thus signals the cultural self-assertion that would come to characterize the Harlem Renaissance. The different directions this self-assertion could take, and the challenges each involved, can be seen in the sonnet translations Cullen and Hughes published in the early 1930s. Where Cullen reinforces the high-cultural credentials of the sonnet to claim membership in a transnational intellectual elite, Hughes introduces vernacular elements to challenge these credentials and position Black oral expression as an alternative cultural standard.

Cullen's *The Medea and Some Poems* (1935) includes not only the eponymous translation of Euripides's tragedy but also three sonnets from Baudelaire's *Les fleurs du mal*: the cat sonnets and "La mort des pauvres," which ambivalently praises death as salvation for the poor. The authors, texts, genres, and languages Cullen selects for translation stand metonymically for high culture. By associating with these canonic sources, he makes a claim for equality that, like Johnson's, hinges on his own position as poet and translator. Cullen strives to make his poetry indistinguishable from the major representatives of European high culture, and thus to become part of that cultural elite himself. This strategy requires him to work by implication and avoid explanatory gestures like Johnson's. Cullen does articulate the strategy elsewhere, for example, in his reports from France, where his translations of Baudelaire seem to have been inspired.

In one of the travel reports he wrote for *The Crisis* in the late twenties, Cullen reports a conversation with the German-French writer Claire Goll. An enthusiast of African American literature, "Madame" Goll reproaches Cullen for writing about Keats, Endymion, and Jupiter instead of tapping the resources of authentic Black life. "It is on the tip of my tongue," he comments, "to ask why Keats himself should have concerned himself with themes like Endymion and Hyperion, but I am drinking Madame's tea" (568). The anecdote articulates Cullen's conception of great literature as a universal sphere that is by definition transnational and transracial. At the same time, it voices his concern that access to this sphere may be hampered by racial prejudice. The punch line alleviates this concern as it shows Cullen superseding his host's prejudice through his wit and his familiarity with the literary tradition. Here too the message is reinforced by genre and language: Cullen presents himself as an educated gentleman traveler in the nineteenth-century tradition and demonstrates his ability to outwit a respected foreign writer in her own language.

The same strategy underlies his sonnet translations, whose politics unfold not in their semantic content but by metonymic implication. In publishing a series of translations from Baudelaire, Cullen measures his poetic skills against one of the most respected figures in the history of the genre. He also adopts his precursor's voice and message, thus claiming for Black poets like himself the thematic range, canonic status, and universal significance traditionally ascribed to white poets such as Baudelaire. The vision underlying these translations is that of a literary canon that includes all races and nations. The political implication is that existing cultural and aesthetic norms need not be changed for such a universal canon to emerge. If anything, Cullen's fidelity to the sonnet form reinforces these norms, but it also reinforces the demand that he, and by implication other Black poets, be admitted into the canon now that he has fulfilled them.

Translation supports this demand in that it allows Cullen to enlist Baudelaire—and the cultural capital he carries—explicitly and directly. At the same time, translation exposes a problem of Cullen's political strategy: in staking his—and by extension Black—access to high culture on the ability to meet standards set by others, he risks accentuating the very differences he seeks to overcome. Poets are expected to develop a distinct poetic voice, so if the standards do not reflect their experience, they will need to deviate from the standards to become recognized as serious poets in the first place. As a Black poet playing to white standards, Cullen wrestles with this problem throughout his oeuvre. Its mechanisms are particularly visible in his translations because translation exposes this double bind: the original text presents a fairly strict standard while also requiring the translating poet to bring his own interpretation to the text.

The implications of this double bind can be traced in Cullen's translation of "La mort des pauvres," a hymn to death as deliverance from life's hardship and injustice. Baudelaire's original thrives on the ambivalences of this proposition. It heightens the tensions between life and death, agency and sufferance, injustice and deliverance. Cullen's translation, by contrast, thrives on its polished language. It often sacrifices tension to ensure stylistic adequacy to the admired original. As a result, Cullen departs from the semantic content of the original and offers a reinterpretation in which the central agency is no longer death but the salvation that awaits in life after death. Where Baudelaire's opening declares death the source not only of consolation in life but of life itself—"C'est la Mort qui console, hélas! et qui fait vivre" (340)—Cullen reduces its agency by emphasizing what awaits after it. He glosses over the decisive twist at the end of Baudelaire's line by turning it into a relatively weak prelude to the second line, whose pun further belittles the seriousness of Baudelaire's invocation: "In death alone is what consoles; and life / And all its end is death" (255). This takes Cullen's poem in a quite different direction. Where Baudelaire ends with a vision of death as the door to "unknown heavens" (*Cieux inconnus*), Cullen refocuses the concluding tercet on a conventional scene of divine salvation where a reassuringly Christian "God" welcomes his "sheep" to "Paradise" (255)—concepts that do not appear in Baudelaire's original. Cullen effectively replaces the tensions that sustain the original with a conventional genteel idealism. This puts more pressure on the formal authority of the sonnet, which Cullen seeks to assert by turning Baudelaire's slightly skewed *ccd ede* rhyme scheme into a perfectly regular *efg*. This too can be read as a reductive gesture, of course, so that the very attempt to standardize reveals the double bind Cullen is confronting. Not even the sonnet offers the kind of unambiguous standard on which his politics of form relies: on the contrary, it turns out to elude the very standards it is supposed to represent.

Langston Hughes, who developed an interest in both the sonnet and translation in the early 1930s, sought to avoid these difficulties by reversing the standards. Instead of fitting Black poetry to the sonnet form, he incorporated the sonnet into the Black vernacular. The inspiration for this strategy might have come from Nicolás Guillén, the Afro-Cuban writer Hughes met in 1930 and began to translate soon after (Kutzinski). A wide-ranging experimental poet, Guillén was schooled in the European tradition but modified its forms with the rumba and son rhythms of the Afro-Cuban community. An early manifestation of Hughes's engagement with Guillén's hybrid poetics is his translation of the love sonnet "2 semanas," which appeared as "Two Weeks" (*p. 43*) in the March 1933 issue of *Opportunity*.

Guillén's poem ironically subverts the conventions of the love sonnet by paralleling an inconsequential fourteen-day love affair with the fourteen lines of the sonnet. Where Guillén retains the classic Petrarchan form, Hughes enhances the vernacular quality of the poem by loosening the rhyme scheme and meter. He opens the poem in tetrameters that grow into pentameters in syncopated fits and starts. He even omits parts of Guillén's lines to create this irregular rhythm, thus conveying the flippant mood of the original with more radical formal means. Hughes's most emphatic departure from the original is his inclusion of the colloquial "Facts are," which opens the summary of the love affair in the concluding tercet. Such vernacular elements grate with the highly formal, even stilted rendering of such lines as "A blush made red each pallid little cheek" (line 6). As a result, Hughes's translation does not succeed in creating the organic blend of formal and colloquial language that characterizes his best poetry. Nevertheless, "Two Weeks" has a significant place in American literary history in that it marks the first step toward a Black vernacular sonnet. Where earlier African American poets, including Johnson and Cullen, had retained the elevated diction and standard form of the sonnet, Guillén's experiments with the form pointed Hughes to its potential for a vernacular poetics that refused both the pejorative associations of Black dialect and the impositions of the European tradition. Hughes would return to this idea in "Seven Moments of Love: An un-sonnet sequence in Blues" (1940) (*p. 43*), whose blend of sonnet and blues elements broke fresh ground in American poetry (Müller 75–82).

The significance of Hughes's translation is not limited to genre history. "Two Weeks" also engages contemporary debates around the politics of Black writing, from Cullen's cosmopolitanism to the reemerging interest in African American folk culture. Hughes employs his mediatory position as a translator to negotiate between these positions. "Two Weeks" is among the first of his many translations from Spanish and French that explore the affinities of Black oral expression beyond boundaries of language and nation. It positions the sonnet form not as the badge of the cosmopolitan elite but as a transnationally shared form that enables poetic communication across these boundaries. Hughes prefaces his translation with a note that introduces Guillén as a "Havana poet" to readers of *Opportunity*, signaling the lateral bonds his translation work establishes among vernacular poets whose ethnic backgrounds force them into marginal yet more productive positions in American culture. In contrast to Cullen's orientation toward the European tradition, Hughes's transnationalism has closer affinities to Pan-American and Pan-African programs of decolonial resistance. He appropriates the sonnet to challenge the very cultural norms that the form represents for Johnson and Cullen. What the three poets share is their interest in challenging narrow notions of cultural authenticity and the racial hierarchies that sustain them. Johnson, Cullen, and Hughes recognized that the sonnet offered an effective framework for these goals—and that translation amplified its effectiveness.

—

Works Cited

Baudelaire, Charles. *Les fleurs du mal.* 3rd ed., Calmann Lévy, 1896.

Cullen, Countee. *My Soul's High Song: The Collected Writings of Countee Cullen.* Edited by Gerald Early, Doubleday, 1991.

Edwards, Brent Hayes. *The Practice of Diaspora: Literature, Translation, and the Rise of Black Internationalism.* Harvard UP, 2003.

Gentzler, Edwin. *Translation and Identity in the Americas: New Directions in Translation Theory.* Routledge, 2008.

Guillén, Nicolás. "Two Weeks." Translated by Langston Hughes, *Opportunity*, 11 Mar. 1933, p. 88.

Hughes, Langston. "Two Weeks." *The Poetry of the Negro 1746–1949*, edited by Langston Hughes and Arna Bontemps. Doubleday, 1951, p. 379; archive.org/details/poetryofthenegro009355mbp/page/n399/mode/2up.

Johnson, James Weldon. "Plácido." *The Crisis*, vol. 23, no. 3, 1922, pp. 109–11.

Kutzinski, Vera. *The Worlds of Langston Hughes: Modernism and Translation in the Americas.* Cornell UP, 2012.

Müller, Timo. *The African American Sonnet: A Literary History.* UP of Mississippi, 2018.

Regan, Stephen. *The Sonnet.* Oxford UP, 2020.

Robbins, Hollis. *Forms of Contention: Influence and the African American Sonnet Tradition.* U of Georgia P, 2020.

Claude McKay's Lonely Planet
The Sonnet Sequence and the Global City

WALT HUNTER

The poetic sequence "Cities" (1934) is a peculiar kind of guide to Claude McKay's forced exile from the United States and Jamaica. From Fez to Cadiz, Barcelona's Barrio Chino to Harlem's Lenox Avenue, "Cities" charts the wayward course of McKay's obligatory internationalism as the itinerant sonneteer witnesses the "embattled workers' day" in Saint Petersburg on May 1, 1923, and the consolidation of Nazi power in Berlin in 1934. "Cities" transforms the modernist "unreal city" of isolation, in which, as Eliot writes, "each man fixe[s] his eyes before his feet" ("The Waste Land" 39), into the riotous city of a revolutionary crowd, where McKay finds "man drawing near to man in close commune" (230). As a kind of sequel to McKay's volumes of Jamaican dialect poems in 1911–12 and to *Harlem Shadows* in 1922, the "Cities" cycle extends and complicates McKay's earlier work with the ballad and the sonnet. This essay looks first at the way McKay channels a visionary power through the sonnet's monumental architecture, then moves outward into the sequence as a whole to explore some ways of thinking about the poems as a linked set of cityscapes. Ultimately, the poetic organization of "Cities" constructs an exemplary form of political organization, in which the collaborative efforts of marginalized individuals transform the space of the city through their creative activities.

The long period of McKay's "vagabond internationalism"—to use Brent Hayes Edwards's term—produced not only a series of well-known novels (*Home to Harlem*, *Banjo*, and *Banana Bottom*) but also some less widely read experiments in poetry (187). While McKay's earlier sonnets form a loose affiliation of poems, "Cities" is quite clearly conceived as a coherent sequence. What did the sonnet sequence as a genre offer to McKay as he attempted to capture the lives of those in cities in the decades between the wars? "Cities" certainly departs in some obvious ways from the tradition of sonnet sequences. Unlike most of Petrarch's *Canzoniere* or Shakespeare's sonnets, McKay's poems are titled for and situated in determinate places. They take on the dimension of space as well as time. In McKay's sequence, the fractured temporality in Petrarch, Sidney, Spenser, Donne, or Wroth shifts axes and becomes a series of loosely connected places.

But the order of "Cities" does not match up with the route McKay actually traveled. The "Cities" sequence is carefully composed, and McKay's actual stops are rearranged. While McKay himself begins in New York, travels through Paris and Marseille, and ends up in North Africa, "Cities" starts in Barcelona, moves through Tangier, Fez, Marrakesh, Tetuan, Xauen, and Cadiz, heads east to Berlin and Moscow, and finishes in the metropole: Paris, London, and New York. The decision to reverse the itinerary reflects McKay's understanding of the sonnet sequence as an engine for dynamically transforming the space of the city into a series of interconnected "squares" for the political organization of a crowd. McKay draws attention away from the city's stone reality and toward its potency, its spontaneous reconstitution as a space for play, dance, and magic. In her work on global cities, Saskia Sassen writes, "The Street can... be conceived as a space where new forms of the social and the political can be *made*, rather than a space for enacting ritualized routines" (574; emphasis in original). This understanding of the city street as a place for play and improvisation helps to explain why McKay begins the sonnet sequence with Andalusia instead of Eastern Europe. The Teutonic facades of 1934 Berlin, with their "ruthless Nordic style" and "massive grandeur," serve as foils for the mosaics of Spain and North Africa (229).

The power to organize the cities in a sequence comes from the visionary energy McKay locates in the masses gathering outdoors and taking over the streets. McKay's poems from the "Cities" sequence capture more than a shared vulnerability; they throb with a shared ecstasy that brings people together. "Barcelona" provides one example of how the sonnet form expands to represent the experience of the crowd in the streets (223). McKay's sonnets in *Harlem Shadows* often gain their force from the necessity of invective and ruthless critique. In contrast, the octave from "Barcelona" develops an incantatory mode as "the folk... come together / From pueblo, barrio, in families... In spreading rings they weave fine fantasies / Like rare mosaics of many colored lights." The comradely crowds in the sonnets for

Cadiz, Fez, and Marrakesh also bear evidence of a kind of spiritual occupation, represented in the poems as fantasy, fever, dream, dance, magic, and prayer. The speaker moves through various states of being smitten, haunted, and charmed. Bells ring as he passes among mosaics, tapestries, flowers, and fountains. There is a dreamlike state of inertia in the sequence as a whole, which, for all its itinerancy, never really seems to get anywhere. Edwards is surely right to argue that the characters in McKay's novel *Banjo*, set in Marseille, form a "global community of the dispossessed" (199). In McKay's sonnets from the same period, we also find a global community of the ecstatically possessed: the crowd, the throng, the multitude, the mob, and the mass in various states of haunting, charming, dancing, singing, and blocking traffic.

The crowds that fill these poems are not so much manic as "mantic," the term used to refer to the Greek account of poetic inspiration. In the sestet of "Barcelona," McKay writes of "the magical Sardana" that "sweeps the city in a glorious blaze," its workers' laughter "Crescending like a wonderful hosanna." In her work on lyric possession, Susan Stewart revives the Platonic account of *enthousiasmos*, the process by which poetry passes along a chain of magnets from the god to the poet. For Plato, this process means that the poet gives voice to knowledge that he does not in fact have but that comes from outside. "The meaning of possession," Stewart argues, "does not reside simply in the idea that the poet's utterances are not *original* or *reasoned*. Rather, such utterances pass through the speaker by means of an external force. One is 'beside one's self'" (112; emphasis in original). In "Barcelona," the word "sardana" refers to the Catalan dance in which everyone holds hands in a ring. The sardana functions as a kind of horizontal possession, replacing or supplementing Plato's vertical account of the chain leading from god through rhapsode to poet to audience.

McKay links the possession of the crowd not to irrationality and chaos but to the spontaneous generation of artistic and political organization. These terms seem like odd ones to apply to the strict design of the fourteen-line form, but there have always been other ways to consider the sonnet than through the usual analogies of imprisonment, restriction, and monumentality. Metaphors of imprisonment are not the only kind of metaphors scattered across the history of the sonnet. Wordsworth might have called the sonnet a cell, but he also referred to it as a key and a trumpet and a glowworm. These nouns make the familiar analogies between the sonnet's formal elements and its thematic concerns a little more complicated. McKay thinks of the sonnet in the same ways as he thinks of the poetic and artistic creations of the global multitude: as a tapestry, a mosaic, a dance, and a city.

In "Cities," each sonnet shares the same pattern of rhyme, which is neither strictly English nor Italian, but rather an invention of McKay's own: *abcd bcda efg fge*. Outside of the "Cities" sequence, I'm aware of no other sonnet of McKay's that employs this scheme. The *abcd* quatrain is a particularly odd way for a sonnet to begin since it resembles four lines of blank verse. By the time the eighth line of the octave arrives, the long-delayed *a* rhyme of the stanza ("nights"/"lights") is that much more pronounced. By deferring the recognition of rhyme, each sonnet gradually lets itself be taken over or seized by the pattern, which builds fervently into the sestet. In the city, McKay suggests, the appropriate metaphor for rhyme is not the "chain" or the "fetter" but rather the "crescending...hosanna" that ends the sestet in "Barcelona." McKay's global city sonnets trope the rapture of the crowd through the metrical fall from blank verse into a rhyming trance.

There is one more way in which the sonnet sequence lends itself to a special kind of vatic amplification in the context of the global city—and for this we have to look not within a particular sonnet but between and among the sonnets as a group. Through the sharing of topos and trope as well as rhyme scheme, McKay's distant cities are not so much distinct plot points as overlapping territories. We are not traveling between the cities or from city to city but rather within a shared space that comes into being through their juxtaposition, a space that has no evident geographic name or concept. Focusing on a given topos (the lyre, the fountain, the tapestry) groups certain cities together in ways that exceed geographical, political, or cultural contiguities. When we encounter a fountain or a tower, for instance, a path lights up that takes us back through others.

The poetics of overdetermination, of excess, and of exuberance found in "Cities" helps to explain why McKay begins with "Barcelona": praising the Moorish and African influences on Spain allows him to emphasize thematically the cultural permeability of the city. By shifting the metaphor for the sonnet from the "room" to the "city," McKay makes the monumentality of the sonnet seem plastic and recombinative, as though the various parts of the city might be reassembled into other as yet unimagined commons. Sonnets, like cities, might preserve their individuation even as they call back and forth to one another using the same figures and tropes. Cities, like sonnets, bear witness not only to the pressure against a restrictive form but also to the potential for an international spirit to expand beyond a discrete textual or physical space.

When McKay returns to Harlem at the end of the "Cities" sequence, his focus remains on the creative production of the revolutionary crowd. In "Note of Harlem," a series of three sonnets, the optimism of Andalusia clashes with the "heart-breaking spectacle" of America. "Harlem" finds the poet listening to music in a bar and wondering how such music could be possible among "the outcasts of the earth": "How can they thus consent to joy and mirth / Who live beneath a world-eternal ban?" (237). Unlike many of the sonnets from this period, "Harlem" answers the poet with a marvelous couplet: "The gifts divine are theirs, music and laughter, / All other things, however great, come after." Far from a naïve bacchanalia or a party at the end of the world, the "gifts divine" of the sonnet's plastic structure usher forth a poetry forged in the streets of a global city never yet to be mapped except in the sonnet sequence itself. That the ruination of the cities through which McKay travels—Marseille, most notably—will be so swiftly to follow only magnifies the intensity of his revolutionary songs.

Works Cited

Edwards, Brent Hayes. *The Practice of Diaspora: Literature, Translation, and the Rise of Black Internationalism*. Harvard UP, 2003.

Eliot, T. S. *The Complete Poetry and Plays, 1909–1950*. Harcourt Brace, 1980.

McKay, Claude. *Complete Poems*. Edited by William Maxwell. U of Illinois P, 2004.

Sassen, Saskia. "The Global Street: Making the Political." *Globalizations*, vol. 8, no. 5, 2011, pp. 573–79.

Stewart, Susan. *Poetry and the Fate of the Senses*. U of Chicago P, 2002.

John Wheelwright, Sound Engineer

MATTHEW KILBANE

The life and poetry of John Wheelwright (1897–1940) testify to a subterranean link between two ostensibly very different cultural forms, the sonnet and radio broadcasting. To set about unfolding this surprising affiliation is also to assume the delightful responsibility of introducing readers to an irresistibly idiosyncratic modern poet little read these days, one for whom the sonnet and radio were objects of characteristically ingenious aesthetic investment. In the 1930s, Wheelwright's artistic commitments to these sonorous technologies—first to the poetic form and then to the communications medium—found their authorization in one and the same deeply felt requirement: the desire to engineer a politically usable modernist poetry. In the final years of that decade Wheelwright believed he had located at last, in the radical implications of radio broadcasting, a socialist horizon for modern verse. And yet his earlier innovations in sonnet form so vividly reveal the initial stirrings of this quest that the largest stakes of these printed sonnets are most clearly apprehended in the light shed by his later career on the air. To read his sonnets well, in other words, we must read with an ear to radio.

For that reason it makes sense to begin in 1938 at the University Club in Boston's Back Bay, where for several months that autumn Wheelwright ran a weekly poetry program on the World Wide Broadcasting Foundation's noncommercial shortwave station W1XAL (later WRUL). According to its funders at the Rockefeller Foundation, W1XAL had been since 1935 "the only station in the United States with national coverage... devoted exclusively to educational programming" (Rockefeller 326).[1] Transmitting 50,000 watts across four shortwave bands, W1XAL was by the late 1930s a leading "university of the air," disseminating "New England enlightenment" with the collaboration of faculty from Harvard and other universities to listeners across the country and, increasingly in non-English languages, around the globe ("Quicker" 54). To recite poetry into a W1XAL microphone was to hitch a ride on a powerful cultural apparatus, one that other entities such as the Rockefeller Foundation, the Pan-American Foundation, and the federal government were simultaneously using, in Good Neighborly fashion, to secure US interests abroad.[2] It is high testimony indeed to W1XAL'S soft power that in May 1938, when congressional efforts to establish a government-owned shortwave station "to counter the heavy-handed propaganda of the Nazi and Fascist competition" were quashed by major networks, the *Daily Boston Globe* could point with beaming hometown pride to W1XAL, already pouring a star-spangled "deluge of high-powered thought... into the ether for a world audience" (Lyons).

Given W1XAL's educational mandate and its high-cultural affiliations, it's hardly unusual that some of this "high-powered thought" issued from poets. It's a good deal stranger to find a poet like Wheelwright in the mix. Those listeners tuning in from Peru, Trinidad, or New Zealand were doubtless unfamiliar with W1XAL's poetry impresario, but Bostonians may have recognized Wheelwright, less perhaps from his poetry than from his minor cultural celebrity, the baffling figure he cut in a city so indelibly his milieu (Lyons). "What Dublin was to Joyce," recalled his friend Winfield Townley Scott, "Boston was to Wheelwright" (Scott 189). When remembered today, Wheelwright's life is often recalled as a spectacle of contradictions.[3] A direct descendent on his father's side of the Antinomian rebel Rev. John Wheelwright (1592–1679), and on his mother's side of the merchant Peter Chardon Brooks (1767–1849), once New England's wealthiest man, even as his family's finances deteriorated rapidly in the poet's lifetime, Wheelwright could boast of near perfect Brahmin pedigree (Wald, *Revolutionary*, 42).[4] But he also relished confounding this upper-crust exemplarity. As a young man grieving his father's suicide, Wheelwright rejected the Puritan faith of his ancestors for a very high church Anglicanism, and after his political radicalization in the early 1930s, set himself the task of squaring Anglican and apocryphal Christian traditions with a drop-dead serious dialectical materialism.[5] He describes his third and final collection of poems, *Political Self-Portrait* (1940), which marshals St. Paul alongside Lenin and references to the "Apostolic Orders" alongside exhortations to class war, as "a self-portrait of one who has found no way of turning, with Scientific Socialism, from a mechanical to an organic view of life than to draw from moral mythology as well as from revolutionary myth" (*Collected* 149).[6]

Wheelwright's Marxism is not of intellectual interest only, however. To a degree greater than many other committed artists of the period, Wheelwright involved himself actively in radical organizing, first with the Socialist Party and then as a founding member of the Trotskyist Socialist Workers Party, penning circulars, picketing, and stumping on the soapbox. This political education taught Wheelwright to inventory his own contradictory social position with incisive critical candor: "Scientific Socialism, Anglicanism, New England seaboard, Harvard College, the haut bourgeois, my family, have given me allegiances or rather prejudices which are revealed in my writing" (qtd. in Damon and Rosenfeld 321). Wheelwright's poetry, with its ragged scrim of densely allusive and exuberantly rhetorical verbal action, arises from an arduous dwelling in the contradictions that his own diverse "prejudices" threw up before him. In the aesthetic field, these contradictions closed ranks into an organizing conflict between the poetic techniques of an autonomous bourgeois modernism, on the one hand, and a Marxist politics that claimed a primarily didactic role for art, on the other. Wheelwright's first collection, *Rock and Shell* (1933), announced his basic poetic program: "the uses of poetry are: to sound, to show, to teach" (*Collected* 57). According to the poet's own sense of modern poetic progress, now that imagism and free-verse measures had submitted "the first two of these" (sounding and showing) to "complex clarification," "the didactic… must undergo proportionate handling" as writers press modernist techniques into the service of associative argument, moral thought, and political instruction. Elsewhere he describes this didactic art, in a suggestive misspelling, as an "idealogical music," a mode of poetic writing that may eschew logical argument in its sonorous, sensuous appeal—"disassociation of associated ideas and the associated of the disassociated"—but that must remain at all points answerable to some fundamental content, idea, or argument such as one finds in the substantial prose glosses accompanying the poems in each of his three books (Damon and Rosenfeld 324).

Throughout the 1930s, Wheelwright went in search of vehicles for this "idealogical music," media in which to reconcile his fractious social alignments. The radio, as we shall see, was one such medium. But before he hitched himself to the shortwaves, Wheelwright lavished his imaginative attention on another, softer-spoken sonorous technology, publishing some of the decade's most formally inventive American sonnets. These efforts culminated in Wheelwright's second book, *Mirrors of Venus: A Novel in Sonnets* (1938). The thirty-five quasi-autobiographical poems narrate in extremely elliptical fashion the early death of a friend, the tumultuous trajectory of another adult friendship, and—in Wheelwright's own gloss—the speaker's growth "in faith from Immortal Selfhood to Eternal Solidarity." As "Phallus" (*p. 42*) indicates, the book is also a hermetically queer text, one whose distending figurative mirrors refract intense concern with the erotics of same-sex friendship.[7] These themes are both obscured and developed—developed in their very obscurity—by complex formal protocols. Wheelwright runs the sonnet through thirty-five distinct permutations. We find strict Petrarchan and Shakespearean forms everywhere, "varied, twisted, transformed, and restored," in R. P. Blackmur's words, alongside inverted, curtailed, and extended sonnets, many of them ingeniously rhymed, others constructed from elegant blank verse or Wheelwright's own roughshod metrics (114). Wheelwright himself asserts that a sonnet sequence of "'perfect' sonnet after 'perfect' sonnet... is a bore," "induc[ing] hypnosis by monotony," and that poets ought to "spend their melodic skill to put thoughts into relief" (*Collected* 63). What deserves special remark is the conspicuous *visibility* of this technical apparatus. In the short prose glosses untangling his hyperbaroque rhetoric, Wheelwright repeatedly draws attention to his formal techniques, as when he notes how a "distorted rhyme scheme in the octave... throws the thought back and forward" or spells out how one sonnet's counterpointed structure parodies A. E. Housman (*Collected* 71, 85). Meanwhile all the rhyming sonnets have their schemes proudly indicated by number in the right margin.

To place a prose gloss (an investment in overt meaning) alongside such spectacular displays of technique is to insist on and even dramatically inflate a tension between the sonnets' idea of their content and the idea of their form. The sonnet's job is then to mediate this tension. In Wheelwright's definition, "the Sonnet weds thought form to verse form within a compass little extended beyond the span of instinctive thought" (63). The notion of a marriage between form and content is utterly commonplace, of course, but Wheelwright pursues this union in a perverse fashion: by driving meaning and *technique* in diametrically opposite directions—by insisting that the poem offers didactic meaning and then submitting that prose sense to a punishingly fussy formal apparatus. The sonnet polarizes form and content, technique and meaning, and the charge produced thereby is the poetic quiddity he calls "instinctive thought."

Consider "Phallus," the book's Shakespearean sonnet. In Wheelwright's gloss, the poem exists to argue "against doubt and distrust in company and separation" (94). All this simple idea needs, it would seem, is proper aesthetic packaging. "Friends need not guard each other as a jealous / Moslem must segregate his odalisque," the sonnet begins, "no more than one need see the symbolled phallus / while meditating at an obelisk." Setting aside the Orientalism marring these lines, a rough paraphrase ("friends don't need to be jealous of each other's time any more than one need read a penis into an obelisk") makes clear that the speaker associates the pursuit of deeper meaning with the possession of the beloved friend. The middle octave unfurls a tortuous figure for the way physical proximity would ruin a relationship otherwise sealed and nurtured by distance—the way "companionship" like a sharp spear or "wedge... whittled by common task and play... would split the pledge / which kisses tallied once in valediction" (lines 6–9). Recalling the vehicle of the preceding metaphor, we may wonder whether the penetrating pursuit of deeper meaning doesn't also contribute to the friendship's ruin, especially when that coded meaning involves sex between men. In any case, the poem snaps imperiously shut with a couplet of superb epigrammatic force: "Habit is evil,—all habit, even speech; / and promises prefigure their own breach." To ventriloquize once more: "Let's not get so habituated to each other. Let's not even speak every day. Anxious promises do more damage than good. And—perhaps—don't go hunting for symbols and meaning in everything I say or do."

There's a reason I have indulged the critical faux pas of presuming to paraphrase this poem. Wheelwright uses the compacted form of the sonnet, and the coiled conceits he spring-loads inside it, precisely to "unhabitualize" speech to a degree that we fairly lose its sense. At the same time, in his own prose glosses and in his statements elsewhere on the importance of didacticism, Wheelwright insists there *is* didactic meaning to be had here. The sonorous machinery of the sonnet is designed to transform this glossable content into sensuous sense, or "instinctive thought." In this way, a poem such as "Phallus" denaturalizes and estranges speech with the goal of making us feel ideational content on the bodily pulse—indeed, to purify it of "evil."

As it happens, Wheelwright will say much the same thing about radio, "the sternest and most refined test that poetry has ever undergone" ("Verse" 1). Years before his career as a poetry jockey on the airwaves, Wheelwright had defined effective verse as "an engineering of sound which, when it rises to poetry, engineers meaning" (*Collected* 155–56). When he began broadcasting first on Boston's WORL and then on W1XAL, Wheelwright determined that his sonic engineering of modern poetry's "high-powered thought" would require that he activate radio's political utility. It was apparently Wheelwright's leftist editorializing that turned a respectable entrée to New England letters into a source of displeasure for the higher-ups at the World Wide Broadcasting Foundation.[8] Damon and Rosenfeld recall the airing of "anti-war poems, pieces of social satire, [and] political burlesques in verse," though it was also the case that Wheelwright framed otherwise innocuous poetic fare in ways that emphasized its political possibilities (322). Contextualizing *The Waste Land* for WORL listeners in 1938, for instance, the noninterventionalist Wheelwright suggests that Eliot's presumably "'post war'" poem "may however soon be called 'pre war'": "The undefined fear, the self-pity, the unrealizable nostalgia of our war-haunted era form Eliot's subject matter" ("Poetry Noon Hour").

Wheelwright was not alone in singling out W1XAL as an object of political utility. In fact, the station's institutional profile makes Wheelwright's firing a singularly unsurprising conclusion to his short tenure on air (Hilmes 118). Since W1XAL had been a key apparatus in the soft power campaigns of Roosevelt's Good Neighbor Policy, including those efforts to combat "Axis propagandistic inroads into the hemisphere" when the war began in September 1939, the station—redubbed WRUL—was the "first to go 'all out' in the active defense of democratic principles" (Cramer 78; Clements 175). Perhaps most incredibly, beginning in 1940 the British Security Coordination, an undercover MI6 outfit operating in the United States, adopted W1XAL—now redubbed WRUL—unbeknownst to its listeners and indeed apparently to its own staff, as one of its "chief venues for placing news stories designed to outrage US public opinion against the Axis forces" (Hilmes 117).[9] As a result, well before the wartime State Department commandeered WRUL and all other shortwave stations in 1942, when the station began broadcasting for the Office of War Information and the Voice of America, a *Life* magazine profile could declare, with good cause, "The Nazis Hate and Fear Boston's WRUL."[10]

Though W1XAL/WRUL's engagements with wartime propaganda postdate Wheelwright's poetry show, the station's enormous potential for political intervention was readily in evidence by the fall of 1938. Wheelwright's firsthand experience with this particular social application of radio technology—an institution authorized for cultural and educational objectives and operationalized for propaganda—strongly inflected his own sense of radio's utility for poetry. In a later essay, "Verse + Radio = Poetry,"

Wheelwright announces that by the late 1930s, the passage from verse to poetry, from sound to socially salient meaning, is now impossible without radio's capacity to actualize poetry's didactic potential. Like nothing else, radio can reconcile the political necessity for a radically didactic poetics with the aesthetic demands of modernist poetry. Wheelwright claims that radio's sonorous address uniquely suits the kind of associative argumentation at which good—that is, properly didactic—political poetry excels: "Exactly as it is hard to follow a logical argument over the air, so is an associational convincing. Here again is poetry so fitted for radio that broadcasting purifies it (almost automatically) by making its most characteristic elements the most effective" ("Verse" 4). Wheelwright's confidence in radio's amenability to poetic logic leads him to assert that "over the radio" ostensibly "difficult" poets such as "John Donne and Hart Crane are clear and simple" ("Talking" 3). Though far from persuasive, the claim is worth pausing over for how boldly it contravenes received ideologies of modernism, namely, the antirhetorical autonomy of the artwork and its presumed opposition to mass-mediated culture. For Wheelwright, poetry and radio meet precisely on the basis of their mutual serviceability as vehicles for the illogical but interested appeal increasingly associated, between the wars, with political propaganda. In the spirit of swift caricature, we might call this Theodor Adorno's worst nightmare: the unholy marriage of all that makes radio perilous for critical democracy (its mystifying, sensuous, irrational address), on the one hand, with a loathsome didacticism that disengages what is authentically critical about lyric aesthetics, on the other.

Just like the sonnet, then, radio magically mediates didactic content and poetic technique. Reading backward from his later embrace of the radio, we see how the "instinctive thought" formulated in Wheelwright's sonnets gropingly anticipates the higher tech "idealogical music" of radical poetry on the radio. In both cases, the signal virtue of these sonorous technologies is their ability to extend the social life of demanding modernist forms. If neither of these arguments are necessarily convincing, it's significant nonetheless that Wheelwright assigns sonnets and radio such similar—similarly central, similarly fantastical—functions in his poetics. On the furthest horizons, this conjunction has implications for how to think about lyric as a material-technical practice, about the historical impact of radio on poetry in the 1930s especially, and also, of course, about the luminously compacted surfaces of Wheelwright's sonnets. On that score, I'll conclude with reference to "Father," one of the most beautiful sonnets in *Mirrors of Venus*, wherein once more we find prodigious technical resources marshaled in a moving demand for precisely unmediated speech. The sonnet concerns Wheelwright's deceased father, an architect whose several notable structures in Boston, including the Longfellow Bridge, are the poem's setting. Impasto word-painting of the turreted bridge and the oily Charles give way, in the final stanza, to a stirringly direct appeal for fatherly speech. "Speak. Speak to me again," the poet writes, "as fresh saddle leather... to a hunter smells of heather" (*Collected* 78). And for more than speech:

> Come home. Wire a wire of warning without words.
> Come home and talk to me again, my first friend. Father,
> come home, dead man, who made your mind my home.

Composed by a poet who lived his relatively short life surrounded by a cityscape his father's architectural mind quite literally made, the sonnet can be read as a moving brief for "instinctive thought." This urgent mental content is technologized in just the spirit of Wheelwright's eventual turn to radio, to a "wire of warning without words," one high-powered enough to inhabit the "mind" as familiarly as one does a "home."

Notes

1. See Hilmes 115–20; Cramer.

2. On W1XAL as a vehicle for the Rockefeller-funded "Pan American Broadcasting Project," see Cramer. The "Good Neighbor Policy" is the name of the Roosevelt administration's diplomatic framework of strategic nonintervention in Latin American (1933–45).

3. See, for instance, John Ashbery's comment, in a 1990 Charles Eliot Norton lecture dedicated to the poet, that "in person as well as in his writing, Wheelwright was literally a set of walking contradictions" (79).

4. As the most thorough treatment of Wheelwright to date, Wald's *Revolutionary Imagination* remains the indispensable guide to the poet's life and art.

5. Edmund March Wheelwright (1852–1912), a celebrated architect, died in a Connecticut sanitarium, where he had been institutionalized for two years for "extreme depression" (Wald, *Revolutionary* 44).

6. Before *Political Self-Portrait*, Wheelwright published two collections: *Rock and Shell* (1933) and *Mirrors of Venus* (1938). All three books were brought out in small runs by the Boston publisher Bruce Humphries. James Laughlin at *New Directions* published a slim posthumous *Selected Poems* in 1941, but it was not until 1972 that the full *Collected Poems* appeared, complete with Wheelwright's final volume, *Dusk to Dusk*, as well as additional uncollected poems.

7. On the subject of Wheelwright's sexuality, see Wald, "Wheelwright and His Kind."

8. While the archival evidence is limited, Damon and Rosenfeld agree that Wheelwright's "dismissal from W1XAL seems to have been at least partly a matter of his political views, both presumed and imagined" (317).

9. See also Boyd.

10. See Hilmes 118.

Works Cited

Ashbery, John. *Other Traditions*. Harvard UP, 2000.

Blackmur, R. P. "Nine Poets." *Partisan Review*, vol. 6, no. 2, 1939, pp. 108–14.

Boyd, William. "The Secret Persuaders." *The Guardian*, 19 Aug. 2006, www.theguardian.com/uk/2006/aug/19/military.secondworldwar.

Clements, Robert J. "Foreign Language Broadcasting of 'Radio Boston.'" *The Modern Language Journal*, vol. 27, no. 3, 1943, pp. 175–79.

Cramer, Gisela. "The Rockefeller Foundation and Pan American Radio." *Patronizing the Public: American Philanthropy's Transformation of Culture, Communication, and the Humanities*, edited by William J. Buxton. Lexington, 2009, pp. 77–99.

Damon, S. Foster, and Alvin H. Rosenfeld. "John Wheelwright: New England's Colloquy with the World." *The Southern Review*, vol. 8, no. 2, 1972, pp. 310–28.

Hilmes, Michelle. *Network Nations: A Transnational History of British and American Broadcasting*. Routledge, 2012.

Lyons, Louis M. "After Leap of 300 Miles Boston's W1XAL Covers World." *Daily Boston Globe*, 22 May 1938.

"Propaganda from the U.S.: The Nazis Hate and Fear Boston's Station WRUL." *Life*, 15 Dec. 1941, pp. 43–46.

"Quicker Fox." *Time*, 11 July 1938, p. 54.

The Rockefeller Foundation. *Annual Report*. Rockefeller Foundation, 1938.

Scott, Winfield Townley. "John Wheelwright and His Poetry." *New Mexico Quarterly*, vol. 24, 1954, pp. 178–96.

Wald, Alan M. *The Revolutionary Imagination: The Poetry and Politics of John Wheelwright and Sherry Mangan*. U of North Carolina P, 1983.

———. "Wheelwright and His Kind." *Spoke*, no. 3, 2005, pp. 194–208.

Wheelwright, John. *Collected Poems of John Wheelwright*. Edited by Alvin H. Rosenfeld, New Directions, 1972.

———. "'Poetry Noon Hour,' Introductions for Readers." John Wheelwright Papers 1920–1940. Box 33, Folder 5, John Hay Library, Brown University, Providence, RI.

———. "Talking Machines." John Wheelwright Papers 1920–1940. Box 36, Folder 5. John Hay Library, Brown University, Providence, RI.

———. "Verse + Radio = Poetry." John Wheelwright Papers 1920–1940. Box 37, Folder 8. John Hay Library, Brown University, Providence, RI.

The Resonances of McKay's Sonnet Voice, Then and Now

DONNA DENIZÉ

The present historical moment in the United States is beset with political, socioeconomic, and cultural dissension. Among the issues contributing to this discord is the resurgence in the country of blatant racial violations as evidenced in overt white supremacist demonstrations, rhetoric, and violence; the alarming incidents of police brutality meted out with impunity on Black bodies; and the recent attempts to render null and void the right of the minority population to vote, to participate in the democratic process on which the country largely bases its prideful greatness. These present-day afflictions, highlighting the deeply entrenched racism that divides the nation, leads citizens, especially those who feel marginalized, to reflect on the avowal in the Declaration of Independence that all men are created equal and to question whether this symbolically contractual pledge means that all citizens are entitled to equal rights. Such an appeal to the Declaration invariably induces a glance backward to further reflection on the historical moments that have brought the nation to the present racial impasse: colonialism, slavery, Jim Crow, followed by the civil rights movement, and the hard-won declaration of the Civil Rights Act in 1964. Today, however, the emergence of the Black Lives Matter movement and, in fact, the very necessity for such a movement, makes one wonder what and how much has changed for Black people in US society. The question brings to mind racially probing poems by the West Indian / African American poet Claude McKay. In three of his most well-known sonnets, "The Lynching," "America" (*p. 35*), and "The White House," McKay sets forth an excoriating discourse that confronts the country's racial problem as pertinently today as it did in the 1920s when he wrote them.

In 1996, Barbara Jackson Griffin's "The Last Word: Claude McKay's Unpublished 'Cycle Manuscript'" states: "During the summer of 1943, five years before his death and one year before his baptism into the Roman Catholic Church, Claude McKay began his 'Cycle Manuscript,' a collection of fifty-four new and old poems, mostly sonnets. He would never see it published. 'Too bitter and personal,' claimed the editor at Harper's, and Dutton's said his sonnets were not poems at all" (41). Two factors are most revealing: McKay wrote many more sonnets than the reading public is aware of, and Black artists' voices were usually read by white critics not as valid artistic expressions but as assertions of individual personality and grievance, as "bitter," and inexplicably angry. The editor of Harper's also called the poems unacceptable because they were "personal." In this light, consider what Lynne Magnusson says about understanding context in Shakespeare's sonnets in her essay "Modern Perspective": "These sonnets are not the unaddressed speeches of an anonymous 'I.' They are utterances in which it matters who is speaking, to whom, and in what situation.... We as readers cannot come to know this 'I' without making an active effort to figure out the context and follow the conversation" (359). From this standpoint, it would appear that McKay's sonnets were critically rejected because their "I" was not anonymous enough. Contextualized historically and sociopolitically, however, the "I" in these sonnets can hardly be said to be merely personal or inexplicably angry, then or now. The recent, tragic deaths of Ahmaud Arbery, Breonna Taylor, George Floyd, the human violations they expose to the world, plus the international protests they have provoked—all these factors not only invoke McKay's artistic craft, they demand his polemics. To the extent that the current social unrest and political uncertainties in society call to mind a bygone time in American history, "The Lynching" (1920), "America" (1921), and "The White House" (1922), in indicting violence against Blacks in the early 1900s, seem to have anticipated its continuance over the last hundred years. Pointed and passionate, McKay's poems reject the way Black voices were marginalized, relegated to an outpost of the nation, the rising American empire. Of course McKay was not the first to employ the sonnet as the means of sociopolitical protest: Shelley's "Song to the Men of England" indicts the privileged classes for exploiting the working class and calls on the working class to resist their oppression, and Wordsworth's "The Banished Negroes" and

"To Toussaint L'Ouverture" were written at a time when events in France threatened to derail democratic ideals that powered the Revolution of 1789. Like the Romantics that influenced him, McKay saw the sonnet as an effective means for social protest and egalitarian principles. Paradoxically, while the formulaic nature and structural limits of the sonnet form seem suited to the expression of the inescapable societal strictures that characterized African American life, the same sense of restriction provides a symbolic boundary against which to frame both the violence of racial oppression and the artistic and psychological liberation to be found in resistance to this oppression. It is compelling, therefore, that McKay chose the sonnet to address the racial contradictions, complexities, and anxieties that plague American society.

For most European immigrants coming to America in the late nineteenth and early twentieth centuries, two areas of major concern were social adjustment and economic security. For McKay and other Black immigrants, there was an added problem: discrimination based on the color of their skin. A Jamaican immigrant who in 1912 arrived in America at the age of twenty-three, McKay was both stunned and affronted by the racial discrimination he witnessed as well as experienced, especially nationwide race riots during the 1919 Red Summer. At the same time, there was global unrest as world leaders attempted to broker world peace through the League of Nations at the close of World War I. Today, exacerbated by the difficult issues of immigration, especially of nonwhite peoples from formerly colonized places such as South America, Africa, Asia, and the Caribbean, current racial discourse has intensified. In recent years, attempts to solve the problem by viewing it as a geographical and cultural border issue have merely deepened the racial anxieties in the country, putting to question such oversimplification of the racial divide that defines the nation. Given the social and political echoes of McKay's time in our present moment, and given the discursive resonances of his poetry in contemporary racial debates, I would like to examine McKay's "The Lynching," "America," and "The White House" in the context of the racial tensions that continue to fracture contemporary American life.

A curious and uncanny temporal nexus seems to link the three sonnets to events of 2020. The first of these links is a striking coincidence: McKay wrote "The Lynching" in 1920, and George Floyd was killed in 2020, exactly a century later. The policeman's cutting off of Floyd's breath by kneeling on his neck is a form of lynching. McKay's poem opens:

> His Spirit in smoke ascended to high heaven.
> His father, by the cruelest way of pain,
> Had bidden him to his bosom once again (176)

"The Lynching" was published in 1920, a time of political and social turbulence. In the second decade of the twentieth century, the nation witnessed the Wilson administration segregate the offices of the federal government, *The Birth of a Nation* become a blockbuster, and the number of lynchings increase in the years following World War I (Yellin 103–5). In addition, global unrest had domestic repercussions: a worldwide pandemic had killed more than twenty million people, including over half a million Americans; W. E. B. DuBois at the 1919 Pan African Congress in Paris protested the power of colonialism abroad while disagreements over the Versailles Treaty split the nation at home; and debates over immigration excited nativist resentments (McGerr). Much of this came to a head in 1919–20 as the Red Summer of racial unrest culminated in the Chicago race riots and the Red Scare fueled antilabor, anticommunist, and anti-immigrant sentiment (Gage). In 1921, the Tulsa Massacre left dozens, even hundreds, of African Americans dead in the streets and an entire section of that city burned to the ground (Ellsworth). By employing an ironic twist in "The Lynching," McKay further draws on the traditional Christian imagery often used in Renaissance sonnets, and this twist conveys the human perversion that gives rise to racial violence. There are echoes of the Passion of Christ and of the tension in the Christian images: the crucifixion, the father calling "to his bosom once again his son," while the "awful sin" of hate against the son "remained still unforgiven" (line 4). Does "the father" here mean God? Since the word "father" is not capitalized, there is an interesting ambiguity and conflation; one logical reading would be that the Black man has been sacrificed and martyred in the service of public—that is, "white"—good. Although there are intimations of the speaker's passion as in the traditional sonnet, ironically, the passion in "The Lynching" is not about the speaker's unrequited love but about the cold heat of others' hate in "eyes of steely blue" (line 12) (note the pointed absence of maternal or "feminine" affect in the women's gaze). It is important to note, therefore, contrary to the dismissive critical labels that McKay's work garnered, such as "personal" and "bitter," the artistic control and precision with which McKay adapts these sonnet forms and the discursive ends to which he does so. To a large extent, the appropriation of sonnet forms may suggest the making of poetic order out of variance, suggesting further that lynching is a form of ritualized disorder. In addition to the high numbers of lynchings in 1919, both

1919 and 1920 saw increased racial violence against Blacks (Tuttle), so certainly McKay wrote the three sonnets at a critical period in American race relations. Another historical coincidence contextualizes McKay's 1921 "America." At the time of this writing, the country faces the question of what path it will choose as its national identity: one of inclusion, democratic rule, and a legacy of rich human diversity or one of autocratic rule, fascism, and white supremacy. Consider catch phrases such as "America First" and "Make America Great Again" and even the question of who is an American, popularized with the birther myth in the months leading up to the election of Barack Obama. All these factors bring my discussion to the present moment, which is fraught with the blatant resurgence of racial conflict, white supremacist rhetoric, incidents of police brutality, and voter suppression. So the sonnet "America" seems prescient. Published in 1921, "America" sets up a dilemma through binary oppositions—rejection vs. attraction, violence vs. nurture—ending the poem with a foreboding apocalyptic vision. The male speaker depicts the country as a woman:

> Although she feeds me bread of bitterness,
> And sinks into my throat her tiger's tooth,
> Stealing my breath of life... (153, lines 1–3)

One cannot help but notice how images keep shifting and how the speaker, through the sonnet form, negotiates the tension between conflicting emotions—passions evoked by prejudice and injustice as well as by the great promise of equality, freedom, and innovation, patent traits of the American dream. In fact, one of the poem's most challenging features is its shifting images: from a masculine speaker to the feminine America, from the hardness of walls and stone to the fluid images of tides, and from the yearning of the poem's "I" to the cruel rejection by the beloved America. Although love, like Cupid, is unpredictable and cruel, the speaker's steadfast love for America ennobles him, and he stands "as a rebel fronts a king in state /... with not a shred / Of terror, malice, not a word of jeer" (lines 8–10). In the Black American experience, the "I" struggles between strength of independence and conviction and racism's suppression of strength and independence. In the oxymoronic phrase, "cultured hell," one notes the double consciousness and ambiguity out of which McKay speaks.

His use of the word "darkly" to describe his vision of the days ahead is significant: both the future of the poem's speaker and the nation are dark, and of course, the speaker himself is dark-skinned. The only certainty in the sonnet's ending is uncertainty, as seemingly firm images of granite and stone in America's "priceless treasures" are built on shaky ground—sand. Nevertheless, the speaker "loves" America and tries to work with her. His sentiment is not hate but indeterminacy about America and the speaker's "place" in a nation whose "place" itself is compromised by racial hatred. In this sonnet, the Petrarchan tradition of unrequited love—so often expressed by earlier sonneteers—is turned to a social and political object: the speaker loves and expresses devotion to the country, the very same country that rejects him. On what foundation is America built, the poem is asking, and if it is merely a country of images, of hollow monuments, one cannot help but hear echoes of Percy Bysshe Shelley's sonnet "Ozymandias," where all that was held by its creator as permanent and indestructible now sinks beneath the sand. In "America," McKay interrogates the original landscape of the sonnet and captures the historical moment, not only of 1921, but also of our own time; the moral contradiction of white supremacy in an avowed democracy and the ambiguity that results.

Just as the speaker in McKay's poem opines that racial hatred is "Stealing my breath of life," the words "I can't breathe," spoken by Eric Garner and George Floyd—two more Black bodies in a seemingly endless list of African Americans falling victim to racial violence in the twenty-first century—have been chanted now by millions of antiracists the globe over. How fitting then that McKay closes "America" with an apocalyptic vision; if we avoid dealing with hate or racism or fail to eliminate them, then hate steals the breath not only of George Floyd and Eric Garner but also the very breath of American life.

Finally, McKay wrote "The White House" in 1922, marking a third coincidence that McKay's poem previsions. The speaker feels excluded from the White House, the seat of democratic principles and governance: "Your door is shut against my tightened face / And I am sharp as steel with discontent" (lines 1–2). Although the White House can be read as an iconic reference to white supremacy, a house is also a domicile, a place where a family or people live or where people meet for a communal activities. At the same time "house" can also mean a dynasty, which suggests power and authority. This sonnet is a stark indictment of the betrayal of traditional democratic ideals of American identity—political and socioeconomic freedoms, exposing the selectivity with which they are applied. These national egalitarian ideals were then, as they have been ever since, not the social reality of African Americans burdened by legalized segregation, redlining, and other discriminatory practices. Excluded from the house, the family, the nation where all citizens ideally "reside," the speaker knows it will take a "superhuman power" to endure and resist the "potent poison" of this "hate" (lines 11, 14). Further, he suggests that the authorized hypocrisy that this system of inclusion/exclusion necessitates "poison[s]" the "heart" of both the oppressor and oppressed. The freedom, equality, and inclusiveness that McKay advocates reveal a fundamental and important connection between the Jamaican poet and his African American peers in the Harlem Renaissance, a connection rooted in the problems and effects of European colonialism.

This link speaks to the passion with which McKay aligns himself with the African American struggle. The geopolitical and psychological tie makes brothers of diaspora Blacks, scions of a system that found trafficking in human bodies indispensable. In addition, colonialism is about creating boundaries, building walls, limitations, and setting up social and political hegemonies or dominions. In this sense, McKay is made subject to the African American condition. African American literature challenges hegemony by indicting it and advocating liberation. McKay's sonnets are passionate, intensely critical of an unjust society that meets the needs of one group at the expense of another, and the poems suggest that such change will require "an organic change in the structure of present-day society" (Effendi 43). Science has long since proven that we are one human race and that once we accept this truth, we will not have to keep our hearts "inviolate / Against the potent poison of... hate" (lines 13–14)—of racism. McKay's words are as relevant today as when he wrote them more than a century ago.

Works Cited

Du Bois, W. E. B. *The Souls of Black Folk*. Fawcett Publications, 1961.

Effendi, Shoghi. *The World Order of Bahā'u'llāh Selected Letters*. Bahā'i Publishing Trust, 1991.

Ellsworth, Scott. *Death in a Promised Land: The Tulsa Race Riot of 1921*. Louisiana State UP, 1992.

Gage, Beverly. *The Day Wall Street Exploded: A Story of America in Its First Age of Terror*. Oxford UP, 2009.

Griffin, Barbara Jackson. "The Last Word: Claude McKay's Unpublished 'Cycle Manuscript.'" *MELUS*, vol. 21, no. 1, 1996, pp. 41–57.

Magnusson, Lynne. "A Modern Perspective." *Shakespeare's Sonnets*. Edited by Barbara Mowat and Paul Werstein. Simon and Schuster, 2004.

McGerr, Michael. *A Fierce Discontent: The Rise and Fall of the Progressive Movement in America, 1870–1920*. Oxford UP Press, 2005.

McKay, Claude. "America." *Harlem Shadows*. Harcourt, Brace, and Company, 1922, p. 6. Rpt. *Complete Poems by Claude McKay*. Edited by William J. Maxwell. U of Illinois P, 2004, p.153.

———. "The Lynching." *Harlem Shadows*. Harcourt, Brace, and Company, 1922, p. 5. Rpt. *Complete Poems by Claude McKay*. Edited by William J. Maxwell. U of Illinois P, 2004, p. 176.

———. "The White House." *The Liberator*, May 1922, p. 16. Rpt. *Complete Poems by Claude McKay*. Edited by William J. Maxwell. U of Illinois P, 2004, p. 148.

Tuttle, William M. *Race Riot: Chicago in the Red Summer of 1919*. U of Illinois P, 1966.

Yellin, Eric S. *Racism in the Nation's Service: Government Workers and the Color Line in Woodrow Wilson's America*. U of North Carolina P, 2013.

WHOSE SONNET?

Whose Sonnet?
(A Transgression)

CARL PHILLIPS

I want to speak briefly about the sonnet as a site of resistance or rebellion and about its appeal especially to writers historically marginalized because of race, gender, and queerness. The first challenge for the historically marginalized poet, when dealing with the sonnet, is how to make it one's own, and the obvious way is at the level of content: insert your own thoughts, your own culture and its concomitant perspective, and you will have, say, a queer, Black sonnet. But has one made it one's own? Isn't the form itself still there—don't the trappings at least have to be, for it to be recognized as a sonnet in the first place? This is the challenge Adrienne Rich addresses, in her idea of a "common language." I've always taken her to mean that she longed for a language that wasn't freighted with whiteness, maleness, heteronormativity. Her initial solution appears in "Snapshots of a Daughter-in-Law" (not a sonnet), where she plays free verse against traditional iambic pentameter and where she also punctuates the poem, throughout, with citations from male writers in the long English tradition and from female writers overlooked, historically. In this way, Rich acknowledges the tradition and inserts another one, meanwhile also inserting her own sensibility and her own prosodic rebellion, grazing up against the pentameter tradition, only to veer abruptly away from it. But the poem is still in English, and Rich is still working within the very tradition that has historically not included her or has at best only patronizingly done so. Indeed, Rich's method of approaching and withdrawing from prosodic tradition is itself consistent with the male, white prosody of vers libre as outlined by T. S. Eliot. Likewise, then—back to the sonnet—if I write a sonnet, I haven't broken the white, hetero cage, as it were; I've simply written my Black, queer perspective from *within* the cage. How to reckon with that?

One might ask, by the way, why even bother with the sonnet, if it comes with all this baggage? I think the reason is that, among fixed forms, it's maybe the shortest form that allows for such range when it comes to modes of thinking. The sonnet's compression—its more or less fixed length—offers the challenge of / opportunity for economy of thought, or the expression of thought. The form itself is what allows for dialogue, dramatic situations, philosophical meditation, even storytelling. While the sonnet is technically a stichic form (that is, there are no stanza breaks), it is rightly also called strophic by prosodists such as Paul Fussell, who points out in his *Poetic Meter and Poetic Form* that the rhyme schemes of both the Italian and the English sonnet create the equivalent of stanzaic division at the level of rhyme (110). So, we hear, in an English sonnet, for example, three quatrains and a couplet, while what we see on the page is a stichic form. What this means is that, if we agree with Fussell when he says that "Stichic organization has been found most appropriate for large, expansive narrative, dramatic, and meditative actions," whereas "strophic organization…has been found most appropriate for dense and closely circumscribed moments of emotion or argument" (110), in the sonnet we have the opportunity for all of these possibilities—the sonnet can be didactic or narrative (with the resonances that accompany those genres), and at the same time it can provide the emotional gesture, the psychological gesture of short lyric—both gestures are themselves also forms of narrative, narrative being about trajectory, including the gesture, say, of moving from joy to sorrow and back.

So much for the sonnet's capacity to contain different modes of thinking. The sonnet also has a greater tolerance for innovation—while retaining its essential formal structure—than do many fixed forms. We see this as early as Shakespeare, who seems constantly to be challenging himself to newer versions, now a twelve-line sonnet, a fifteen-line sonnet, sonnets entirely enjambed, or never, or sonnets governed by anaphora. This is entirely aside from what we could say about metrical variation. But the sonnet is always recognizable, despite the innovation. You can remove the rhyme, the meter of a sonnet, and it's still possible to retain the sonnet's mode of delivery of information, its logic, its argumentation. This isn't so for the villanelle or sestina, for example. Nor for the limerick. Nor for the rondeau.

Those are some of the appeals of the form, and why should these be limited to one type of writer? Just because it was made by certain people doesn't give them exclusive rights to it. But even with this availability, what is it about the sonnet that seems especially to appeal to historically marginalized writers? I believe that the sonnet's openness to a range of epistemological modes, along with its capacity for innovation, is part of the answer. If I am able to exercise my own sensibility, in terms of content *and* form, then I don't have to worry that I'm being co-opted by whiteness, say, as a Black poet. Instead, I'm using what's been handed down to me, but to my own purposes and in my own inflections—this doesn't make it exclusively mine, which is to say, we are no further ahead than Rich was, but unlike Rich we aren't aiming for a common language; rather, as incongruous as it may seem, I'm making of the sonnet a conversation that insists on the inclusion of *my* language, as manifest not just through words but through experience. It's a bit like racism in the United States—a very long tradition indeed, woven into the very fabric of the nation—it *is* the fabric of the nation; my speaking up, my refusal to be invisible, and my insistence on being visible when and how I choose, all of these prevent history from being a one-sided unassailable fact and instead make of history an organic, restless choiring of provocation, recognition, dissent, nostalgia, inquiry, argument, an ever-shifting pact: we agree that something happened, but what, and how, and who is saying so, who gets to?

I've already mentioned how, having decided to engage with the sonnet, historically marginalized writers will often choose subject matter unique to themselves, in a sense insisting on a place at the table by sitting down at the table. This is certainly a form of resistance, though I think the challenge is how to make this form of resistance new over time. As an example, it's fine for Countee Cullen to write a sonnet as a statement that a Black man is able to write a sonnet and has the right to do so; it's fine for Claude McKay to use the sonnet to depict Black life as a way of insisting that Black life both exists and is a valid subject for the sonnet. Those were radical gestures back then. It's harder to be radical about race in the sonnet when that has itself become a long tradition—though it can be done, as we see in the sonnets of such practitioners as Terrance Hayes and Patricia Smith (see *pp. 105* and *92*).

But resistance can also occur—both Hayes and Smith are aware of this—at the level of form itself. I've already noted that Shakespeare himself was constantly innovating as he produced his sonnet sequence. And there are plenty of variations of the English sonnet since Shakespeare, including the Spenserian sonnet, the sixteen-line sonnets of George Meredith's sequence *Modern Love*, Gerard Manley Hopkins's curtal sonnet, sonnets comprised entirely of heroic couplets, nonce sonnets such as Robert Frost's "The Oven Bird," terza rima sonnets such as—Frost again—"Acquainted with the Night." More contemporarily, there are Lyn Hejinian's sonnets in *The Unfollowing* (p. 74), composed entirely of non sequitur statements, troubling the idea of how information gets delivered in the sonnet versus in the brain; Diane Seuss meanwhile, in her *Still Life with Two Dead Peacocks and a Girl*, invents a sonnet that abandons rhyme scheme but adheres to fourteen lines, and each line is seventeen syllables long, what Allen Ginsberg called an American Sentence, which he first introduced in his 1994 *Cosmopolitan Greetings*.

Just when I think there's nothing new to do with and to the sonnet, I'll see something new again. Most recently I've been spending time with a sonnet from Cathy Park Hong's *Engine Empire*, "Seed Seller's Sonnet"—thirteen lines, line length all over the place, narrative on the surface, oddly confessional and associative as well, ending with an allusion to John Berryman's *Dream Songs* (making me wonder if those are also their own kind of sonnet). Another fascination has been Jennifer Chang's "Whoso List to Hunt," a sort of exploded sonnet in fourteen prose monostichs, some sections including quotations from the original Wyatt sonnet, one section all white space.

I could say a lot about each of these poems, but I want to consider instead how the sonnet seems specifically wired for rebellion. It's an idea I've been playing with and nudging forward, one I haven't come across before, though I'm no trained scholar of sonnets or of anything else prosody related. I think the sonnet is unique as a form that has disruption built into it from the start, and I believe this explains a big part of the form's appeal to historically marginalized writers in particular. I'll grant that what I'm going to point out is subtle, and I don't know that a lot of writers—or any?—think about this aspect of the sonnet, but it feels, if not consciously thought about and through, like George Herbert's description of prayer in his own sonnet called "Prayer": it's maybe just "something understood." (I can't resist mentioning that Herbert's sonnet is composed entirely of fragments, not a single complete sentence—this strikes me as a radical innovation for the seventeenth century.)

Fussell points out that the structures of the Italian and English sonnet regulate the poem's logic or manner of thinking. He's looking primarily at structure as established by rhyme. By that thinking, we see how the Italian sonnet divides into two uneven parts because the first part is governed by a rhyme scheme *abba* that semantically implies two related thoughts, each folding back on itself before unfurling again to fold back; comparatively, the scattering of rhymes in the second half, the sestet, feels like a distillation of the octave's solidity—as Fussell puts it, in a rare moment of what feels like real excitement, it is not unlike sexual climax, the buildup followed by release. He goes on to say that something similar happens, but more hurriedly, in the English sonnet, where the rhyme creates a structure of three quatrains—and since the rhymes change from quatrain to quatrain, there is more of an implied forward movement of thought, and the fact that each part *is* a quatrain suggests an argument whose movements are equal in size; then we get the Fussell release from that pattern, in the concluding rhyming couplet.

As I say, Fussell looks at structure as established by rhyme patterns. I am more interested, lately, in the rhymes themselves. A different way to look at the Italian sonnet, for example, is as circularity being abandoned for radiality, routine or regimen for (given the various options for the rhymes of the sestet) unpredictability, and finally introversion for extroversion. *A* and *b* are thrown aside—rebelled against—for *c* and *d* and (potentially) *e*. This feels different to me from the release of sexual climax or, to borrow another of Fussell's images, different too from inhaling and exhaling. It feels, sonically, like stability yielding to restlessness. I hope it's clear that I'm not simply replacing Fussell's metaphors with an analogous one of my own—instead, I'm proposing the opposite. The move from sexual excitement to climax is the reverse of stability to restlessness, while neither breathing in nor breathing out can be said by definition to correlate automatically with stability or restlessness; if anything, the two acts work in tandem, calm breathing means calm inhalation and exhalation—likewise, when it comes to frantic breathing, the franticness applies to both actions.

What I'm saying may be easier to demonstrate with the English sonnet. Fussell says that this sonnet essentially has two parts—a twelve-line section of three quatrains, and a two-line couplet for the second part. The point of release, for him, is between the final quatrain and the couplet. But looking at the rhyme alone, I'd say there are three moments of release, one after each quatrain. Yes, the pattern of quatrains remains intact, but each quatrain abandons the earlier rhymes for a new set, ending in a couplet whose rhymes have never been seen in the poem. The double quatrains of the Italian sonnet feel like stability because the same rhymes are adhered to; in the English sonnet, the rhymes are constantly shifting. Yes, there is a pattern of interchanging rhymes, but the rhymes themselves keep changing—in this way, the English sonnet is laced throughout with sonic restlessness, and that restlessness is, incongruously, never resolved at the level of sound. The shift from interspersed rhyme to the two rhymes of the couplet being brought together without intervention is indeed a movement toward consolidation—it sounds like closure. But the couplet's rhyme is new, is a step away from the earlier rhymes—and this, combined with its being a couplet instead of a quatrain—makes the couplet the most rebellious component of the English sonnet: each quatrain rebels sonically; the couplet is a rebellion of sound and of established form.

How different this is from, again, the villanelle and the sestina, both forms that require retrieving the rhymes (or repeated words, in the case of the sestina) by the poem's end and organizing them in a final stanza—which is to say, those forms tend toward consolidation in terms of sound; the sonnet tends toward dispersion, sonically, even as it structurally aims to deploy an argument that leads to something like conclusion or proof.

One could argue that all of this falls away once we remove rhyme from the sonnet. But I think it's possible that the inherent sonic restlessness of both sonnet forms, apparent in their respective traditions, still lingers in the psychology of the sonnet as we've come to understand it over time. That's at least what draws *me* to the sonnet. Rebellion is one form of restlessness; innovation is another. To me, the sonnet is an ideal form for historically marginalized writers since it contains the very restlessness that is part of the condition of being marginalized—in that sense, this very old, very white tradition does in fact include something of my own experience already—and its openness to innovation means we feel free not just to speak of our own experiences but also to speak of them in a particular personal way, letting our differences manifest themselves in terms of formal invention, all while upholding the essential form of the sonnet, though to varying degrees. The patriarchal tradition remains there; the difference is that, in engaging with the particular manifestation of that tradition that we call the sonnet, we don't have to look exclusively through the lens of that tradition as handed down to us—instead, we get to look back at it and interrogate it and reshape it—and, having reshaped it, we re-see it through the lenses of our own experience. That is, as I understand it, how revolutions—what the sonnet invites—begin.

Works Cited

Fussell, Paul. *Poetic Meter and Poetic Form*. McGraw-Hill, 1979.

The Sonnet As

Neuroqueerness in the American Sonnet

NATHAN SPOON

While cognitive disabilities are not new, neuroqueerness is both a new and highly suggestive term. Nick Walker, who, along with fellow autistic scholars Athena Lynn Michaels-Dillon and M. Remi Yergeau, is responsible for proposing the term, defines "a neuroqueer individual" as "an individual whose identity has in some way been shaped by their engagement in practices of neuroqueering." Walker states that "neuroqueer is both a verb and an adjective," referring to practices and describing things "associated with those practices." "I originally conceived of *neuroqueer* as a verb: neuroqueering as the practice of queering (subverting, defying, disrupting, liberating oneself from) neuronormativity and heteronormativity simultaneously."

This essay explores ways self-distraction, playfulness, mutuality, and self-assertiveness show up in poems by Robert Frost, E. E. Cummings, Charles Bernstein, and torrin a. greathouse, four American poets that, because of either ADHD, autism, or dyslexia, express neuroqueerness while using the sonnet. Also, as a poet who has published many sonnets, I believe it is relevant to mention the aspect of having an insider's view, as I have, myself, been diagnosed with each of these disabilities. It is in this circumstance that I value, learn from, celebrate, and share perspectives on these poems.

Before the development of various diagnoses, neuroqueer poets would have been unaware of the scope of their differences and of their identities. Others commenting on their works would have been unaware of these as well. While it is impossible to diagnose deceased writers, understanding cognitive diversity and disabled identity presents readers today with an opportunity to consider poems from the past in a new light. Crucial to rereading such works is recognizing how, in addition to writing divergently, neuroqueer individuals read divergently and in ways allowing for connections and insights that would less likely be made by neurotypical readers. On this point, I often suspend my knowledge of readings offered by neurotypicals so I can read more in my own way, which may then be taken as disruptive, messy, irrelevant, or even foolish, but which is what I have to offer. When such readings are applied to the works of neuroqueer poets, they may have their own inherent relevance for the ways they connect poems back to their poets' disabled embodiments. For readers without neurological differences, this is exactly the challenge when reading a few of the poems here, which have been read and commented on in so many ways that do not take neurological difference into account that existing commentary can be a barrier to understanding the identities of the poets and how these identities may factor into the poems. Additionally, neuroqueer literary works provide opportunities for typical readers to learn about their own contributions to what has been termed the "double empathy problem" (Milton 883), which refers to the two-way street of communication between typical and atypical individuals. The typical majority generally imagines that atypical individuals need to adapt if they wish to be understood, when, in fact, typical individuals are equally failing to understand atypical people.

Having a multiply divergent brain means that I will frequently jump topics or interrupt myself in poems, due to ADHD, sometimes even leaving sentences or lines of thinking incomplete, as if they are partial images in a collage. I have a strong inclination for seeing patterns and drawing connections, even where others are unsure there is a connection. I have, due to dyslexia, a pronounced ability to see the whole of a poem when encountering each next part. Especially while writing a poem, I have a strong sense of how the next word, phrase, or aspect contributes to the whole, to the degree that I write my poems beginning to end as a single draft. I also often queer poems that are otherwise conventionally grammatical by leaving out all punctuation except for periods, used even when the sentence is a question. My motivation is a need to bend "correct" language into something that fits with my own way of existing.

The following sonnets stand out to me for ways their language operates and for ways they use aspects of creativity that are important to my own neuroqueer writing. I regularly self-distract in poems by imagining, for example, a future that is accepting of cognitively disabled people, as I do in my sonnet "The Republic of Tenderness." I use playfulness in sonnets such as "Kiddo" (*p. 109*) to make space for my different ways of structuring poems and as a way of embracing what Jennifer White-Johnson has termed "autistic joy." I embrace mutuality by writing poems that embrace indeterminacy, inviting readers to close circles of meaning if they wish to do so. I also use self-assertiveness, in poems such as "Be Monster" (which is not a sonnet) or "Rolling with the Schadenfreude" (which is a sonnet), as a way of countering voices that are harmful for the ways they view disabled people as burdens, echoing eugenics.

Self-Distraction

As Robert Frost, who "was dropped from school for what we call daydreaming" (Torrance 49) once explained, "Dartmouth is my chief college, the first one I ran away from. I ran away from Harvard later but Dartmouth first" (Frost, *Robert Frost, Speaking*, x), These incidents are only a few among many indicators that Frost, if living today, might be diagnosed with ADHD. And yet by cultivating and channeling his remarkable creativity (another indicator), Frost wrote many relatable, complex, strange, and memorable poems, including, from his first book, "Mowing." With its irregular and swaying patterns of rhyme and meter, "Mowing" is, as Peter Howarth notes, "a fourteen-line meditation on the way poetry and mowing are both kinds of self-distraction."

In the poem's first six lines, the narrator is remembering an experience of mowing with a focus on his scythe and the sound it is making, while the final eight lines present a case for understanding mowing and poetry as grounded in the everyday world. At any rate, "There was never a sound beside the wood but one, / And that was my long scythe whispering to the ground." Who knows what (the narrator claims to know "not well") it was whispering? Isn't self-distraction about temporarily and constructively stepping away from the emotional? The overwhelming? What am *I* doing *here*? Being unable to always be in the actual place engaging with the real thing, it would certainly be nice to let my mind drift instead, while remembering being in silence near the woods and getting physical, by mowing and then leaving "the hay to make." Reading this sonnet as a cognitively disabled person, I cannot help thinking of spoon theory and crip time and the different ways disabled people manage time, energy, and resources. I very much know the need for physical exertion and how, by producing the neurotransmitters the ADHD brain so frequently craves, such exertion can bring about an increase of calm and the experience of getting deeply lost (and found!) in hyperfocus.

Playfulness

In their essay "E. E. Cummings and Dyslexia," J. Allison Rosenblitt and Linda S. Siegel suggest that "Cummings was probably mildly dyslexic." Instead of concealing his disability by conforming to traditional expectations, as Frost did, Cummings was a poet who made use of his variation of neuroqueerness. "you shall above all things be glad and young" is a poem that seems to revisit and rewrite some dynamics from the biblical account of the Garden of Eden. In it, Cummings takes a playful approach to grammar and, especially, to punctuation.

This sonnet, written in blank verse, is tidily comprised of a couplet, a quatrain, a couplet, a quatrain, and a final couplet. It begins with what is presented as the fragmentary end of a sentence and ends with what might be an unfinished sentence because it lacks end punctuation. Between these bookending fragments are two complete sentences. The first addresses how things will be if you are young and, after a semicolon, how things will be if you are glad. The second, longer sentence is also in two parts linked by a semicolon, and each of these parts is made up of two parts linked by a colon. Leading up to its first colon, this sentence mentions the need "girlboys" have for "boygirls," and after the colon the narrator states, leading up to and beyond the semicolon, "i can entirely her only love // whose any mystery makes every man's / flesh put space on; and his mind take off time." After this, Cummings uses two more lines, with the narrator advising the addressee that thought in love would require God's forgiveness as well as God's mercy to spare the lover, to reach the final colon and then two more lines, warning of knowledge, with its illusions of progress (described ominously as a "foetal grave") and "negation's dead undoom," to complete this sentence.

While it irked the critic R. P. Blackmur, who summarized Cummings's poetical approach as "baby talk," the playful queering Cummings engaged in, particularly with the typography of his poems, can be understood as a wonderful display of embracing and centering dyslexic challenges and traits that might have easily been sources of embarrassment and even shame.

Mutuality

"Questionnaire" (*p. 90*) by the dyslexic poet Charles Bernstein comes with directions: "For each pair of sentences, circle the letter, a or b, that best expresses your viewpoint. Make a selection from each pair. Do not omit any items." The purpose of these directions is to present the prospective material in a way that allows for the creation of an individualized text. This you-have-already-chosen-your-own-adventure-due-to-the-ways-you-are-wired-and-otherwise-disposed-so-make-your-selections-now poem allows its reader (or hearer) to keep selected options and disregard any other possibilities. With the directions given and the options presented, the poet recedes. Or does he?

A puzzled scientist writing about the "scattered thoughts" in the *Diary* of dyslexic scientist Michael Faraday concluded that "from the morass of articulated and unarticulated principles, concepts, observations and physical facts, Faraday suspended the need to understand and simply acknowledged the thoughts which came into his head. The coherence of ideas was not imposed by any prior framework but was allowed to emerge from the chaos of thoughts he experienced" (Crawford 220; qtd. in West 139). The pairs of sentences in Bernstein's text seem at first to have a coherence, and then, suddenly, they begin turning in various ways. Why did he put *these* options together like *this*? From an individual encounter with the rudimentary "morass" of the options Bernstein offers, an individualized poem emerges.

Self-Assertiveness

To be autistic is to be complicated. It is also to live, according to etymology, in *autos* (self). The term was put forward while autism was being conceptualized as "a condition in which fantasy dominates over reality" ("Autism"). Despite increased understanding of autism and autistic people, this outmoded conception, which comes from the *OED*'s origin note, still holds. Being a person who is viewed as disconnected from reality and pathologized for having sensory-motor and social style differences is challenging.

Nonetheless, to begin her "Ars Poetica *or* Sonnet to Be Written across My Chest & Read in a Mirror, Beginning with a Line from Kimiko Hahn" (*p. 128*) torrin a. greathouse borrows the words of another poet to say, "I could not return to the body that / contained only the literal world." The narrator of greathouse's poem, after mentioning demands to "sever" the body, a disabled body, during the act of writing and after being "taught that it does not belong," has an epiphany: "look, here it is, real // & irrefutable." This articulation of the discovery of a body that is "real // & irrefutable" is in stark contrast with the *OED* entry. greathouse's narrator next mentions that beneath the "dark calligraphy" of this sonnet lies "music unhinged // from inside a gaping mouth, a body—*mine* (emphasis in original)." Even the poem

> can't be read without
> it: crippled, trans, woman, & still   alive.

Conclusion

While neuroqueer writers have always existed, the conditions I have taken as examples are all new in the sense that they are now being framed by diagnostic criteria and medicalizing language. Perhaps because of this newness—and despite the significant research that has gone into understanding these conditions—there has been, by comparison, little scholarly work exploring neuroqueerness and neuroqueer identities in connection with poetry. This lack of a body of knowledge can make access to publication and other types of visibility in poetry difficult for cognitively disabled poets. Circumstances are particularly dire for autistic individuals who, for example, face an unemployment rate of 80 percent, and who, based on my own observation and experience, face even higher rates of exclusion in the field of poetry. It is worth noting how companies across the corporate world are actively addressing this disparity even as so few efforts are being made in poetry and literature. Given all this, there is considerable opportunity for all of us to engage in working toward greater understanding and acceptance of poetry expressive of neuroqueerness.

Works Cited

"Autism, *N.*" *Lexico*, www.lexico.com/definition/autism/.

Bernstein, Charles. "Questionnaire." *Girly Man*. U of Chicago P, 2006, pp. 67–68.

Blackmur, R. P. "Notes on E. E. Cummings' Language." *Form and Value in Modern Poetry*. Forgotten Books, 2018, pp. 287–312.

Crawford, Elspeth. "Learning from Experience." *Faraday Rediscovered: Essays on the Life and Work of Michael Faraday, 1791–1897*, edited by David Gooding and Frank A. J. L. James. Macmillan, 1985, pp. 220–27.

Cummings, E. E. "you shall above all things be glad and young." *The Columbia Anthology of American Poetry*. Columbia UP, 1995, p. 437.

Frost, Robert. "Mowing." *The Columbia Anthology of American Poetry*. Columbia UP, 1995, pp. 306–7.

———. *Robert Frost: Speaking on Campus*. Edited Robert Connery Latham. W. W. Norton, 2009.

greathouse, torrin a. "Sonnet to Be Printed Across My Chest & Read in a Mirror, Beginning with a Line from Kimiko Hahn." *Kenyon Review*, Sept./Oct., 2019, kenyonreview.org/kr-online-issue/2019-septoct/selections/torrin-a-greathouse-763879/.

Howarth, Peter. "The Modern Sonnet." *The Cambridge Companion to the Sonnet*, edited by A. D. Cousins and Peter Howarth. Cambridge UP, 2011, pp. 225–44, Cambridge Companions to Literature.

Milton, Damien E. M. "On the Ontological Status of Autism: The 'Double Empathy Problem.'" *Disability and Society*, vol. 27, no. 6, Aug. 2012, pp. 883–87.

Rosenblitt, J. Allison, and Linda S. Siegel. "E. E. Cummings and Dyslexia." Annals of Dyslexia, vol. 70, no. 3, Oct. 2020, pp. 369–78.

Torrance, E. P. *Education and the Creative Potential.* Minneapolis, MN, U of Minnesota P, 1963.

Walker, Nick. "Neuroqueer: An Introduction." 2 May 2015, updated and revised summer 2021, neuroqueer.com/neuroqueer-an-introduction/.

West, Thomas G. *In the Mind's Eye: Creative Visual Thinkers, Gifted Dyslexics, and the Rise of Visual Technologies.* 2nd ed., Prometheus, 2009, p. 139.

White-Johnson, Jennifer. "Autistic Joy as an Act of Resistance." 25 Oct. 2019, www.thinkingautismguide.com/2019/10/autistic-joy-as-act-of-resistance.html/.

"From the you to me"
Interpersonal Exchange in Margaret Walker's
For My People Sonnet Sequence

ARIEL MARTINO

Margaret Walker described the year that she spent at the Iowa Writers' Workshop from 1939 until 1940 as one that nearly killed her (Jackson 104). The harrowing experience produced her debut poetry collection *For My People*, which won the prestigious Yale Younger Poets Prize in 1942. It also earned her a teaching position at Jackson State University and propelled her to eventually return to Iowa to receive a PhD in 1965. Walker's misery at Iowa bears the traces of the storied program's intense pedagogy, one that was founded on a restrictive notion of craft that required the student refine tirelessly through editing and careful attention to form. In *The Program Era* Mark McGurl describes pedagogy before the 1960s as one that teaches the student to refine from the experiential adage "write what you know" to a highly stylized, modernist expression: a process that "[begins] in 'self' but ending in disciplined 'impersonality'" (130). This would suggest that, as much as *For My People* is an exuberant expression of Black subjectivity, it is also the product of the thematic concerns that occupied faculty and directors at Iowa and a carefully wrought collection of modernist poetry.[1] Walker was undoubtedly interested in the potential for the literary to transform, just as she was invested in relocating and communicating aspects of the African American vernacular tradition. Recruited as a Southern regional poet, she was reportedly expected to produce "authentic" manifestations of Black culture—as she does in the folkloric ballads that comprise the second section of *For My People* (Thomas 82). But she also includes stirring political calls that have, since the collection's publication, been aligned with the project of cultural expression. Walker used *For My People* as a place to both represent Black people as politically engaged, and also to work out a form of politics that could account for such engagement. In the sonnet sequence that closes the collection, she locates political recognition in an interpersonal exchange, employing the sonnet's conversational structure and the sequence's iterative organization to signal that this recognition is contingent, ephemeral, and ongoing.

Walker invokes the underlying tension of the sonnet—the restrictive pull of prescribed form and the broadening push of unending expressive possibility—to mark Black life as worthy of artistic elevation and political recognition. She further marks her reclamation of the sonnet form as squarely in line with a Black literary tradition. As Hollis Robbins notes, "with its venerated status, its genteel appeal for editors and publishers, and its comfortable fit at the bottom of a newspaper column, the sonnet form was the single most popular form for African American poets in the first half of the twentieth century" (7). So, just as Walker's highly celebrated use of the ballad form in *For My People* can be seen as the result of her education in the history and significance of the form in English literature and also an assertion of extant ballads within the African American and Black diaspora vernacular tradition, her use of the sonnet amplifies an extant but underexamined movement to remake the form. Timo Müller encourages us to think of the African American sonnet as a contested space, demonstrating that African American "authors conceived the sonnet as a space that can be occupied, reshaped, expanded" (5). Building on Robbins's and Müller's capacious sense of the African American sonnet as a form that is politicized in its inception, I want to suggest that Walker's poetics and politics were wrought from a series of contradictions: a middle-class upbringing in impoverished Alabama, radical political contacts, and highly traditional training in English literature at Northwestern University and the University of Iowa. Her readers, both contemporaneous and more current, tend to see the formal training she received and her middle-class background as a container for her radicalism. It was as if her use of form was a mask that slipped unseemly content past the literary tastemakers, both Black and white. Her use of the sonnet helps us to see the ways in which form is inextricable from content. The politicized content of the sonnet sequence that closes *For My People* is enhanced by the politicized gesture of a Black woman using a rarified form. By invoking the sonnet, Walker marks herself as conversant in a tradition that, as stated above, involves the developing Black aesthetic but also includes the much longer, whiter, and more Western history of the sonnet. For Walker, it was not so much a matter of Anglo-European form with African American content; her poetry insists that African American formalism is capable of communicating a politics.

Walker's formulation of political recognition is, at this point in her career, abstract and in formation; as a result, it has been deemphasized in favor of a more general description of her expression of Leftist politics. In his account of the period during which Walker wrote, Lawrence Jackson identifies Walker as "the product of the same ambitious Southern Black middle class that produced Chester Himes, William Attaway, and Sterling Brown" and marks the publication of *For My People* as a moment in which she "turned fully toward the working class for her material" (104). Jackson's evaluation directs readerly attention to the content of Walker's poems—the depictions of working-class folk in her ballads, the interpolation of a proletarian voice in poems such as "We Have Been Believers" and "Today," and the strident demands outlined in "For My People." Lorenzo Thomas similarly locates a politics in Walker's collection, drawing out the contrast between her training as a regionalist and the technical feats she goes to in order to impart a forward-looking conception of what the Black literary aesthetic can look like. He writes, "Margaret Walker exhibits a determined optimism that transcends political movements in its deepest implications" (Thomas 81). Jackson highlights the political content of Walker's poetry, while Thomas thinks about the implications of using such content, one that gestures toward a more equitable standard of excellence. But both men exclude the collection's sustained use of the sonnet form and, as a result, miss the extent to which the collection dwells in what Thomas names "political movements." Walker is concerned with the granularity of lived experience and she views such experience as the basis of a politics.

Accounts of Walker as political do redress an earlier misreading of the granularity of her poetry, which had often been read as adherence to the modernist standard of the particular as basis for the universal. *For My People* was published when Walker won the Yale Younger Poets Prize, joining the ranks of Muriel Rukeyser and James Agee, who had been awarded the prize in the preceding decade, and William Meredith, Adrienne Rich, and W. S. Merwin, who would go on to win the prize in the next.[2] In the introduction to *For My People*, Stephen Vincent Benét was tasked with contextualizing Walker's work, both in terms of its continuation of an already distinguished literary tradition, one that valued modernist universality above all else, and also with recognition of Walker's place as the first Black poet to win the prize. Benét's approbation, coupled with his pointed insistence that to celebrate Walker's work simply because she is Black is "meaningless patronage," structured readings of the collection, again appealing to the work's proficiency and its ability to invoke the universal. "Poetry must exist in its own right," Benét insists, and Walker's poems are "the song of her people, of her part of America" (6). Benét goes on to praise Walker's "deep sincerity," her use of voice, and the impossibility of reading her verse "unmoved," qualities that aid in her depiction of the lives of Black people. Benét's introduction initiates a tension between his insistence that Walker's poems be recognized for some abstract sense of quality and his implication that her "sincerity" could only come from a racialized writer. The bulk of his introduction focuses on the titular poem, a dense, ten-stanza call for Black empowerment. But his insistence on the generic excellence of Walker's poetry defangs even the political content of the obviously political poem.

Reading Walker today, we must reclaim her politics and also think about her political views as shifting across the collection. *For My People* is comprised of three sections: the first includes the title poem and nine other poems in an elevated, collective, or historical register; the second includes ten ballads, sometimes in dialect, drawn from African American folklore; the final section includes six sonnets, each one individually titled but often containing language that links one poem to another. Already we are encouraged to read the six poems not only sequentially but as part of a network of meaning wherein the images of one poem refer back to and also alter those that came before. While each poem is distinct and each section employs different formal strategies, all are concerned with the lived reality of the Black experience, an inherently political proposition in a poetry collection. The title of this essay comes from the collection's final poem "The Struggle Staggers Us" (*p. 52*) where Walker writes, "There is a journey from the Me to You/ There is a journey from the You to Me / A union of the two strange worlds must be" (58). Embedded in those three lines, Walker delineates a politics that begins in individual lived experience and becomes politicized in the moment of encounter. The "union" that she imagines at the collection's close is one in which the Black subject is recognized as human, treated with dignity. This recognition, the collection suggests, happens at the level of the formal and the interpersonal.

More than any other poem in the collection, "Iowa Farmer" sketches the contours of Walker's imagined "union," modeling the political recognition she desires. As the third poem in the sonnet sequence, "Iowa Farmer" stands out as much for its unique content as it does for its anomalous form.

Most of the other poems adhere closely to the Shakespearean sonnet form. Only "Iowa Farmer" and the poem that follows it, "Memory," depart from a recognizable sequence of end rhymes. This links the two poems, and while "Memory" is about dispossession and isolation in the city, "Iowa Farmer" is about the self-determination of the Midwestern farmer. Walker begins the poem by reflexively introducing her encounter with the farmer as a dialogue: "I talked to a farmer one day in Iowa" (55). The spareness of this overture, the way that it is devoid of context, gives the encounter an abstract, almost allegorical air. The farmer is reduced to type, but the evocativeness of that type already suggests something about the practices and values that the speaker will go on to extoll in the remainder of the poem. Walker ends the poem with an imaginative transition from the conversation—which is not recounted—to the recollection that drives "Memory," the poem that follows it: "Yet in the Middle West where wheat was plentiful / where grain are golden under sunny skies / and cattle fattened through the summer heat / I could remember more familiar sights" (55). "Memory" picks up amid this reverie, contrasting the idyllic, fecund Midwestern summer with the "cold and blustery" cityscape. But temporality is key: during the moment of Walker's encounter, there is productive communion, one that contains a kernel of a politics.

The glancing moment of connection described in "Iowa Farmer" both models a desired form of individual self-possession and suggests a mutuality in that self-possession. Put another way, it is a mutual acknowledgment that a speaker-subject like Walker's—a Black woman—could experience the same degree of autonomy as a white farmer. The speaker recounts, "there was no hunger deep within the heart / nor burning riveted within the bone, / but here they ate a satisfying bread" (55). The envy in this description is almost palpable. The elements missing from the farmer's life—hunger and burning—echo the language she uses to describe the condition of impoverished subjects elsewhere in the sonnet sequence, drawing a stark distinction between the farmer's self-possession and the precarity of life without land and livelihood. The conversation that takes place between the farmer and speaker is not recounted, but she gives us images of security and home throughout the sonnet that demonstrate the assuredness of his position. The farmer "knew his land"; there is "love for home / within the soft serene eyes of his son"; and "His ugly house was clean against the storm" (55). Despite the lack of aesthetic appeal to his house, it is safe and functional, beloved by his children and provides the "satisfying bread" the speaker later admires. Her description projects a sense of security that extends beyond the farmer himself. The importance of the son—his love and security—

cannot be understated. He offers both a vision of a stable family structure, absent in the rest of the sonnet sequence, and a sense of futurity. What the speaker desires is the farmer's self-possession *and* the ability to pass that self-possession along to future generations.

Though race remains implicit in the poem, the farmer's whiteness and Midwesternness are crucial in the politics that Walker generates. The intersubjective journey that forms the crux of her case for Black humanity depends on an appropriation of aspects of humanity that come from outside. In this case, it is the quintessentially American dream of land ownership and self-sufficiency. The poem could be a critique of the aspects of American policy that have occasioned Black dispossession—the broken promise of "forty acres and a mule," segregation, discrimination in housing and employment—but it is notable that Walker meets the farmer with admiration and not scorn. It is a sort of ducking under the fence of structural racism, imagining a world in which such conditions do not inhibit the Black subject from enjoying the same self-possession and the freedom that seems to go along with it. Walker writes that the farmer "spoke with pride and yet not boastfully / he had no need to fumble for his words" (55). Given the interpersonal connection that the poem crystallizes, we might see Walker's speaker(s) throughout *For My People* performing a similar function. Of course, poets must always "fumble for [their] words" in the sense of crafting a poem, but the declarative tone throughout Walker's work, what Benét called in the introduction "sincerity," reveals her determination to state her case outright. Black life, she says, is worthy of admiration. Her encounter with the farmer models the "journey from the Me to You," but her collection models the "journey from the You to Me," wherein the reader is invited into conversation with Walker. *For My People*, and particularly the sonnet sequence that ends it, may fall short in its abstraction, but it is radical in its imagining of an intersubjective construction of humanity. Walker imagines a political sphere that is public—not a governmental apparatus but society as a public. For her, the social is political.

Notes

1. Mark McGurl summarizes the tension in the directorial poles of the Iowa Writers' Workshop as a discrepancy between Midwestern regionalists' emphasis on the "technology" of the literary and the Southern writers' emphasis on "tradition." He notes that the Midwestern regionalists "looked outward and sought prestige through expansion" and the Southern regionalists "insisted that the regionalist project must turn inward and achieve literary excellence through exclusion, through the willed imposition of limits" (151).

2. Muriel Rukeyser won in the Yale Younger Poets Prize 1934 for *Theory of Flight*; James Agee won in 1933 for *Permit Me Voyage*; William Meredith won in 1943 for *Love Letters from and Impossible Land*; Adrienne Rich won in 1950 for *A Change of World*; W. S. Merwin won in 1951 for *A Mask for Janus*. The prize helped to establish the early careers of several figures who would go on to define modern poetry.

Works Cited

Benét, Stephen Vincent. Foreword. *For My People*, by Margaret Walker, 1942. Yale University Press, 1989.

Jackson, Lawrence. *The Indignant Generation: A Narrative History of African American Writers and Critics, 1934–1960*. Princeton UP, 2011.

McGurl, Mark. *The Program Era: Postwar Fiction and the Rise of Creative Writing*. Harvard UP, 2009.

Müller, Timo. *The African American Sonnet: A Literary History*. UP of Mississippi, 2018.

Robbins, Hollis. *Forms of Contention: Influence and the African American Sonnet Tradition*. U of Georgia P, 2020.

Thomas, Lorenzo. *Extraordinary Measures: Afrocentric Modernism and Twentieth-Century Poetry*. U of Alabama P, 2000.

Walker, Margaret. *For My People*. Yale UP, 1989.

The Sonnet Is Not a Luxury

LISA L. MOORE

"I went to Catholic schools, you see," says Audre Lorde. "Now smartness was not as important as being good, and I was *really* bad." In the 1996 documentary *Litany for Survival: The Life and Work of Audre Lorde*, we hear of a series of schoolgirl crimes, but the one Lorde knows will really shock us is the story of her first published poem. Eyebrow raised, lip curled, hands imitating the disapproving gestures of the nuns, Lorde loves the irony of claiming a very traditional verse form, the sonnet, as the height of bad-girl bravura:

> I learned about sonnets by reading Edna St. Vincent Millay's love sonnets and loving them and deciding I was going to try.... I was editor of my high school magazine and I wrote a poem about love. And... the faculty advisor said it was a bad sonnet. And I really knew that it was a good one. But I knew that she didn't like it because of the things that I said in it. So I sent it off to *Seventeen* magazine and they bought it. And I made more money from that one poem than I made for the next ten years. (Griffin and Parkerson)

Audre Lorde's poems, usually associated with the directly political and confessional open forms of second-wave feminist poetry and the vernacular and confrontational styles of the Black Arts Movement, have been overlooked as part of the history of the sonnet. Indeed, although Lorde's poems are "widely anthologized, honored by numerous awards, and praised by contemporary poets," they have "received little critical attention" (Rudnitsky 473).[1] Lorde's perhaps unexpected interest in the sonnet challenges critics to "look to the insides of archives and bodies of work themselves in their original contexts" when reading Black poetry. Elizabeth Alexander cautions us against reading such poems "just as we receive them…with the hard-to-avoid periodizing, tidying-up impulses of the presents in which they are made" (88). Lorde's first publication, which does not appear in any of her collections, is a poem I do not want to see lost to history or dismissed as juvenilia. Alexander reminds us: "it is testimony, or the text itself, that takes us inside the black interior, a moment, a movement." Lorde's first published poem takes us inside the Black interior of the modern sonnet, its revision, rejection, and revival. As part of the work of what I call elsewhere "a lesbian history of the sonnet," this essay centers the queer, Black, and feminist energies of this compact, powerful, and explosive form.[2]

Lorde's first published poem, "Spring," is attributed to "Audrey" Lorde" (her given name) in the popular fashion periodical *Seventeen* in April 1951. It begins: "I am afraid of spring; there is no peace here, / The agony of growing things is in my veins." Appearing as it does in a fashion magazine with, that month, a pink cover showing a white boy and girl, the poem surprises with its emphasis on death, burial, a speaker sobbing with fear. In the biographical statement that appears on the same page as the poem, "Audrey Lorde" describes herself as a collector of "folk songs… and old books." She mentions a special "prize" from her "searches through Fourth Avenue bookshops," "an ancient and yellowed copy of the romantic Poets." Just a few months past seventeen years old herself, Lorde is already developing a complex sense of the multiple sources of her poetic vocation. Describing her interest in "folk songs," Lorde claims membership in not only the Greenwich Village beatnik scene she was already exploring with Hunter High School classmate and future Beat poet Diane di Prima but also the blues and folk vernacular traditions brought into the literary mainstream by Langston Hughes and other poets of the Harlem Renaissance, whom Lorde knew through her participation in the Harlem Writers Guild. Finally, she claims lineage from the English Romantic poets, a bold assertion for a young woman who whose photograph appears on the facing page in this white-dominated magazine.[3]

Lorde herself later attributed her reluctance to claim the influence of Black writers to the misogyny and homophobia she found among advocates of both the Harlem Renaissance of a generation before her and the Black Arts Movement of her own generation. "I was not a popular Black poet," she said in an interview, "because some of the things I said ran very counter to… the line in Black poetry at the time. And there was a lot of sexism involved.… Also because I was a lesbian,… I was suspect. I have always been suspect in different situations" (Chawla 126). She also spoke, more obliquely, about how her complex sense of Black identity was inflected by her decade-long marriage to a white man, Ed Rollins, with whom she had two children, and her long partnership with a white woman, Frances Clayton. But Lorde may also have been comfortable claiming an Anglo-European poetic lineage because of her Caribbean heritage. Much of the English poetry Lorde valued as a child came to her through her parents, their own tastes shaped by their colonial schooling in Grenada. Lorde did not view Shakespeare, the Romantic poets, T. S. Eliot, and Edna St. Vincent Millay as off limits or their achievements as out of reach. In writing a sonnet and working hard to publish it, then, Lorde defiantly marked and also obscured her complex personal and poetic lineages.

A distinctive formal feature of Lorde's sonnet is her use of the chiasmatic refrain, in which the first line is repeated and reversed in the final line: "I am afraid of spring; there is no peace here" becomes "There is no peace here. I am afraid of spring." This strategy may recall Millay, who often repeated first lines as final lines, though not with this bravura use of chiasmus. (Millay's "Dirge without Music" begins with the phrase "I am not resigned" and ends "And I am not resigned.") Critic Cheryl Wall, however, gives us a different lineage for this rhetorical strategy. She describes the blues technique of "worrying the line," whereby a musician repeats a line or phrase with a difference. This kind of repetition, Wall argues, is "a metaphor for lineage and "for the "literary traditions" of African American women writers (Wall 8). Repeating a refrain with a difference can be an Anglo-European folk song move; it can be an homage to an admired woman poet; or it can be a blues move. Lorde's poem seems to want us to hear all three and more. For example, her use of off-rhymes (winters/hinder, hair/here) evoke the "skillful consonant-only rhymes" of Gwendolyn Brooks (Howarth 237).[4] Audrey Lorde's "Spring," then, introduces a poet who claims multiple lineages in a popular venue aimed at young women readers.

Sonnets by African American writers were in wide circulation during Lorde's school years, especially Claude McKay's "If We Must Die" (*p. 35*), which Winston Churchill is said to have quoted in an address to the House of Commons during World War II.[5] The sonnet form had been a flashpoint in the debates of the Harlem Renaissance of the 1920s (Howarth 235). The "folk poetics" of Langston Hughes were a conscious riposte to the more bourgeois forms and themes of his rival, Countee Cullen. "Cullen, however, thought that Hughes' poems had fallen into the same racial trap that Dunbar's dialect poems had" (Howarth 236). In the 1930s, such writers as Sterling Brown, Melvin Tolson, and Georgia Douglas Johnson engaged in both the political resistance advocated by Hughes and the exploration of subjectivity of the traditional lyric. Black sonnets in this period "were exceptional sites for the appearance of anti-lynching discourse" in popular Black periodicals such as *The Crisis* and *Opportunity* (Woodson 74). The rivalry between Hughes and Cullen has shaped our understanding of received forms in the poetry of the Harlem Renaissance, but Jon Woodson argues that the blues and the sonnet both engage in the project of "the transformation of abjection, trauma, and inarticulacy into personhood, autonomy, and vocal citizenship" (12). Woodson refers to both genres as forms of "black self-fashioning" (70).

In fact, by 1930, when thirteen-year-old Gwendolyn Brooks wrote her first sonnet, "The Hinderer," a poem about racism at her Chicago high school, "she might easily have regarded it as an African American form" (Ford 354). Brooks, of course, became the best-known Black woman poet of the period of Lorde's own young womanhood and a virtuoso of the sonnet form. Brooks's verse epic, *Annie Allen*, won the Pulitzer Prize for poetry in 1950, the first time the prize had been awarded to an African American author. The volume contains a noted sonnet sequence that Brooks describes as a "sonnet-ballad." In a 1970 interview, Brooks talks about consciously modifying the sonnet form in the iconic sequence, "Gay Chaps at the Bar," from her 1945 volume, *A Street in Bronzeville*: "A sonnet series in off-rhyme, because I felt it was an off-rhyme situation" (Brooks, "Interview" 10). Off-rhyme in particular had been employed by modernist sonnet writers such as Cummings to deform and wake up the sonnet. So "when she set about writing sonnets in the forties and fifties," Karen Ford argues, "Brooks recognized the form as simultaneously American, African American, Anglo-European, traditional, and modern" (355).

Brooks's sonnets opened up "the possibility of modernist interior representations to transcend the often stereotypical portrayals of African Americans," and their form is not incidental, according to Elizabeth Alexander: "The sonnet is a 'little room,' and Brooks reveals the equivalent of painted tableaux" in her sonnet sequences and sonnet-ballads ("Toward" 15, 16). In Brooks's hands, the sonnet becomes "a square window or doorway, a look suddenly in, and then deeply in" to both domestic and psychic interiors (16). Brooks famously gave up received verse forms after being challenged to do so by students at historically Black Fisk University when she visited there in 1967, but for the rest of her career, the sonnet continued to be Brooks's touchstone, representing "the very question of poetic form" (Ford 345). Indeed, Brooks casts off formal verse in the name of the sonnet, saying in 1969, "this does not seem to me to be a sonnet time" (*Conversations* 68; qtd. in Ford 352). But Brooks's about-face on form is more equivocal than it appears from this statement, for she continues to defend the sonnet even while rejecting it, for instance, when she writes, "I have written many more sonnets than I'm sure I'll be writing in the future, although I still think there are things colloquial and contemporary that can be done with the sonnet form" (*Conversations* 45; qtd. in Ford 346). Brooks's equivocation is understandable, for the sonnet again came under fire in the 1960s from Black Arts Movement writers for many of the same reasons given by the Fisk students. Ishmael Reed wrote in *The Black Aesthetic*, "Some slaves excelled at 'Sonnets,' 'Odes,' and 'Couplets,' the feeble pluckings of musky Gentlemen and slaves of the metronome" (Reed 381; qtd. in Ford 367). The Black Arts critique of white aesthetic norms often paired, as here, the deathliness of subservience to white culture with its queerness, the "feebleness" of its masculinity. In her defiant way, by contrast, Lorde may have liked the sonnet's associations with queerness and femininity and carried forward Brooks's discovery that formal limitations "need not be seen as a constraint but rather as a way of imaging the racial self unfettered, racialized but not delimited" (Alexander 5).

Although Lorde went on to write in many styles, including long multi-part poems and the book-length poetic novel *Zami*, sonnet form remained visible in her work in revised and revolutionary forms. For example, the fourteen-line "Now," from *The New York Head Shop and Museum* (1974), insists, from its title forward, on its own contemporary urgency and relevance: "Woman power / is / Black power..." The series of declarations that open the poem create a sestet with epistrophe instead of rhyme, so that the remainder of the poem serves as a kind of octave. Layered on top of this implicit Petrarchan form, a Shakespearean-style couplet ("I am / are you") is pulled back by the stanza break to lines 12 and 13. And lines 8 and 9 ("my heart beats / as my eyes open") function as a volta as the multiple, compressed meanings are opened up by the poem's unpunctuated line breaks. The lines could be understood as: "Human power is always feeling. My heart beats as my eyes open." Or "Always feeling my heartbeats. As my eyes open, as my hands move. " Or "Always feeling my heart beats as my eyes open." As Peter Howarth has said of the modernist innovations of E. E. Cummings, Lorde too stretched "the boundaries of the form...abandoning octaves, sestets, full meters, predictable rhymes and any formal pressure to begin at the beginning, or come to rest at the end of a line" (233).[6]

Perhaps, while Gwendolyn Brooks was disavowing the sonnet form in which she had written her masterpieces, Audre Lorde, whose ars poetica is usually taken to be "the master's tools will never dismantle the master's house" ("Master's Tools" 95) was writing unmarked, avant-garde sonnets. The statement about the master's tools, made famous on bumper stickers and bookmarks around the world, was first articulated in a talk Lorde gave at a New York University conference in 1979.[7] It's often forgotten that Lorde's remarks that day are not, first and foremost, about poetry. They are about racism in the white women's movement, and in particular, the absence of Black women and lesbians from the other panels at the conference, as if, Lorde says, "lesbian and Black women have nothing to say on existentialism, the erotic, women's culture and silence, developing feminist theory, or heterosexuality and power" (94), some of the topics of the other, all-white, all-straight panels. Feminism is not only ineffective but damaging, Lorde contends, when "the tools of a racist patriarchy are used to examine the fruits of that same patriarchy" (94). The master's tools—the exclusion of the perspectives of "those of us who stand outside the circle of society's definition of acceptable women"—are only appealing to women who "still define the master's house as their only source of support" (95).

"Their only source of support." Lorde strategically deployed what might be called the master's tools throughout her life and work—but in the service of those, like her, seeking to create a home outside the master's house or find their own room within it. Lorde got a master's degree in library science in the 1950s and used her modest but steady income as a public librarian to support herself and her children from 1961 to 1968. She taught at elite private schools and at various branches of the City University of New York throughout the 1970s. Lorde inhabited and studied patriarchal and racist institutions, as we all must and do, and used their resources to challenge their exclusions from within. But of course her interventions were possible only because of the work she did to create alternative family forms, raising children first with a white man and later with a woman partner and participating in radical political communities, for example, in her collaborations with Gloria Anzaldua, Cherrie Moraga, Adrienne Rich, and Barbara Smith. Lorde traveled as much as she could afford, living cheaply in Mexico as a teenager and Germany in her forties and visiting Cuba, West Africa, and South Africa before spending the last years of her life on the Caribbean island of St. Croix with her lover, the Crucian activist and scholar Gloria Joseph. Her forms of knowing came out of all this.

Lorde's deeply informed work as a poet is an important lineage by which the sonnet was carried forward to its current renaissance among Black writers, especially Black queer and women poets. Just as Audre Lorde said, "I have always been suspect," the sonnet form has always been suspect too.

The sonnet, in the hands of these writers, is not the master's tradition. The form has been distinctively shaped for contemporary poetics as a feminist, queer, and African American form, as an expression of a "black interior." A lesbian history of the sonnet allows us to perform that act of respectful looking that Elizabeth Alexander describes this way: "To SEE, to lay eyes on these 'black interiors,' is at first startling. Then it is amazing" (19). The form invites complexity and contradiction because "sonnets can *think*. This is precisely [what gives] the sonnet its political force" (Ford 357). As one of the legacies of Audre Lorde, the sonnet is not a luxury.

Notes

1. Another excellent essay on Lorde's poetics also appeared in *Callaloo*: Keith Leonard, "Which Me Will Survive: Reclaiming Identity, Rethinking Audre Lorde," vol. 35, no. 3, summer 2012, pp. 758–77. Poet and scholar Alexis Pauline Gumbs is currently working on a much-anticipated biography of Lorde.

2. See Lisa L. Moore, "A Lesbian History of the Sonnet," *Critical Inquiry*, vol. 43, no. 4, summer 2017, pp. 813–38.

3. Pamela Jones of the Dance Theater of Harlem appeared on the cover of *Seventeen* in January 1972. The issue also includes an interview with and photograph of Yolanda King, "Martin Luther King's Daughter: People Expect Me to Be A Saint," *Seventeen*, vol. 31, January 1972, pp. 1, 92.

4. Important works on the African American sonnet include Hollis Robbins, *Forms of Contention: Influence and the African-American Sonnet Tradition*, U of Georgia P, 2020, and Timo Müller, *The African American Sonnet: A Literary History*, UP of Mississippi, 2018. Lorde's poems are not discussed in either book.

5. David Caplan says in a footnote that this "oft-repeated story" is "hard to either verify or disprove." *Questions of Possibility: Contemporary Poetry and Poetic Form*, Oxford UP, 2004, p. 141.

6. In Lorde's "Now," the dramatically shortened line seems to have been a direct influence on Lucille Clifton's sonnet-like, fourteen- and fifteen-line poems, such as "homage to my hips" and "the death of fred clifton" in which some lines consist of only one word.

7. The essay was based on a speech Lorde gave at the New York University Institute for the Humanities Conference in 1979.

Works Cited

Alexander, Elizabeth. *The Black Interior: Essays*. Graywolf Press, 2004.

Brooks, Gwendolyn, and George Stavros. *Conversations with Gwendolyn Brooks*, edited by Gloria Wade Gayles, UP of Mississippi, 2003.

———. "An Interview with Gwendolyn Brooks." *Contemporary Literature*, vol. 11, no. 1, 1970, pp. 1–20. *JSTOR*, www.jstor.org/stable/1207502.

Chawla, Louise. "Poetry, Nature, and Childhood: An Interview with Audre Lorde." *Conversations with Audre Lorde*, edited by Joan Wylie Hall. UP of Mississippi, 2004, pp. 115–27.

Ford, Karen Jackson. "The Sonnets of Satin-Legs Brooks." *Contemporary Literature*, vol. 48, no. 3, 2007, pp. 345–73. *Project MUSE*, doi:10.1353/cli.2007.0037.

Griffin, Ada Gay, and Michelle Parkerson, directors. *A Litany for Survival: The Life and Work of Audre Lorde*. PBS, 18 June 1996.

Howarth, Peter. "The Modern Sonnet." *The Cambridge Companion to the Sonnet*, edited by A. D. Cousins and Peter Howarth. Cambridge UP, 2011, pp. 225–44.

Lorde, Audre. *Conversations with Audre Lorde*, edited by Joan Wylie Hall. UP of Mississippi, 2004.

———."The Master's Tools Will Never Dismantle the Master's House." *This Bridge Called My Back: Writings by Radical Women of Color*, edited by Cherrie Moraga, Gloria Anzaldua, and Barbara Smith. Kitchen Table Women of Color Press, 1983, pp. 94–101. Reprinted in Audre Lorde, *Sister Outsider: Essays and Speeches*. Crossing Press, 1984.

———. "Spring." *Seventeen*, Apr. 1951, p. 137.

Reed, Ishmael. "Can a Metronome Know the Thunder or Summon a God?" *The Black Aesthetic*, edited by Addison Gayle. Doubleday, 1971, pp. 381–82.

Rudnitsky, Lexi. "The 'Power' and 'Sequelae' of Audre Lorde's Syntactical Strategies." *Callaloo*, vol. 26, no. 2, 2003, pp. 473–85. *Project MUSE*, doi:10.1353/cal.2003.0055.

Tinsley, Omise'eke Natasha. *Thiefing Sugar: Eroticism Between Women in Caribbean Literature*. Duke UP, 2010.

Wall, Cheryl A. *Worrying the Line: Black Women Writers, Lineage, and Literary Tradition*. U of North Carolina P, 2005.

Woodson, Jon. *Anthems, Sonnets, and Chants: Recovering the African American Poetry of the 1930s*. Ohio State UP, 2011.

Mapping Radical Poetic Geographies

The Sonnets of Frank X Walker and Maggie Anderson

JODIE CHILDERS

Countering stereotypical and superficial depictions of contemporary Appalachia, the poets Frank X Walker and Maggie Anderson construct innovative sonnets that resist reductive, monolithic notions of place and identity and illuminate a multivalent Appalachian culture informed by the diverse individual family stories and collective traditions that shape the region.

In the American imagination, the poetic voices that highlight the complexities of Appalachia (a geographical expanse that touches on thirteen states) are too often overshadowed by derogatory stereotypes of the region disseminated through television and film. According to the sociologist Rebecca Scott, "Appalachian stereotypes conflate the land and people with dark, trash-filled hollows sheltering isolated incestuous communities" (37). These images have material consequences to a region that suffers under a legacy of extractivism, environmental degradation, and systemic poverty. The historian Ronald Eller argues that these stereotypes "blame the victim for Appalachia's problems," which enables "the rest of America to keep the region at arm's length, rather than to confront the systemic problems of a dependent economy, environmental decay, and institutional weakness that challenge mountain communities today" (x).

For poets on the margins of American society, the sonnet can serve as a space to express and enact resistance to dominant discourse, a site to exploit the tension between adhering to literary traditions and rebelling against them. The founder of the Affrilachian Poets collective, Frank X

Walker, experiments with the sonnet to invent what he terms the "Affrilachian sonnet," a novel poetic form rooted in Black Appalachian identity and history. Challenging patriarchal conceptualizations of work, Maggie Anderson employs the sonnet to preserve a feminist family lineage of labor in the West Virginia coalfields. Harkening to literary conventions while also defying them, both Walker and Anderson reinvent the sonnet on their own terms, mapping radical poetic geographies in contemporary Appalachia.

Born in Danville, Kentucky, Frank X Walker is a prolific poet and interdisciplinary artist with an expansive oeuvre, tackling a range of themes from the autobiographical to the historical. In 1991, he coined the neologism "Affrilachia," a portmanteau that gave voice to the intersecting experience of Black and Appalachian identities and laid the groundwork for a powerful movement in the arts that continues to grow and thrive. As Walker explains in an interview, "part of what we've done as Affrilachians is commit to this idea of making the invisible visible, giving the muted a voice, because we always felt like that. The structure was designed to make us feel invisible" (Umar). Building on Walker's vision, the collective of Affrilachian Poets "render the invisible visible" by celebrating "a multicultural influence, a spectrum of people who consider Appalachia home and/or identify strongly with the trials and triumphs of being of this region" ("Affrilachian Poets Defined"). In 2000, Walker published *Affrilachia*, a collection of candid lyrical poems that reflect on race, place, and identity. Through subsequent volumes of historically informed poetry, including *Buffalo Dance: The Journey of York* (2004), which was awarded the Lillian Smith Book Award, Walker has used the persona poem to foreground figures from African American history, "rescuing muted and silenced voices" (Walker, "An Interview" 33). In 2007, Walker and the poet Nikky Finney launched the literary periodical *Pluck! The Journal of Affrilachian Arts and Culture*, and in 2018, the University Press of Kentucky published the anthology *Black Bone: 25 Years of the Affrilachian Poets*. The history of the Affrilachian Poets has also been documented in the film *Coal Black Voices*, which Walker coproduced.

In 2016, Walker turned to the sonnet in *The Affrilachian Sonnets*. A unique experiment in style, form, and content, this book inaugurates a new and distinctive form of Walker's own design in dialogue with striking wood engravings by the artist Joanne Price. While the sonnets in this collection follow the fourteen-line structure, they do not conform to conventional patterns of rhyme and meter. In an interview with Bruce Dick and Forrest Yerman, Walker explains how he conceived the structure for these poems: "I felt that I wanted to take something traditional and morph it back toward something useful to me. So to call it an Affrilachian sonnet means that I get to define it, and it doesn't have to fit the traditional Italian or Shakespearean sonnet forms" (Walker, "Still Chasing" 409). In one poem from this collection, "Gunning for Bear," Walker delineates the Affrilachian sonnet through the process of creating it. Redefining conceptions of the lyric from its powerful first line, the speaker imagines John Henry (the African American steel-driving folk hero) as a poet, using "his hammer and determination to beat quatrains" (lines 1–2). The speaker declares that the music of John Henry's labor is, in fact, "a sonnet" much like the "Olympic Sonnet" of Jesse Owens or the "fierce love and mid-song sermons" of Nina Simone (lines 6–7). Enumerating a list of Black innovators and artists in a range of creative fields, Walker goes on to showcase Affrilachian voices, whose sonnets span the globe, from the lyrics of Bill Withers to the sounds of Rhiannon Giddens and the Carolina Chocolate Drops. Walker's sonnet not only makes Black identity and history in Appalachia visible but also contests the notion that the Appalachian region is solely rural, as he highlights, for instance, August Wilson (who was born in Pittsburgh and wrote extensively about the city) as an Affrilachian author whose plays are "a crown of sonnets" (line 10). As Walker points out, "mass media has sold the world an image of the region that is all White, dirt poor, illiterate, and devoid of culture, but knowing that both Pittsburgh and Birmingham are in Appalachia destroys that myth" (Walker, "An Interview" 33). As he redraws the map of Appalachia, Walker also reinvents the sonnet, creating a poetic form that is rooted not in literary tradition but in the radical power and courage to break societal and aesthetic rules. The final three lines of "Gunning for Bear" make an argument for what kind of work an Affrilachian sonnet does in the world:

> Any black poem with too much pluck to be Petrarchan
> That looks trouble, a problem, a challenge, an obstacle, or
> A bear in the eye and doesn't run, is an Affrilachian Sonnet. (12–14)

Through this final proclamation, Walker does not just transform the superficial structure of the sonnet, he also imbues the sonnet with a radical, new spirit. At the center of this sonnet is a love that is synonymous with courage, enacted by an artist who stares "a bear in the eye" and doesn't back down. The poem begins with an epigraph from the iconic sonnet "If We Must Die" by Claude McKay: "Though far outnumbered let us show us brave." McKay's sonnets serve as the paradigmatic example of the creative fortitude that animates the Affrilachian sonnet. For Walker, a sonnet is a bold and daring endeavor; it acts even as it contemplates, it labors as it sings.

While "Gunning for Bear" branches outward, connecting Affrilachian identity to an expansive transnational network of artistic innovation, Maggie Anderson draws on the domestic sphere, excavating her family history in "Sonnet for Her Labor" (*p. 86*). For Anderson, who was born in New York but moved to West Virginia at the age of thirteen, Appalachia's position on the outskirts of American society has served as a source of both creative inspiration and freedom. In an interview with John Hoppenthaler, Anderson discusses how marginality has fueled her creative process: "Living in the margins for much of my life (as a woman, as a lesbian, and as a poet with deep roots in Appalachia) I have come to (or have had to) understand the possibilities that can come from living on the edges, with little side trips to the mainstream from time to time" ("Maggie Anderson Interview"). Although Anderson typically writes in free verse in a colloquial style and has even expressed suspicion about the exclusivity of formal verse, she has also composed several sonnets during her career including "Sonnet for Her Labor," published in her *A Space Filled with Moving* (1992). This sonnet is one of her most celebrated works and has been anthologized in several collections of Appalachian and working-class literature.

"Sonnet for Her Labor" is a poem about invisibility—the invisible labor and invisible lives of Appalachian women—a portrait of her Aunt Nita's life and death, encapsulated within fourteen lines. The first eight lines of the sonnet establish the setting, both physical and emotional. Nita's daily life is relegated to the domestic sphere, her vision constrained by the surrounding mountains: "My Aunt Nita's kitchen was immaculate and dark, / and she was always bending to the sink" (lines 1–2). Yet it is not only the shadow of Laurel Mountain but the looming presence of extractive industry that impinges on the home, as the "coal dust" brought in by the men each day tarnishes the home and must be wiped away from countertops. Nita's daily life consists of cooking and cleaning, but in the third quatrain, the domestic routine is problematized by Nita's death, which is described as subtly as all the details in the poem, from mixing batter to hauling water. The sonnet moves from cleaning to cooking to death seamlessly. The enjambment between the ninth and tenth lines carries one day into the next, giving the sense of the inevitable movement of time: "One March evening, after cleaning, / she lay down to rest and died."). The drama of the volta is minimized, maximizing the emotional impact. The cause of death is not discussed. This is an elegy, but there is no raging against the dying light; Nita's death is the problem of the poem, yet the language used to describe it is quiet and unexceptional. Her death is as ordinary as her daily labor.

Following the rhyme scheme of the Shakespearean sonnet while actively stripping the poem of literary pretension, Anderson honors Nita's life not only in the poem's content but through its aesthetic. Anderson uses slant rhyme and enjambment, which give the poem a prosaic, imperfect feel that creates a tension between the conversational tone and the carefully crafted form. The story behind the construction of the sonnet also illustrates how Anderson's writing process was dialogical and collaborative, inviting Nita's voice into the work. Regarding the sonnet, Anderson recounts: "My Aunt Nita was the one in my family who showed the most interest in my writing. She liked to read my poems (my poems from high school English classes—my bad adolescent love poems!) but she always wondered why my poems did not rhyme. Years after her death, I decided to write a poem to honor her and the life of hard labor she lived for only 52 years. Of course, *this* poem would have to rhyme" (Letter to Margaret Voorhees, 17 May 2009; qtd. in Voorhees). The push and pull between the direct rhyme and off rhyme exhibits respect for Nita's aesthetic wishes while also enacting moments of poetic rebellion, paralleling the tension between the power of the central figure and the containment of her mind and body trapped within patriarchal structures. In the final couplet, Anderson introduces another shift in the poem, as the speaker steps outside the interior space of the home and reflects on Nita's life from an omniscient perspective. Denise Levertov observes that the goal of the poem "is to awaken sleepers by other means than shock" (412). The final couplet of Anderson's sonnet does this magnificently as it grapples with the enormity of Nita's life and death: "No one said a word to her. All that food / And cleanliness. No one ever told her it was good" (lines 13–14). Anderson resists forgetting but also refuses to romanticize or construct a hagiography. The sonnet does not build to a grand crescendo in the final couplet but instead resolves as humbly as Nita's life.

According to poet Diane Wakoski, "American poets celebrate their differences (regional and otherwise) and almost always connect them to the bigger myths of the culture." While Frank X Walker and Maggie Anderson begin with the specificity of Appalachia as a starting point, their sonnets interrogate power and history in American society more broadly. Yusef Komunyakaa observes that American poets "internalize the landscape, how we see and face the world, that's the lens we see through. Again, this idea of celebrating and confronting, that's part of it as well." It is in this lyrical gesture of "celebrating and confronting" that these unique sonnets by Walker and Anderson emerge, affirming the dignity and diversity of Appalachian subjects and stories.

Works Cited

"Affrilachian Poets Defined." *Affrilachian Poets*, libraryguides.berea.edu/c.php?g=816791&p=6039891#s-lg-box-19202550.

Anderson, Maggie. "Maggie Anderson Interview with John Hoppenthaler." *Connotation Press: An Online Artifact*, Nov. 2017, www.connotationpress.com/hoppenthaler-s-congeries/2017/november-2017/3128-maggie-anderson-poetry.

———. "Sonnet for Her Labor." *Windfall: New and Selected Poems*. U of Pittsburgh P, 2000.

———. *A Space Filled with Moving*. U of Pittsburgh P, 1992.

Coal Black Voices. Directed by Jean Donohue and Fred Johnson. Produced by Frank X Walker. Media Working Group, 2006.

Eller, Ronald D. Foreword. *Back Talk from Appalachia: Confronting Stereotypes*. Edited by Dwight Billings, Gurney Norman, and Katherine Ledford. UP of Kentucky, 2001, pp. ix–xi.

Komunyakaa, Yusef. "What Is It to Be an American?" Interview by Ishion Hutchinson. *Poets.org*, Academy of American Poets, 14 Oct. 2016, poets.org/text/yusef-komunyakaa-and-ishion-hutchinson-what-it-be-american.

Levertov, Denise. "Statement on Poetics." *The New American Poetry, 1945–1960*, edited by Donald Allen. University of California Press, 1999, pp. 411–12.

Scott, Rebecca. *Removing Mountains: Extracting Nature and Identity in the Appalachian Coalfields*. U of Minnesota P, 2010.

Spriggs, Bianca Lynne, and Jeremy Paden, editors. *Black Bone: 25 Years of the Affrilachian Poets*. UP of Kentucky, 2018.

Umar, Akhira. "'We're Here': Affrilachians Make Visible the African Americans in Appalachia." *Kentucky Kernel*, 17 Mar. 2020, www.kykernel.com/lifestyle/were-here-affrilachian-poets-make-visible-the-african-americans-in-appalachia/article_548beae8-68a2-11ea-a0dc-43ed6436c238.html.

Voorhees, Kathryn. "Maggie Anderson: Appalachian and (Almost) Uncorseted," *Mezzo Cammin, Women Poets Timeline Project*, www.mezzocammin.com/timeline/timeline.php?vol=timeline&iss=1900&cat=40&page=Anderson.

Wakoski, Diane. "Q & A American Poetry: Diane Wakoski." *Poetry Society of America*, poetrysociety.org/features/q-a-american-poetry-1/diane-wakoski.

Walker, Frank X. *Affrilachia*. Old Cove Press, 2000.

———. *Buffalo Dance: The Journey of York*. UP of Kentucky, 2004.

———. "Gunning for Bear." *The Affrilachian Sonnets*. Larkspur Press, 2016.

———. "An Interview with Frank X Walker." An Interview by Jabari Asim. *The Crisis* (Baltimore, MD), vol. 20, no. 3, 2013, pp. 32–33.

———. "'Still Chasing These Words': A Conversation with Frank X Walker." Interview by Bruce Dick and Forrest Yerman. *Appalachian Journal*, vol. 38, no. 4, 2011, pp. 408–22. *JSTOR*, www.jstor.org/stable/41320269.

Subverting the Tradition in *The Tradition*

Jericho Brown's Reconceptualization of the Sonnet

MICHAEL DUMANIS

In a 2019 conversation with Candace Williams in *The Rumpus*, poet Jericho Brown declares that he is "completely in love and obsessed with the sonnet.... I mean, I'm educated in the sonnet. It's been pushed down my throat the entirety of my life. There's something in me that doesn't like that, and doesn't trust that, because I'm a rebellious human being. I need to be a rebellious human being because I'm black and gay in this nation and in this world which has not been good to me or anybody like me. I have this responsibility to be skeptical, even of what I love."

Three years earlier, in the Spring 2016 issue of *Bennington Review*, Brown published a fourteen-line poem that was not included in his subsequent Pulitzer Prize–winning collection *The Tradition*. Here is the poem in its entirety:

Independence

I am not your Thomas Jefferson.
I am not your Thomas Jefferson.
I am not your Thomas Jefferson.
I am not your Thomas Jefferson.

I am not your Thomas Jefferson.
I am not your Thomas Jefferson.
I am not your Thomas Jefferson.
I am not your Thomas Jefferson.

> I am not your Thomas Jefferson
> I am not your Thomas Jefferson.
> I am not your Thomas Jefferson.
> I am not your Thomas Jefferson.
>
> Watch me fuck up your architecture
> Just as I built Monticello with my hands.

    The poem's architecture has much in common with the architecture of an English sonnet—three quatrains followed by a couplet, a declarative rhetoric, a synthesis of the poem in the final two lines. The regular rhyme-like repetition of the first twelve lines also serves to create a metrical pattern, albeit a trochaic tetrameter—*I*-am *not*-your *Tho*-mas *Jeff*-er-son—rather than an iambic pentameter. This poem recalls the Terrance Hayes's "Sonnet" from *Hip Logic*, which repeats the line "We sliced the watermelon into smiles," without volta or variation, fourteen times. In Hayes's poem, however, the first-person collective point of view asserts identity through the continual action of slicing the watermelon. By contrast, Brown's speaker asserts his identity through telling us who he is not—and also through one past action: the actual physical labor that is neither credited nor rewarded when the neoclassical architect of Monticello and America get to inhabit and claim ownership over what is considered Jefferson's particular home (though of course plenty of slaves resided on the estate as well).

    In the poem's closing, an opposition is set up between "your architecture," the preconceived blueprint, and "my hands," the means by which something is actually made. Monticello, with its lofty, evocative name of Italian origin, connotes a stately work in a grand tradition. What Jefferson is ultimately most famous for is a declaration, a speech act through which he asserts liberty from an oppressive ruler. This new declaration in verse not only asserts independence from tyranny but also refuses to be conscripted into the American project, committed instead to subverting it and making it its own.

    In this sense, the vulgarity, "fuck up," at the poem's close demonstrates full linguistic freedom and a break from constraint and convention. When the speaker asks the putative descendants of Thomas Jefferson to watch him "fuck up" their architecture, he is referring not only to the physical structure of Monticello but also the sociopolitical architecture of a nation that creates a space easier for some to inhabit than others as well as to the architecture of a poem. The speaker not only destabilizes and challenges a historical tradition where workers were enslaved and devalued while slaveowners were heralded as visionary architects but also subverts the closed poetic form par excellence of Western tradition, queering the sonnet by rejecting the customary linear argument of its quatrains, flipping the meter from iambic to trochaic and refusing the expected end rhyme in the couplet.

There is a sexual dimension to this sonnet as well, a promise of ravishment. The words that break us free of the poem's first twelve lines are literally "watch me fuck." The speaker will not reveal himself through abstractions or naming but rather through the operations of the body. Following this, the emphasis moves from the conceptual (architecture) to the physical—"Monticello," "my hands." We transition from the voyeurism of the penultimate line to the labor of the last, through the correlative conjunction "just as," in which it's hard not to also hear "justice." Meanwhile the spondee "*fuck up*" actually messes up the otherwise trochaic patterning of its line (*watch* me...*ar*-chi-*tec*-ture).

The reader, particularly if they are hearing the poem read out loud, not just seeing it on the page, only discovers that "Independence" is a sonnet with the closing couplet. There is no overt indication of the poem's form in its preceding twelve lines. The same can be said of "The Tradition" *(p. 113)* the title poem of Jericho Brown's latest book, which begins with the planting of flowers and swerves at the end into an enumeration of the dead. The sonnet's caesura-heavy last line—"*John Crawford. Eric Garner. Mike Brown.*"—is comprised of the names of three Black American men murdered by the police. Mike Brown's surname rhymes with "cut down" in the preceding line, a phrase that seems to be about flowers in a garden being culled until the final line's devastating revelation. Prior to the rhyming couplet, "The Tradition" doesn't overtly announce itself as a sonnet—although there are structural elements that elegantly delineate quatrain groupings within the block stanza: the first lines of the first two quatrains begin with the italicized names of flowers, and the first two quatrains' last lines also end with the italicized names of flowers. The ninth line ("Men like me and my brothers filmed...") breaks the pattern, a volta of sorts, beginning a sentence that stretches through five of the remaining six lines of the poem, speeding up through shorter lineation and abrupt enjambment. This mirrors the action of the poem's second half, where a video of the blooming flowers is shot, then sped up, evoking recent videos capturing the killings of Black men by police. The final line reverts to the use of italic, though the flowers have blossomed into men cut down in their prime.

The triad of men at the sonnet's close echoes the triad of flowers that begin the poem in the similarly caesura-heavy first line of fragments. The words of the last line are clipped, guttural, culturally American, final in their brevity and abruptness. By contrast, the flowers in the first line are Latinate, polysyllabic, euphonious rather than mournful: "*Aster. Nasturtium. Delphinium.*" The sonnet that ends with a rhyming couplet begins with a rhymelike pattern of assonance, where the sound of the word "aster" is replicated immediately in the first two syllables of "nasturtium," and the last syllable of "nasturtium" is echoed in the end of "delphinium." And yet the sonnet's final line changes the significance of the named flowers, turning them from opulent decorative flourishes into a funereal display, and the poem into a dirge.

The classical, sophisticated-sounding names of the flowers in the first line make the men who garden falsely assume that planting these beautiful-sounding flowers would give them possession, agency, power over the land and their destinies: "We thought / Fingers in dirt meant it was our dirt, learning / Names... in elements classical / Philosophers said could change us." As in "Independence," an opposition is set up between those performing manual labor and those who profit from its spoils: those with their "fingers in dirt" versus the property holder, an invisible landowner who presumably has no physical contact with the soil. The gaze is toward the bounty of Heaven, with "*Aster*" and later "*Star Gazer*" and later "*Cosmos*" evoking the celestial, and even the "*Delphi*" within "*Delphinium*" gesturing toward the ancient Greek sanctuary sacred to Apollo. Yet this is a poem not of transcendence but rather of Apocalypse, a poem "where the world ends." Significantly, the last flower planted at the close of the first eight lines is "*Baby's breath.*" Life begins, the video speeds up, and we read the names of the men who have died.

The title "The Tradition" suggests a multiplicity of traditions at once. There is the historical lineage of men who create beautiful gardens that are not for them to inhabit and enjoy, generations of unheralded anonymous men—first the "dead fathers" who toiled in the fields and now their children dying under an even hotter sun—men who erect Monticellos for the pleasure and possession of others. There is the tradition in this country of de jure slavery and then the de facto enslavement and subjugation that followed it, and the tradition of treating Black lives as less significant and, in the scheme of things, anonymous (until the poem insists on leaving us with the dead sons' names). There is also the received European, then American, and then, as a means of decolonization, African American tradition of sonnet writing in which the master's tools are used to dismantle the master's house, in which the sonnet form is put to new use, distorted, fucked up, repurposed.

Of the multiple fourteen-line poems within Brown's *The Tradition*, particularly striking is Brown's invented sonnet variant, the duplex, a form that Brown describes as part sonnet, part ghazal, part blues—marrying the quintessential Western form with the quintessential Urdu and Persian form and a quintessentially African American form. There are five duplexes in the book, the fifth a cento assembled from Brown's other duplexes. In an interview I conducted with Brown for *Bennington Review* before the book's publication, he said:

> Here are some of the questions I was asking myself. What does a sonnet have to do with anybody's content? And if the presumed content of a sonnet is that it's a love poem, how do I subvert that? How do I trick that out? And how do I nevertheless make it a love poem? And if I'm Jericho Brown, what is a Jericho Brown sonnet? That gave rise to my desire to create a new form for this book, which is the duplex.... I do feel like a bit of a mutt in the world. I feel like a person who is hard to understand, given our clichés and stereotypes about people. So I wanted a form that in my head was black and queer and Southern... Since I am carrying these truths in this body as one, how do I get a form that is many forms?

The duplex, or as he called it, the Jericho Brown sonnet, is also a mutt. (See *p. 112* for a related poem by Brown.) Its fourteen lines are organized into seven discrete closed couplets, every other one indented as though in call and response. The first line of each couplet approximates or repeats verbatim the last line of the couplet before it, so that their end words echo. The closed couplets, as in a ghazal, behave as though they can be their own two-line poems, only linked to the other couplets through the repeating diction that holds them together. As a result, the effect is decidedly nonlinear, fragmentary, disjunctive, destabilizing, protean. The indentation of alternating couplets further reinforces a sense of slippage, instability, and turning. In a way, the duplex recalls yet another non-Western form, the pantoum, since lines from one stanza are repeated in the next stanza, acquiring new significance as the text around them changes, and each step forward is partially undone, until we end up where we began, a circular journey.

One of Brown's duplexes also begins the way a ghazal traditionally does, with a *matla*, a first couplet using the same end word in both of its lines: "Don't accuse me of sleeping with your man / When I didn't know you had a man." In a poem about homosexual encounter, the phrasing of the first couplet literally lays one man underneath another. The second couplet, which partners the second line of the first couplet with a new line ("The moon flowed above the city's blackout") lays the end word "man" over "blackout," a word that merges blackness with "out" in its modern connotation. In the poem's last couplet—"What's yours at home is a wolf in my city. /You can't accuse me of sleeping with a man," the speaker's lover transforms, through the wildness of his sexuality, into a wolf, which absolves the speaker from the accusation—from the lover's partner and implicitly from a homophobic society at large—that he is sleeping with another man. The poem also uses the duplex's repetitive diction and recontextualizing couplets to emphasize the likeness of speaker and lover. Both are overly young and unreasonable. In this instance, as elsewhere in Brown's duplex sonnets, the couplets begin to take on the properties of coupling, two lines held together, then one line leaving its partner for a new couplet.

The type of dwelling this duplex form is named after is a bit of a mutt as well, one's own home but really half of a home, sharing a wall and a yard with another, a space that is simultaneously discrete and communal, a site of economic liminality where one is no longer in a landlord's apartment but not entirely on one's own. It seems no accident that the first of the duplexes in the collection begins by explicitly connecting the structure of poetry to the structure of a house: "A poem is a gesture toward home."

Brown's duplexes engage in Shakespearean reversals, chiasmus, and double entendre. For instance, in the line "No sound beating ends where it began" in the first duplex in the collection, "sound" can be the noun and "beating" can be the word modifying the sound, so that the sentence asserts that music takes you from one place to another. And simultaneously "beating" is the noun and "sound" is a modifier for the violence, as earlier in that same duplex "my tall father / Hit hard as a hailstorm. He'd leave marks." In his *Bennington Review* interview, Brown goes on to say of the duplex, "It rhymes because you're repeating the lines, and it turns, so it's definitely a sonnet. Part of the reason why I wanted to invent a form is because I want full participation for myself, but also for anyone who's writing after me, in the tradition. And the way that you become a part of it is that you literally deal with it. You participate by writing in received forms, but also by creating forms for others to receive, and also by subverting forms, by thumbing your nose at them."

Works Cited

Brown, Jericho. "Independence." *Bennington Review*, issue 1, Apr. 2016, www.benningtonreview.org/brown.

———. *The Tradition*. Copper Canyon Press, 2019.

Dumanis, Michael. "Jericho Brown in Conversation with Michael Dumanis." *Bennington Review*, issue 6, 2019, www.benningtonreview.org/jericho-brown-interview.

Hayes, Terrance. "Sonnet." *Hip Logic*. Penguin Books, 2002, p. 13.

Williams, Candace. "Gutting the Sonnet: A Conversation with Jericho Brown." *The Rumpus*, 1 April 2019, therumpus.net/2019/04/the-rumpus-interview-with-jericho-brown/.

Deafing the Sonnet

MEG DAY

Creative writing, as both a field and an industry, is steeped in ableism and audism. That is, it prioritizes nondisabled, neurotypical poets and poems and pretends we are neither present as your contemporaries nor holding the whole of the canon on our shoulders, rooted as we are—Blind, Deaf, and Mad among us—in the very bedrock of lyric history. And despite our belief in the capacity of literature to teach empathy and drain ignorance, poetics reiterates ableism and audism at rates and in ways that, while creative, rival Hollywood. We have mythologized hearing poet Allen Ginsburg as the father of American Sign Language poetry and honored countless collections—by nondisabled poets borrowing Deaf and disabled experiences—with the field's most respected awards. We are ground zero for blind love, deaf heaven, phantom limbs, and paralyzing—no, crippling—fear.

Contemporary poetics has taught us to anticipate a nondisabled readership or no readership at all. The irony, of course, is that nondisabled writers are the ones to join our disabled lineage of dis-kin such as Homer and Milton, Dostoyevsky and Borges, Woolf, Joyce, O'Connor, Lorde, Butler—I could keep going, but I don't have to: if one in five Americans is disabled, then I'm already speaking to my kin and comrades. We're here, despite the illusion that erases us.

In this essay, I wish to be a poet and not a scholar, which is to say I wish to speak more to the *making* aspect of poetic craft and less to the *made* thing of literature. As a Deaf poet who is also queer and trans, I wish to take a break from being analyzed by that which already dictates so much of my creative mind and the ways it is permitted to move on and off the page. But I resist, in particular, the critical gaze that evaluates one's capacity for participation in poetics; one might assume—based on popular, phonocentric definitions of poetry, or the Norton Anthology's table of contents—that Deaf poets writing in English simply don't exist. I wish to passively refute that idea with the fact of my corporeal form, so that we might engage actively instead in what might be possible when Deaf and disabled poets are not regulated by the limitations of the nondisabled imagination and allowed, without having to reiterate our existence, to freely make.

There is not enough space in this essay for me to lead you gently through a Disability 101 primer, so let's just assume we are in agreement about the following: "disability" is not a bad word; disabled lives are essential, not expendable, and absolutely worth living and protecting; disabled pride includes resisting the cure model that seeks to eliminate us and therefore resists the contemporary eugenics movement, which stretches from the medical industrial complex through to the academic one and right into poetics; disabled people should be the ones to tell our own stories and be participants in legislation that impacts our lived realities; and accommodations, while often treated as a privilege and a burden, are not only a legal obligation but a human right.

This essay is meant to be about Deafing the sonnet. But the problem with Deafing the sonnet is that I would have to then concede that the sonnet is first and foremost a hearing form. And why shouldn't it be? Aren't they all? Doesn't all of poetics rest on the assumption that lineation and meter set poetry apart from prose by prioritizing musicality and sound? In Hirsch's *The Essential Poet's Glossary*, the entry on sound poetry reads, "Sound is crucial to poetry and thus, in one sense, all poetry is sound poetry, except, perhaps, deaf poetry" (Hirsch 299). But there is no entry on deaf poetry, which is a digression we don't have space for. So, implies without imagination, sound is crucial to poetry. And don't hearing people assume that Deaf people have no access to or concept of sound? And even if we did, certainly we were not the ones to invent poetic form. Right?

Eugenics is, first and foremost, a kind of thinking. As a young poet, I was told—as I imagine many young poets are instructed—I must master the sonnet. And in the same breath, I was told I would never get it right because I can't hear rhymes and I can't scan for meter by ear. There is a difference between difficulty and inaccessibility. There is a difference between challenge and exclusion. The academy disagrees, obviously, because the academy pursues capitalistic perceptions of value and worth via rigor and standardization, valorizing the overcoming narrative with the lie of bootstraps in hand. The academy charges you money to prove you are disabled enough to require reasonable accommodations, but then punishes you for costing them money in order to receive what is perceived as an advantage over others.

And so what does this have to do with the sonnet? After years of late nights in graduate lounges memorizing lists of hearing rhymes, trying to get the vowels on the page to match the vowels in my mouth so my mind might replicate them fluently and exactly? If it is that there is a difference between difficulty and inaccessibility, then there is a difference between the American sonnet and the hearing one. It's just one way—but likely the most popular—in which the joy and power and potential of inherited poetic form has been weaponized to gatekeep Deaf poets writing in English from inclusion through anything but Hirsch's nonindexed afterthought. If mastery of the sonnet remains a steadfast and sometimes compulsory membership admission to participation in American poetics, then so be it. We will Deaf the sonnet, or we will prove it has been Deaf all along:

One: To engage the sonnet is to engage in a conversation with history. I refuse to imagine there is no Deaf sonnet before me. I refuse to imagine there were no Deaf hands in the baton pass between Giacomo da Lentini and me. And look: only six pages deep on the google search and Keats is translating the sixteenth century's Pierre de Ronsard, who left the military for poetry because of his deafness. And look: he's writing sonnets.

Two: As a Deaf American living in a phonocentric, audist country obsessed with sonics and frustrated by any minor inconvenience, repetition is my birthright. *What did you say? I'm sorry, what did you say? I missed that—what did you say?* Hearing babies are taught ASL; Deaf babies are implanted with cochlear implants; you can major in American Sign Language, but I can't get an interpreter for my course on genealogy of the lyric. Everything is a slant rhyme when you're Deaf, even the politics that dictate your exclusion. Over and over. *Abab. Cdcd.* We know this pattern by heart.

Three: The sonnet, as it turns out, is a really lovely and torqued version of the traditional and ableist narrative arc: rising action, climax, then resolution. Have a problem? Fix it. Have a disability? Eliminate it. Eugenics is first and foremost a way of thinking. But the sonnet asks questions, turns inward for answers. The sonnet—forgive me for personifying it so liberally—turns but trusts itself. Can change. Has pride.

Four: The sonnet is received, like any fixed form, as a material consideration in poetics; if you can imbue in the very structure of things—the corporeal form—a reminder of its origins and its makeup, then you can avoid, as I have attempted, wasting time reiterating your own existence and instead get down to the things you wish to say.

Which is why, five: Deaf poets should simply choose new ears. I have one set, given at birth, that engage the hearing invention of silence in complex and felt ways. But as they say, if you don't have homemade, store bought is fine: so I have another set of ears that make me cyborg, digitally connecting me to more and different interpretations of vibration and pitch, certain voices on certain words. I have another—a far more comprehensive set!—in whatever vessel arrives as my ASL interpreter, whether it be in flesh or on screen. And I have one more still in my hearing service dog who keeps me out of danger and notifies me of both dropped keys and approaching cars. Accommodation is a way of life. Access is a human right. And so why shouldn't I borrow a hearing poet's ear the way Deaf poet Sam Rush recently said they borrowed a hearing bystander's ear at a party to confirm there was no one in the bathroom. Why shouldn't we make access our own form and then receive it?

For the last two years, I've been working with Donne's *La Corona*, and by "working with" I mean I've been using his sonnets as an auditory prosthetic and pirating his rhymes. Donne as assistive device, as a fifth set of ears, is newer territory for me; I'm more comfortable writing queer responses into his framework or finding respite in the company of another poet frustrated by existence. In my poem "Boy Corona" (*p. 124*), I've pirated and preserved all of Donne's end rhymes for the entirety of the crown: if I use Donne's rhyme, I don't have to worry about not knowing anymore how these words actually sound; I can focus on what it does to the body, how it transforms. Given that my sequence is also about the push-pull of a kind of physical conversion, the exercise is, like my own language, multimodal and expansively nonlinear. Donne as adaptive device is Donne as accommodation. Donne as a new pair of ears that allows me to engage my Deaf reality enough that I do not have to saturate the poem with the difficulty of audism or argue with you about whether poetics requires a hearing version of sonics to succeed. Instead, my Deafness remains in the materiality of the sonnet itself.

Donne's rhymes, like the best of adaptive technology, are reliable—reliable but inventive, exact but also bent, staggered, hidden. Why can't we have fun? He braids rhymes through syllabic packing and pairs it with audacious metaphysical conceits, pushing the words into the line instead of letting the line push back. The body is in control, not sound. And so it is with the sonnet: Donne's internal rhyme unifies the verse and creates in the reader a sense of expansion—both of breath and of self—and yet it is firmly contained. The experience of reading Donne's sonnets aloud without sound is transformative. I'm a student of it. I want to better understand how he makes the body sing.

Working with Donne's sonnets gives me great flexibility in that way: he develops his arguments through paradox, he exhausts rhymes until they are made anew. His rhythm is strong lined and beat centered, and yet his poems make manifest the momentariness of being alive and being in love with being alive and of being ashamed of being so in love with being alive given how awful—and often godforsaken—it turns out embodiment can be.

And so perhaps Deafing the sonnet is really just a matter of casting off the internalized poetic ableism of phonocentrism and pursuing accommodation through what we know best: the phenomenology of rhyme, the felt sense of it, the kind the sonnet offers. What it means to wrap your mouth around a vowel that repeats, tightly, and turns on itself. A new understanding of *internal* rhyme—not the hidden repetition of assonance, but the linked physical movements such recurrence requires. The sonnet is a form that provides textual access to what we are: a living body, a container of conflicting truths, tightly packed in the push-pull of call and response, of repetition that reflects back a bodily reality, even if you can't hear it. Hillary Gravendyk reminds us that we should avoid "lurking critical notions that a poetics of disability is always registering the effects of an 'unstated physical condition'" (7), and while I wish for a poetics in which self-assertion and disclosure of disability is not necessary to avoid nondisabled appropriation or ongoing erasure, perhaps accommodation—as a form—can register not just the effects but the presence and the power and the joy of our unstated but obvious Deaf and disabled existence and can allow, too, the mastery and pleasure of participating in a revised poetics that has been rightfully ours all along.

Works Cited

Day, Meg. "Boy Corona." *The Nation*, Feb. 3, 2021, www.thenation.com/article/culture/boy-corona/.

Gravendyk, Hillary. "Chronic Poetics." *Journal of Modern Literature*, vol. 38, no. 1, 2014, pp. 1–19. *JSTOR*, www.jstor.org/stable/10.2979/jmodelite.38.1.1.

Hirsch, Edward. *The Essential Poet's Glossary*. Houghton Mifflin Harcourt, 2017.

WRESTLING WITH
THE LANGUAGE AND TRADITION

Wrestling with the Language

Dialect and Form in Paul Laurence Dunbar

HOLLIS ROBBINS

In London on January 28, 1898, Paul Laurence Dunbar wrote to Alice Moore, his fiancée, that he had finished a dialect love poem called "Dely" and now wanted to try his hand "at a bit of a sonnet" to "balance the effect" (Metcalf 403). I've long wondered what he meant by this. For Dunbar—the first important poet whose sonnets feature a distinctly Black American voice—to provide a clear link between his dialect practice and sonnet practice is provocative and, perhaps, unintuitive. Sonnets are widely considered a prestigious form and dialect a lowly genre. What does it mean that they are related? The strict systems of rules, voice, and tradition of sonnets and dialect may be closer than we've assumed, and we might attend more closely to literary associations in dialect.

The orthographic task for dialect writers is to produce a set of directions—grapholects—for a reader to read aloud that seem to be a reproduction of another person's voice. The term "grapholect" refers to the visual aspects of both standard English and literary dialect. You have to deconstruct and sonically reconstruct words. Good writers of dialect understand how educated readers translate dialect grapholects by working to sound out unorthodox spellings and unexpected apostrophes. Poets use eye rhymes, spelling "is" as "iz" or "once" as "wunce," which not only makes things easy to sound out but also alerts readers that the tone of the speech is something other than conventional speech.

The reader of dialect focuses on denotation through sounding out a dialect grapholect ("ez yushal" for "as usual") rather than connotation. Readers preoccupied with denotation tend to suppress paths of connotation. Dialect poetry thus seems deceptively simple; the "unlettered" poetic speaker produced by reading aloud seems unconnected from literary history. The language of dialect poetry is in a state of play but not a play that suggests literary associations. Black dialect poetry is accordingly not critiqued as part of a historical tradition or studied by scholars for allusions or influences.

Consider the dialect love poem that Dunbar hoped to "balance" with a sonnet. "Dely," published several months after the date of the letter in *Lyrics of the Hearthside* (1899), is seven eight-line stanzas of alternating trochaic tetrameter/trimeter about a dark woman the speaker compares to a summer's day:

> Jes' lak toddy wahms you thoo'
> Sets yo' haid a reelin',
> Meks you ovah good and new,
> Dat 's de way I 's feelin'.
> Seems to me hit 's summah time,
> Dough hit's wintah reely,
> I' s a feelin' jes' dat prime—
> An' huh name is Dely.
>
> Dis hyeah love 's a cu'rus thing,
> Changes 'roun' de season,
> Meks you sad or meks you sing,
> 'Dout no urfly reason. (187)

We see painstaking adherence to strict rules of punctuation and orthographic tradition, even while grammar and spelling appear to flout convention. Consider what's spelled right: "you" and "new." Look at the words "haid" and "season" and "urfly." Both "season" (and "reason") are spelled correctly to make pronunciation by an educated reader invariant. The goal is reducing variation in spoken performance. The more successful dialect is—the more it can be read smoothly—the more production will seem like reproduction.

"Dely" fits the courtly love tradition well. The poetic speaker praises his beloved, compares her to a warming liquor, a summer's day, and, in the last stanza, a religious blessing. Why isn't it read that way? Did Dunbar know it wouldn't be read as a kind of sonnet? Did he understand all too well that tradition in dialect poetry resides in simply standardizing the grapholects ("dat" for "that," "huh" for "her") rather than reading for allusion or historical tradition?

The sonnet Dunbar wrote the following day was most likely "Sonnet (On an Old Book with Uncut Leaves)," also published in *Lyrics of the Hearthside* (83). If the speaker of "Dely" memorializes his beloved by titling the poem after her and repeating her name seven times, he articulates no interest in the permanence of publishing—there's no Shakespearean gesture of words lasting though eternity or earning a readership or public acclaim. The speaker of "Sonnet," by contrast, clearly holds the counterbalancing view:

> Emblem of blasted hope and lost desire,
> No finger ever traced thy yellow page
> Save Time's. Thou hast not wrought to noble rage
> The hearts thou wouldst have stirred. Not any fire

Consider the moments of nonstandard diction in the lines that follow:

> Save sad flames set to light a funeral pyre.
> Dost thou suggest. Nay—impotent in age,
> Unsought, thou holdst a corner of the state
> And ceasest even dumbly to aspire.
>
> How different was the thought of him that writ. (lines 5—9)

"Dost," "holdst," "ceasest" are deployed for poetic effect, creating a speaker who would use such archaisms. The difference between "writ" and "'roun'" in "Dely" is that "writ" presents itself as a deliberate poetic choice by the poet and "'roun'" presents itself as the voice of an unlettered speaker transcribed by the poet. Erik Redling notes that scholars "often attach the authenticity of a black literary dialect to the ethnic black identity of its author.... Black dialect grapholects thus can frequently be perceived as serving as metaphors of black vernacular speech and its attributes" (26). This is an understatement. For a poet such as Dunbar, experienced in dialect grapholect, there is no essential difference between "I's feelin'" in "Dely" and "thou holdst"—neither represents standard English speech: both are poetic conventions. But a sonnet in his day didn't expect the reader to reproduce the speaker's voice the way a dialect poem does, and this is the balancing act with which Dunbar was wrestling.

It is likely that Charles Chesnutt read Dunbar's sonnet and patterned his short story, "Baxter's Procrustes" (1904), about a book with uncut leaves, on it. Dunbar writes in his letters to Alice about his competition with Chesnutt on who was becoming the more important dialect writer. "Houghton, Mifflin & Co are to bring out a collection of 'Conjure stories' of his," Dunbar writes in September 1898, hearing that Chesnutt had been encouraged by *Atlantic* editor Walter Hines Page to write more dialect work, including a novel. "Now that another Richmond has come on—a Richmond so worthy of my mettle, too,—'a horse, a horse!'" (Metcalf 681–82), turning to Shakespeare to describe a dialect competition. Dunbar read widely and deeply while honing his dialect craft: Shakespeare, the Brownings, Bulwer-Lytton, Rider Haggard, Kipling, Riley, Tennyson, Whittier, Longfellow. Shakespeare helps the process of writing dialect.

Why was Dunbar balancing dialect with sonnet writing? He was not schooled in iambic meter and his early sonnets are halting and unsure. Wallace Thurman noted that Dunbar was "the first Negro poet to be emancipated from Methodism, the first American Negro poet who did not depend on a Wesleyan hymn-book for inspiration and vocabulary" (556). Unburdened by schooling in iambs, Darwin Turner argues, Dunbar experimented with dactylic feet and "favored patterns of skillfully combined anapests and iambs," particularly in his dialect productions (62). Dunbar's facility with iambic pentameter came after his dialect exertions and his experiments in finding the right voice for his sonnet speakers. "I did the sonnet yesterday which I said I was going to do and I want to write another today," Dunbar writes to Alice the day after writing the sonnet on uncut leaves (Metcalf 410). That sonnet was probably "Harriet Beecher Stowe," published in *Century Magazine* (1898):

> She told the story, and the whole world wept
> At wrongs and cruelties it had not known
> But for this fearless woman's voice alone.
> She spoke to consciences that long had slept:
> ....
> And blest be she who in our weakness came—

Something crucial occurs in this poem. The pronoun "our" in the twelfth line quietly indicates the poetic speaker's membership in the race liberated by Stowe's writings. The speaker is Black. The speaker of Dunbar's most important sonnet, "Robert Gould Shaw" (1900), is racially unmarked, but the enslaved Americans Shaw fought to free are marked by punctuation to guide pronunciation—one might say dialect—in the second quatrain:

> What bade thee hear the voice and rise elate,
> Leave home and kindred and thy spicy loaves
> To lead th' unlettered and despisèd droves
> To manhood's home and thunder at the gate?

Note "th' unlettered." Something similar occurs in the last quatrain of "Douglass" (1903):

> Oh, for thy voice high-sounding o'er the storm,
> For thy strong arm to guide the shivering bark,
> The blast-defying power of thy form,
> To give us comfort through the lonely dark.

With "o'er" we see how Dunbar's dialect work inflects his sonnets. Given Dunbar's long experience removing letters and replacing them with apostrophes in dialect poetry to "mimic" nonstandard speech, can we really see the practice used in "traditional" poetic practice as simply removing syllables for metrical consistency?

Recent criticism of Dunbar's work by Nadia Nurhussein and others has uprooted and rerooted Dunbar in an era of dialect writing as poetic craft, allowing us to question a reciprocal relationship between the craft of writing dialect and writing sonnets. Nurhussein argues that treating "dialect orthography as a mask under which authenticity can be found also simplifies the subtleties of orthographic experimentation, and what it can manipulate readers into doing" (92). Nurhussein interrogates Alice's claim that "it was in the pure English poems that [Dunbar] expressed himself" (97). In his letters to Alice, Paul Dunbar rarely uses dialect; when he does, he typically puts it in quotation marks: "I recited 'po'try' about you," he writes at one point (Metcalf 192). More pointedly, Dunbar defends his dialect writing in a letter to Frederick Douglass's widow, Helen, saying "I am sorry to find among intelligent people those who are unable to differentiate dialect as a philological branch from the burlesque of Negro minstrelsy."[1] For Dunbar, dialect and sonnets clearly balance each other.

In the 1950s, William Carlos Williams claimed that the diversity of American language encouraged poets to "*listen* to the language" (290). "Dialect is the mobile phase, the changing phase, the productive phase—as their languages were to Chaucer, Shakespeare, Dante, Rabelais in their day" (291). Listening to language offers an "opportunity to expand the structure, the basis, the actual making of the poem" (291). For Dunbar, dialect needed to be recast as poetry that would be read for allusion and tradition and permanence. What better to balance the effect than a sonnet?

Note

1. Paul Laurence Dunbar to Helen Douglass, October 22, 1896, in Paul Laurence Dunbar Papers, Ohio Historical Society; quoted in Bruce, 60.

Works Cited

Bruce, Dickson. *Black American Writing from the Nadir: The Evolution of a Literary Tradition*. Louisiana State UP, 1992.

Dunbar, Paul Laurence. "Douglass." *Lyrics of Love and Laughter*. Dodd, Mead, 1903, pp. 127–28.

———. "Harriet Beecher Stowe." *Century Magazine*, vol. 57 (Nov. 1898), p. 61.

———. *Lyrics of the Hearthside*. Dodd, Mead, 1899.

———. "Robert Gould Shaw." *Atlantic Monthly*, Oct. 1900, p. 488.

Metcalf, Eugene Wesley. *The Letters of Paul and Alice Dunbar: A Private History*. U of California P, 1973.

Nurhussein, Nadia. *Rhetorics of Literacy: The Cultivation of American Dialect Poetry*. Ohio State UP, 2013.

Redling, Erik. *"Speaking of Dialect": Translating Charles W. Chesnutt's Conjure Tales into Postmodern Systems of Signification*. Königshausen and Neumann, 2006.

Thurman, Wallace. "Negro Poets and Their Poetry," *The Bookman*, July 1928, p. 556.

Turner, Darwin T., "Paul Laurence Dunbar: The Poet and the Myths." *A Singer in the Dawn: Reinterpretations of Paul Laurence Dunbar*, edited by Jay Martin. Dodd, Mead, 1975; 59–74.

Williams, William Carlos, "The Poem as a Field of Action" (1948). *Selected Essays of William Carlos Williams*, New Directions (1954).

Sensuous Waste in the Sonnets of Frederick Goddard Tuckerman

ZOË POLLAK

> Yet in such waste, no waste the soul descries
> ....
> For whoso waiteth, long & patiently,
> Will see a movement stirring at his feet
> —Tuckerman, Sonnet V:II

If asked to find a poem that ends with an image of the repellent, most of us would probably turn to a modernist anthology or a twenty-first-century chapbook.[1] Yet writing alongside luminaries of the American Renaissance was a poet who depicted all varieties of natural waste and decay in his sonnets. Many of these sonnets close with arresting portrayals of detritus and disintegration: the "molasses" tint of insect effluvia (III:4, 120), the shattered jaw of a horse (II:V, 102), a berry's blood-colored "spit" (II:1, 99). But while his 1860 volume of poems was esteemed by such icons as Emerson, Hawthorne, Tennyson, and Frost, Frederick Goddard Tuckerman's name rarely appears on contemporary college syllabi. Among the hundreds of poetry anthologies published in the past thirty years, I have located only three that accord Tuckerman significant space in their pages.[2] In fact, the majority of scholars specializing in nineteenth-century American literature remain unfamiliar with his work.

Tuckerman was born in 1821 to a prosperous Boston family of professors, composers, and critics. He attended Harvard alongside Thomas Wentworth Higginson and was mentored by the sonneteering mystic Jones Very. Because he did not need to earn a living, Tuckerman could afford to give up a career in law just one year into practicing. He chose instead to devote his days to literature, astronomy, and botany, pursuing his research with an empirical rigor and methodical eye akin to Henry Thoreau, his famous poet-naturalist contemporary. At twenty-six, Tuckerman moved to the leafy town of Greenfield and spent the rest of his life within eighteen miles of Emily Dickinson.

Just before the Civil War, as Dickinson began replacing the exclamation points that end-stopped much of her early poetry with the trademark dashes that forestall resolution, Tuckerman published a series of Petrarchan sonnets whose closing lines are equally suspended. His formal poetics depart radically from those of his anglophone predecessors and contemporaries, the majority of whom let the prototypical sonnet's logical structure guide their poems from a scene-setting description or observation to an internal meditation, question, or pronouncement. Consider, for instance, one of Charlotte Smith's elegiac sonnets, which begins by depicting the cycle of the seasons but shifts at the volta to lament that human happiness, by contrast, has "no second spring" ("Sonnet I" 57). Or take as example a sonnet of Wordsworth's, which presents the image of a stream, "humbler far than aught," and develops the stream into a vehicle to reflect the speaker's own currents of thought and memory ("A little unpretending Rill" 8).

Tuckerman reversed this trajectory. Rather than transition from description to allegory, he regularly began sonnets with broadly framed metaphysical questions and assertions, only to leave the reader with a graphic image of waste whose connection to the poems' initial musings remains suggestively and unnervingly elusive. One such sonnet, "Sometimes I walk where the deep water dips" (*p. 14*), opens with the restless poet-speaker muttering to himself as he paces the contour of a shore. Its final lines deliver the reader to the face of a rock covered in bird droppings: "And hard like this I stand, & beaten & blind / This desolate rock with lichens rusted over / Hoar with salt sleet, & chalkings of the birds (III:X, 123). To reserve a sonnet's closing lines for a depiction of shit—to speak plainly—is unconventional. Granted, Tuckerman sanitizes the excrement by portraying it as "chalkings." Yet the precision with which his euphemism captures the guano's tint and texture on the rock is immersive and even beautiful; it is almost as though the droppings are artistic creations within the sonnet in addition to comprising the poet's medium. What is the reader supposed to feel on encountering such a sensuous canvas?

Tuckerman's dense coats of description—the russet blooms of lichen, the encrusted salt, the streaks of bird guano—render the rock's surface anything but "desolate." It is as if the speaker started out with a conceit he had intended to develop, one that draws a parallel between the battered stone and his weathered spirit but then gets carried away by his own powers of illustration. The lichen sprouts like rust on the stone, the salt sleet collects as if it were gray hair, and the droppings line the rock's face like chalk. None of these descriptions masquerades as empirical or objective; each contains a metaphor that calls as much attention to the poet's eye as it does to the stone's surface. Yet each visual is too specific and too successful at conjuring an actual rock to function solely in service of the figural. Indeed, by the end of the sonnet Tuckerman has muddied the distinction between tenor and vehicle: right after comparing the rock to his speaker (the rock's "long caverns" are "like tears in me"), he likens his speaker to the rock ("And hard like this I stand"). Where do these circular gestures lead? There is no dearth of routes in this poem; the speaker traces the line of the shore, the path of his "wandering words," the stone's long and worming caverns, and the chalklike streaks on the rock. But unlike Smith's and Wordsworth's sonnets, which make their philosophical destinations transparent, Tuckerman moves toward blindness and opacity.

Traditionally, we would be able to turn to the Petrarchan sonnet's internal structure for prosodic if not thematic closure: a conventional octave offers two airtight, back-to-back envelope rhymes followed by the interwoven chords that seal the sestet. In Tuckerman's case, we cannot rest on this fundamental architecture. Instead, his variant of the form in Sonnet III:X forces us to reach across Italianate divisions and strain to connect the octave's "words" with the sestet's "birds" to make a rhyme that, with one more intervening line, would echo too faintly to be heard. It becomes difficult, then, to reconcile this sonnet's precariously extended aural resolution with what one critic called Tuckerman's "truncated" imagistic endings (Golden 392). Without any exegetical guidance from the sonnet's wayward, fancy-driven speaker, the responsibility of achieving closure lies with the reader. So although we catch ample evidence of the artist's hand in his sharp-eyed metaphors, his habit of drawing back and detaching his speaker from the scene, coupled with the sonnet's attenuated architectonics, thwarts straightforward resolve.

Many of Tuckerman's closing images "trip the reader head and foremost into the boundless," as Frost said all poetry should, and leave us to deal with our discomfort (ix). In a different sonnet from *Poems*, the speaker himself feels his hopes beginning to "decay" as the object he longs to clutch escapes his grasp, and so he "shudder[s] and turn[s] away" from the scene in front of him (II:XXI, 109). Like this speaker, nineteenth-century reviewers balked at Tuckerman's penchant for the elusive. "We fear we must class among those qualities that recommend his lines to the *Atlantic* a certain vagueness and dreaminess that leaves the reader in doubt as to the writer's meaning," remarked the *Springfield Republican*.³ One hundred years later readers still construed Tuckerman's rejection of closure as inexpert and even unintentional. "Hardly one of the sonnets is entirely satisfactory," the *Times Literary Supplement* determined, because "a rhyme misses or the metre falters or—the worst of his faults—the meaning fades into obscurity" (England 251). Yet Tuckerman's insistence on maintaining the kind of ambiguity that can frustrate critics creates possibility. His Keatsian negative capability allows us space to approach his retreats as invitations. In the case of the bird chalkings sonnet, it is up to us whether we choose to settle on the rock face for its own sake or to "stumble" and "strive," like the speaker, to decipher the writing on the wall (or the chalkings on the rock). The conclusion's only certainty is its open-endedness.

To close a sonnet on a subject as unsavory as excrement, without providing an interpretive framework to guide the reader toward resolve, is unparalleled in Tuckerman's century. All the more striking, then, that his sonnet series teems with poems whose speakers meditate on metaphysical abstractions only to stop abruptly on concrete descriptions of spoilage and excretions. These endings are often the most immersive portions of the sonnets, frequently engaging multiple senses at once. One sonnet, for instance, leaves the reader in front of a "smouldering pit" of "Blackness and scalding stench" (II:III, 100), while another ends on a masticated stem of grass "not to be put back, / Or swallow'd in, but sputter'd from the lip!" (V:X, 137). These depictions form the last words of the sonnets' last lines, and without a concluding figurative gesture or the tempering touch of allegory, it is hard to know how to read them.

Tuckerman's imagistic closing lines suspend time within the poem and unmoor us from the sonnet's conventional progression. His choice to culminate on substances that are either disintegrating or physically processed and expelled, without assimilating them into the sonnet's archetypal psychological sequence, forces us to sit with these raw subjects and struggle over how to (re)digest them if we wish to reach a sense of closure. The fact that these poems impart the impression of having stopped prematurely when they conclude on subjects that epitomize cessation is deeply and productively ironic. And given that most of Tuckerman's sonnets end with distended rhymes and dissolving Petrarchan divisions, one could say that the forms themselves are de-composing. His decision to halt poems on subjects that exemplify conclusion—what could embody expiration more excessively than waste and decay?—only emphasizes how pointedly open-ended his sonnets really are.

Whether describing "bypast" flowers that "redden again in rain" (II:V, 101) or a night heron "wading in the swamp" and lighting up the water with the disintegrating feathers on her "phosphoric breast" (V:II, 133), Tuckerman portrays decay as vivid, brilliant, and always active in its existence. His endings suggest that what appears to be spent or finished still has room for development and growth, whether the object of attention be a solid becoming liquid, mold blooming on a surface, or the shifting emotional and philosophical impressions such transformations produce in the reader. These closing lines of Tuckerman's, which make waste unfamiliar and astonishing, encourage us to regard subjects we reflexively avoid and to linger on them longer than we would in life. By retraining us to dignify aspects of nature we normally dismiss, Tuckerman—himself overlooked in the poetic canon—expands the conceptual limits and ethical strictures bounding nineteenth-century anglophone sonnet decorum.

Notes

1. This essay has been crucially informed by conversations with John Shoptaw on Tuckerman and the sonnet.

2. See John Hollander's *American Poetry: The Nineteenth Century* (New York: Literary Classics, 1993), Jonathan Bean's *Three American Poets: Melville, Tuckerman and Robinson* (London: Penguin Books, 2003), and David Bromwich's *American Sonnets: An Anthology* (New York: Library of America, 2007).

3. Houghton MS AM 1349, vol. 9, Houghton Library, Harvard University, Cambridge MA.

Works Cited

England, Eugene. *Beyond Romanticism: Tuckerman's Life and Poetry*. State U of New York P, 1991.

Frost, Robert. *The Notebooks of Robert Frost*. Edited by Robert Faggen. The Belknap Press of Harvard UP, 2006.

Golden, Samuel. "Frederick Goddard Tuckerman: A Neglected Poet." *The New England Quarterly*, vol. 29, no. 3, 1956, pp. 381–93.

Smith, Charlotte. *Charlotte Smith: Major Poetic Works*. Edited by Claire Knowles and Ingrid Horrocks, Broadview Press, 2017.

Tuckerman, Frederick Goddard. Frederick Goddard Tuckerman compositions. Houghton Library, Harvard University, Cambridge, MA.

———. *Selected Poems of Frederick Goddard Tuckerman*. Edited by Ben Mazer. Harvard UP, 2010.

Wordsworth, William. *The Sonnets of William Wordsworth*. London: Moxon, 1838.

Frost in the Company of Shakespeare and Wordsworth

JONATHAN F. S. POST

"Frost is the author of the best sonnets in English written by someone who was not Shakespeare" (xx–xxi). The statement, by David Bromwich, is the kind of summary judgment that the present volume might very well seek to unsettle. But the remark invites us to think what might be the connection between Frost and Shakespeare (and later in this essay with Wordsworth), and here the assertion becomes more interesting.

Frost seems to have signaled this possibility early on in his career in the opening poem from his first volume of poetry, *A Boy's Will* (1913). A sonnet in couplets, "Into My Own" alludes to the familiar line from Shakespeare's Sonnet 116 that closes off the third quatrain of that poem on a triumphantly transcendent note: "Love alters not with his brief hours and weeks, / But bears it out even to the edge of doom." Shakespeare then concludes with the famous couplet: "If this be error and upon me proved, / I never writ, nor no man ever loved." Frost opens his sonnet with a more modest gesture, but the echo from 116 is still striking. He speaks of his wish that "those dark trees"

> So old and firm they scarcely show the breeze,
> Were not, as 'twere, the merest mask of gloom,
> But stretched away unto the edge of doom. (15)

Frost's sonnet turns out to be an early vocational promise, not a statement about love's enduring power but about his own "will" going forward in his evocative pursuit of "those dark trees." If we hear the under-song of Shakespeare's sonnet, we also hear some youthful chutzpah in Frost, even if we leave aside the reference to his forebear's first name in the book's title, *A Boy's Will*.

After several centuries of near silence, Shakespeare's sonnets were everywhere in the nineteenth and early twentieth centuries, but where to go in Frost after this venturesome beginning is more puzzling. Bromwich turns to the late sonnet, "The Silken Tent" from *A Witness Tree* (1942), remarking that "in tone and theme" the poem has "something in common" with Shakespeare's Sonnet 18 ("Shall I compare thee to a summer's day"), but he quickly slides off the comparison with Shakespeare in favor of a learned reference to a line from Donne's *The First Anniversary*—hardly a sonnet—and then leaves Shakespeare altogether by offering a subtle reading of the reflexive imagery in Frost's poem. He concludes with a reference to Keats, reminding us of the curious and capacious ways that sonnets keep invoking their past (xxi, xxii).

What brings Shakespeare's Sonnet 18 to mind is not just the mention of comparable summery seasons but the figure of comparison itself: "Shall I *compare* thee to a summer's day?"; "She is *as* in a field a silken tent" (italics mine). After which, with the seed planted, Frost invites us to witness, in that remarkable, spiraling, single sentence of fourteen lines, the poet hoisting his own perfectly structured Shakespearean sonnet: three quatrains in alternating rhymes; syntax loosely connected by conjunctions at the end of the first and second quatrains; the quiet, momentary pause at the end of the third quatrain, with Frost then tenderly tightening the knot in the concluding couplet, lightly rhyming "air" with "aware." So familiar, yet so different.

What these two poems have in common is a tone of whimsicality ("capriciousness" is Frost's word) generated by the idea of making similes for love, with Frost playing wistfully with the form Shakespeare made famous and also making something of his own out of it. A woman is like a silken tent in a summer breeze, which is like a poem, the one you are reading, and perhaps other sonnets you have read. The poem contains, in fact, a reminiscence of Sonnet 116 in its reference to the tent pole as a "pinnacle to heavenward [that] signifies the sureness of the soul" (302), but Frost's treatment of this figure, the figure his poem makes, is not so determinedly for all time, but, as he famously said, "a momentary stay against confusion" (777). We might think of "The Silken Tent" as a light and delightful airing, more song than sonnet. Aware of his predecessor's weightiness with words, a weight only made greater by the intervening three centuries—"So long as men can breathe or eyes can see, / So long lives this, and this gives life to thee" (302)—Frost chooses a more oblique way of saying as much. His "Silken Tent" is a silken twist.

As in so many things, so in his sonnets Frost is the craftiest of poets. His most Shakespearean themed sonnet, "Design," with its echoes of *Macbeth*, is impeccably Petrarchan; his most Miltonic of sonnets, "Never Again Would Bird's Song Be the Same," about Eve in the garden, is indelibly Shakespearean. Frost clearly enjoyed playing with the sonnet form—"Acquainted with the Night" is a sonnet in terza rima that ultimately forms a rondeau—creating something new out of this witch's broth of old, snatching at a phrase or two, throwing a line to an earlier poem. On the basis of echoes and allusions, he seems to have read Shakespeare's sonnets selectively, even narrowly: darkly in "Design," but no Dark Lady; youthfully at times, as in "Meeting and Passing," but with no "fair youth" or youths or rival poets or Horatian monumentalizing in mind, just the occasional celebration of an unnamed beloved, as in "The Silken Tent," or the named bird or brook as he glances sideways and earthily at traditional representations of inspiration and in doing so, distinctly flattens Shakespeare's sometimes (to the modern ear) overemphatic final couplets.

Frost's Shakespearean interests were largely those of the pastoralist. But they sometimes tended in the direction of the georgic, toward work, not just play, as in "The Silken Tent," occasionally echoing the agrarian note sounded in Shakespeare's early sonnets (Sonnets 1–17), when Shakespeare enjoins his young aristocratic subject to marry: "For where is she so fair whose uneared womb / Disdains the tillage of thy husbandry?" (Sonnet 3). Frost's response to this country sentiment is anything but crude, except perhaps in title only. "Putting in the Seed"—about husbandry in the double sense, and wifery too—is his down-to-earth version of Sonnet 116, Shakespeare's "marriage" poem beginning "Let me not to the marriage of true minds / Admit impediments."

Frost's poem is, at first blush, something of a tug-of-war between husband and wife, between work and play. He's at work and so is she, he outside, she inside. The first line abruptly but informally asserting her agency—"You come to fetch me from my work tonight / When supper's on the table"—might seem a small threat to his autonomy but then gets quickly reconceived as she comes forth in his imagination to enjoy her own solitude and "become like me" (120). Are there impediments, we wonder? Perhaps, but of a playful, ritualistic sort, a kind of game they perform every spring evening that only serves to align the two more strongly in their parallel desire for the world of nature and each other. The line that links them inseparably is the "heavily accented elevated" ninth: "Slave to a springtime passion for the earth" (Poirier 219). It brings the first sentence to a firm conclusion, the two now as one, in this world. The line also introduces a new rhyme into the poem as it strengthens its Shakespearean path of alternating rhymes with a concluding couplet. It's at once a slight hiccup and a true volta. Passion then comes bodying forth in the remaining lines—"How love burns through the Putting in the Seed / On through the watching for that early birth" (lines 10–11)—as it rarely does in Shakespeare's sonnets:

> When, just as the soil tarnishes with weed,
> The sturdy seedling with arched body comes
> Shouldering its way and shedding the earth crumbs. (lines 12–14)

This is marriage that is earthy and fruitful, no tillage or pillage. The sonnet is likewise a sturdy seedling, arching its back slightly at the ninth line, paying homage to the modified Shakespearean form that gave it being, and then shouldering its way like a newborn into full view as it sheds the earth crumbs. If a sonnet can be courtly, likened to a silk tent, so can it sprout up from below. In either case, we're involved in a world of making and remaking. In this, I'm reminded of James Longenbach's comment at the end of *How Poems Get Made* (2018). "Lyric knowledge comes to us in language that is flowing because it has flown" (152). His terms are likewise borrowed. They come from Elizabeth Bishop's "At the Fishhouses," but they capture the sense of the ongoing usability, the historicity, of the English language, not just the diction that gets differently inflected in the vernacular, of which Frost was a master, but also the language of forms too. In this regard, it is worth noting that Shakespeare did not invent the sonnet form in English that now bears his name, but any poet using it, especially a poet as alert as Frost, is conscious of the Shakespeare legacy.

To look beyond Shakespeare is inevitably to encounter Wordsworth in literary history as well as in Frost and to widen our understanding of Frost's sonnet practice. As he noted in a letter of 1917 to Lewis B. Chase, "but before all write me as one who cares most of Shakespearean and Wordsworthian sonnets" (qtd. in Maxson 9). 1917 was also the year that Eliot published *Prufrock and Other Observations*. No doubt Frost's attraction to a sometimes truculent Wordsworth ("Scorn not the Sonnet") sprang from his own defensive attitude toward the form. He was alone among his modernist contemporaries in not only exploring the sonnet but giving it a significant, if not quite canonical, place among his lyrics and dramatic poems. To the eight uncollected sonnets, mainly from his early years, another twenty-eight or so appeared in print, and a familiar handful are always included in the anthologies. Likewise, Wordsworth's undeviating adherence to the Petrarchan format helped to balance out Shakespeare's equally undeviating use of quatrains in alternating rhyme, just as Wordsworth's recouping of the political sonnet from Milton pointed the way beyond the amatory in Frost: toward the commendatory ("A Soldier"), the topical ("The Investment"), and the satirical ("The Planners"). And so too Wordsworth's elevation of nature as a subject matter ("It is a beauteous evening, calm and free") and of the sonnet form itself ("Nuns Fret Not at Their Convent's Narrow Room") must have pleased Frost, whose "Design" calls attention to the sonnet's carefully structured dimensions.

Still, as with Shakespeare, differences abound. Frost's sonnets are more restless and experimental than Wordsworth's, less chaste in their use of form, mode of expression, and subject matter, darker and more deeply ironic in their response to nature. "The sonnet is the strictest form I have behaved in, and that mainly by pretending it wasn't a sonnet," Frost wrote to Louis Untermeyer late in life (qtd. in Maxson 6). One senses the wink here. "Behaved in" is an odd metaphor that captures a sense of the unruly in Frost as much as it points to the restrictions he otherwise pretended weren't there. "There is a singer everyone has heard, / Loud, a mid-summer and a mid-wood bird." This is the familiar, somewhat devious opening couplet of "The Oven Bird." Everyone? Well, every ear-reader for sure,[1] thanks to the percussive stress on "Loud" in the trochaic inversion at the beginning of the second line. Frost's oven bird then quickly declines from singer to the prosiest of birds. "He says that leaves are old and that for flowers / Mid-summer is to spring as one to ten" (116). Nothing flowery here, as the steady beat of Frost's folksy pentameter line, from one to ten, prevents the passing of the seasons from swelling with sentiment. Not that the poetic is altogether out of reach, but it is notably framed in speech not song. "He says... He says... He says." And when it comes time for the poem's volta, if that's what it is, Frost gives us one of the most deadpan turns in English: "And comes that other fall we name the fall." The punctuated full stop here, in the service of a further emphasis on speech, keeps the sestet close to the ground. "The bird would cease and be as other birds / But that he knows in singing not to sing." He behaves, in other words, by not behaving like the usual bird (or poet) fitted out for country verse, and he does so, moreover, in a sonnet with a specially designed, unusual rhyme scheme.

In more than one sense, Frost's poem, like the bird, is a prosaic counter to the Romantic sublime, and much of the poem's meaning—and the pleasure we take in it—is in accounting for this deviation from convention. Must a poem about a bird be a celebration of song? Or can it hew closer to the ground, like the scythe in "Mowing," another of Frost's celebrated poems, and unruly in a different fashion. It is a sonnet that doesn't quite behave like one, and not just because it plunges headlong into its subject by overriding the pentameter line until the fifth. Its rhymes are arbitrary, unpatterned (Maxson 7). This departure from the norm has encouraged purists like H. A Maxson to discount both this poem and, for reasons of length, the fifteen-line "Hyla Brook" (*p. 28*), from sonnet consideration. But anthologists and critics rarely do. An intensely appreciative Seamus Heaney, for one, throws the rulebook aside in declaring that the melodies of "Mowing" "possess a wonderful justifying force, and remind us that Frost is, among other things, one of the most irresistible masters of the sonnets in the language" (291). Irresistible in part because Frost resists the high-flown rhetoric of a Wordsworth, as does Heaney, so influenced by Frost, not by rejecting it outright but by folding it into the less poetic vocalizations where the truth of the poem is said to reside: "It was no dream of the gift of idle hours / Or easy gold at the hand of fay or elf: / Anything more than the truth would have seemed too weak / To the earnest love that laid the swale in rows" (Frost 26).

Frost is speaking about the mower, but he might as well be addressing the poet and his "earnest love" for his craft as lays his lines in rows, even those that sometimes deliberately contain "feeble-pointed spikes of flowers." In almost every memorable sonnet, Frost says something memorable about what he is saying in the poem. In "The Oven Bird": "The question that he frames in all but words / Is what to make of a diminished thing"(116). Not just the diminished thing that is the mid-summer, mid-wood bird, but the sonnet form as Frost employs it. For that reason perhaps and not because of an inability to count, readers often accord "Hyla Brook" sonnet status, so busy is it talking, in complex rhyming patterns, about the subject of inspiration right from the beginning: "By June our brook's run out of song and speed" (115). The question, again, is what to make of a diminished thing, a question amplified three-fold in the sestet of "Design" and underlying as well the challenge implied in the title to that gorgeous late sonnet, "Never again would bird's song be the same" (275). Why not, we ask? And Frost tells us, elaborating on a series of thoughts about the relationship between words and sound, speech and song, which goes to the core of his aesthetics.

In these self-reflections on the sonnet, Frost reminds us of the reflexive Wordsworth of "Nuns Fret Not," who celebrates the sonnet's safe space ("'twas pastime to be bound / Within the Sonnet's scanty plot of ground"

(5). But Frost's ruminations, like his scythe, are more glancing, less safe, his walls more porous than a convent's, admitting sounds that constantly disrupt the familiar patter of poetic feet. One way to think about the history of the sonnet is to regard key moments of transition in reshaping the courtly into the vernacular. Shakespeare represents one of these watersheds, more so than Sidney, Milton another (despite being quickly swept under the rug by Bromwich), and Frost yet another, in a variation on the Wordsworth of the *Lyrical Ballads*, by insisting that we hear the plain regional markings of a *New* England voice. Heaney understood as much about Frost's contribution when he invites us to participate in the opened ground of his own rich, northern Irish dialect in "The Glanmore Sonnets." But Heaney goes one step further. He insists that we attend to the excavation of words themselves and their change in meaning over time. The line of influence I am tracing here is one reason why Frost remains central to current sonnet practitioners who want to stamp the form with more than their own voice.

Note

1. Frost's concept of the "ear-reader" is developed by William H. Pritchard, "The Grip of Frost," *The Hudson Review*, vol. 29, summer 1976, 185–204.

Works Cited

Bromwich, David, editor. *American Sonnets: An Anthology*. New York: Library of America, 2007.

Frost, Robert. *Robert Frost: Collected Poems, Prose, and Plays*. Library of America, 1995.

Heaney, Seamus. "Above the Brim: On Robert Frost." *Salmagundi*, no. 88–89, fall 1990–winter 1991, pp. 275–94.

Longenbach, James. *How Poems Get Made*. W. W. Norton, 2018.

Maxson, H. A. *On the Sonnets of Robert Frost: A Critical Examination of the 37 Poems*. McFarland, 1997.

Poirier, Richard. *Robert Frost: The Work of Knowing*. 1977. Stanford UP, 1990.

Shakespeare, William. *The Complete Sonnets and Poems*. Edited by Colin Burrow, Oxford UP, 2002. Oxford World's Classics.

Wordsworth, William. *The Complete Sonnets of William Wordsworth*. Moxon, 1838.

Strange Voltas

MICHAEL THEUNE

Formally, virtually every sonnet is, at least in part, a concrete poem that looks like a sonnet. When one sees a block of text, one can tell pretty quickly whether it's a sonnet, or a near sonnet. A sonnet, however, is not only a formal but also a structural construct, if by structure one means, specifically, the pattern of a poem's turning. A sonnet in English consists not only fourteen lines of (perhaps) iambic pentameter (perhaps) in a rhyme scheme. A sonnet also contains at least one significant turn—a significant shift in rhetorical and/or dramatic trajectory—called a volta. Many commentators have recognized the importance of the volta to the sonnet. Paul Fussell states that the volta contributes "something indeed indispensable to [a sonnet's] action" (116). Phillis Levin even goes so far as to call the volta "the seat of [the sonnet's] soul" (xxxix).

Taking the volta into consideration, one sees a sonnet differently: not as a static block of text but as a reactor, catalyzing and channeling flows of linguistic energy. On a heat map showing where the dynamic action of a sonnet takes place, the white heat would be at the volta. Typically, this means that the heat map would glow brightest in the Petrarchan tradition at the turn from octave to sestet, or else, for a Shakespearean sonnet, at the turn into the final couplet.

Although this understanding advances conceptualization of the sonnet's workings, it still is too staid, nesting the crucial volta in some fairly predictable ways. Commentators are still coming to more systematically realize that—as the large-scale shift from its Italian to its English position indicates—the location of the volta has in fact long been not something settled but rather another occasion for poetic experimentation. In "On Sonnet Thought," Christina Pugh states, "Whether it occurs before the closing couplet in the Shakespearean sonnet, before the sestet in the Petrarchan scheme, or elsewhere in a sonnet, the *volta*'s often breathtakingly indefinable pivot remains a vital component of the governing structure" (361).

This essay will consider voltas that occur "elsewhere" in sonnets in order to demonstrate that even the placement of the turn has long offered opportunity for innovation and, in so doing, will offer new ways to appreciate some more recent American sonnets. It will reveal that, while sonnets always ask readers to expect the unexpected, readers need to be alert to the shifting volta, which not only amplifies surprise but also contributes greatly to a sonnet's signification by underscoring or undercutting—enacting or effacing—meaning.

Poets have been experimenting with the volta's location almost since the sonnet's birth. Much of the prose of Dante's *La Vita Nuova*—a sequence of poems to and about his beloved Beatrice along with a running commentary on the verse—involves the poet's explication of his poems, and this explication is largely specifically structural, helping readers to better engage the actual sinewy rhetorical and dramatic dynamism of the sequence's lyrics—most of which are sonnets—rather than merely impose stereotypical expectations on them. Translator Barbara Reynolds suggests that Dante is trying to instruct readers who are acquainted and preoccupied with the features of poetic form so they may read his poems more vitally and accurately. Reynolds states that Dante "evidently thinks it necessary to make clear to fellow-poets and instructed readers where the counter-divisions occur. Perhaps he considered that preoccupation with the *form* of poetry or with its embellishments was tending to obscure lucidity of thought" (18). Reynolds pursues this thinking, noting that Dante is offering readers a chance to read over his shoulder as he instructs, " 'What I want you to notice is the articulation of the thought-content, for this is by no means always identical with the structural [i.e., formal] articulation...' " (18).

Some canonical British poems include surprisingly situated voltas. George Herbert's "Prayer (I)" is one such poem. "Prayer (I)" dramatically enumerates the many things prayer might be and also endeavors to determine what prayer, in fact, is. The poem is not clear where it is going—indeed, it quickly comes to seem confused, lost in its own inventiveness, overwhelmed by possibilities. This sense is underscored by the fact that no significant turn occurs where it might be expected. The speaker's efforts, however, are not in vain: just a mere two words from the poem's end, there's a sudden comprehension: prayer is "something understood"—a profound, quieting miracle that echoes a prayer's ultimately submissive *so be it, Amen.*

William Wordsworth's "Surprised by Joy" offers another example. Early in his career, Wordsworth wrote a number of poems that expressed his exuberant reactions to the natural world. One such poem begins, "My heart leaps up when I behold / A rainbow in the sky." Wordsworth's "Surprised by Joy" opens with just such a moment, and then—in one of the earliest major turns in the history of the sonnet—the speaker turns to share his joy with a loved one (in this case, the poet's daughter Catherine) only to remember at the second line's "Oh!" that she is not there, that she has died. After this powerful turn away from the physical act of turning, the vast majority of the poem becomes an awful reckoning with the mind's ability to recuperate from and even take sublime pleasure after such loss. In this way, the sonnet, stunned and saddened but also wiser, enacts its own chastening.

While it might be tempting to create a tidy historical narrative by saying that, in a way similar to Shakespeare's remixing of Petrarchan sonnet structure, American sonneteers took the English sonnet and made it their own by experimenting in vastly new ways with the placement of the volta, this just is not the case. But it is the case that, even if not exactly pioneers when it comes to resettling the volta, American sonneteers—and very likely, sonneteers of other nationalities—continue the experiment, toying with where the volta occurs, playing with the sonnet's pattern of expectation to create new, special effects. Three examples follow.

Gwendolyn Brooks's "the rites for Cousin Vit" (*p. 54*) contains another of the earliest major voltas in a sonnet: it occurs about halfway through the second line. Initially, the reader learns that Cousin Vit—placed on a "casket-stand"—has died. However, "the rites for Cousin Vit" quickly leaves its elegiac mode to turn into a poem celebrating the life of Cousin Vit, a figure of vitality—she's portrayed as someone who loves to dance and socialize. The sonnet honors its subject by both stating that her liveliness cannot be contained—"She rises in the sunshine. There she goes"—and enacting it: Vit is so powerful she even breaks the sonnet structure, forcing the sonnet to turn almost immediately from death to resurrection.

Bernadette Mayer's "Sonnet (You jerk you didn't call me up)" (*p. 79*) initially offers some terrific torquing energy, though in some somewhat predictable ways. The speaker lambasts her (potentially soon-to-be former) lover for his inattentiveness. She complains that even other imperfect lovers such as the ancient Roman poet Catullus—who wrote a poem that begins "Odi et amo," "I hate and I love"—at least were still drawn into the drama of passion, unlike her stunted, sophomoric dude-bro, who seems willing to "settle for a couch / By a soporific color cable t.v. set" on which he watches *G.I. Joe* cartoons. The speaker uses this argument to try—at what turns out to be the sonnet's first big turn—to get the lover to "Wake up!" and then challenges him: either "make love" or settle in for another night of masturbation. Though the speaker says this cheekily as "or die at the hands of the Cobra Commander." Cobra Commander is the enemy of the cartoon hero G.I. Joe, and sex is sometimes referred to as *la petite mort*, the little death, so this playful allusion also can be read as onanistic: petite morting in hand-to-hand combat with the king of snakes.

So, by line 14, the traditional end of a sonnet, Mayer's poem is already sassy and hilarious and structurally gratifying. But then it gets even better. There's unresolved dramatic tension after the close of line 14: the sonnet actually waits for an answer! Nothing happens. Fed up, then, there's a final turn: "To make love, turn to page 121. / To die, turn to page 172." That is, the poem makes clear that if the dude-bro doesn't understand passion, perhaps he'll understand the language of a child's choose-your-own-adventure story. But of course, there's likely really no longer a choice: the speaker is through wasting time on someone she is clearly greater than and, so, over with.

Phillis Levin notes that "though a poet will sometimes seem to ignore the *volta*, its absence can take on meaning, as well—that is, if the poem already feels like a sonnet" (xxxix). Few engage the refusal to turn as obviously and as funnily as Ron Padgett in "Nothing in That Drawer." Padgett's sonnet consists of fourteen lines, each of which reads, simply, "Nothing in that drawer." Padgett's high-concept poem stays interesting for as long as it does mainly because its nullity intrigues in the sonnet's field of expectation. Each turn from line to line allows one to hope for something new to break the monotony, and beyond that, one may wish for a structural, voltaic turn at the octave's end or else heading into the couplet—or anywhere else, for that matter!—but it doesn't come. Padgett's nothingness is thus greatly amplified and transmuted into comedy by being played on the instrument of the sonnet's expectations.[1] Ellen Bryant Voigt states that "the sonnet's *volta*, or 'turn,' usually at line 9 or line 13, has become an inherent expectation for most short lyric poems" (164). While this certainly is correct, the fourteen-line poem generally is a clear formal indication that a reader is in the territory of the sonnet and therefore should be especially alert for turns, expecting the unexpected, prepared for structure's surprises. These dynamic actions might occur where long-standing traditions would place them—as Voigt writes, "usually at line 9 or line 13" (164)—but it also simply is the case that the history of sonnet writing is rife with important experiments in the placement of the volta. Sonneteers have long known of the volta's potency and therefore know of the power that can be generated by moving it around in the sonnet, or even, in Mayer's case, pushing it beyond the bounds of the sonnet altogether, or else, in Padgett's case, eliminating the volta and coyly using the sonnet's anticipation for the purpose of playful subversion.

Much more might be done to explore the dynamics of structural turning in sonnets, generally. How else do poets use the sonnet's patterned structural expectations to deliver their own singular surprises? How do poets orchestrate major and minor voltas in sonnets? Given the sonnet's brevity and the tendency to see—wherever they occur—one or two (or maybe three) significant turns in any one sonnet, is it possible, as poet Terrance Hayes suggests, that there could be a new kind of sonnet that could contain "a clamor / Of voltas" (*p. 105*).

When it comes to thinking specifically about the placement of the volta in the sonnet, more might be done, as well. Emerging poets need to recognize more fully the variety of options they have in terms of the location of the volta. By better understanding the dynamic, experimental nature of even this aspect of sonnet tradition, they will be better equipped to more fully participate in and continue to transform the sonnet's trajectory. Even expert commentators might be more attuned to experiments with and the effects of voltaic placement. In the excellent *The Making of a Sonnet*, editors Edward Hirsch and Eavan Boland include a section called "The Sonnet Goes to Different Lengths" to highlight the sonnet's formal variety (293–336). Although Hirsch and Boland thus recognize formal experiments with the sonnet, they do not in any way highlight structural experiments of the kind on display in this essay, and in fact, their discussions about the volta generally reinforce standard expectations: the turn will occur between octave and sestet, or final quatrain and couplet. There should, however, also be a selection of sonnets called "Strange Voltas," which gathers sonnets that experiment with the sonnet's structural components, including with where sonnets turn.

The poems gathered in this essay might be considered initial entries for just such a selection, one that will grow for each reader as they engage more sonnets and so encounter more specimens. An increased sensitivity to the effects of voltaic location might then be shared by all those who care about and work with contemporary sonnets and the sonnet tradition and thus lead to even more alert engagements and grander and/or subtler experiments.

Note

1. See also Rebecca Morgan Frank's discussion of this poem in her essay in this volume.

Works Cited

Brooks, Gwendolyn. "the rites for Cousin Vit." *Blacks*. Third World Press, 1987, p. 125.

Fussell, Paul. *Poetic Meter and Poetic Form*. Revised ed., McGraw-Hill, 1979.

Hayes, Terrance. "The song must be cultural, confessional, clear." *American Sonnets for My Past and Future Assassin*. Penguin Books, 2019, p. 46.

Herbert, George. "Prayer (I)." *The Temple: Sacred Poems and Private Ejaculations*. Ferrar, 1633, p. 43.

Hirsch, Edward, and Eavan Boland. *The Making of a Sonnet: A Norton Anthology*. W. W. Norton, 2009.

Levin, Phillis. Introduction. *The Penguin Book of the Sonnet: 500 Years of a Classic Tradition in English*. Penguin Books, 2001, pp. xxxvii–lxxiv.

Mayer, Bernadette. "Sonnet (You jerk you didn't call me up)." *A Bernadette Mayer Reader*. New Directions, 1992, p. 93.

Padgett, Ron. "Nothing in That Drawer." *Great Balls of Fire*. Coffee House Press, 1990, p. 5.

Pugh, Christina. "On Sonnet Thought." *Literary Imagination*, vol. 12, no. 3, Nov. 2010, pp. 356–64.

Reynolds, Barbara. Introduction. *La Vita Nuova* by Dante Alighieri. Translated by Barbara Reynolds, Penguin Books, 1969, pp. 11–25.

Voigt, Ellen Bryant. *The Art of Syntax: Rhythm of Thought, Rhythm of Song*. Graywolf Press, 2009.

Wordsworth, William. "My Heart Leaps Up." *Poems*. Vol 1. Longman, Hurst, Rees, Orme, and Brown, 1815, p. 3.

———. "Surprised by Joy." *Poems*. Vol 2. Longman, Hurst, Rees, Orme, and Brown, 1815, p. 191.

Partial Visibility

Short-Lined Sonnets

LESLEY WHEELER

For a short form, the sonnet makes an extraordinary amount of room for rebellion. The device of the volta presents an opportunity to overthrow established perspectives, metaphors, and meanings. The American sonnet has accrued a supplementary history of making struggle visible. The Black American sonnet epitomizes this through poems emphasizing liberty and transgression that chime with each other over centuries (Müller 6–8). Intersecting with Black poetry, sonnets of queer love manifest marginalized communities and marshal arguments for justice (Caplan 61–86). American sonnets of the last hundred years apply dissident spirit to the form itself through disorienting enjambments, destabilized meters, and slant rhymes. The sonnet's brevity presents another opportunity for disruption: it can correlate with experiences of smallness and secrecy. Elizabeth Bishop's "Sonnet" (*p. 48*) and Adrienne Su's "Four Sonnets about Food" (*p. 101*) render a brief form even briefer to represent cultures of silence.[1] These short-lined sonnets use negative space to imply the pressures on women to minimize their bodies and conceal desire. Refusing to be entirely seen by the sonnet, the authors find fresh ways of focusing on joy.

Bishop's "Sonnet" appeared in the *New Yorker* in 1979, three weeks after her death, and later in her *Collected Poems* (192). The title highlights the poem's resemblance to the inherited form but also draws attention to Bishop's transgressions. Composed in four-to-seven syllable lines, "Sonnet" uses five or six rhymes that are so slant—such as "mercury" and "bird"—that a reader might not register them if the poem were titled differently. As Lloyd Schwartz wrote in the *Atlantic*, internal rhyme is just as prominent as end rhyme. Further, most of the rhymes occur on unstressed syllables, contributing to the poem's falling rhythms. Trochees and dactyls predominate, although no pattern is consistent enough that "Sonnet" could be called metrical.

Further, Bishop relocates the volta. The first sentence of "Sonnet," beginning with the word "Caught" followed by an em dash, is comprised of six lines, and the second, beginning with the word "Freed" followed by an em dash, of eight. This inversion of octave and sestet is key to the poem's meaning. From her first collection forward, especially in "The Man-Moth" and "The Gentleman of Shalott," Bishop used "inversion," a sexology term indicating gender role reversal, to encode what readers might now call queerness. Inversion also enters the poem through a description of a mirror from whose beveled edges a "rainbow-bird" escapes, suddenly able to fly "wherever / it feels like." Ending on the word "gay" with an exclamation point, the poem is often read as a coming out poem.[2] Bishop's formal nonconformity and use of structural inversion reinforce that interpretation.

The imagery of Bishop's poem involves tools for measurement: spirit-level, compass, thermometer, and the mirror itself, a means for gauging proximity to ideals of beauty. First these devices trap the "creature divided," then they break, releasing exuberant energy. "Sonnet" imagines freedom from measure, including poetic measure, but Bishop does this by rendering the "narrow room" of the sonnet yet narrower.[3] Intensification of the form's compression somehow enables liberation, like a spring contracting so it can expand with greater force. Sonnets are always powered by concentration, but this tighter ratcheting evokes the concealment of the metaphorical closet and has a gendered element, reflecting pressure on women to occupy minimal space. Bishop imagines haunting then fleeing the thin edge of the sonnet's mirror, seeing the form but refusing to be seen by it.

Instead of mechanical metaphors, Adrienne Su invokes cooking's distillation processes to convey the power of smallness. Again, gender and sexuality are part of the soup. "Four Sonnets about Food" appears in Su's first book, *Middle Kingdom*, amid poems concerning marriage. The sonnets portray a domestic arrangement similar to heterosexual marriage, emphasizing constraints experienced by both partners but especially the woman speaker. Su gives constraint a visual marker by characterizing the relationship in the sonnets' only set of parentheses:

> (I say "him" only
> because it is a man
> in my house

>   who eats and a woman
>   who goes about
>   the matter of sustenance) (66)

He consumes food prepared by a woman. Su depicts love that seems to be defined by a traditional gender script: a woman stays home and cooks while a man commutes to earn money.

Sacrifice underwrites the woman's actions. Creatures die and become sustenance for a man referred to as a "mighty / predator," and Su calls dinner an "offering" (65–68). Further, she identifies with sacrificed animals in the lines "Who feeds / another is like bones / to him who eats" (66), echoing other poems in the book about girls slimming themselves down to a "bony" condition or responding to surveillance by diminishing themselves, as in "Eighteen-Year-Old Biography" (9). Self-reduction also manifests in the pronouns. Bishop's "Sonnet" never uses the first person. Likewise, Su avoids self-reference as the woman disappears into her task: scallops are seared and ginger grated without anyone claiming agency. This changes in the fourth sonnet, yet even there, the "I" is concerned with the speaker's future death and absence, when she won't be able to offer dinner or, metaphorically, her body. As in Bishop, this shiftiness suggests a "slippery and elusive" projection of self, but this time in relation to Asian American identity and literary traditions (Jeon 989). As Dorothy Wang writes, "the minority poet and subject is, in effect, split from herself, becoming both first and third person" (448).

In "Four Sonnets about Food," the lines are boiled down like "bird bones" used to make stock (65). The word "bird" brings an icon of lyric poetry into the kitchen, but this poet turns song into food by presenting single-sentence poems resembling recipes or menus. The self-effacing speaker harmonizes with the shortened lines. She is also rooted in a version of Chinese American womanhood that Su evokes as a learned performance. Earlier in this collection, "Miss Chang Is Missing" defines the stereotype:

>   dark-eyed, supernatural, ginseng-
>   otherworldly. Likely to one day
>   walk off the earth and into the sky. (20)

"Four Sonnets about Food" seems to comply with a pressure to diminish or vanish outright. "I can't always be," Su writes in the last sonnet of the sequence, foreshadowing death in the way she breaks the line.

Yet Su's "small soul" materializes into a "warm body" with a physical destiny in "red clay." She manifests tenderness by presenting her beloved with a nourishing meal instead of declarations. This final section also involves direct expression of emotion: "I am afraid," it begins. Su's grounding of the act of cooking in love constitutes a volta from the impersonality of the preceding sonnets, a turn between poems rather than within them. Through a potentially self-abnegating brevity, Su reverses the narrative she suggests elsewhere, beginning with invisibility and ending in embodied feeling. On the plate and in the poem, food appeals to the senses, conjuring physical presence despite the inevitability of loss. Su's elliptical verse emphasizes gesture over explanation.

Su and Bishop misuse the sonnet because poetry can only partially reveal love's largeness, which remains occluded or at least partly unspeakable. Identity, likewise, is incompletely legible, expressible mainly through exquisite control and self-limitation. In its partial mirroring of a well-known form, a short-lined sonnet uses negative space—the part of the line left unwritten—to imply forces arrayed against speech. Yet both these poems prioritize pleasure over critique. They offer resistance through concentrated and vibrantly colorful presence.

The compression experiment can be pushed even further. Seymour Mayne's "word sonnets," in an outer-limit example, consist of fourteen words. The sonnet, however, casts just the faintest shadow on Mayne's invention; without rhyme, meter, or turn, his poems resemble haiku. Bishop and Su encode their response to a challenging and potentially oppressive inheritance by rendering their resistance to tradition prominent, but it isn't total. Making space for queer love without shame and for the distilled power of smallness, they are virtuoso in defiance: super sonneteers.

Notes

1. Another practitioner of the "minimalist sonnet" is Mona Van Duyn; see *Firefall*, Knopf, 1993, p. 83n1.

2. See Brett C. Millier's discussion of the poem's "mischievously disguised confessions of alcoholism and homosexuality" in *Elizabeth Bishop: Life and the Memory of It*, U of California P, 1993, p. 546.

3. See Müller on the "long, influential tradition of conceiving the sonnet in spatial terms," a tendency crystallized by Wordsworth's "Nuns Fret Not at Their Convent's Narrow Room," p. 6.

Works Cited

Bishop, Elizabeth. *The Complete Poems 1927–1979*. Farrar, Straus, Giroux, 1979.

Caplan, David. *Questions of Possibility: Contemporary Poetry and Poetic Form*. Oxford UP, 2005.

Jeon, Joseph Jonghyun. "Asian American Poetry." *Cambridge History of American Poetry*, edited by Alfred Bendixen and Stephanie Burt. Cambridge UP, 2015, pp. 978–1002.

Millier, Brett C. *Elizabeth Bishop: Life and the Memory of It*. U of California P, 1993.

Müller, Timo. *The African American Sonnet: A Literary History*. UP of Mississippi, 2020.

Schwartz, Lloyd. "Elizabeth Bishop's 'Sonnet,' Introduction." *The Atlantic Online Poetry Pages: Soundings*, March 29, 2000, www.theatlantic.com/past/docs/unbound/poetry/soundings/bishop.htm.

Su, Adrienne. *Middle Kingdom*. Alice James Books, 1997.

Van Duyn, Mona. *Firefall*. Knopf, 1993.

Wang, Dorothy. "Asian American Poetry and the Politics of Form." *The Cambridge History of Asian American Literature*, edited by Rajini Srikanth and Min Song. Cambridge UP, 2015, pp. 437–53.

Sonnets and/as Boxes

Ken Taylor, Joseph Cornell, and the New Lyric Studies

NATE MICKELSON

A themed exhibition of Joseph Cornell's boxes opened at The Stable Gallery in New York City in December 1955. Titled "Winter Night Skies," the show featured boxes filled with cut-outs of astrological figures, star charts, wire grates, painted wooden dowels, drinking glasses, and other materials (Solomon 238–40; McShine, plates 210–15). Frank O'Hara, then a reviewer for *Art News*, responded by writing a fourteen-line poem titled after the artist (Gooch 260; Solomon 238). Organized in two equal sections, the poem approximates the elusive effects of looking at Cornell's work. The first half describes a kaleidoscopic scene where "violet / light pours" across a sky that is also a room (*Collected Poems* 237). In the second half, the poet finds himself "a little too / young to understand" the "near distances" the boxes contain (237). O'Hara gave instructions to print the poem "like boxes" (Solomon 238; O'Hara, *Collected Poems* 537). It appears in two equal sections with extra spacing to stretch the lines exactly square at the margins. Full sentences wrap across line endings with no observable patterns. If the poem is not quite a sonnet, it is also not quite a box. Despite its appearance on the page, "Joseph Cornell" lacks the conceptual dimensions of the artist's boxes. Rather than opening "near distances" for the reader to explore, syntax and typography signal that the poem should be read sequentially, from the beginning of line 1 to the end of line 14. As we follow its associative leaps, the poem stays on the page rather than entangling us in a more complex structure.

Ken Taylor takes up a similar experiment in his 2016 collection *self-portrait as joseph cornell*. The book features seventy Italian sonnets. Labeled as figures 1–70, each poem is printed on the right-hand side of a two-page spread with a title, caption, and checklist, like the wall labels in a gallery or museum, right-justified just below. The book is organized in three sections with headings borrowed from Cornell's works: "thimble forest"; "objects (roses des vents")"; and "habitat for a shooting gallery." The captions and checklists indicate overlapping groupings of poems and identify source materials ranging from personal memories to geographic locations to artistic influences. These elements and the collection's overall layout function as paratextual structures that provide supplemental coordinates for reading (Genette 407–10). By dispersing our attention from title to poem to caption to checklist, they entangle readers in experiences of associative looking. They invite us to look at the sonnets as if they were assemblages displayed in a gallery. We look at and into them, like O'Hara looking into Cornell's boxes, and involve ourselves in the "near distances" that emerge between their components.

The poem "first the trees, now this" appears under the label Fig. 16 in *self-portrait*. Like several others in the collection, it was published initially in a small magazine. (Taylor credits twenty-four different earlier venues on the collection's copyright page.) As a stand-alone sonnet, the poem assembles everyday impressions from a domestic scene. A father stands in his kitchen grinding walnuts while his daughters play in the yard. The father's reflections resolve, at the turn of the sestet, into parental responsibilities. He hears the younger girl, who had been playing with a neighbor, approach the other: "sister: *smell my face, i smell like boy*" (44, italics in original unless otherwise noted). This is the poem's concluding line. Taylor's repetition of "smell" and his elision of the article "a" before boy, reinforce the girls' playful innocence. These elements foreground the children's bodies and suggest complications of gender and sexuality. The line's tonal layering recalls the father's intuition, from the poem's opening lines, that the "shapes of leaves are trying to tell me / something different" (44). His daughter's words interrupt—or perhaps respond to and fulfill—his reflections.

The caption and checklist that accompany "first the trees, now this" provide an expanded structure for interpretation. Taylor states the poem's title and identifies its materials: "Newburyport pesto, *fille du feu*, ½ dozen icing cakes on slot machine" (44). The French phrase calls to mind Gérard de Nerval, the author of a collection of short works about young women, *Les Filles du feu*. Nerval was among Joseph Cornell's favorite writers and a model for his practice of gathering objects and "mental picture[s]" for his works on walks through New York City (Solomon 91). The allusion associates the younger daughter, or *fille*, in Taylor's sonnet with Nerval and also with the young women Cornell featured in his boxes. The box known as *Bébé Marie,* for example, consists of a girl's doll standing in a forest of twigs painted in glittery silver (McShine, plate 8). The slot machine in the poem's checklist refers to another series of boxes that share the general title *Medici Slot Machine* and feature reproduction portraits of child nobility alongside "popular amusements," such as letter blocks and penny candy machines (Solomon 137). Paratextual references to Cornell encourage us to consider the sequential narrative of "first the trees, now this" as a series of stills. The daughters playing in the sestet appear against the octave's background of leaves and then recede, like *Bébé Marie,* behind the branches the father sees through their kitchen window. The younger daughter's "shy rendezvous" with the neighbor and her report to her sister suggest pairs of figures, girl-boy and girl-girl, in an assemblage that includes a walnut, icing cakes, and the "scroll cutouts" of an "epiphone acoustic guitar" (Taylor 44).

The materials identified in the captions and checklists give the sonnets of *self-portrait* a handmade quality. Their presence encourages readers to drift away from sequential reading. Even as we engage in conventional interpretive work, Taylor encourages us to look at the sonnets as gatherings of elements that never fully cohere.

Cornell repurposed some of the boxes he used in his work and constructed many himself, taking care to strip, paint, varnish, and distress them to produce a patina of age (Simic 63). As a result, the boxes engage viewers in various ways, for example, as containers, frames, shrines, games, and puzzles. The poet Charles Simic proposes that they serve more mystical purposes as well, defining liminal spaces, "a safe haven, a nook, [or] a place out of sight," where the artist and viewers of his works can explore states of altered awareness (68). As "vehicle[s] of reverie," the boxes invite private responses that carry us into our own fears, fantasies, and desires (Simic 46). Cornell invokes these possibilities and more in a journal entry where he describes his trove of materials as a "diary journal repository laboratory, picture gallery, museum, sanctuary, observatory,... the core of a labyrinth, a clearinghouse for dreams and visions... childhood regained" (qtd. in Simic 37).

O'Hara explains the disorienting effects of looking into Cornell's boxes in a September 1955 review of a show at the Stable Gallery. Though the boxes "can be described in detail," O'Hara explains, the "effect of their beauty was so singular as to defy description" ("What's with Modern Art"). As in the boxlike "Joseph Cornell," the poet describes his experience in the negative. Though the boxes are filled with identifiable components, the meanings and associations they call to mind proliferate rather than resolving into articulable wholes. O'Hara suggests in his review that the boxes can be viewed as works in themselves and as intermediary structures viewers look at and into to access their components. As Mary Ann Caws suggests in her edition of Cornell's journals, the boxes "invite us to peek, to peep, and finally yield to our imagination" to such a degree that we end up meeting ourselves "in the confines of this tiny frame, this box, this microcosm of complicity" (36). O'Hara's reticence may be a response to (and avoidance of) just this kind of unanticipated meeting.

Caws, O'Hara, and Simic's descriptions of looking into Cornell's boxes center on the complex relations between their material structures and aesthetic forms. Each writer responds to the dynamics of nearness and distance that bind the boxes' components and engage the viewer's attention. Proponents of the New Lyric Studies advocate a related approach to reading. They ask critics and readers to maintain distinctions between "two interrelated and historically specific elements of the text: generic form and material form" (Eckert 973). These distinctions are necessary because contemporary practices of reading, especially in academic settings, subsume divergent poetic experiences under and into the larger category of the lyric. This "lyricization," as Mary Poovey terms it, overwrites the particularities of individual poems with abstractions (qtd. in Jackson 182). As Virginia Jackson explains, these abstractions include the idea that all lyric poems depict subjective experiences and that readers are listeners overhearing private speech (183, 185). Jackson's work calls attention to poems' material circulation and the range of responses they occasion. As she and Yopie Prins explain in the introduction to *The Lyric Theory Reader*, their work aims to disrupt the assumption that lyric poetry is a "stable term" and make space for "other ideas of poetry and its possibilities" (8).

Jonathan Culler, whose work Jackson and Prins cite in their introduction and include in the anthology, engages with another kind of materiality: the "characteristic extravagance" of lyric language (Culler 202). He observes that everyday language tends to lock speakers and listeners into particular times—present, past, or future tense—and perspectives or subject positions—first, second, or third person. Lyric language disrupts these effects by drawing attention to language's "material dimensions" and the ways these dimensions block access to readerly "identification and displacement" (205). Lyric poems are extravagant in Culler's view because they entangle us in processes of subject formation we otherwise take for granted. Building on this observation, he proposes that readers might use lyric poems as tools for considering the affordances and constraints of "dwelling in a particular language" (205).

Reading Taylor's sonnets with Culler's insights and the New Lyric Studies framework in mind brings forward their associative complexities. For example, if "first the trees, then this" can be read in the conventionally lyricizing way of reconstructing the late afternoon situation, it can also be read in terms of its linguistic extravagance. The younger daughter's repetition of the word "smell," for example, signals how discourses of sex and gender intervene in childhood identity formation. Similarly, the poem can be interpreted through the private emotions it displays and the intimacy it sets in motion within the family and between poet and reader. Especially in the form it takes in *self-portrait*, the sonnet also invites us to approach it as a Cornell-like box we might look into or a "microcosm of complicity" where we might meet ourselves in chains of associations. The collection's paratextual structures disperse readerly attention over an array of focal points: the texts of the poems, the captions and checklists, and the blank pages. This dispersal draws attention to the sonnets' "material conditions" and the "forms, shapes, and rhythms" of the routines of interpretation they engage and disrupt (Eckert 976; Culler 205).

Three sonnets in *self-portrait*'s middle section assemble future possibilities for poetic and lyric reading. Each explores a method of divination: looking at entrails, consulting an oracle, and watching birds. The first of the three, "haruspex decision tree," is a gathering of fragments separated by slash marks. The fragments accumulate toward an italicized final couplet: "*from what we call poetry a cock crows / away off there at the break of something*" (90). Taylor pitches these lines as wisdom. Their allusion to *Hamlet*, where a cock crows in the first scene, signals difficulties ahead. But other elements indicate more hopeful trajectories. For example, Taylor links a "hovercraft" to the font type "helvetica" as some kind of "zen koan" in the octave and describes a "splinter of faith" in the sestet involving a sauce-stained lottery ticket and a working-class uprising (90). The caption and checklist suggest three overlapping scenes of reading: a "fortune cookie," with its associations to casual predictions; a "peep show," which could signify vice or a child's picture show; and a symbolic "Red Lizard" (90). These scenes suggest ways that readers might break away from the tragic portents of "what we call poetry" by following different paths.

The possibility of breaking from sequential reading emerges in the second of the three poems, "medicine man," as well. The poem connects the landscape of precontact North America with a visit to the shrine to Apollo at

Delphi during a period when classical Greece and the Indigenous civilizations of the Americas were each thriving, "450–420 B.C." (98). Positioning readers on "thresholds / built on geometric before polis & alphabet," the sonnet invites us to look out across landscapes of rising smoke and temple ruins (98). As in "haruspex decision tree," Taylor involves us in these acts of looking by using the collective pronoun "we": "we lift shadows to act out a crow eclipse: / resound votive gifts to *naos* & first stones" (98). If we can reconstruct the scene of a speaker visiting Delphi, we can also step back from lyricized reading to follow other associations. For example, the "*romantic vapor* on limestone" in the poem's checklist connects back to the smoke of the ritual offerings and the sound of a "blowing sax" (98). The allusion to jazz suggests Harlem's Apollo Theater as another "several / rhythm temple" we might explore (98). This new location suggests the "ionian sea shine" and "thresholds" noted elsewhere in the sonnet are music, the Ionian mode, or major scale, and the "geometric" improvisations it enables.

Taylor entangles readers even more deeply in the relationships between listening to music and looking for signs in the third divination poem. Titled "taking the auspices"—after the practice of augury, or observing birds to predict future events—the sonnet calls to mind the many boxes Cornell devoted to birds, including *Habitat Group for a Shooting Gallery* (McShine, plate 23), the work Taylor takes as the title of *self-portrait*'s third section. The sonnet features a variety of birds, including hawks, wood thrushes, geese, quail, owls, robins, and buzzards. Four poets join the menagerie. Taylor introduces them in the sonnet's seventh line, "baraka said duncan said pound," and the accompanying checklist, "*N. Mackey's trout* on tenor sax, 8 × 6" (100). The poets' last names route our attention from the text of the poem to the paratextual structures that frame and contain it. Different interpretive trajectories come into view. For example, just as we might derive symbolic meanings from the birds flying around the poem's fourteen lines, we can also look at them as material musical symbols, as Taylor instructs in the caption: "*write birds in their treble scale*" (100). If they are notes arrayed on a staff, in turn, the sonnet's list of poetic influences also becomes a kind of chord or melody the poet is listening for and striving to play.

The paratextual structures of Taylor's sonnets disrupt sequential reading by activating these networks of associations. They open "near distances" like the ones O'Hara, Caws, and Simic discover in Cornell's boxes and extend the insights of the New Lyric Studies by inviting readers to practice associative entanglement as a method of interpretation. Looking into

Taylor's sonnets as if they were boxes suggests new directions for the form. Their paratextual materials indicate that sonnets can function as gathering points, or nodes, for assembling poets' and readers' ongoing associations. Cornell invites viewers to assemble the works his boxes contain by elaborating on the meanings their elements make available. Sonnets, or poets who write sonnets, can do the same. They can array their materials in ways that encourage us to meet ourselves in their structures and construct futures that cut across the confines of formal order.

Works Cited

Caws, Mary Ann, editor. *Joseph Cornell's Theater of the Mind: Selected Diaries, Letters, and Files*. Thames and Hudson, 1993.

Culler, Jonathan. "Why Lyric?" *PMLA*, vol. 123, no. 1, 2008, pp. 201–06.

Eckert, Lindsay. "Reading Lyric's Form: The Written Hand in Albums and Literary Annuals." *ELH*, vol. 85, no. 4, winter 2018, pp. 973–97.

Genette, Gerard. *Paratexts: Thresholds of Interpretation*. Translated by Jane E. Lewin, Cambridge UP, 1997.

Gooch, Brad. *City Poet: The Life and Times of Frank O'Hara*. Harper Perennial, 1993.

Jackson, Virginia. "Who Reads Poetry?" *PMLA*, vol. 123, no. 1, pp. 181–87.

Jackson, Virginia, and Yopie Prins. General Introduction. *The Lyric Theory Reader: A Critical Anthology*, edited by Virginia Jackson and Yopie Prins. The Johns Hopkins UP, 2015, pp. 1–8.

McShine, Kynaston, editor. *Joseph Cornell*. The Museum of Modern Art, 1980.

O'Hara, Frank. *The Collected Poems*. Edited by Donald Allen. U of California P, 1995.

———. "What's with Modern Art?" *Jacket*, vol. 6, Jan 1999, jacketmagazine.com/06/ohara.html.

Simic, Charles. *Dime-Store Alchemy: The Art of Joseph Cornell*. New York Review Books, 1992.

Solomon, Deborah. *Utopia Parkway: The Life and Work of Joseph Cornell*. MFA Publications, Boston, 1997.

Taylor, Ken. "first the trees, then this." *Gigantic Sequins*, vol. 3, no. 1, 2011. Rpt. in *And Other Poems*, andotherpoems.com/2012/11/13/ken-taylor/, and in *self-portrait as joseph cornell*, p. 44).

———. *self-portrait as joseph cornell*. Pressed Wafer, Brooklyn, 2016.

Standing in One Place to Move

The Repeated-Line Sonnet

REBECCA MORGAN FRANK

Repeated-line sonnets hold a distinctive position in American poetry: there are not many of them, but they are memorable and sometimes controversial, instigating arguments over whether they are poems, much less sonnets, at all. Yet the sonnet form is itself a historical repetition, one that extends rhetorical traditions of repetition. Anaphora, locked into the front of the line and away from the strictures of a sonnet's rhyme scheme, is ubiquitous, ranging from a few initial repetitions to dominant repetition, such as in Shakespeare's Sonnet 66, in which ten lines begin with "and," or Robert Burns's first sonnet, "A Sonnet upon Sonnets," which begins seven lines with "fourteen," concluding, "Fourteen good measur'd verses make a sonnet." The line could be a tagline for the American sonnet, give or take the fourteen and the meter, though Burns could hardly have anticipated the repeated-line sonnets of contemporary American poetry. The American sonnet has long embraced epistrophe in the absence of rhyme, such as in the repeated "you" line endings in John Ashbery's "At North Farm," or Bernadette Mayer's "Sonnet: 'name address date,'" which ends "and a tooth / for a tooth / is a tooth."

When anaphora and epistrophe meet, and a poet repeats the same full "good measur'd verses" fourteen times, is this automatically a sonnet? Does saying something fourteen times have particular meaning or effect? Does such fourteen-line repetition work differently than repetition in a poem such as James Tate's "Lewis and Clark Overheard in Conversation," which repeats "then we'll get us some wine and spare ribs" twenty-three times? I would argue yes to each of these questions. Repetition's reverberation within the not-so-narrow room of the sonnet proves, yet again, the form's expansiveness and its ability to contain critiques of itself. Poets continue to speak back to, and through, the sonnet in distinctive ways in the repeated-line sonnet, but two distinctive lineages of hybridity emerge. In one vein, the materiality of texts and musical saturation deconstruct both meaning and form, while in the other, traditions of formal hybridity in African American poetry create meaning through repetition as a participatory mode.

An example of the first is "Sonnet: Homage to Andy Warhol" in which Ron Padgett responds to Warhol's movie *Sleep*, which loops shots of Warhol's lover, poet John Giorno, sleeping. The sonnet repeats not only one line but one letter: "Zzzzzzzzzzzzzzzzzzzzzzzzzzzzzzzzzzzz" (Padgett, "Sonnet" 13). According to Daniel Kane, "Like Warhol's mechanical reproductions of everyday objects and images, this reproduction of a single letter emphasizes process and surface, thereby denying symbolic significance to a sacral word or image" (117). Kane's argument can be expanded: the repetition also denies the symbolic significance of the sonnet form itself. The reproduction of the letter *z* maintains a sense of the sonnet's sonic repetition while engaging in performative ambiguity: do you read the poem as nasal snoring sounds or the distinctly visual cartoonish sound of the repeated letter? Either way, the poem works as a visual joke, both amplified by its sonnet form and aimed at it.

Does such heightened repetition disrupt the sonnet's built-in inclination toward closure, or does closure happen anyway, arriving by virtue of the form, the visual frame or naming frame of a sonnet, which transmits that the end is near? In *Bean Spasms*, Ron Padgett's playful and irreverent collaboration with Ted Berrigan, this sonnet is renamed "Sonnet for Andy Warhol" and paired on the page with "Sonnet," which solely repeats the line "Nothing in that drawer" fourteen times (54); the titles and the visual field signal the form in both poems. Padgett later notes the materiality of "Sonnet": "Perhaps my 'sonnet' was more of an anti-sonnet, with a tinge of the concrete poem about it; that is, the poem itself looks something like a chest of drawers, each line being a different drawer" ("The Other Room"). In his 1969 collection *Great Balls of Fire*, Padgett retitles this sonnet "Nothing in That Drawer" (5). While the title no longer instructs the reader, the form is still conveyed on the page through visual repetition: we see the shape of a sonnet and thus recognize impending closure, reassured that repetition will not be infinite.

When the poem is heard rather than seen, the original titular framework of "sonnet" still provides anticipated relief. Padgett's updated title revokes this. In his Academy of American Poets Poet-to-Poet series reading of the poem, Padgett talks of repetition as sonic play: "When I was little, I used to have fun, uh, just saying the same word over and over and over and over until it sounded weird." He then repeats the word "bottle" many times, adding, "if you do that long enough the word just gets completely weird and funny and interesting." The experience Padgett describes is called "semantic satiation," which the American Psychological Association defines as "the effect in which a word seems to lose its meaning after it has been repeated many times in rapid succession." Yet such satiation can't drive the Warhol sonnet, which includes no words, and in the case of "Nothing in That Drawer," the effect is closer to that of "saturation," as used by Barbara Herrnstein Smith in her discussion of the effects of systematic repetition in *Poetic Closure*: while such repetition tends to give stability to the structure of which it is a part, the further it is extended the more desperate becomes our desire for variation or conclusion. This latter effect is comparable to what Gestalt psychologists call 'saturation,'... In connection with the saturating effect of musical repetition, Leonard Meyer points out that the listener's reaction will depend upon the degree to which he perceives the repetition as "'meaningful'" (42). In short, stability gives way to desperation, but the reaction is based on the listener's or reader's assessment of the poet's intent, for as Meyer himself says, "Our expectation of change and our concomitant willingness to go along with the composer in this apparently meaningless repetition are also products of our belief in the purposefulness of art and the serious intents, the integrity of the composer" (135). In the case of Padgett's sonnets, the reader needs to be in on the joke and on board with the aesthetic move of deconstructing such purposefulness or seriousness itself or the result is the "boredom, fatigue, impatience, or flight" that Herrnstein Smith warns can supplant closure (42).

But what if change is built into repetition itself? Padgett also acknowledges Gertrude Stein's influence on "Nothing in that drawer" and concludes that "a repeated word or phrase sounds different from the previous one" ("The Other Room"). Stein herself argues that there is no true repetition: "[repetition] is very like a frog hopping he cannot ever hop exactly the same distance or the same way of hopping at every hop. A bird's singing is perhaps the nearest thing to repetition but if you listen they too vary their insistence. That is the human expression saying the same thing and in insisting and we all insist varying the emphasizing" (288). If vocal performance of repetition creates change, perhaps a repeated line is not repeated after all. Even poems read silently are experienced through the temporal experience of reading, which implies movement rather than stasis. We are not frozen in time: the poem moves us forward. But is the line losing or gaining meaning through "desperation" and "insistence," to use Stein's terms? In the case of Padgett's poems, dissolution seems inevitable.

Other repeated-line sonnets, however, build meaning through their insistence, particularly when read within the lineage of hybridity in the African American sonnet. Consider Langston Hughes, who mashes up the blues and sonnet in his "Seven Moments of Love: An un-sonnet sequence in Blues" (*p. 43*) using anaphoric repetition, or repetition with change: "Don't have to go to church. / Don't have to go nowhere" or "What do you mean, why I didn't write? / What do you mean, just a little spat?" Then there is Gwendolyn Brooks's "the sonnet-ballad," which joins the sonnet and ballad, repeating the full opening line as the closing line: "Oh mother, mother, where is happiness?" In Brooks's poem, the language has not changed, but the meaning has. While similar modes of repetition predate the twentieth century, by acknowledging the sonnet's intersection with the ballad and the blues in the poems' titles, Hughes and Brooks signal that they are invoking more communal forms. They thereby move us from the singular voice and address of the sonnet and plant the expectation of refrain, which can embody call and response or other forms of communal participation that evoke questions of communities and their boundaries. Such participation and allusion offer the change and meaning for which we become "desperate."

While the postmodern repetitions of Padgett and Warhol dig at the sign, in "Sonnet," from *Hip Logic*, Terrance Hayes is signifyin(g) in the vein of Henry Louis Gates with the use of the repeated line "We cut the watermelon into smiles." As Stephanie Burt notes, Hayes "play[s] on racist stereotypes that associate rural black Americans with watermelon and fixed grins, and on the assumption that all sonnets say or mean the same thing. He also points back to the black writer Paul Laurence Dunbar's famous stanzaic lyric of 1896: 'We wear the mask that grins and lies.'" Hayes references and reframes the past even as he reflects on its continuance with the repeated line. What is the effect? This returns us to Meyer's commentary on repetition saturation depending on meaningfulness to the receiver. What is the saturation point in this poem and who has reached it? Who is this "we" in the poem? This sonnet reaffirms the differing experience of those slicing and those observing, even as all readers inhabit the language through the communal act of repetition.

The formal tradition of the chant provides a lens with which to address how this communal act may be differently embodied. According to Aldon

Lynn Nielsen, "Chant... in order to be *heard as* chant, must be present itself as the at least vaguely familiar, the already heard, for it must have presupposed the possibility of reiteration, response, recall, rerapping. It is not chant if not repeated, nor is it orature unless it is transmitted, remarked, redeployed. Each member of the inheriting chain of tradition repeats the chant in a different voice, replays it in a different register, alters its rhythmic patterns" (30; italics in original). Nielsen's argument invites us to consider whether we are part of the inheriting chain, and, if so, where we are in that chain. As a reader, are you part of the "we" of Hayes's sonnet? Am I? The subjectivity of the sonnet stares back at us—the singular, too often assumed to be universal, disrupted. The poem serves as both testimony and interface of divergent experiences. Even as the sonnet brings the appearance of closure, of relief, with its final, fourteenth line, the subject pushes back at this, denying the relief of clear closure. Oppression is circular, cyclical, ongoing. While the poem ends in fourteen lines, it echoes on, continuing past the frame of the sonnet indefinitely. There is no relief from the repetition because the conditions of the poem have not changed. Meaning is imbued in the repetition, and meaning is amplified by an ending that defies closure.

A more recent addition to the repeated-line sonnet tradition is Nate Marshall's "African american literature" (*p. 127*) from his 2020 collection *Finna*. Marshall repeats the line "I like your poems because they seem so real" (81) thirteen times before subverting the repeated-line form in the final line. As J. Howard Rosier argues, "the monotony serves as both example and exercise; the poem's speaker simultaneously mimics the exhaustion of the white gaze while preserving his autonomy through writing in traditional forms." Marshall is a rapper as well as a poet; thus, this sonnet evokes yet another musical form as he ends the poem with the musical "cut" as the final turn. For those still asking the question of whether these repeated-line fourteeners are sonnets, I will give Marshall the last words with that final cut, the turn of the fourteenth line of his sonnet: "F'sho, good look, this also a sonnet."

Works Cited

APA Dictionary of Psychology, American Psychological Association, dictionary.apa.org/semantic-satiation.

Ashbery, John. "At North Farm." *A Wave*. Viking Penguin, 1984, p. 1.

Berrigan, Ted, and Ron Padgett. *Bean Spasms*. Granary Books, 2012.

Brooks, Gwendolyn. "the sonnet-ballad." *Blacks*. Third World Press, 1994, p 112.

Burns, Robert. "A Sonnet upon Sonnets." Scottish Poetry Library, www.scottishpoetrylibrary.org.uk/poem/sonnet-upon-sonnets/.

Burt, Stephanie. "Voluntary Imprisonment." *Slate Magazine*, 28 May 2019, slate.com/culture/2019/05/terrance-hayes-sonnet-poetry-stephanie-burt.html.

Gates, Henry L. *The Signifying Monkey: A Theory of Afro-American Literary Criticism*. Oxford, UP, 2014.

Hayes, Terrance. "Sonnet." *Hip Logic*. Penguin Books, 2002, p. 13.

Hughes, Langston. "Seven Moments of Love: An un-sonnet sequence in Blues." *Esquire*, 1 May 1940, classic.esquire.com/article/1940/5/1/seven-moments-of-love.

Kane, Daniel. *All Poets Welcome: The Lower East Side Poetry Scene in the 1960s*. U of California Press, 2003.

Marshall, Nate. "African american literature." *Finna*. One World, 2020, p. 81.

Mayer, Bernadette. "Sonnet: 'name address date.'" *A Bernadette Mayer Reader*. New Directions, 1992, p. 26.

Meyer, Leonard B. *Emotion and Meaning in Music*. U of Chicago P, 1966.

Nielsen, Aldon Lynn. *Black Chant: Languages of African-American Postmodernism*. Cambridge UP, 1997.

Padgett, Ron. "Nothing in That Drawer." *Great Balls of Fire*. Coffee House Press, 1990, p. 5.

———. "The Other Room Interview Series: Ron Padgett." *The Other Room*, 2009, theotherroom.files.wordpress.com/2009/11/the-other-room-interviews-ron-padgett.pdf.

———. Poet-to-Poet: Ron Padgett Reads "Nothing in That Drawer," Academy of American Poets, 2014, vimeo.com/137139097.

———. "Sonnet: Homage to Andy Warhol." *Film Culture*, no. 32, 1964, anthologyfilmarchives.bigcartel.com/product/film-culture-no-32-1964.

Rosier, J. Howard. "Talk It Out." *Poetry Foundation*, www.poetryfoundation.org/articles/154055/talk-it-out.

Smith, Barbara Herrnstein. *Poetic Closure: A Study of How Poems End*. U of Chicago P, 1968.

Stein, Gertrude. "Portraits and Repetition." *Lectures in America*. Beacon Press, 1985, pp. 165–206.

Tate, James. "Lewis and Clark Overheard in Conversation." *Selected Poems*, Wesleyan UP, 2013, p. 90.

"This resonant, strange, vaulting roof"
Contemporary Sonnets beyond Iambic Pentameter

ANNA LENA PHILLIPS BELL

When poets speak of breaking the form of the sonnet, which some do fairly often of late, one implication is that the form is inflexible and, thus, brittle—any little shift will shatter it. The phrase also connotes a violence that can read as gendered: it can suggest that the form is merely a vessel the poet pours his genius into, and that, it turns out, genius needs no vessel, or looks better in one that is broken, coerced, or violated. I'm more interested in poets' radical expansions on the form—in shifts that enlarge or transform the sonnet but leave its form felt. Rather than attempting to break the vessel, a number of contemporary poets are employing less-than-usual materials for its construction. Among the most exciting of these, to my ear, are meters other than iambic pentameter.

Antony Easthope, in *Poetry as Discourse*, calls English poetic discourse since the Renaissance—and by extension, iambic pentameter—"an epochal form, co-terminous with the capitalist mode of production and the hegemony of the bourgeoisie as the ruling class" (24). In a poetic context in which most metrical work is still overwhelmingly iambic—and in a sociopolitical context in which labor and leisure are still overwhelmingly defined and confined by capitalist structures—noniambic materials surprise. They may make room for radical modes of being and saying, a possibility realized by US poets from Langston Hughes to Edna St. Vincent Millay to Patricia Smith. They make it possible to think and feel with the sonnet in new ways, and they help in exploring vital subject matter: expanding traditions of storytelling, addressing aspects of race and gender, evoking new, or old but newly found, ways of inhabiting the world. A feminist reading might consider these shifts not just as expansions but as alterations or repairs—(a)mending an object toward a new purpose or longer usefulness. The following four examples from poems by US sonnet makers, each in a different meter, offer distinct possibilities for the form.

Falling Meters

Annie Finch's noniambic sonnets, along with her extensive, groundbreaking scholarship on meter, open new possibilities for expressing women's power and vulnerabilities through the form. In "Wild Yeasts," from her 2003 collection *Calendars*, she uses dactylic pentameter to suggest the energy and mystery of making bread—a biological process humans use for our purposes but that feels indeed wild, mysterious, not entirely within our ken. The poem does not tell us much in the way of setting, but it shows us a single speaker kneading a single loaf of bread to be shared—a solitary act of craft that will lead to communion. Though this work might be done with iambs, the sprawl and spill of Finch's dactyls allow the "breath of the wildest yeast" to "roar."

Rhymewise, the poem has three quatrains and a final couplet, but its stanzas are divided as a Petrarchan sonnet. The sestet begins with a question:

> How could I send quiet through this resonant, strange, vaulting roof
> murmuring, sounding with spores and the long-simple air,
> and the bright free road moving? (p. 70)

The answer is action: "I sing as I terrace a loaf / out of my hands it has filled like a long-answered prayer" (lines 11–12). In the sestet I hear not only a bread-making but a poem-making argument. "This resonant, strange, vaulting roof / murmuring, sounding with spores and the long-simple air, / and the bright free road moving" (lines 9–11) feels like an apt description of metrical work, revealing it to be less constraint to be followed or broken by the poet than process, voyage, substance, transformation. To "send quiet," the poem implies, needs singing; meter requires the interplay of soft spaces and stresses, beats and offbeats.

Another argument this poem (and many others) makes for metrical patterning: having gotten off to an earnest start, within the song, there's room to mess around. In the final line of "Wild Yeasts," the position of "refracts" as an iambic substitution embodies its meaning—the rhythm turns back, much as the instant of eating the bread will recall its making. In the last two feet of the closing couplet, like the dough, the meter rises: "Now the worshipping savage cathedral our mouths make will lace / death and its food, in the moment that refracts this place."

In his Spenserian sonnet "Doppelgangbanger" (2017), Cortney Lamar Charleston uses long lines of falling meter to evoke a teenager's rebellion against received ideas about how Black men should be in the world and a mother's concern for her son's safety. The poem's flexible mix of trochaic and dactylic meter, in lines of mostly seven beats, allows a conversational beginning that places us immediately in the scene of the speaker's memory: "Fox Valley Mall, technically in Aurora, attracts slightly / rougher edges— *ya mans right here*, stoners, guapo boys / and black" (lines 1–3). The rhyme scheme enhances the poem's energetic metrical moves, shifting effortlessly between falling and rising rhyme: in the first quatrain, for instance, slightly/ boys/lightly/decoy.

Regular trochees (with an implied offbeat after "this") in short, snappy sentences reinforce the strictures of the advice the speaker receives from a mall cop he encounters with his mom: "*Straighten this. Pull up that. E-NUN-CI-ATE.* I peep his ploy" (line 7). Briefly the speaker inhabits this same meter, before returning to more complex patterns for his (internal) retort: "But I don't need telling. If I'm a stereotype, / I be branded Sony, Bose—not some shit Zenith did" (lines 10–11).

The penultimate line moves into anapestic pentameter, a brief interlude in rising rhythm that heightens the return to falling meter that follows. And the final line's rapid, almost dipodic trochaic septameter lends even more weight to the poem's devastating conclusion: "yet still, mom looks like she wants to light flame to my hide; / she don't want me stunting as some stat been shot and died" (lines 13–14). The hero of this poem's heroic couplet is not the speaker but his mother, her anger with and fear for her son as poignant as his razor-sharp evocation of those feelings.

Rising Meters

Anapests are sometimes said to rollick. Whether I like this, I'm not sure; it suggests an absolute about their character that elides their more subtle qualities. Anna Maria Hong's "Nude Palette" (*p. 102*) from her 2020 collection *Fablesque*, begins in anapestic tetrameter: "What a muse, what a mess, this state of undress." An unfamiliar phrase in a familiar cadence quickly becomes a familiar lament, the meter and the near rhyme of muse/mess setting up not an opposition but a transformation. Hong's anapests catapult us into a plethora of -*ess* rhymes, both internal and at line ends; their effect is less rollick than overwhelm, in which the speaker nonetheless remains in control of the narrative.

The combined effect is of excess, a chaos that's both fertile and, possibly, more than the speaker can easily bear. "An embarrassment of purchase, promise," the eighth line puts it, shifting chameleonlike in the direction of iambs before diving back into triple meter in the next line: "Hello, virtuoso, you had me at emo" (line 9). Here the rhyme shifts too, into a surfeit of *o*'s. The *-ess* returns only in the final line of the poem, where it envelops (clothes?) the *o*'s: "*en masse, in toto.* Oh, no. Say yes." The poem might seem to have abandoned its anapests at the end, but it has only raised the stakes. The pause after "*en masse*" and the parallel pause after "Oh, no" take the place of unstressed syllables, emphasizing the drama of the poem's conclusion, allowing the last four syllables to hold even more weight. In those final two feet, the contrast or transformation—or two-things-true-at-once—echoes the juxtaposition of the poem's first two feet. The pause after "no" reinforces the shift from no to yes, even as it affirms each inclination.

Chad Abushanab's ballad sonnets—a form that without question wins the Best Spoonerism prize—move in the tradition of Gwendolyn Brooks's "the sonnet-ballad," telling their brief, piercing stories with iambic tetrameter rather than Brooks's pentameter. In Abushanab's "Here on Earth" (2019), the meter combines with *abab* quatrains and plain, clear syntax and vocabulary to also suggest a relation to Robert Frost. "The field behind our house tonight," the poet begins,

> reminds me of an empty bed,
> with drifts of snow like wrinkled sheets
> and shadows where you laid your head.

The tetrameter's quiet regularity helps portray a speaker whose understatement makes their grief only clearer. In pentameter we might feel a more conversational tone, one more confident or explanatory; in "Here on Earth," the speaker measures out words and phrases as if counting sheep—or days. In the fifth line, the first metrical substitution—a spondee that in a louder poem might barely register—suggests the speaker's desperation: "A month and six days since you left."

This poem also plays with the heightened possibilities for interaction between sentence and line that a shorter-than-pentameter line can allow. The first stanza is a single sentence. The next two lines comprise one sentence, after which follows the shortest sentence yet: "Sleep won't come." That acephalous iamb reads as a little joke by a speaker who's being kept up by their thoughts.

The tetrameter also makes possible a brilliant enjambment before the poem's final line. In a pentameter frame, the penultimate line would read, "and brace myself to face the numb white space." But the tetrameter pushes "white space" off the cliff, conferring extra emphasis on "numb." This makes possible a quietly heartbreaking caesura after "white space," after which the poem turns from its view of the field outside to the empty bed inside: "and brace myself to face the numb / white space, the bed you're missing from." Abushanab's final couplet, two feet shy of heroic, is one for an age of antiheroes.

In a brief survey, it is possible to suggest just a few of the modes that meters beyond iambic make room for. Rooted in oral tradition and showing up in poems whose authors are keenly aware of the ways a poem on the page is embodied through speech or other physical means, these meters call us toward poetic ways of being that are variously interior, collaborative, inquisitive, incisive, and—okay, yes—rollicking. Inhabiting our bodies, they move us to new understanding, enhancing their poems' complex subject matter. As we continue to enlarge and amend the sonnet, work like this stands as an invitation to make new metrical experiments.

Works Cited

Abushanab, Chad. "Here on Earth." *Ecotone*, vol. 15, no. 1, issue 28, 2019, p. 128.
Charleston, Cortney Lamar. "Doppelgangbanger." *Ecotone*, vol. 13, no. 1, issue 24, 2017, p. 33. Rpt. *Doppelgangbanger*, Haymarket Books, 2021.
Easthope, Antony. *Poetry as Discourse*. Taylor and Francis, 2013.
Finch, Annie R. C. "Wild Yeasts." *Calendars*. Tupelo Press, 2003, p. 70.
Hong, Anna Maria. "Nude Palette." *Fablesque*. Tupelo Press, 2020, p. 52.

Kay Ryan's Miniature Sonnets

DIANA LECA

Hunting for sonnets in *The Best of It* (2010), which won Kay Ryan the Pulitzer Prize for Poetry, you'll often come up a little short, at twelve or thirteen lines. Other times, you'll find you've just slipped over. Whatever the number, it is by minifying the lines—each rarely longer than six syllables—that Ryan rejigs the sonnet form so effectively. While it might be tempting to refer to these narrow poetic stacks as not-quite-sonnets, this would be to overlook the outsized effect of Ryan's reduction. The miniature, as Steven Millhauser argues in "The Fascination of the Miniature," is not "merely minute"—like a bottle cap or an ant. Rather, it is minute *in relation* to something else, and it is this "discrepancy of size" that "shocks us into attention" (128–29).[1] We might think, he suggests, of a dollhouse and its minuscule teacups or, as Ryan notes in an essay on miniatures, an inscribed grain of rice.[2] Like her small sonnets, such artifacts grab our attention because they are the scaled-down versions of something bigger.

But how do miniatures hold this attention once they've snatched it? Millhauser claims that it is by the intricate precision of their construction—by presenting a never-before-seen level of detail. "The more precise," he writes, "the more wonder-compelling" (132). And the eerier, too. After all, exactitude's tendency toward exposure brings with it both thrills and qualms: "If your line is about three words long," Ryan has said, "nearly every word is on one edge or the other. You can't hide anything" (Halstead; qtd. in Fagan 269).[3] By allowing us to see the conventional sonnet's mechanisms close-up, miniatures such as "New Rooms" (*p. 80*) "Snake Charm," and "Doubt" reveal the form to be far more peculiar than is traditionally assumed.

Countless critics have been lured by Ryan's ultrasmall sonnets into counting not just lines, a normal enough thing to do with sonnets, but also words, letters, and punctuation marks. Take a look at "Say Uncle" (*p. 80*) the opening poem of Ryan's eponymous 2000 collection:

> Every day
> you say,
> *Just one*
> *more try.*
> Then another
> irrecoverable
> day slips by.
> You will
> say *ankle*,
> you will
> say *knuckle*;
> why won't
> you why
> won't you
> say *uncle*? (*Best* 149)

Overshooting by a line, this semisonnet is typical of Ryan's art in many ways: it's metrically irregular, but with a distinctive taste for monometer; it mixes dead-straight masculine rhymes (day/say; try/by) with wonky feminine ones (ankle/knuckle) and nested off-rhymes (another/irrecoverable); it supercharges line endings and uses a playful tone that gets a little pensive, if not mildly sinister, on rereading. Indeed, to "say uncle," according to the *Oxford English Dictionary*, is "to acknowledge defeat, to cry for mercy," late nineteenth-century North American slang denoting submission.

Like "Say Uncle," moreover, Ryan's sonnets tend to occupy space as compact columns. This slender shape, along with their Skeltonic leanings (trimmed lines, frequent chiming), suggests light verse, as the poems "inch downward with off-beat charm" (Spiegelman 165). But they are harder to categorize definitively. Langdon Hammer calls Ryan's poems "roughly sonnet-sized blocks" (177)—and the "roughly" interests me as much as the "blocks." Surely, what Hammer has in mind is "approximately"—that is, they are pretty much sonnets. With "Say Uncle" in mind, connotations of "ungentle" or "violent" might arise too. But it is the third meaning of "roughly" that is most suggestive for my purposes: "without care, skill, or finish; in a crude or imperfect manner."

We might in fact think of Ryan's sonnets as "odd boxes"—as the title of an early poem directs us to do. These not only resemble and frequently *feature* small containers (a fish tank, a "square foot" garden) and other small quadrangular contraptions (jewelry boxes, envelopes), they also reflect on themselves *as* boxes of various sorts. This is not at all unusual for sonnets, if we recall Wordsworth's nun's "narrow room" or Spenser's "little space"— to name only the most familiar. But while Ryan's sonnets appear like tiny, cozy nooks, they have nothing restful about them. Take, for example, "New Rooms," the first poem in her collection *Erratic Facts* (2015):

> The mind must
> set itself up
> wherever it goes
> and it would be
> most convenient
> to impose its
> old rooms—just
> tack them up
> like an interior
> tent. Oh but
> the new holes
> aren't where
> the windows
> went. (1)

The short lines reveal ledge after ledge, and the dipodic metre—albeit irregular—creates the swift, perilous rhythms more typical of nursery rhymes. Bits of "New Rooms" seem strangely out of place, moreover, such as the final rhyme (tent/went). You *hear* the rhyme, but on the page it is found— rather awkwardly—in the first position rather than the terminal. So, if the prerhyme "convenient" can be said to set up the "epigrammatic clinch" of the couplet, it's only to the ear (Hurley and O'Neill 81). Other rhymes, too—must/just and goes/impose/holes/windows—pop up irregularly, so you never know when to expect them.

Providing a little extra confusion, the volta (of sorts) is not where you're meant to find it. It is first teased, though not delivered, in the seventh line with the dash and the dangling "just" and entirely absent from its usual position on the ninth. The "turn" appropriate to the sonnet—its "most unique and distinctive aspect," according to Annie Finch—seems to have disappeared.[4] There is, however, a decisive shift in thought and in grammatical mood, from the wishful subjunctive ("it would be") to the indicative.

Signaled by the "Oh"—an interjection J. H. Prynne calls a "near-inarticulate particl[e] of speech" (140) and which, in classical rhetoric, is used as a figure for turning—the volta arrives halfway through the tenth line. It is this misplacement, both in the sense of being the wrong position and temporarily lost, that makes the sonnet so unnerving.

As a miniature, "New Rooms" lacks comforting unity and, in its halting cadence and scattered rhymes, fails to provide the regular, "stepped progression toward the closing couplet" that is characteristic of the sonnet (Preminger and Brogan 1168). The instability perceptible underfoot is, of course, also the sonnet's subject. Without hitching onto David Mason's life-based reading, which interprets "New Rooms" in light of Ryan's loss of her partner, Carol Adair (672), it's still possible to recognize the sonnet's anxiety around acts of misplacement. Mason directs the reader's attention to *Erratic Facts*' dedication to Adair, but we might consider another paratextual item, namely, the epigraph. It reads, simply: "erratic: (n) *Geol.* A boulder or the like carried by glacial ice and deposited some distance from its place of origin."[5]

As Mark Fisher notes, the eerie is marked not only by "disappearances" but also by "geological anomal[ies]" and by "an intensely atmospheric terrain" (122)—all of which Ryan's small sonnets raise. Staying with "New Rooms" a little longer, consider the terminal line, constituted by a single word: "went." Dislodged from the previous line, the diminutive line takes on a kind of solidity as the sonnet's resting point. This seeming fixity, however, conceals movement through its etymological kinship with the word "wend" (to turn, to alter the position of, to turn round or over). In the final line, there's not only the shift in tense but also, and critically, a turn toward the state of singleness. A sonnet, says Finch, has "the ability to keep a moment, to hold a feeling or experience and turn it around in the light of our awareness until many facets are evident" (1). This process, in "New Rooms," is continuous. In fourteen short lines, the absent one is at once held, turned over, and left to slip away on glacial ice. In Ryan's sonnet, someone or something went—and keeps on wenting.

Is this comforting? Hardly. Grief's bewilderments give this "odd box" its slender shape, its turn on "Oh," and the ghostly final line, which takes on the qualities of yet another volta, enabling the sonnet's final wrench. Although Millhauser maintains that dread and terror belong to the gigantic and not to the miniature (which for him "charms" and produces a softer sense of "wonder" and to which we "yield" in "sensual self-surrender," 130), there is clearly a confounding effect to Ryan's small sonnet—however funny it might also be. In her *Paris Review* interview, Ryan is asked about whether it bothers her that critics conceive of her poems as compressed, answering: "compression is the opposite of what I do: what interests me is so remote and fine that I have to blow it way up cartoonishly just to get it up to visible range."

Magnification indeed always accompanies the miniature. But the blown-up is not always risible—haplessly and helplessly clumsy in its inflation, as in a cartoon. As she writes in her essay "To Be Miniature Is to Be Swallowed by a Miniature Whale," magnification can be "destabilizing, dizzying, sickening" (*Synthesizing* 281). In *A Philosophical Enquiry into the Sublime and Beautiful*, Edmund Burke argues: "Whatever therefore is terrible, with regard to sight, is sublime too, whether this cause of terror be endued with greatness of dimension of not, for it is impossible to look on anything as trifling, or contemptible, that may be dangerous" (47).

Burke's main example is a serpent—a creature that regularly crops up in Ryan's work. Her sonnet "Snake Charm," published in *Flamingo Watching* (1994), describes the small, stealthy snake that "improves everything it catches":

> This snake is reckless,
> with no concern for balance. It can
> slide over any surface, a silent line,
> an endless pattern, a generative rhyme. (*Best* 72)

As if in response to Frost's "Design" (1936)—a sonnet featuring a spider and concluding "If design govern in a thing so small"—Ryan's ode to "a fingerling snake," a mere three inches long, is also an ars poetica. As Doris Davis puts it, "a reader might add that Ryan herself is the snake charmer in the way that she tames this irregular sonnet about a snake and throughout her work digests and refashions imagistic chunks of the commonplace to render her own 'generative rhyme'" (279). Yet this doesn't quite capture the weirdness of Ryan's diminutive sonnets, which by their very smallness, their unruliness (with "no concern for balance"), their slipperiness, and the spookily silent and endless way they go on and on—"slid[ing] over every surface"—have the effect of what Marc Botha calls "the minimal sublime" (12).

It might be unsurprising that a sonnet about a serpent could bring on the thrill of terror, but for Ryan an egg is just as good. To explore a little further what Willard Spiegelman calls Ryan's unsettling "cockeyed vision" (163), I'd like to turn to another sonnet, "Doubt." The poem begins with a view of a chick urgently "chip[ping] its way out" of an egg and ends with an ominous "stranger's knock" (*Best* 86). The last lines observe: "you know it is the Person from Porlock / who eats dreams for dinner, / his napkin stained the most delicate colors." This is, as some will know, an allusion to Coleridge, who describes being interrupted by a stranger's visit while composing "Kubla Khan" in 1797—the intrusion proving infelicitous and impeding the conclusion of the poem ("Fragment"). Ryan brings the Porlock man *into* her sonnet, one anxiously concerned with finish—and with finishing, as is clear from the first line: "A chick has just so much time." It's perhaps tempting to stress the "so" here—that is, to imagine a chick having endless time, *so* much time, to while away its chick hours. But taking the first three lines together ("A chick has just so much time / to chip its way out, just so much / egg energy to apply to the weak spot"), the temporal urgency of the task becomes apparent, and the reader is invited to reconsider the chick's desperate situation by promoting not the "so" but the "just."

Ryan uses meter to reinforce this feeling of unease—both the chick's and the discombobulated reader's. Although we're treated, periodically, to a fluid trimeter ("at twice the rate of work") or a nearly perfect iambic pentameter ("you know it is the Person from Porlock") and thereby lulled into the familiar and satisfying rhythmical motion of a conventional sonnet, Ryan swiftly interrupts and jumbles the meter again with a lopsided, unrhymed final couplet ("who eats dreams for dinner, / his napkin stained the most delicate colors"). Elsewhere in the poem, she opts for polysyllabic rhymes of Byronian brio: *Who can? / albumen* and *any of us / Orpheus*, along with that key rhyme: knock/Porlock, which rhymes an ictic "knock" with the disyllabic "Porlock," a type of rhyme frequently used by Donne, and later, by Pound. As Spiegelman notes, Ryan is "a master of the off-balance, slightly syncopated rhyme that both hides and reveals depths of anxiety, muted horror" (164). Just as with "New Rooms," Ryan's rhymes in a poem about artistic anxiety and dying dreams are so effective because they are erratic and incomplete, glowing all the more brightly (and in all their delicate colors) when they do pop up.

"Doubt," in other words, proves equal parts unsettling and charming. Balancing these feelings in her diminutive sonnet, Ryan evokes what Fisher calls "the peculiar appeal that the eerie possesses" (13). For Fisher, the eerie is concerned with very basic questions of presence and absence: why is *something* there where we wouldn't expect anything at all (say, a stone circle in the middle of a field), or why is there *nothing* where there should be something (as in an amnesiac's uncomprehending gaze)—that's the eerie.[6] Ryan's sonnets make eeriness a formal property: rhymes crop up where we don't expect them (tent/went) or fail to materialize where they should, as in the closing couplet of the Porlock poem; a perfect meter will loosen to nothing or, conversely, will firm up into something momentarily familiar. Even more crucially, a final fourteenth line will be withheld as in "Bitter Pill" (*Best*, 18), or a single word will be conjured up to fill it.

It might be tempting to think that by upsetting so many conventions, Ryan's sonnets put off, irritate, or distress readers. But as Fisher rightly argues, we often take pleasure in the eerie, which has a "positivity, a languorous and delirious allure" (122). It's there in the dreamy logic of the Porlock sonnet. It's there too in the one about the mind wandering through new rooms or about the silent fingerling snake endlessly generating its rhymes. To borrow then from George Saintsbury's reflections on doggerel—or "bad" verse—it's not as if Ryan aims to pen a conventional sonnet but fails to achieve the expected standards (392). Instead, she willfully shortens and tightens and tinkers and miniaturizes, so that the wonderful strangeness of the sonnet form is illuminated all the more clearly.

Notes

1. The examples are Millhauser's.
2. Ryan alludes to Walter Benjamin's admiration of "two grains of wheat with the whole *Shema Israel* inscribed on them" ("To Be Miniature," p. 281).
3. Fagan also cites John Freeman's apt observation, in his *Los Angeles Times* review of Ryan's *The Best of It* (25 April 2010), that "true wisdom... never simplifies but rather sees complexity with an unsettling clarity. This is why, when we describe poems by Frost or Dickinson, we reach for the word 'eerie.'"
4. I'm grateful to the audience member of the "Sonnets from the American" conference who prompted me to think further about the disappearance of the volta.
5. The definition is from the *Collins English Dictionary*.
6. The examples are Fisher's (12).

Works Cited

Botha, Marc. *A Theory of Minimalism*. Bloomsbury, 2017.

Burke, Edmund. *A Philosophical Enquiry into the Sublime and Beautiful*. Edited by Paul Guyer, Oxford UP, 2015.

Coleridge, Samuel Taylor. "Of the Fragment of Kubla Khan." *Christabel, Kubla Khan, and the Pains of Sleep*, H. Didier, 1816, pp. 51–54.

Davis, Doris. "The Imaginative Nature of Kay Ryan's Poetic Bestiary." *CEA Critic*, vol. 77, no. 3, November 2015, pp. 278–83.

Fagan, Deirdre. "Kay Ryan and Poetic Play." *CEA Critic*, vol. 79, no. 3, November 2017, pp. 267–74.

Finch, Annie. "Chaos in Fourteen Lines: Reformations and Deformations of the Sonnet." *Contemporary Poetry Review*, December 2009, www.cprw.com/Misc/finch2.htm.

Fisher, Mark. *The Weird and the Eerie*. Repeater Books, 2016.

Halstead, Richard. "Kay Ryan Rises to the Top despite Her Refusal to Compromise." *Marin Independent Journal*, Sept. 23, 2007.

Hammer, Langdon. "Poetry in Review." *The Yale Review*, vol. 99, no. 1, 2011, pp. 176–89.

Hurley, Michael, and Michael O'Neill. *Poetic Form: An Introduction*. Cambridge UP, 2012.

Mason, David. "Against Identity." *The Hudson Review*, vol. 68, no. 4, winter 2016, pp. 669–79.

Millhauser, Steven. "The Fascination of the Miniature." *Grand Street*, vol. 2, no. 4, 1983, pp. 128–35.

Preminger, Alex, and T. V. F. Brogan, editors. *The New Princeton Enyclopedia of Poetry and Poetics*. Princeton UP, 1993.

Prynne, J. H. "English Poetry and Emphatical Language." *Proceedings of the British Academy*, 1988, pp. 135–69.

Ryan, Kay. *The Best of It: New and Selected Poems*. Grove Press, 2010.

———. *Erratic Facts*. Grove Press, 2015.

———. Interview with Sarah Fay. *The Paris Review*, no. 187, winter 2008, www.theparisreview.org/interviews/5889/the-art-of-poetry-no-94-kay-ryan.

———. "To Be Miniature Is to Be Swallowed by a Miniature Whale." *Synthesizing Gravity; Selected Prose*. Grove Press, 2020.

Saintsbury, George. *A History of English Prosody: From the Twelfth Century to the Present Day*. Vol. 1, MacMillan, 1923.

Spiegelman, Willard. "Kay Ryan's Delicate Strength." *The Virginia Quarterly Review*, vol. 88, no. 3, 2012, pp. 159–67.

Restaging the American "Freakshow" in *Olio*

Tyehimba Jess's Syncopated Sonnets

MARLO STARR

In her foreword to *Mother Love*, which revives the Persephone myth in a sequence of modern sonnets, Rita Dove describes the sonnet form as a harmonious "intact world" (xi). Any variation of strict Petrarchan or Shakespearean norms, meter, and rhyme scheme, then, "represents a world gone awry." Considered an icon of Western culture, the sonnet is often associated with conservatism and canon worship: its "prim borders," as Dove calls them, mark the boundaries between society's centers and peripheries, between received and forgotten histories (xii). Yet within the African American poetry tradition, the sonnet has long been a vehicle of protest and open critique. As Antonella Francini argues, tracing the sonnet's appearance from the Harlem Renaissance to the works of Dove and Yusef Komunyakaa, Black poets have replaced the theme of love and reinstated the sonnet in its medieval form: like Dante's verses, the sonnet in African American traditions often functions as a public forum where the speaker asks for a reply from a specific audience (37). Building on the Black revival of the form as a discursive space, Tyehimba Jess's *Olio* (2016) forcefully reimagines the sonnet as a mode of public address and imperative, implicating its reader in the production of American history.

Jess's Pulitzer Prize–winning collection is a feat of archival recovery and formal acrobatics. Like its title, which the book's frontispiece defines as a hodgepodge of miscellaneous elements or the second act of a minstrel show, *Olio* draws on vaudeville tropes, playfully ironizing the history of American minstrelsy. From the outset, the book's narrative voice, which takes on the persona of a P. T. Barnum–like showman, invites the audience to take in the spectacle: "Fix your eyes on the flex of the first-generation-freed voices," he beckons, "Weave your own way between these voices" (3). Like a ringmaster parting the circus tent, the narrator turns to directly address the audience as the book moves from one "act" to the next. Even the cover, which displays the word "olio" in the shape of a minstrel mask, an additional *o* hanging in an open mouth, gazes back at the reader with its two *o* eyes (Rutter 178). These textual and paratextual markers consistently call attention to the role of audience participation, creating an ongoing dialogue between reader and text.

The 230-page poetry volume, which spans the end of the Civil War through the beginning of World War II, follows twelve African American performance acts and historical figures, including Booker T. Washington, Paul Laurence Dunbar, and Scott Joplin, and a cast of blues and ragtime musicians. Contrapuntal—or in the author's own description, "stichomythic" ("Dogbytes Interview")—with poems arranged in alternating lines of dialogue, Jess's figures face off with canonized white writers. In one section, the pianist "Blind" Tom Wiggins confronts Mark Twain on the page, and in another, Henry "Box" Brown, who escaped slavery by shipping himself in a crate to Philadelphia, "blues the blackface" of John Berryman (1). Appropriating the minstrel voice of Berryman's Henry-persona in the *Dreamsongs*, Jess converts nine of the Berryman's caudate sonnets into "freedsongs" sung by his reincarnation of "Box" Brown.

The collaged narrative winds through multiple forms: haiku, double shovel, and syncopated ghazal, as well as prose letters and interviews, but the book's most dominant form is the sonnet and the poet's tour de force: the syncopated sonnet. Through syncopation, Jess multiplies the Shakespearean sonnet form to create multivoiced poems that can be recited like hymns sung in round, duets, or simultaneous voices singing in competing lyrics. While these sonnets appear in various sections of the book, sometimes framed by more traditional sonnets, I focus on their densest presentation through the lives of Millie and Christine McKoy.

The McKoy twins, born into slavery in 1851, were conjoined twins fused at the lower spine. They were submitted to regular medical scrutiny and leased to traveling freakshows starting at the age of two (2). Following emancipation, they would go on to travel the world as singers under the stage name "The Two-Headed Nightingale" and would eventually purchase the land of their former plantation. Jess charts their biography across five syncopated sonnets, beginning with "Millie and Christine McKoy" (*p. 99*). Mirroring the twins' conjoined bodies, the poem brings together two sonnets, with separate lines on the left and right sides and shared lines that fall in the middle. With Millie's lines on left and Christine's on right, the poem offers multiple modes of reading. Read as a duet, from the top—left to right, the poem takes on a doubled Shakespearean rhyme scheme:

We've mended two songs into one dark skin	We ride the wake of each other's rhythm
bleeding soprano into contralto	beating our hearts' syncopated tempo

(41)

Two chains of slant rhyme—(*a*) "skin," "rhythm," "stem"; and (*b*) "contralto," "tempo," "rose"—set the pattern in motion, which then continues for the rest of the poem: *cc dd cd ee ff ef gggg*. Yet because each individuated line operates independently, they can be rearranged in infinite ways, like notes that can be played in any order. Read first down the left side and then down the right, the rhyme pattern changes to a back-to-back Shakespearean scheme, with alternating rhymes until the ending couplet, but the sonnet can also be read clockwise, counterclockwise, backward, in reverse, and crisscrossing diagonally from left to right and back. Jess calls these various modes "interstitial" and "anti-gravitational"—pick up at any point in the poem, and it still reads as syntactically coherent; while some of these variations change the rhyme scheme, the pattern remains regular (222).

The next poem, "Millie-Christine: On Display," which begins with a shared line and then straddles to opposite sides of the page, offers more prismatic dimensionality. When Jess performs the poem—which deals with the series of medical examiners and scientists who prod the twins "from spine to loin" like "prize bovine"—he reads down the shared, middle lines first and then reads again from bottom to top, incorporating Millie and Christine's individual lines along the way (45). In his review of *Olio* for *The Stranger*, Rich Smith observes that in "Millie-Christine: On Display," the different directions of reading allow for diverse interpretations: "Read the left side and the right side together, and you have a defiant poem about how the conjoined twins see themselves not as 'freaks' but rather as a miracle created by God. However, when you read the poem down the page and then back up the page, the tone and the point of the poem shifts... into a kind of prayer of gratitude." In this way, the poem enacts *Olio*'s overriding themes, recombining to open up infinite possibilities of meaning but also emphasizing alternate and contrapuntal ways of reading history.

Before the final poem in the sequence, another layer of framing hints that the syncopated sonnet is not merely an act of formal pyrotechnics.

Another flourish adds metacommentary that subtly implicates the reader: the backside of a foldout page opens to show a fourteen-inch-wide block of text marching from one edge of the page to the other. Unpunctuated sentences running together strain the reader's attention and mimic a breathless ringmaster hyping the crowd before the big reveal:

> step right up ladies and gents boys and gals and see the two headed nightingale the McCoy Twins never before seen on this continent a double dose of darkie believed to be one of a kind... it's here for sale for a low low price as you can look them up and down and side to side and backwards and forwards... step right up fine people examine her side to side and backwards and forwards and diagonally you can see the conjoined twins' entwined humanity laid bare for you to read nature's dark strange story in their twin bodies step right up ("McCoy Twins Syncopated Star" 60)

The foldout acts as a curtain to further entice the audience, recalling turn-of-the-century "freakshows" that made spectacles of differently abled and Black female bodies. Disability studies scholar Rosemarie Garland Thomson explores the history of the freakshow in nineteenth-century and early twentieth-century America, contending that the spectacle of the nonnormative body worked to consolidate the sociopolitical status quo: by fetishizing visible disabilities, the freakshow created "freaks" in order to exaggerate the "perceived difference between the viewer and the showpiece" (62). Garland Thomson writes: "The freakshow gave the American citizen a ceremonial cultural forum in which to examine apprehensions about the grand democratic experiment and the citizen's relationship to it" (80). In *Olio*, Jess recreates the freakshow that turned the McKoys' bodies into human curiosities but collapses the distance between spectacle and spectator by making the audience an active participant in the construction of the sonnet sequence. When the curtain is drawn back, a *Transformers*-style megasonnet unfolds. The five syncopated sonnets, which appeared separately in the previous pages, are now laid out on a single spread and arranged in the butterfly shape of artist Jessica Lynne Brown's accompanying illustration. The star of sonnets defies hierarchy because the poems can be read across the page diagonally, from top to bottom, side to side and backward and forward, as the "ringmaster" promised. The reader is made coauthor: whichever direction the reader chooses to move through the sonnets determines the final outcome, and the interactive feature of the sonnets highlights processes of selection and omission within the construction of narrative.

Throughout *Olio*, the unseen narrator frames each section through a similar tone of ironized minstrelsy. A long list of racial epithets is prefaced with

"GUARANTEED! *ALL TITLES HISTORICALLY ACCURATE!* GUARANTEED!"—the triple exclamation points and repetition accentuating the irony (133). The appendix (which is itself filled with hidden prose poems marked by internal rhyme), includes reader instructions for the book's even more interactive features: three perforated pages that can be torn out and folded into various shapes, like origami. "Step right up!" the ringmaster again commands, and "let your scissors rend the paper" (213, 218). The dialogue between Paul Laurence Dunbar and Booker T. Washington's double shovel can be folded into a cylinder, a torus, or a Möbius shape, so that the lines match up in different ways, creating infinite ways of reading the poem. The ringmaster-narrator eggs the reader on: "Still, there's more to be told from the fixture of masks so flexible—find the caesura and make it fold so Dunbar and Booker are back to back against the stacked lynch mobs they hold inside" (214). While humor is often used to dispel discomfort, the kitsch of the tear-out pages also emphasizes the reader's role as contributor: after folding, readers discover that they have unwittingly cornered the two figures against the lynch mob.

Later, instructing the reader to create a Möbius strip for the Bert Williams / George Walker comedy duo, the narrator comments: "One's words flow into the other's and back again, and on and on like an ever-bending act, a joke that never (ever?) never ends" (217). Jess is at his most playful here, but the high-stakes game of formal innovations—revising the sonnet and the book itself as an object—does not belie the atrocities at the core of *Olio*. Instead, they reveal historical continuities that undermine national progress narratives that wish to relegate America's legacy of slavery to another century.

Works Cited

"Dogbytes Interview: Tyehimba Jess." *Cave Canem: A Home for Black Poetry*, cavecanem poets.org/dogbytes-interview-tyehimba-jess/.

Dove, Rita. *Mother Love: Poems*. W. W. Norton, 1996.

Francini, Antonella. "Sonnet vs. Sonnet: The Fourteen Lines in African American Poetry." *RSA Journal*, vol. 14, 2003, pp. 37–66.

Jess, Tyehimba. *Olio*. Wave Books, 2016.

Rutter, Emily Ruth. "The Creative Recuperation of 'Blind Tom' Wiggins in Tyehimba Jess's *Olio* and Jeffery Renard Allen's *Song of the Shank*." *MELUS*, vol. 44, no. 3, Sept. 2019, pp. 175–96, doi:10.1093/melus/mlz026.

Smith, Rich. "The First 4-D Book of Poetry: Tyehimba Jess Has Done the Unimaginable with *Olio*." *The Stranger*, winter 2017, www.thestranger.com/art-and-performance-winter-2017/2017/12/06/25595148/the-first-4-d-book-of-poetry-tyehimba-jess-has-done-the-unimaginable-with-olio.

Thomson, Rosemarie Garland. *Extraordinary Bodies: Figuring Physical Disability in American Culture and Literature*. Columbia UP, 2017.

HOME, INTERIORITY, INTIMACY

Broken Hearts and Broken Homes
The Desolation of the American Sonnet

STEPHEN REGAN

One of the most striking qualities of the sonnet form is its capacity for profound thought and imaginative reach within the seeming constraints of a small number of lines and a prescribed set of metrical and rhythmic expectations. This formal characteristic, with its inverted relationship between scale and scope, continually invites comparisons of a visual and architectural kind, and one of the most familiar structural metaphors through which the sonnet is depicted is that of a small room. From its inception in Renaissance Europe right through to the present day, the sonnet has been likened to a room—one that might be intricately and ornately designed as part of the "house of life," one in which love and domestic harmony might prosper, and one that serves to stimulate rather than confine imaginative vision. Examples abound in the tradition of the English sonnet, all the way from John Donne ("We'll build in sonnets pretty rooms") to Wordsworth ("Nuns Fret Not at Their Convent's Narrow Room") and Elizabeth Barrett Browning ("this close room" in *Sonnets from the Portuguese*). More recent examples of the sonnet-room equivalence can be found in the work of Kate Bingham, whose *Archway Sonnets* (2020) is a book of poems in which the open bedroom window and the closing front door are the frames through which she imaginatively enters and leaves her local London neighborhood.

American poets have extended and complicated the preoccupation in sonnet writing with small rooms and domestic spaces, often in surprising and disturbing ways. We might go so far as to say that one of the distinguishing features of the American sonnet is its radical destabilization of the familiar structural equation between the sonnet form and the house / the home / the room, so that what emerges is a distinct preference, not for the well-furnished house of life or the pretty room, but for the deserted building and the sorrowful home. Frequently, the implicit harmonious relationship in the European sonnet between a secure domestic space and love's fulfillment is flagrantly disrupted. It might be that in seeking to assert a measure of difference and independence from their European counterparts, as well as in seeking to convey a sense of struggle for cultural, domestic, and national security, American writers are much more inclined to give voice to feelings of dislocation and desolation, and to write candidly and dejectedly about broken homes and broken hearts.

We can begin to map a tradition or subgenre of American sonnets of domestic desolation that would include the deserted homes of Frederick Goddard Tuckerman, Edwin Arlington Robinson's "Haunted House," Edna St Vincent Millay's "Sonnets from an Ungrafted Tree" (*p. 37*), Robert Lowell's "To Speak of Woe That Is in Marriage," Sylvia Plath's "Aftermath," and James Merrill's sonnet sequence, "The Broken Home" (*p. 62*), to mention just a few examples. In many ways, Tuckerman is the exemplar of a way of writing sonnets that combines formal elegance with melancholic reflection on broken homes. Tuckerman's sonnets are notable for their desolate domestic settings, alluding mysteriously to terror and anguish in "An upper chamber in a darkened house" and mourning the loss of the occupants in a "red house" poignantly remembered as "Absent of beauty as a broken heart" (26).

The compactness of the sonnet form is used to great effect in Tuckerman's creation of melancholic vignettes, so that curtailment of a story becomes an essential part of the mystery. It's also worth noting how, despite the impression of formal elegance, the sonnet form bends strangely and unexpectedly in response to the painful perception of broken homes and broken hearts. In "An upper chamber in a darkened house," for instance, we move from an opening Petrarchan quatrain (*abba*) to a Shakespearean quatrain (*cdcd*) in the octave, and then to a completely irregular sestet in which one word stands out because it doesn't seem to belong there. It doesn't rhyme with any other word in the sestet. That word is "think" (*7*).

The quality of deep thought induced by meditation on desolate domestic detail is evident too in the sonnets of Edna St. Vincent Millay, especially in the sequence "Sonnets from an Ungrafted Tree," published in 1923. This is how that remarkable sequence opens:

> So she came back into his house again
> And watched beside his bed until he died,
> Loving him not at all.

That "not at all" is devastating but so too is the pathos in the image of "The winter rain" that "Splashed in the painted butter tub outside" (606). In Millay's poems of disappointed love, the equation between the constraints of daily life and the constrained but ultimately liberating form of the sonnet is repeatedly emphasized. The sonnet is often a way of coping with the dark. In the sonnet that begins "When I too long have looked upon your face," there is a decisive turning from the light. Just as Robert Frost confesses to having been "acquainted with the night" in a terza rima sonnet, so Millay must "become accustomed to the dark." The sestet opens with a line that immediately conveys a sensitive apprehension of how form is integral to meaning: "Then is my daily life a narrow room" (578).

Marital discord conveyed through the framing device of a single room also distinguishes Robert Lowell's disturbing sonnet, "'To Speak of Woe That Is in Marriage,'" though the disappointment is expressed in more candidly sexual terms and intensified through references to the husband's alcohol abuse. The poem was originally part of a longer composition ironically titled "Holy Matrimony" and eventually found its position in the closing pages of *Life Studies* (1959), along with those other poems of personal and sexual distress, "Man and Wife" and "Skunk Hour." The compactness of the sonnet conveys a desolate sense of domestic tension and impending breakdown, especially in its relentless couplets that seem to comment ironically and bitterly on the vanquished ideal of a married couple. The sonnet opens, however, with an image of the open bedroom windows, shifting ambivalently between suggestions of oppressive heat and the possibility of a new and fruitful life:

> The hot night makes us keep our bedroom windows open.
> Our magnolia blossoms. Life begins to happen.

Thereafter, any promise associated with the open bedroom windows is brutally crushed. What exists of "home" is routinely presented in negative terms, as with the hopeless rhyme of "home disputes" and "prostitutes," and with the alarming way in which the husband's "swaggering home at five" is immediately followed by the wife's "only thought," which is "how to keep alive" (190). There is a striking disparity between the scholarly apparatus of the poem—its Chaucerian title, its murky origins in Lowell's reading of Catullus 76, and its spliced quotation from Schopenhauer)—and its desperate, colloquial immediacy. Lowell's rhetorical skill in handling the sonnet form is clearly evident in his compelling presentation of the wife's voice and the rhetorical assurance through which he simultaneously catches romantic longing, complaint, and fear. When the sonnet first appeared in *Partisan Review* in 1958, it was not enclosed in quotation marks. The later addition presents the entire sonnet as reported speech and reinforces the impression of the poem as an unedifying domestic narrative that emerges fittingly, if disturbingly, from the bedroom.

In the same year that *Life Studies* was published, Sylvia Plath composed the chilling sonnet "Aftermath," which was later collected in *The Colossus and Other Poems* in 1960. Plath's sonnet house is a burned-out ruin, to which an audience lusting for excitement and scandal is compulsively drawn, much as "The peanut-crunching crowd" moves in on the speaker of "Lady Lazarus" (244). As with the later poem, Plath deftly blends the domestic and the mythological, amplifying a personal tragedy through association with a memorable archetypal figure. The occupant of the ruined house is seen as a descendant of the abandoned Medea in Euripides's tragic drama, with the appellation "mother" and the distinctive "green smock" strangely at odds with the dark, destructive history of her classical predecessor:

> Mother Medea in a green smock
> Moves humbly as any housewife through
> Her ruined apartments (114)

Plath's rhyme scheme evades any association with either Petrarchan or Shakespearean models, following a stark pattern of alternating rhyme words, as if aiming for but not entirely achieving *abababab* in the octave and *cdcdcd* in the sestet. The rhymes themselves are purposefully strained and the rhythm hindered by a predominance of restrictive nine-syllable lines. Plath published very few sonnets, although she used the form extensively in her student days, but "Aftermath" is striking and imposing in the way it views a tragic scene from the perspective of a bystander and in the way it displaces the familiar house or room of sonnet tradition with a burned-out ruin.

Perhaps the most ambitious and most accomplished instance of how a troubled exploration of domestic space generates formal experimentation in the modern American sonnet can be found in James Merrill's sequence of seven sonnets, published in *Nights and Days* in 1966. Merrill's title for the sequence, "The Broken Home," is a euphemism for a child's traumatic experience of family disintegration following his parent's separation. At times, the sonnets resort to the numbing, deadening language of casual cliché, as when recalling "A marriage on the rocks" (198). At the same time, of course, "A marriage on the rocks" might well be an appropriate 1960s updating of the old Petrarchan conceit of shipwreck. The impulse behind the sequence is to discover a finer apprehension of loss and dissolution than is available in ready-made phrases and to register this with greater linguistic precision: "The flame quickens. The word stirs," as the speaker confides in the opening sonnet (197). What makes this such an accomplished sonnet sequence is the way in which the child's anguished relationship with his parents is conveyed through overlapping frames of reference that are at once historical, mythological, and psychological. His father is a World War I pilot turned businessman on Wall Street. His mother is a suffragette, who is expected to be content "giving birth / Tending the house, mending the socks" (198). At the same time, his parents are variously seen as Father Time and Mother Earth, and as tragic actors in a modern Oedipal drama. There is a brilliant economy of style in the fractured narrative of the sequence, much of it made possible by the pervasive imagery of the broken home. The fifth sonnet begins with the child's memory of his mother and father after a party at the house: "Tonight they have stepped out onto the gravel. / The party is over. It's the fall / Of 1931. They love each other still" (198). The usual happy associations of "stepping out" are undermined by the abrasive "gravel." The party is over in every sense and the seasonal fall of 1931 is the setting for both the end of a marriage and the economic decline of the 1930s.

The ambitiousness of writing a painful autobiographical narrative in a sonnet sequence (a formal arrangement more usually associated with happy resolution) is reminiscent of George Meredith's *Modern Love*. In Merrill's sequence, however, the child's troubled consciousness is at the forefront of the narrative and painfully exposed through architectural details as we move through the rooms of the broken house. The child remembers how "A lead soldier guards my windowsill," the windowsill serving as a psychic threshold, but he only finds that "Something in me [his heart presumably] grows heavy, silvery, pliable." He finds companionship with a red dog, an Irish setter, and in the final, seventh sonnet of the sequence, "A child, a red dog roam the corridors, / Still, of the broken home." Like those desolate rooms in Tuckerman's sonnets, the child's old room, with "Its wallpaper— cream, medallioned / With pink and brown" is a place of nightmare.

We come back to the window frame of the broken house in the final sonnet. It seems fitting that the house has been turned into a boarding school, where another child "may actually be allowed / To learn something." Looking out the window, that other child might "Watch a red setter stretch and sink in cloud" (200). There is just a touch of humor as the dog and the sun become one in the image of the "red setter," but there's also a necessary letting go. The final sonnet avoids the clinching effect of a rhyming couplet, settling for a more distant rhyme between lines 11 and 14, "allowed" and "cloud."

Each of Merrill's seven sonnets tries out a different formal arrangement at the level of line and meter, as if trying to repair the broken home. These are innovative and versatile structures, and they constitute a poetic landmark in demonstrating how sonnets and sonnet sequences can accommodate modern narratives of disappointed and disrupted lives. "The Broken Home" is a striking instance of the intense relationship that we often find in American sonnets between the sonnet space and desolate domestic settings. It reminds us that, despite the long-established association of the sonnet with structural and emotional ideals of unity, harmony, and resolution, American poets have often employed the form, with powerful effect, in a troubled exploration of broken homes and broken hearts.

Works Cited

Lowell, Robert. *Collected Poems*. Edited by Frank Bidart and David Gewanter, Farrar, Straus and Giroux, 2003.

Merrill, James. *Collected Poems*. Edited by J. D. McClatchy and Stephen Yenser, Knopf, 2001.

Millay, Edna St. Vincent. *Collected Poems*. Edited by Norma Millay, Harper and Row, 1956.

Plath, Sylvia. *Collected Poems*. Edited by Ted Hughes, Harper and Row, 1981.

Tuckerman, Frederick Goddard. *The Complete Poems of Frederick Goddard Tuckerman*. Edited by N. Scott Momaday, Oxford UP, 1965.

Helene Johnson's "Barbaric Songs," "Choked"

ELEANOR WAKEFIELD

Helene Johnson, born in 1906, was among the younger poets of the Harlem Renaissance. Today, Helene Johnson suffers from relative neglect, which impoverishes our understanding of both the Harlem Renaissance and the possibilities of the sonnet form. Though her free-verse poems are more often anthologized, her sonnets offer complex, sometimes deliberately ambiguous portrayals of Black women's interiority. In particular, two of her sonnets, "A Missionary Brings a Young Native to America" (1928) (*p. 46*) and "Sonnet to a Negro in Harlem" (1927) (*p. 46*), show how the shared contrast between sonnet and "song" reveals one way that Johnson exploits the nuances of the form to simultaneously embody and critique the American sonnet tradition. This essay explores what the sonnet form contributes to the understanding of Black figures in America who are not (yet) American, asking how the form embodies and also creates this vision of America in contrast to an African or otherwise exoticized home. The poems use different rhyme schemes and depict different types of Black characters in America, raising different questions about assimilation, among other things, but the shared theme of song within the sonnet structure provides a way of imagining the creation of a place in America.

The sonnet invites contrasts and tensions, emphasizing them formally in fact, and Johnson uses that effect to distance speaker from observation and form from what the poem represents; the form is aware of its history and its work in creating poetic meaning. In "A Missionary Brings a Young Native to America," first published in *Harlem*, the contrast between speaker and subject of the poem (here in the object position) is put in religious terms, with America represented by the missionary of the title who has brought a "young native" to this continent; in "Sonnet to a Negro in Harlem," which appeared in both *Caroling Dusk* and *Ebony and Topaz*, the contrast between America and the man's "home" (Africa or perhaps the Caribbean) is visual and aural, in how the man looks and sounds walking down the street. These poetic subjects, neither in the subject position of the poem, are not allowed to speak in the sonnet form, in these instances an American form, representing the tenets of a culture they do not yet fit into. Both poems mention the "songs" of the characters. Their songs differentiate them from the people around them, but the poetic form does not give voice to those songs.

Though the sonnet is etymologically a "little song," a phrase that may call to mind spontaneity, it is now more associated with its constructedness or deliberation. Of course, the constraint of the form need not be limiting, but the form's associations with control, tradition, and labor are distinctive. (This also generally separates the sonnet from many lyric poems, especially those by female poets, that critics historically dismissed as songlike, thereby also dismissing the skill required to write them.) Thus, "song," here and more broadly, connotes something closer to "natural" (or even primitive, suggested by the adjective "barbaric" in "Sonnet to a Negro in Harlem") in that it may not have been learned or may be from a folk tradition, and something not yet worked into a particular shape. This distance between the song and the sonnet features prominently in both poems, emphasizing a related distance between speaker/observer and the observed immigrant character whose songs are mentioned but not represented on the page.

The physical presence of the Black body combines with a deep emotional ambivalence about Christianity in "A Missionary Brings a Young Native to America," which imagines one woman's experience of the mythologized journey to "salvation" in America. In this poem, the subject struggles, caught between her traditions and freedom on the one hand and the constraints of this new faith on the other. Never using the first-person pronoun, the sonnet does not grant the young "native" the authority to speak in its form. The form itself can be seen as the "belt / Of alien tenets" that "choked the songs that surged / Within her" (lines 7–9). In this sentence, however, the poem also shows the effort the native is putting into adapting to her new setting and the religion that brought her to it: she tries to pray even when she is alone. Despite her attempts, the conflict between her instincts and what she has been instructed to do extends into the night; her recitation of prayers is superficial, and when she does sleep, she dreams "unholy dreams." The poem ends with her "waiting for the light" (line 14), which ambiguously calls to mind both enlightenment and death, and links to the violent "steel-spiked wave of brick and light" earlier in the poem. As she wrestles with her position now in America, what it is possible to hope for is left unclear.

"A Missionary" is neither English nor Italian in structure; instead, it is composed of an *abab* quatrain and two quintains (*cdcdc* and *efefe*); this formal experiment emphasizes the flexibility of the form even as it reinforces the constraint within which the "young native" is bound. Its rhyme scheme is somewhat subtle—internal rhymes, alliteration, and assonance call attention away from end rhymes as the primary aural effect. Throughout the poem, enjambment emphasizes and enacts the speaker's struggle to fit within the perceived confines of a form that is unfamiliar; the syntax works against the line endings to heighten the tension of the native's internal contortions. Where an Italian sonnet generally has a volta, a break in stanzas and ideas between lines eight and nine, this poem enjambs those lines, forcefully frustrating the expectation of a volta. An English sonnet would have its turn after line 12, and this poem does offer a final image that suggests a summary there, though lines 13 and 14 are not separate syntactically from line 12 and its preceding lines. Lines 10–12 establish the scene before the final summary appears, unrhymed:

> And as the moon grew large and white
> Above the roof, afraid that she would scream
> Aloud her young abandon to the night,
> She mumbled Latin litanies and dreamed
> Unholy dreams while waiting for the light.

So in these structural ways, the expected form of a sonnet is reshaped to contain the struggles the native is experiencing; it adapts, as sonnets do, but in denying readers some expected patterns, it demonstrates unease with which the native adapts to her new environment. The formal variation suggests that just as the content of this poem challenges the traditional structure, the natural inclinations of the native—the songs inside her—challenge the "alien tenets" of her new church and country. And the sonnet's inherent flexibility allows those contrasts to be legible. Putting "songs" into even lines, capturing emotional, physical experiences unique to Black Americans, democratizes the sonnet form. The "Latin litanies," also not given voice, remind us that the sonnet has been and is a genre of the common people, not (only) the elites, whether in Italy or in America, and the poet's skillful inhabiting of the genre with Black bodies and songs reiterates that long tradition.

Like "A Missionary Brings a Young Native to America," "Sonnet to a Negro in Harlem" engages directly with race and place, using the American sonnet to contain the "song" of an objectified character whose voice is not presented. In this poem, the form's inherent concision and duality amplify the internal and external conflicts the speaker experiences as she observes the "Negro" walking down a Harlem street. Though a poem ostensibly about the man walking, like Petrarch's sonnets this one reveals as much about its speaker as its subject, with the speaker presenting the man's body and gait in a received poetic form that can be interpreted as constraining him, as does his new setting.

Formally, of course, it is important that Johnson chose the sonnet to memorialize this image; long associated with unrequited love, the sonnet is also a form of memorial, and in this instance it operates on both levels. While white writers had embraced the sonnet for long enough that by the early twentieth century it carried elite, memorial connotations, Black writers in Harlem took up others of Dante's early purposes of the genre: its ability to speak for and to a particular group, its possibilities for vernacular and highly targeted in-group speech. In describing the man, she calls on the blazon tradition's catalogue of attributes, which can be read as objectifying and even doing violence on the body described but which in this sonnet works to make the reader see and appreciate the Black male body. At the same time, though, putting the description of the man in the second person—"You are disdainful and magnificent" (line 1)—puts the reader in the position of the man. This puts a community of readers in a position of understanding themselves as the man and the observer, seeing through the poem's perspective both views.

The language of the poem returns again and again to the anger of the Negro in Harlem at his situation, which comes to be both the scene described and the poetic form that creates it; paired in nearly every line with his beauty, this anger addresses the political and artistic situation of Black people, particularly poets such as Johnson herself. The adjectives in the opening lines establish the poem's extended contrast: the general descriptions "disdainful" and "magnificent" (line 1) lead to physical traits "perfect" and "pompous" (line 2). As the poem continues, the man's inability to fit in is both a cause and an effect of this "scorn" (line 12); he is shown rejecting a society that has rejected him by a speaker who professes to admire him. A question left open by the ambiguous description is whether she admires the man in spite of his anger or for it. His contrasts especially are shown in the clause that link the opening pair of quatrains: "Small wonder that you are incompetent / To imitate those whom you so despise" (lines 4–5). The man is unwilling and unable to blend in with white society, but because these lines follow "Your dark eyes flashing solemnly with hate" (line 3), the "small wonder" refers to his own attitude, not the racism of white people (or America more broadly, or even the sonnet tradition). "Incompetent" stands out in this line, a word perhaps borrowed from a former boss, reused to give the man his own narrative of his inability to keep a job here in Harlem. The word also ends the first quatrain, rhyming with "magnificent" from the opening line; his incompetence and his magnificence bracket his identity, and the lines between attempt to resolve that contrast in a way that is sympathetic to him. Seen in the context of a world that was not at all kind to Black men and Black artists, the man's inability to fit in—his magnificence and pomposity—can be read as defensive, the speaker giving him the gloss he needs in the face of larger cultural scorn. At the same time, containing his physical description in the sonnet form, one that women and Black writers sought to inhabit though it was not historically "for" them, emphasizes these contrasts and extends them to the Black poet. But because Johnson's sonnet is clearly competent, the claims about the man's ability or inability to fit in or behave in ways that might be acceptable to the people around him become more complicated. This troubled, circular relationship between his anger and his social exclusion is amplified by the poem's ethnographic approach, wherein the speaker assumes a neutral observer status while also filling in the description with interpretation. The reader, therefore, cannot achieve an objective view of the scene because the sonnet is as much the interpretation of the speaker—and thus about the role of this particular speaker—as it is about the Negro in Harlem.

Like "A Missionary," this poem, with the reference to the subject's "song," emphasizes the multiplicity of modes and voices available to the Black immigrant to America and Black artist in America. In both poems, the song appears near the middle of the poem, structurally contained by the form; in "Sonnet to a Negro in Harlem," the octave, all one sentence, ends with a reference to his home (or an exoticized place he calls to mind for the speaker): "Your head thrown back in rich, barbaric song, / Palm trees and mangoes stretched before your eyes" (lines 7–8). This amplifies the audacity of capturing him in a form traditionally used to memorialize love or admiration, by naming so explicitly his "barbar[ism]" while also reminding us of the subjectivity of the speaker. As in "A Missionary," the song reveals to us that the poem's subject (or, again, object) has a voice, but one that is not usually represented in the sonnet form. In this case the speaker imagines what he thinks, his anger about work, but does not quote him. His "song" thus contrasts with Johnson's way of framing, constructing, arguing—the sonnet itself. The "gait" in line 2 foreshadows the extended image of him walking along the lines of the sonnet, but the last four lines especially call attention to form: using "footprint" and "feet," we see his movement compared to the poet's construction of the poem. This further calls attention to the observer's role in creating the man as a figure and in creating the forward propulsion of the poem, which ultimately functions recursively—the image of walking along suggests a straightforwardness that does not apply either to the man's assimilation or to the way sonnets reveal their meaning. The line "Why urge ahead your supercilious feet?" (line 11) asks the man and the poet this rhetorical question, characterizing the feet as too good, in line with other moments in the poem—"You are too splendid" (line 14). The poem suggests that if the feet and lines represent the sonnet, then the man as a figure may not fit within its form, even while presenting him, piece by piece, in this form of adoration. There is a simultaneous suggestion that in his attempt to fit in, his disdain will be evident, pointing to the poet's play with the form as, perhaps, full of "scorn" (line 12). Whether the speaker or poet feels scorn for the sonnet or not, the form clearly creates an opportunity to explore what it means to inhabit a space—literal and poetic—not always welcoming to someone like the man or the speaker. The form embodies tradition and imposition in a useful way, contrasting and creating tension with the figure of the Black man (and the Black, female poet) in America.

Both poems would reward much deeper analysis, but in brief, in both sonnets the Black character embodies a "song," a memory of a place, and a way of being, all of which do not comfortably fit in America, which Johnson uses the sonnet form to demonstrate. Both poems distance speaker and subject (and reader), complicate identity categories, invite scrutiny of the poetic form and its history, and much more. The specific contrast between an embodied song and the sonnet form giving voice to an American speaker observing the Black subjects (or rather objects) adds tension to these already rich, complex poems. Johnson's work contributes to this discussion of innovative continuation of the sonnet tradition by adding to and complicating ways of forging female poetic identity: who the Black female artist is and who she can be are related but distinct questions from who the white female artist is and who she can be in the early twentieth century, and who the Black male artist is and can be. Additionally, the variety of Johnson's sonnet forms highlights experimentation and the adaptability of the form; close reading of her work enriches our conception of both the time period and the genre.

Works Cited

Johnson, Helene. "A Missionary Brings a Young Native to America." *Harlem: A Forum on Negro Life*, 1928. Rpt. *This Waiting for Love: Helene Johnson, Poet of the Harlem Renaissance*, U of Massachusetts Press, 2000, p. 40.

———. "Sonnet to a Negro in Harlem." *Caroling Dusk: An Anthology of Negro Poets*, edited by Countee Cullen, Harper and Brothers, 1927, p. 217; *Ebony and Topaz: A Collectanea*, edited by Charles S. Johnson, Opportunity, 1927, p. 148, rpt. *This Waiting for Love: Helene Johnson, Poet of the Harlem Renaissance*, U of Massachusetts Press, 2000, p. 43.

Mitchell, Verner D. *This Waiting for Love: Helene Johnson, Poet of the Harlem Renaissance*. U of Massachusetts P, 2000.

But Could a Dream

Form and Freedom in Gwendolyn Brooks's
Domestic Sonnets

TESS TAYLOR

In a landmark interview about artistic practice in 1969 with George Stavros in Madison, Wisconsin, Gwendolyn Brooks said of art: "You just can't stay in your comfortable old grooves. You have to extend yourself. And it's easier to stay home and drink beer" (2). In this conception, Brooks's version of comfort is "staying home," and her art is "extending yourself," presumably moving *beyond* whatever home is. Art asks us to travel, move beyond comfort, unsettle ourselves, realign our familiar. But what does traveling mean here—and now? How do we travel? By what means do we productively unsettle ourselves? The question has new resonance when we consider that so many of Brooks's poems are actually about literal homes or homelike public places. Her poems circle neighborhoods, exteriors, alleys, inhabitants, businesses, but also actually map the inside of homes themselves. In fact, in that same 1969 interview, Brooks described her work this way: "I believe I have written more 'kitchenette building'-type poems than I have written about birds singing and feeling sorry for a girl who's temporarily overwhelmed by grief" (12).

Indeed, rather than leaving "home," Brooks's art of unsettlement actually emerges from exploring and voicing home or homes, in making poetic maps of familiar and lived-in spaces. In fact, it's arguable that Brooks's project is to explore her own domestic vernacular, to play the very grooves of neighborhoods and people that represent and embody her sense of community, home, and belonging. Brooks's whole work exists and is framed with contexts of gender and racial and class boundaries that limit the freedoms to travel, leave, explore, and move away from such "homes." Brooks often explores the confinements of the places she writes about, whether the ruts of segregation and racism, or the confining experiences of class and gender, or both. The speakers of Brooks's poems are often reacting to forms of confinement, "involuntary" places where the domestic is a received rather than chosen space.

How do you unsettle yourself while staying home? How do you play your life's given grooves against themselves? As I write in the ninth month of a pandemic, when many of us have been asked to "stay home" for nearly a year now, these questions feel newly resonant. I'm about to spend a few moments in the grooves of Brooks's domestic sonnets, asking how she uses the sonnet form to dramatize domestic containment—fixed enclosures, whether comfortable or not—and also to hint, in the same quarters, at the way the sonnet itself can offer both lyric transit, lyric unsettlement, and lyric liberation. I'm interested in how Brooks's sonnets harness the tension of lyric both to stage protest and to introduce some possibilities of freedom. In a related groove: I speak from a certain frequency. I offer these thoughts on confinement as I write at 6:30 am in a garage office which is also, I feel I should report, a much-used laundry room.

The sonnet, I think, always carries with it the whiff of its courtly history, even when that history is subverted, upended, repurposed. In fact, the chance to subvert the sonnet's trailing history is also one of its excitements. To reinvent a form successfully is to charge it both forward and backward in time, electrifying it anew. When Terrance Hayes constructs his *American Sonnets for My Past and Future Assassin*, and his speakers address the changeable and violent force of American racism, we cannot help overhearing the way Wyatt or Dryden or Shakespeare crafted the echoing mask of the sonnet's rhymes to address the elusive, changeable lover. In his later address, Hayes echoes and subverts this tradition: We no longer speak to the unseen lover but to the unseen assassin, who is outer, but also inner; other, but also self. Hayes's work reminds us at every turn that the courtly lover may be gone, but we now live in an endless fraught dialogue with racism's recurring destructive force. The very way that the sonnet has already spoken sets up this reverberation in its current speech. Hayes's poems compound both meaning and resonance through this long echo.

Brooks's sonnets are no less revolutions and reframings of their tradition. They craft what Courtney Thorsson calls a "black aesthetic of the domestic" (149). Brooks's sonnet masks act as sites from which to create and fathom personhood, subjectivity, desire, and rage. In writing poems for home, for cramped spaces, in the voices of women, and for the fury of a dream deferred, Brooks crafts both a speaker and its audience, widening the sonnet's range, setting down new stakes for it. Brooks's sonnets create rooms in which new speakers and new spaces can be heard and seen. They also create sites at which speakers can reflect on questions of confinement and escape.

I have picked three domestic sonnets as examples so we can walk in their grooves, examining a range whose composition spanned twenty years. These are "kitchenette building" from *A Street in Bronzeville* (1945) (*p. 54*), "the sonnet-ballad" from *The Anniad* (1949), and "my dreams, my works, must wait till after hell" from *Selected Poems* (1963).

The first, "kitchenette building," an early sonnet, isn't quite a proper sonnet. It only has thirteen lines. It begins in the voice of a chorus:

> We are things of dry hours and the involuntary plan,
> Grayed in, and gray. "Dream" makes a giddy sound, not strong
> Like "rent," "feeding a wife," "satisfying a man." (3)

What do we make of this sonnet—or almost sonnet—that *almost* lets a dream sing inside rooms that are *almost* apartments? What do we make of this domestic interior, in which we overhear voices of speakers, who are not even sure they can call themselves speakers, open by calling themselves "things"? Who speak in a chorus of voices, as if distinction itself were too much luxury?

These are not quite sonnet's subjects: A building, its inhabitants, and the strange, possible, uncertain space by which dream allows us to feel human at all. On the level of form, we're in uncertain space as well: Although this thirteen-line poem is a not-quite sonnet, it gains its energy from its nearness to sonnet, from its proximity and also abnegation of the fourteenth line woven through. We hear the aural possibility of sonnet set in long syllabic lines that easily could be but have not been relineated. The poem's opening tercet has thirty-eight syllables, two short of the forty that would lend themselves to iambic quatrains. Those leggy lines have fourteen and twelve syllables, while in the rest of the quatrains, the lines have ten or eleven syllables. The poem's second stanza is not a tercet but a quatrain, again hoveringly suggesting sonnet space. Could a dream live inside this poem? Similarly, could this poem be a sonnet? Maybe. Maybe not. But I would say that in truncating the sonnet, Brooks's plan feels not involuntary but precise.

Meanwhile, the poem does give voice and make room for something "white and violet," something "warm." There is, despite all, a distinctive twisting wish inside these lines. The possibility of the dream questions and turns against its own question, much as Keats's "Bright Star" proposes that the lover become a distant priestly star but also remain within the mortal frame of fickle human breath. This wish and counterwish, this act of volta, embodies an act of sonnet, as well. In "kitchenette building," the sonnet gives breath-space to the half-dream that might be taken away.

It is a strange thing that the act of wishing within in a sonnet seems to create such outsized space. Just as when we say "don't think of a white horse," the horse is invariably all the more there, this insertion of the dream—which we may only have lyric time for, or indeed *no* time for—is one of the lingering effects of this poem: the white and violet dream may follow you all day, simply because the poem has suggested so convincingly that it cannot. Even in 1969—after she never wrote sonnets again—Brooks suggested this as the template for the kind of poem she'd be working on for the rest of her life.

Brooks conceived of another poem as sonnet-ballad in "Appendix to the Anniad: leaves from a loose-leaf war diary," from *The Anniad*, published in 1949, four years after *A Street in Bronzeville*. That poem, "the sonnet-ballad" begins "Oh mother, mother, where is happiness? / They took my lover's tallness off to war / Left me lamenting" (51). Both title and subject remind us of another way that Brooks remakes her sonnets: by reminding us of the sonnet's less courtly cousin, the ballad. This sonnet is more formally familiar than the thirteen-liner "kitchenette building." In fact, it's a perfect Shakespearean sonnet and is even about love. But in framing these verses as sonnet-ballad, Brooks earths them into a folksier register. The ballad tradition and the sonnet tradition deal in thwarted love. The prime difference between a sonnet and a ballad is that the capacious ballad can always accept another improvised folk verse, while the sonnet, in its tidy courtly rooms, must end. Yet this sonnet, simply by being in the voices of women or in the voice of a woman who is losing her love, tips its register toward a tradition filled with the laments of anonymous women. I have to say: I don't know whether this sonnet is "domestic" per se, though I suppose when I imagine a daughter talking to her mother, the mere presence of women talking suggests domestic space. I'll add another wrinkle: It's interesting that Brooks has also claimed this register for an epic, *The Anniad*. And Annie's sonnet refers to a larger, historic tragedy: love in a time of war. So not only is Brooks proposing that the sonnet be ballad, she is proposing that the domestic be epic, as well. Brooks adopts this form by blurring registers. Brooks's sonnet is meant to be both ballad and epic at once.

Despite their different uses of the sonnet form, both "kitchenette building" and "the sonnet-ballad" are motored forward by the conditional tense, the tense of wishing, the tense of something hoped for or intuited rather than present. Both use the conditional tense to dramatize not only confinement inside the sonnet but also to imagine ways outside that confinement. Just as Brooks writes "But could a dream" (about the white-and-violet sprig inside "kitchenette building"), in "the sonnet-ballad" she writes, "Some day the war will end, but oh, I knew / When he went grandly out that door / That my sweet love would have to be untrue." The war will end, but how will the lover have changed? We hang in the zone of waiting, trying to map a happiness that may or may not ever come to exist. No less than in "kitchenette building," this sonnet's speaker circles an elusive domestic dream.

In closing, I turn now to one of the last sonnets Brooks ever wrote, published in 1963 and also squarely about the perils of confinement, about the labors of waiting, and of dreams deferred. That poem, "my dreams my works must wait till after hell," begins

> I hold my honey and I store my bread
> In little jars and cabinets of my will. (23)

The speaker notes "I am very hungry. I am incomplete" (line 5). This is a poem of plosion of tight and furious half rhyme. In contrast to the two previous sonnets, which inhabited a chorus style "we" or voiced the song of a lover, this is a sonnet of direct and personal address. It is the attempt of a self, an "I," to persevere in the face of both disappointment and fury, and it forges that perseverance in figures of the preserve. How do we persevere? How do we preserve ourselves when we are told endlessly to wait? How and when do we get back to the stored thing? This sonnet crafts a small explosive container of tumbling, plosive half rhymes, where any "I" who speaks this poem will find their own tongue exploding against their mouth. This is dramatic language at the extreme: tilted forward by a constellation of *h*'s, *t*'s, and *d*'s, and our very tongues are held and lidded by their pressure on our teeth. In embodying this confinement down to the level of syllable, this sonnet performs fury, pushing against the tightness of some seemingly indefinable time, which asks us to defer both honey and our bread for some lingering, disconcerting, incompleting hell.

We are in a season when many of us, any of us, some more than others, may recognize the fury of this speaker. This poem has companioned me these long months, when so many dreams have been deferred and lidded, and when it is not clear when or what lives we will ever resume. And while the kitchenette building sends up a dream as a possible wish, this poem only asks that we keep our "eyes pointed in," hoping that someday we can get back to the "honey and bread" and someday the jars we unlatch will be sweet again. Perhaps, when that moment comes our "taste will not have turned insensitive" (line 13). How then, is it, that in simply reciting these furious words, I am unlidded and feel held in my rage?

In her 1969 interview with George Stavros, Brooks said: "The poet deals in words with which everyone is familiar. We all handle words. And I think the poet, if he wants to speak to anyone, is constrained to do something with those words so that they will (I hate to use the word) mean something, will be something that a reader may touch" (2). What if, in fact, the words, in their touch, create their reader? What if the very sounds and rhythms of words can remind us, inside ourselves, that we are human? What if the right words provide the tools by which we may both recognize and unsettle home?

In 1983, Brooks would say "my works express race and focus on rage" (Thorsson 155). In 1969, Brooks was already being asked to define the relationship between that rage and lyricism. She wisely sidestepped the idea that there is a binary distinction between them. This lyric is about as good a vessel for anger as one can hope for. It also contains the hint of a prayer that what we unlid, whenever we may unlid it, may still be good.

When I exit the room where I have written this essay about sonnets, I will reenter the ninth month of the pandemic, and the small catastrophe of my home—a bungalow where two parents struggle to work full-time jobs even part time and two children also need care. The dishes are not done; the laundry is strewn; my son doesn't understand fractions. My daughter is lonely. The domestic will be all present and the thin scrim of this "writer's life" will fall away, perhaps for days. I'll run the machines, sweep the floor, pull out odd bits to craft into dinner. The writing I'll do will be to make lists with care, because grocery store lines are long, manageable if (only if) you get there on a weekday or order in groceries, which sometimes I can, for which I am grateful. I will clean my house, for which I am grateful. There is huge privilege in having a house to clean and the possibility of ordering groceries. Also, the furious longing of these hard days, the cut of them: sometimes mopping the floor after the kids are in bed or waiting in line at the market for food, I hear the voice in my head turn and mock me: "But, do you know how many women's lives have ever been only this—market and cleaning, cooking and mopping, keeping children alive?" And, then with a sneer: "How dare you have once thought your life could be different?" And this voice is not wholly wrong, even though it is not kind.

Still, the tight fury of this sonnet! The way in which it is motored forward by its deferred longings, by its bid to unlid those longings, even in such space. It is a jar for anger and honey. This is verse that can companion us, sliding from "incomplete" to "Wait" (lines 5, 7) and "hurt" to "heart" (lines 9, 11). In it I can feel my almost unspeakable domestic grief, a grief I might otherwise not dare to language, being as it is, domestic. I am grateful to this sonnet, these sonnets, their dreams and rooms. I keep my eyes pointed in. But while I do, such poems are honey and bread.

Works Cited

Brooks, Gwendolyn. "kitchenette building." *Blacks*. Chicago: Third World Press, 1987, p. 20. Rpt. *Selected Poems*. Perennial Classics, p. 3

———. "my dreams my works must wait till after hell." *A Street in Bronzeville*. Harper and Brothers, 1945. Rpt. *Selected Poems*. Perennial Classics, p. 23.

———. "the sonnet-ballad." *Annie Allen*. Harper and Brothers, 1949. Rpt. *Selected Poems*. Perennial Classics, p. 51.

Brooks, Gwendolyn, and George Stavros. "An Interview with Gwendolyn Brooks." *Contemporary Literature*, vol. 11, no. 1, 1970, pp. 1–20. *JSTOR*, www.jstor.org/stable/1207502.

Thorsson, Courtney. "Gwendolyn Brooks's Black Aesthetic of the Domestic." *MELUS*, vol. 40, no. 1, spring 2015, pp. 149–76, doi.org/10.1093/melus/mlu062.

Gwendolyn Brooks's Esoteric Sonnet "A Lovely Love" as an Alchemical Metatext

JON WOODSON

The earliest African American, modern, esoteric sonnet was Gwendolyn Bennett's "Sonnet 1" (1927), a reworking of Elizabeth Barret Browning's "I thought once how Theocritus had sung." A member of A. R. Orage's esoteric movement that operated under the guise of the more mainstream Harlem Renaissance, Gwendolyn Bennett adapted the pattern for writing esoteric prose fiction to writing sonnets. The four maxims that underpin the esoteric project are "to know, to dare, to will, and to keep silent" (Levi 30). The ability to write while keeping silent depends on the use of code. Bennett's repurposing of the sonnet to communicate doctrines of spiritual development served as a model seven other writers of esoteric sonnets—Melvin Tolson, Owen Dodson, Frank Yerby, Margaret Walker, Helene Johnson, Gwendolyn Brooks, and Robert Hayden. Taking up a vigorous experimentation where Bennett had left off, Gwendolyn Brooks moved well beyond Bennett's straightforward reversal of Browning's familiar love poem.

Gwendolyn Brooks's sonnet "A Lovely Love" (*p. 55)* is composed of an overlay of five separate semantic levels. This interpretive scheme is only approximate and is merely a suggestion of Brooks's complex intertextual and hypertextual web of associations. First, lyrical realism is anchored in biography and stereotype, where Brooks's father is a janitor. Second, a defining Roman and Greek myth incorrectly substitutes the janitor's javelin for a discus. Third, a Messiah theme, where young love is considered as infinite, does not explain how the birth of the Messiah is comparable to the flight of the panicked lovers.

Additionally, Shakespearean themes and prosody are the determining factors in Brooks's sonnet, which signifies on Shakespeare's "lovely boy" sonnets. It would require an exhaustive study to determine how that intertextuality operates. For now, we can point out that the "lovely boy" section of Shakespeare's sonnets begins with Sonnet 126, a sonnet so irregular that it has continually perplexed Shakespearean scholars; Brooks's is also a deviant sonnet, with both a volta and a parting couplet and fifteen lines. Brooks's curious title makes another connection to Shakespeare's sonnet. Despite the contradictory notion that the lovely love being described in Brooks's poem is transcendent, when it is put next to the love in the Shakespearean cycle, everything must be reevaluated. Shakespeare's sonnet cycle is notorious for not being lovely: one section of the poems describes a homosexual love affair, while another describes an affair with a Black prostitute afflicted with a venereal disease.

Brooks's sonnet reiterates the rhetoric of Shakespeare's sonnets in a slantwise fashion. Brooks's first line twice presents the "let" found in twenty-three of Shakespeare's 154 sonnets. The comedic contrast between Brooks's rhetoric and Shakespeare's is clearly mocking. Brook's furtive teenage lovers first declare for improvised hideaways—alleys, a hall. Another arrangement is found in line five, "Let it be stairways," and then the imperative mood of "let me not" is playfully reversed by "Not lit" in line eleven. Brooks's vocabulary is unusual, yet the 108 words of Brooks's surface text harbor nineteen of Shakespeare's words—thought, played, found, make, fall, kiss, kindness, lovely, love, star, above, wise, men, either, coming, must, catch, here, run.

Having broached the subject of Shakespeare's 154 sonnets, we must consider how Brooks stands in respect to them. In the 154 sonnets of the 1609 quarto, the first 126 are addressed to a young man; the last twenty-eight are either addressed to or refer to a woman. Margaret Healy notes that "Shakespeare's enigmatic dark lady makes her abrupt entrance in Sonnet 127, immediately compelling the question, why is she 'black'? This is, of course, a witty strategy, 'cocking a snook' at Petrarchan norms and allowing the poet to demonstrate his considerable prowess, subverting the usual blazon with 'dun' breasts and 'black wires' (Sonnet 130, lines 3, 4) and shaping novel beauty in his lines" (98). On its surface, Brooks's sonnet challenges easy interpretation since the multiple levels of social definition—age, race, gender, and morality—fly in the face of the assertion that the lovers are "definitionless." The lovers themselves flee because they are all too aware of the degree to which they lack the sublime state of being above definition.

Other elements of Shakespeare's writings also intrude on Brooks's sonnet. Though critics have not mentioned it, we cannot help but experience the sonnet as a parody of *Romeo and Juliet*. The end word of line seven, "shocks," reminds us of the famous soliloquy in act 3 of *Hamlet*.

Finally, the presence of spiritual alchemy in Brooks's sonnet represents the most complex inclusion. In the first place, alchemy is unfamiliar to most critics of modern poetry; a subset of this unfamiliarity is that most critics do not know that alchemy can be chemical, spiritual, or simultaneously spiritual and chemical. In addition to those ambiguities, the association of Shakespeare and his sonnets with spiritual alchemy is unknown to most critics of modern literature, as well as to most Shakespearean scholars. In *Shakespeare, Alchemy, and the Creative Imagination*, however, Margaret Healy states that "we should definitely take more notice of the numerous Shakespearean hints and prompts and look less 'head on' in order to uncover the spiritual and philosophical meanings playing beneath the 'strange' literal layer of his sonnets. For Renaissance culture, truth was always hiding in askew ('askance,' Sonnet 110) perspectives" (168–69). While "it is strangely rare to meet literary scholars who have glanced at the *Hermetica* or read Pico's *Oratio*, let alone alchemical poetry" (Healy 209), Brooks was aware of Shakespeare's investment in spiritual alchemy in his sonnet sequence and indicates as much in her sonnet: indeed, one important aspect of Brooks's sonnet is its subtle betrayal of Shakespeare as a fellow alchemist.

Returning to the semantic layers, the sonnet's lyrical realism can be penetrated by applying Healy's point that the literal layer is a screen for Shakespeare's esoteric presentation to Brooks's poetry as well. Intentional mistakes were used in the esoteric texts written by the followers of A. R. Orage to establish that the texts were written in code and that they contained esoteric information. It is only within matters as familiar as myth that mistakes can be made. Greek and Roman myth serves as an index pointing to the sonnet's true nature. Brooks's sonnet presents the myth of Hyacinth in lines two and three. The mistake is that Brooks supplies a javelin, while in the myth Hyacinth is struck and killed by a discus. Lines four, six, and fourteen continue to toy with the myth, for "make the petals fall," "where you have thrown me," and "catch" allude to the accidental death of Hyacinth.

The Messiah theme has extensive contingencies. The title of the sonnet also points to a complex range of esoteric associations. The letters *lv* allude to the Hebrew number 36 (*lamed vau*), an index for the tzadikim. In the lore of Kabbalah, the tzadikim are the thirty-six concealed righteous women and men whose role is to maintain the planet and save it from destruction (Zwerin 3). The specific task in which Brooks and her tzadikim circle was engaged was the creation of a modern secular messiah, which is why the Nativity takes up three of the sonnet's fourteen lines. A. R. Orage believed that, as modern tzadikim, his esoteric group was charged with arranging an enactment of an "objective drama" that would change world history for the better. The Orageans believed that there had been two earlier messiahs brought about by two earlier "Objective Dramas" (King 163–64). The first was Osiris, the handiwork of the ancient Egyptian priests; the second messiah was Jesus, the handiwork of the Essenes. The Orageans were largely disguised as Marxists, and as such they made two attempts to erect a modern messiah. The first two attempts failed; the third attempt abandoned Marxism and, according to the Orageans, set up Martin Luther King Jr. as a prominent civil rights leader. King's assassination constitutes an unknown: in accounts of the messiah conspiracy in Oragean fictions, *Judas, My Brother* (1968) by Frank Yerby and *Jesus Came Again: A Parable* (1956) by Vardis Fisher, the messiah is supposed to survive. We can infer from the later account provided by Ralph Ellison's *Three Days before the Shooting* (2010) that King's assassination was unplanned and that it disrupted the entire Oragean project (Woodson, *Notes* 138–46). Crucially, Brooks's sonnet was written during King's career but before his death. In Brooks's sonnet the indices for the three messiahs are too numerous to fully account for in this brief exposition. The Egyptian index that points to Osiris is found in line fourteen, where "us here" may be read as Horus, the reborn Osiris. The "splintery box" in line five alludes to the box in which Set imprisoned Osiris. The "stairway" in line five is the heraldic ladder of Osiris, which is also called a stairway in the *Pyramid Texts*: "A stairway has been laid down for you away from the Duat and toward the place where Orion is, and the Sky's Ox shall receive your arm" (Allen 232). The index that points to Jesus appears on the literal level of the poem, in the "swaddling clothes" (line 10), "wise men" (line 12), and "fondling star" (line 11). The name of the third messiah, King, is made insubstantially present in the sonnet by virtue of a diffuse sounding of *k*'s and *-ing*'s throughout the poem.

The elements of Shakespearean themes and prosody in Brooks's sonnet are divulged through the poem's vocabulary, allusions to the "Sonnets" and to the plays, and through various forms of wordplay. Nearly every word in Brooks's sonnet is severally cross-referential. For instance, "shocks," beyond its association with *Hamlet*, when combined with sphere in "atmosphere" (line 15), phonetically forms Shakespeare's name as "shock sphere." Reading "shock sphere" through an esoteric lens suggests that Brooks recognized that Shakespeare's sonnets described his spiritual transformation through alchemy.

The coded semantic level makes available the spiritual alchemy in the poem. Spiritual alchemy is a practice that reasserts an alternative meaning to the contents of chemical alchemy. Brooks's complex treatment of this topic beggars description: nearly every word is an index leading to an element associated with alchemy. The poem may be an initiatory text, though it presents the reader with such a comprehensive and obscure supply of alchemical references as to not be readily understood. Brooks supplies the word "alchemy" in line thirteen through the cabala, the phonetic-syllabic-omnidirectional-discontinuous code used by Medieval alchemists. The first syllable of alchemy, "al," resounds throughout the opening lines: "alleys," "hall," "fall"; the last two syllables are sounded by "coming" in line thirteen. Texts written by Orage's followers always include the word cabala, though as in the case in Brooks's sonnet, it is nearly indecipherable, since the word is itself written in the code—"catch" (line 14) combined with "people" (line 13). When read closely, Brooks's sonnet divulges the names of alchemists, the names of alchemical texts, important alchemical concepts and processes, the components of the alchemical laboratory, and the fundamental principles of the alchemical process.

Alchemy takes its origin from the Emerald Tablet attributed to the Egyptian god Thoth (also called Hermes Trismegistus). Brooks gives this source phonetically in line two as "epithet and thought," where Thoth is equivalent to "thought" and "epithet" is a clue to the relevance of equating "thought" and "Thoth." Line one of the sonnet names two major compendiums of esoteric information: "alleys" alludes to Rene Alleau's *History of Occult Sciences* (1966), and "hall" alludes to Manly Hall's *The Secret Teaching of All Ages* (1928). In addition, "sought" in line three alludes to Mary Anne (South) Atwood's *A Suggestive Inquiry into the Hermetic Mystery* (1850). These texts inscribe their presence on the esoteric form of the poem. The words "definitionless" and "sphere" are distinctive terms found in the Alleau and Hall volumes. "Definitionless" and "sphere" in the final line connect to "alleys" and "hall" in line one by drawing an apprehensible X across the words of the sonnet, turning the material text itself into a cosmic alchemical emblem. As a final imposition, Brooks's sonnet draws a line from "sphere"/fear upwards and across to "alleys"/Alleau as a way of tracing the entire atomic project back to the tragic successes of chemical alchemy. This is Brooks's way of designating spiritual alchemy as the means of countering the historical source of destruction represented by the catastrophic atomic transformations made possible by chemical alchemy. "Hall" is one of the most potent words in the sonnet, for it is combined with another word that makes visible an important level of the poem: "definitionless." Brooks looks to Manly Hall's use of "definitionless" in his discussion of "the mysterious tenth sphere or cosmic egg—the definitionless Cipher of the Mysteries" (*Secret Teachings of All Ages* 272).

Wordsworth has famously related the Romantic sonnet to a room. Brooks associates the esoteric sonnet with the cosmic egg, which is also the alembic or alchemical urn. South's hermetic text introduces an alchemical urn (*A Suggestive Inquiry* 13), indicated by an anagram found in line thirteen—"run." Thus, Brooks's esoteric sonnet-urn-egg is a microcosm, the totality of everything.

Brooks's sonnet presents the entire esoteric historical project of the Orageans, who planned to save the earth by creating a secular messiah. The coded closing line of the sonnet, "Definitionless in the strict atmosphere," deciphers to warn that the earth will be destroyed by atomic war—"Fear atomic destruction": the implication is that unless the new messiah is brought into being, there is no hope for human survival.

Works Cited

Allen, James P. *The Ancient Pyramid Texts*. Society of Biblical Literature, 2005.

Atwood, Mary Ann (South). *A Suggestive Inquiry into the Hermetic Mystery With a Dissertation on the More Celebrated of the Alchemical Philosophers, being an attempt towards the recovery of the ancient experience of Nature*. Trelawny Saunders, 1850.

Brooks, Gwendolyn. "A Lovely Love." *The Bean Eaters*. Harper, 1960. Rpt. *Blacks*. Chicago: Third World Press, 1987, p. 49.

Goldman, Judith. "On Gwendolyn Brooks's *The Bean Eaters*." *Poetry in 1960, A Symposium*, edited by Al Filreis, special issue of *Jacket 2*, 29 April 2011, jacket2.org/article/gwendolyn-brooks-bean-eaters.

Hall, Manly P. *The Secret Teachings of All Ages: An Encyclopedic Outline of Masonic, Hermetic, Qabbalistic, and Rosicrucian Symbolical Philosophy: Being an Interpretation of the Secret Teachings Concealed within the Rituals, Allegeries, and Mysteries of All Ages*. H. S. Crocker, 1928. Rpt. Philosophical Research Society, 1988.

Healy, Margaret. *Shakespeare, Alchemy and the Creative Imagination*. Cambridge UP, 2011.

King, C. Daly. *The Oragean Version*. 1951. Author's private collection. Rpt. Book Studio, 2016.

Levi, Eliphas. *Transcendental Magic, Its doctrine and Ritual.* Translated by A. E. Waite. G. Redway, 1896.

Melhem, D. H. *Gwendolyn Brooks: Poetry and the Heroic Voice.* Lexington: UP of Kentucky, 1987.

Mootry, Maria K. "'Tell It Slant': Disguise and Discovery as Revisionist Poetic Discourse in *The Bean Eaters*." *A Life Distilled: Gwendolyn Brooks, Her Poetry and the Heroic Voice*, edited by Maria K. Moody and Gary Smith. U of Illinois P, 1987, pp. 177–92.

Woodson, Jon. *Notes on Ralph Ellison's Three Days before the Shooting.* CreateSpace, 2017.

Zwerin, Rabbi Raymond A. "The 36—Who Are They? A Kol Nidre Sermon." Temple Sinai, Denver, www.themathesontrust.org/papers/judaism/thirty-six.pdf.

Three Mothers, Two Eves
Female Virtuosity and Outrage in the American Sonnet

ANNA MARIA HONG

This essay discusses the sonnet as a vehicle for female virtuosity and expression of attendant outrage in various registers, examining sonnets by two twentieth-century maestros of form, Gwendolyn Brooks and Sylvia Plath, along with the very contemporary collaborative sonnets of Simone Muench and Jackie K. White.

I approach this writing as a practitioner, noting the patterns that I perceive in these poets' invocations of the sonnet, and as someone who knows the form from long engagement with its musical and political possibilities. When one is working within the sonnet, one can feel a direct engagement with other constraints and constructs; for example, of gender, race, and class, as embodied by the form's notably male, white, and wealthy European tradition. As Gwendolyn Brooks says at the end of the last poem in "The Womanhood," which concludes her ground-breaking second collection *Annie Allen*, "The toys are all grotesque / And not for lovely hands," adding:

> Let us combine. There are no magics or elves
> Or timely godmothers to guide us. We are lost, must
> Wizard a track through our own screaming weed. (66)

Published in 1949, *Annie Allen* was the first book by any Black writer to win the Pulitzer Prize, and Brooks, of course, earned many other firsts in her illustrious career. The closing lines of "The Womanhood" cap a series of sonnets, ballads, and other poems, beginning with the sonnet sequence, "the children of the poor" in which a young woman contemplates her life, her writing, the destructions of World War II on the home front, and the lives and futures of her children who are not just her biological progeny but whole populations facing constant threat, "adjudged the leastwise of the land" (sonnet 2, line 2) and in need of the poet's empowering "brisk contour" (sonnet 2, line 5), which she delivers in this series, speaking as both a young mother and as an African American writer and activist. I want to examine the fourth sonnet, which confronts the dilemmas of her position head on, beginning with the directives to

> First fight. Then fiddle. Ply the slipping string
> With feathery sorcery; muzzle the note
> With hurting love; the music that they wrote (54)

These opening lines are followed by a series of commands extending the metaphor of playing music in the context of battle, as the speaker dramatizes the challenges to speaking and being heard. The poem is remarkable to me in both its candor—the overt call to fighting, war, and hate—and in its slyness. Even as the speaker privileges the fight in this ars poetica, recognizing the need "For having first to civilize a space" (line 13) that is hostile to her and her peoples' very presence, "Carry[ing] hate / in front of you and harmony behind" (line 14), she mellifluously sears her points home in precise iambic pentameter and a perfectly turned Petrarchan rhyme scheme.

Notably, only a few feet deviate from the iambs. The alliterative spondees of "First fight" and "Win war" add sonic emphasis to those calls to action. The trochee of "muzzle" speaks to a desire to inhibit "the music that they wrote," which I interpret as a reference to the sonnet tradition itself, which must be invoked in a dazzling manner akin to magic: "Bewitch, bewilder" (line 4). By the end of the poem, the fiddle has become a violin, an embodiment of high European culture and tradition, much like the sonnet, which has been deployed in the poem as an instrument of change with "feathery sorcery."

Lines 5–7 ironically instruct the poet/musician to use the form/instrument gently so as not to disturb racialized and gendered expectations of delicacy and acquiescence—"Devote / The bow to silks and honey"—a sentiment that is immediately undercut by the delightfully understated turn of "Be remote / A while from malice and from murdering," as if the speaker is calmly drinking tea while taking a break from a crime spree and not just being distant, as the phrase before the link break would indicate.

Then, literally without missing a beat, Brooks ushers in her call to war with collected resolve: "But first to arms, to armor" (line 9), deploying the doubled sound and meaning in case we didn't get it the first time. This, to me, is the declaration of a pioneer, someone who is well aware of the precarious nature of all her positions as the first to break ground in treacherous territory, the field of literary vantage, which is also her home, as underscored by her fluid manipulation of the sonnet's rigors, and where embracing malice and murderous rage as a necessary starting point liberate the poet-speaker to stake that place. The ironized adherence to expectations in lines 5–7 may be required in order to be taken seriously as a Black American woman poet "Qualify[ing] to sing / Threadwise" in the mid-twentieth century, but the unfettered fury beginning with "First fight" literally envelops these lines.

Speaking of wrath and virtuosity, I'll look next at Sylvia Plath's "Sonnet: To Eva" (*p. 69*) which is among her juvenilia, composed before 1956, when Plath was in her teens and early twenties, probably around the same time as Brooks's *Annie Allen*. Although Plath isn't known for her sonnets, the sonnet predominates in her very early writing, and her early training in the form resonates through her oeuvre, through the gut-punching rhymes and rhythms and drive to finality of *Ariel*.

This Shakespearean sonnet begins in murderous rage with "All right, let's say you could take a skull and break it" (304), the first stanza likening a victim's skull to a smashed clock, expressing a desire to kill time, as well as describing a person who is named in the second stanza simply as "a woman" or women as indicated by the eponymous Eva/Eve who has been "betrayed" in a display of her own broken speech: "inane mechanic whims" and "notched tin platitudes" (lines 7, 11).

These bitterly catalogued remains remain unfixable, neither by "man nor demigod," the inner life scrambled before and after the killing. One can surmise that the killer, the unnamed "you," are the thwarted words themselves, the unsaid, or "jargon yet unspoken," as the lucid description of what can't be articulated occupies the bulk of the poem, though something survives both the curtailed living and the violent undoing. In the sonnet's concluding couplet, "The idiot bird leaps up" and sings the time, rising like an everyday phoenix, unable to keep itself from talking, with the speaker characterizing its song as "lunatic thirteens." Out-of-time music and madness following the traumatic shattering—or what is perceived as madness—are the only places where the woman can speak.

As with the fourth sonnet of Brooks's "the children of the poor," the music itself matters, both contradicting the poem's overt assertions, as the young woman poet eloquently evokes the disastrous effects of suppressed speech, and enhancing the message. Unlike the rest of the poem, which employs irregular meter, the final couplet, where the reeling, irrepressible bird sings, employs nearly perfect iambic pentameter:

> The idiot bird leaps up and drunken leans
> To chirp the hour in lunatic thirteens.

This poem inhabits the sonnet as a kind of corset. Like Brooks, Plath elaborates on the gendered speech/verse that dams and dooms the singer, constricted to speaking only of "weather, / Perfume, politics, and fixed ideals" (line 12), straining against the iambic weft until the couplet's release, when the bird loses its domestic trappings.

And like Brooks, Plath is hyperaware—even from extreme youth—of the forces arrayed against her very act of speaking, describing the brutally high price of speaking as "a woman" (line 5) in gruesome detail. The skull/clock has to be smashed for the bird/true voice to sing its own song, the inhibited person / prim housing destroyed in the process. The bird's/woman's liberated speech is dismissed as insanity, a charge that still resonates today. This poem, to me, also expresses the fury of someone who had something new and urgent to say, someone who broke ground with her skull but hadn't yet found her sustaining people, the article "a" before "woman" emphasizing her solitary state.

Like Brooks and Plath, Simone Muench and Jackie K. White refer often to music, acts of speech, and wielding weapons in their splendid collaborative sonnets, recently published by Black Lawrence Press in the chapbook *Hex & Howl*. One poem from this collection, "Against Teleology," (p. 97) offers another take on the foundational myth of Western literature, opening with these lines:

> They made Eve an event, a teleology
> we've teethed too many mouths upon, jawing
> uneven through supposed apple skin.

I'm at least as demoralized as everyone else is about the viciously racialized and gendered seizures of our current moment, but I am heartened by the differences that seventy years of concerted protest in deed and word can make. This poem begins with the expected ending, the "Event" of woman as endpoint, scapegoat, and fodder for men who have profited from the suppression and ruin of women, and extrudes that story through the sieve of the sonnet's metanarrative song to result in a new tale with a plural "We" as its protagonists.

In this version, judgment rests with the exiled, and it is their divine right, buttressed by the forces of spirit and nature: "We took the garden with us, now the gavel / is our godhead" (lines 11–12). These speakers reject the blandishments and threats that would kill them, aligning themselves instead, in the last two lines, with "the heart's rattle"—musical instrument, internal beat, snake's tail, a thing that unsettles and shakes things up—with bad Halloween apples "razored at our core"—totally tricks!—and things that cut a perpetrator and the bs yet shimmer like new skin—"Full of sharp. Full of sheen."

The poem's last word "sheen" echoes "satin" from the previous tercet, the cloth's shine outlasting its formerly restrictive role, the poem concluding with this slant-rhymed image resonating sonically and visually, emphasizing that this ending is a beginning. Throughout the poem, Muench and White expand the sonnet's sonic net through idiosyncratic rhythm, alliteration ("fang" to "fallout") and internal rhyme ("*sorry*," "glory," "story" and "exodus," "with us"), amplifying the end rhyme, the associations among these words, and the fact that this Eve is not alone. Full of rings like the reverberations of struck gongs or cascading bells, this sonnet builds on the blood work of Brooks's "timely godmothers" and Plath's unnerving bird to transmute misogyny and rage, with its makers reveling in the sonic booms that they together create.

The dual speaker also implies a sympathetic listener. Unlike Plath's solitary bird whose singing is interpreted as lunacy or Brooks's antagonistic audience requiring her to invoke hate as a shield while performing technical wizardry, Muench and White can anticipate being heard as they speak, employing their own music to expand the sonnet to a kind of trumpet, resounding received form and story to herald a newly attuned era.

Works Cited

Brooks, Gwendolyn. *Selected Poems*. Harper and Row, 1963. Rpt. HarperCollins, 2006.

Plath, Sylvia. *The Collected Poems*. Edited by Ted Hughes, Harper and Row; Faber and Faber, 1981. Rpt. HarperCollins, 2018.

Muench, Simone, and Jackie K. White. *Hex & Howl*. Black Lawrence Press, 2021.

A Plummy Sonnet by Mani Leyb

JORDAN FINKIN

Among the many noteworthy names in American Yiddish poetry, that of Mani Leyb (penname of Mani Leyb Brahinski, 1883–1953) stands out. A native of what is now Ukraine, he immigrated to New York in his early twenties. He spent his ailing and largely impecunious life engaged in two pursuits: making a living as a shoemaker and writing poetry. His career in poetry began as part of a group of American Yiddish poets that came to be known as Di Yunge, or "The Youngsters." These were poets drawn neither to the overt emotionalism nor to the labor didacticism of the preceding generation of Yiddish writers in America. Rather, these poets turned their pens to aestheticist—or what some have called impressionist—verse; that is, capturing small emotional inflections or the "mood" of a situation in pared down and often finely wrought lyrics. Mani Leyb's keen eye for emotional nuance translated well to such an aesthetic, and he produced a body of remarkable poems. Leyb was devoted to the idea of simplicity, which for him meant clarity of image and an aversion to the highfalutin. Often this led him to traditional quatrains, folksongs, and unerring rhymes.

Toward the end of his life, however, after a period in which he wrote very little, he turned, as he convalesced in a tuberculosis sanitorium, to composing a series of sonnets that seem to have been intended as a summative expression of his literary project (Wisse 218–23). In an essay on Mani Leyb, his great friend, the poet Reuben Iceland (1884–1955), expressed his "endlessly deep joy" that for however wonderful Mani Leyb's earlier poetry had been, those poems were but preparation for his sonnets, his "crowning achievement" (104–5). Not collected until after his death, these dozens of sonnets cover a wide range of subjects and themes, all of which are informed by an American context.

By way of background, Hebrew, in the fourteenth century, was the first language after Italian in which sonnets were written. Yiddish, however, remarkably does not seem to have seen a sonnet until the 1890s. For two sibling literary traditions, this historical divergence is notable. Sonnets entered the Yiddish literary bloodstream in two separate places. In Europe, poets such as Leyb Naydus (1890–1918) drew their inspiration from European decadence and symbolism (Finkin, *Exile* 53–78). This in turn would lead to some of Yiddish literature's great modernist sonnets. In America, the first significant sonnets were produced by Fradl Shtok (1890–1990); the intensity and emotional complexity of her sonnets laid the foundation for a significant engagement with "the sexual voice" (Hellerstein 199). Equally striking from a historical perspective is the lateness of Yiddish to this form in particular. This is especially notable given both the importance of the sonnet in shaping the idea of high art and Yiddish's reliance on Western literary forms to expand and burnish its own literary history (Finkin, "What" 93–99). If it wasn't the patina of high art that drew Leyb to the sonnet, then what—in the fifty sonnets published posthumously in the collection *Sonnets* (1962) or the sixty-five in his collected works—accounts for his clear attraction? On the surface level, Leyb was certainly drawn to the rhyming opportunities of the form. After all, at the end of the day "the sonnet is a rhyme-scheme" (Scott 244). But as Leyb notes in his ars poetica, "To My Sonnet," artistry needs to be more than the "cunning" trappings of high art rhymestery. Even more than that, his was a project whose aim was to seal the legacy of a poet absorbed in the multifarious idea of legacy (Finkin, "To Organize" 85).

In the American context, one might have expected a certain thrall to the Shakespearean form. Instead, many of his sonnets are Italian. And what's more, in one of his most famous sonnets, "To the Gentile Poet," he dismisses the relevance of the "heir to Shakespeare, to shepherds and knights" for "a poet of the Jews" who is himself "unneeded." "In an alien world I sing the tears / Of the desert vagabond under alien stars" (Leyb 40). The attitude of these lines marks a rich tradition of distinctly American sonneteering. They describe an affinity with other "outsiders" who use a traditional form to critique both what that form has been made to represent as well as their exclusion from that representation. The sonnets of Countee Cullen or Claude McKay, for example, make a natural analog (Osherow 3).[1]

The newly immigrant form in Yiddish seems to have called to Leyb, the immigrant to America. The sonnet's storied freedom within constraint offers the ideal model for the immigrant and outsider voice struggling in America, no matter how successfully. Leyb used that constrained freedom to think through many of the themes that had appeared in his earlier work, but now with a new vitality. He returns especially to the ironies and emotions of domestic life and the sometimes frank eroticism that he had explored in his early poetry.

Let us take Leyb's sonnet "A Plum" (*p. 32*), its English translation in the anthology section of this volume:

A Floym

In kiln ovnt hot der balebos
fun boym a rayfe floym aropgerisn
ineynem mitn blat, un ayngebisn
di toyik bloye hoyt. Hot fun zayn shlos

der shlofediker zaft geton a gos
mit kiln shoym. Un tsu farshlisn
ir gantsn zaft—a tropn nit fargisn—
hot er pamelekh, vi men trogt a kos

mit vayn, in beyde fule hent di floym
gebrakht der vayb un eydl tsugetrogn
tsu ire lipn. Hot zi mit a libn

"a dank"—fun zayne hent genumen nogn
di floym. Biz in di hent iz im farblibn
di hoyt, dos beyndl un tseklekter shoym. (27)

The first feature to note is that while this is an Italian sonnet, the rhyme scheme of its sestet—*cde dec*—is fairly uncommon and unconventional, a hint at a poet feeling around for new space within an established tradition.

The poem begins with a "husband," using with some irony a Yiddish word (*balebos*) indicating "head of the household"; this gives the scene a bourgeois cast. As the poem unfolds, we see the paterfamilias relishing the sensual act of plucking and biting into a ripe plum. Something about the experience impels him to have his wife share in it. The act of gingerly carrying a partially eaten plum in two hands is treated as something almost ceremonial. The overflowing juice is echoed in the enjambment from octet to sestet, words overrunning the line. It is in the volta, as we anticipate some significant shift, that our attention turns from husband to wife. And in that volta, the image of a man offering fruit to his partner reverses the Adam-Eve dynamic. Not only does it intensify the latent erotic charge in Genesis, it also acts as an antidote to late-marriage tensions. The charge of temptation is defused by the knowingness of their relationship, the proscribed made permissible.

Along with the clear play on the Bible, I am tempted to read a parallel American text to Leyb's poem, namely, William Carlos Williams's "This Is Just to Say." This poem presents an ostensible note left by a husband to his wife, mentioning that he ate all the plums in the refrigerator that she had been saving for her breakfast. The selfishness of the husband who couldn't help himself from eating all his wife's plums and who then goes on to rub her nose in it by describing how sweet and tasty they were is subverted by the solicitousness of Leyb's husband who cannot help but share this treat with his spouse. Indeed, the imagist simplicity of the Williams poem, with its one-, two-, and three-word lines, is refuted by the sonnet form itself; the domestic space can be occupied by more than domestic language. The almost comic moment of Leyb's final stanza—the wife's genteel gratitude before she greedily scarfs down the plum—heartens us to the final assessment that all that was left to them was the spent marc—the residue—of their marriage.

This brief discussion directs us to two significant points. First, America releases a protean, Genesis-like energy and opens a space for reimagining and recreating. A plum tree in a would-be middle-class backyard can make of an older married couple a new Adam and a new Eve. Second, Mani Leyb operated within that American space, relocated the sonnet there, and continued the process of "domesticating" it, both in theme and within the Yiddish literary tradition.

Note

1. For cases in point, see McKay's "If We Must Die" (*The Liberator*, July 1919) or Cullen's "Yet Do I Marvel" (*Color*, Harper and Brothers, 1925, p. 3; reprinted by Western Margin Press, 2021).

Works Cited

Finkin, Jordan. *Exile as Home: The Cosmopolitan Poetics of Leyb Naydus*. Hebrew Union College Press, 2017.

———. "To Organize Beauty: The Sonnets of Mani Leyb." *Studies in American Jewish Literature*, vol. 34, no. 1, 2015, pp. 70–93.

———. "What Does It Mean to Write a Modern Jewish Sonnet?: Some Challenges of Yiddish and Hebrew." *Journal of Jewish Identities* vol. 7, no. 1, 2014, pp. 79–107.

Hellerstein, Kathryn. "The Art of Sex in Yiddish Poems: Celia Dropkin and Her Contemporaries." *Modern Jewish Literatures: Intersections and Boundaries*, edited by Sheila E. Jelen et al. U of Pennsylvania P, 2011, pp. 189–212.

Iceland, Reuben. *Fun unzer friling: Literarishe zikhroynes un portretn.* Inzl, 1954.

Leyb, Mani. *Sonetn.* Di Goldene Pave, 1962.

Osherow, Jacqueline. "A Wanderer in the Desert: How a Tubercular Shoemaker Became a Great Yiddish Poet." *Tablet Magazine*, 23 January 2008, www.tabletmag.com.

Scott, Clive. "The Limits of the Sonnet: Towards a Proper Contemporary Approach." *Revue de littérature comparé*, vol. 50, no. 3, 1976, pp. 237–50.

Wisse, Ruth R., *A Little Love in Big Manhattan.* Harvard UP, 1988.

Eulogizing a Generation in Elizabeth Alexander's "When"

ABDUL ALI

Black death has prompted a number of sonnets that have formed a literary record of how the poet reaffirms humanity in the face of racialized violence on the Black body. Whether we are discussing the latest protest—at this writing, it would be on behalf of Breonna Taylor, the African American woman who was murdered in her own home by agents of the state—or the untold number of Black lives that were killed by mobs in 1919 that inspired Claude McKay to write his canonical "If We Must Die" (*p. 35*), the protest sonnet has endured. Taking McKay's sonnet as exemplar, given its status in the canon of African American letters, we see Black death strictly through a masculine lens, calling for a lock-step militarized response to racialized violence that captures a measured scene of Black male rage, creating a template by which Black sonnets discussing Black death are judged. Nevertheless, our scholarly literature is finally catching up to the reality that Black women have been writing sonnets for a long time, dating back to Phillis Wheatley in the eighteenth century. Without the careful reading of Black women poets alongside Black men in our literary discourses on the sonnet, our record of Black life is incomplete, and so much of our humanity erased. There is much delight in reading the ways in which poet Elizabeth Alexander, while responding to Black death, makes some radical revisions on what we call the "protest sonnet."

Alexander and McKay's poems offer a timely juxtaposition as they engage the topic of Black death using the sonnet form, allowing us to measure attitudes about gender performance and respectability as it relates to living and dying. We can almost feel the heaviness of Black death from McKay's "If We Must Die" as death is invoked six times in varied forms: die, dying, dead, death. But as we read further, we understand that death is not the focal point of the sonnet. The question that McKay raises is "how" do we live. Violent death is a risk for Black people in the poem. Hence, the repeated line, "If we must die." McKay, however, treats death not in absolute terms as he invokes the conjunction "if," making it a conditional prospect. "If we must die / let it not be like hogs." Again, McKay is concerned with how Black men live, if we die, extolling courage and honor as virtues to live by. This poem is a call to arms. The speaker takes on the persona of a general preparing his troops for battle. In these fourteen lines, we get a temperature for the year 1919—perhaps one of the bloodiest summers for Black Americans in history—but also for what the model of Black manhood should look like: fearless, ready for battle, poised for martyrdom.

When we read McKay's "If We Must Die" there is little question as to whether it is a protest poem. The sonnet even ends with the words: "fighting back." Elizabeth Alexander's "When" (*p. 98*), however, illustrates Black men as the opposite of soldiers, taking us off the battlefield. The Black men that inhabit this throwback to the 1980s are "divine, spoke French, had read everything" (line 2). These are the Black men that likely attended Yale with the poet. These are post–civil rights Black men who can choose how and where they'd like to fight. It is only toward the poem's final line that we see that the battle that these Black men are fighting is an internal one. Alexander writes,

> [they] photographed well, did not smoke, said "Ciao,"
>
> then all the men's faces were spotted. (lines 13–14)

This final line describes facial lesions that were consistent with those who were HIV+. The image is significant because it pivots the poem. We do not get any mention of death through the entire poem, and yet it waits ominously in the final line. This choice demonstrates Alexander's dexterity as the poem becomes a double-enclosure structurally; it is silent about the AIDS epidemic within the poem the way many of our communities were in the 1980s—and unfortunately, still are today. The last line breaks the silence, exposing and indicting both the speaker's and our community's silence on this taboo topic. So, in this sense, the poem protests in a subtler way, making the protest more powerfully felt. The fighting here is reading, meditating, raising consciousness about taboo topics such as HIV-AIDS, which is a different kind of fighting than that which McKay calls us to do. And yet, his last two words, "fighting back," have resonance and intertextuality with Alexander's "When."

In the poetic cosmos that these two poets create, Black men in both poems are asked to be fearless as they navigate the world. The intertextuality between the poems suggests that there isn't one way of protesting, which also holds true of Black masculinity. In our society of binaries concerning Blackness and maleness, we are often asked to choose one mode—hetero or gay, hunter rather than hunted, above the ground rather than buried in the ground. These binaries collapse in McKay's and Alexander's poems as the greatest articulation of manhood is being brave and fearless. McKay invites his fellow Black men to fight, and if they should die, they will be rewarded with a "noble death." For Alexander, this love of life and fearlessness opens up possibilities for being. The poet writes that Black men of the 1980s have read "Baraka's / 'Black Art': 'Fuck poems/and they are useful'" (lines 10–11), which is arguably the model manifesto for creating poems and performing masculinity during the Black Arts Movement. Alexander also writes that the Black men of the 1980s "drank espresso with Soyinka and Senghor" (line 9) and "tore up the disco dance floor" (line 12). In these lines we see an expansion of Black male identity that is capacious and translocating. This is how free and multifaceted her male subjects are. And yet, tragically, the Black men in both McKay and Alexander poems await death at the conclusion of their poems.

The formal choices of both McKay's and Alexander's poems are what make their sonnets ultimately political. McKay chose to write "If We Must Die" as a Shakespearean sonnet, in iambic pentameter, giving the subjects of racialized violence the literary respectability that comes with this revered European form, thus promising a mainstream audience. The poem was published in *The Liberator* magazine in the summer of 1919, which historians have dubbed "Red Summer," a bloody few months in 1919 where racial violence reached a boiling point, claiming the lives of many African American men, women, and children. The poem was then reprinted in numerous other literary journals outside the United States, bringing international attention to Red Summer. Putting these sentiments in a poem with its music, its grief, and its outrage proved to be an effective tool of protest as well as a monumental literary achievement in American letters.

Alexander's sonnet "When" reads like a list or catalog of cultured Black men that hardly registers as political. But in her employment of the blazon, typically reserved for praising the female body, we see the political work of the poem come into focus. The poet writes:

> In the early 1980s, the black men
> Were divine, spoke French, had read everything,
> Made filet mignon with green peppercorn sauce (lines 1–3)

This different kind of political work that Alexander employs lies in shifting our aesthetic, elevating a marginalized group to divine status. Alexander decenters whiteness, allowing the Black men to live free of racialized violence. It is the world stage of culture, where these Black men are able to be present, showing off their brilliance, linguistic and culinary skills—images that we often don't associate with Black men on the six o'clock news.

Alexander puts Black men in a rare backdrop to show their collective fabulosity, Black excellence, their loving relationships with Black women. By elevating these Black male lives, the speaker compels the reader to be invested in their productivity to the culture and right to live. The poet closes the poem in these two lines:

> [they] photographed well, did not smoke, said "Ciao,"
> Then all the men's faces were spotted.

The white space between the last two lines of the poem creates a dramatic tension for the reader to meditate on both the crowded, multifaceted lives Black men led juxtaposed with the silent killer that was HIV-AIDS, specifically in the 1980s.

A reading of both Claude McKay's and Elizabeth Alexander's sonnets offers an inescapable view of Black death. Notice that in McKay's "If We Must Die," there are no time markers situating the poem in a particular time and place, thus, giving the poem a timeless shelf life, witnessing Black death through the decades—from Red Summer to Emmett Till to Breonna Taylor, capturing our contemporary moment.

In sharp contrast, Elizabeth Alexander's sonnet "When" is necessarily focused on the 1980s. Thirteen lines of the sonnet praise Black men for their divinity, for being extraordinary in every category—well-read, well-traveled, concerned about the transformative powers of Black art—and yet these Black men are not protected from this ubiquitous Black death that ravaged queer communities of the 1980s.

So what is the meaning of all this Black death? Alexander's poem doesn't pretend to have an answer. That is not the purpose of her sonnet. The design of her poem is similar to an unveiling of a life-size work of visual art; the poem seduces us to see all of its bright colors, textures, and unexpected movements, then boom, we are punched in the eye by the big reveal. That is to say, beauty and life are fleeting. And what is the Black artist's responsibility in recording such short-lived beautiful lives?

Claude McKay's Shakespearean sonnet, "If We Must Die" is designed like an argument: there's exposition, metaphors, and a thesis, recognizing the real prospect of death. His proposed solution is confrontation: that we must confront death with courage, with clear eyes, and that we never suffer it quietly. But it is the final line of the poem that signals a resolution: the poet writes, "Pressed to the wall, dying, but fighting back." The act of fighting back—resistance—is our own saving grace.

Juxtaposed, these two sonnets come full circle. McKay warns us not to fear death but cowardice instead. And that resistance should be our weapon of choice. For Alexander, the fight is more about breaking silence, having close engagement with our dearly beloveds, loving them hard and without condition. It is her sonnet of the 1980s that memorializes all those Black queer lives that were ended prematurely because of HIV-AIDS, or arguably, silence. For Alexander, remembering, writing, bearing witness is the weapon of choice against erasure.

Works Cited

Alexander, Elizabeth. "When." *American Sublime.* Greywolf, 2005, p. 10.
McKay, Claude. "If We Must Die." *The Liberator.* July 1919, p. 21. *Poetry Foundation,* www.poetryfoundation.org/poems/44694/if-we-must-die.

Animals and the Self in Henri Cole's *Middle Earth*

YUKI TANAKA

A lyric poem happens in a moment of solitude, away from others. In her book on Shakespeare's sonnets, Helen Vendler singles out this solitariness as a hallmark of lyric poetry: "The lyric... gives us the mind alone with itself. Lyric can present no 'other' as alive and listening or responding in the same room as the solitary speaker" (19). But what would happen if others are insistently present in the same room, and if these others are nonhuman characters? How would their presence change the status of a solitary speaker and hence expand our understanding of the sonnet as a genre?

Henri Cole has been writing free-verse sonnets over two decades, starting most notably with *The Visible Man* (1998) and *Middle Earth* (2003). *Middle Earth* was written during his fellowship year in Japan, the country of his birth. In 2001, Cole returned to Japan for the first time at the age of forty-five and started writing sonnets inspired by his immediate surroundings. From these poems, a new self emerges. In *Middle Earth*, the speaker interacts with animals as though they were his equals. Animals are present in his earlier books, but in *Middle Earth* they have more agency and seem to act on their own will, giving the speaker another perspective from which to see himself. Cole presents himself not in isolation but in relation to others, creating a less solipsistic kind of lyric.

Animals do appear in *The Visible Man*—the first book where Cole openly writes about his homosexuality—but they are often subsidiary to the human drama of desire. "Horses" is a good illustration of the secondary role animals play in this earlier work. The horses are first introduced as real, but they quickly become figurative. The poem begins: "Setting out on my bicycle alone, / I came upon the horses / drenched in bright sunshine" (41). Seeing the contentment of these horses, the speaker imagines himself being transformed into a horse. In the closing lines, the real horses disappear, replaced by a psychological landscape: "Flinching there on my haunches, / nipping the air as if it were green grass, / how I yearned for my neck to be brushed!" (41). The horses in the opening become a metaphor in the end, embodying the speaker's desire to be loved.

In *Middle Earth*, however, animals are more grounded as physical beings. Very often in the book, nonhuman characters insist on being noticed and force their way into the speaker's meditations. The poem, "Necessary and Impossible," ends: "I sit on a rock, / tearing up bread for red and white carp / pushing out of their element into mine" (28). In "Morning Glory," the flower is "climbing toward me" (30). In "Myself with Cats," the speaker observes a feline interaction: a cat "thrusts / his ugly tortoiseshell body against hers, / sprawled in my cosmos" (31). "Melon and Insects" begins: "Pedaling home at twilight, I collided / with a red dragonfly" (33). Some of these encounters are violent ("push," "thrust," "collide"), emphasizing the existence of a physical world outside the self. These nonhuman characters have bodies and can "collide" with the speaker. Their otherness is acknowledged; they are not easily subsumed into the speaker's thinking and feeling.

The presence of these creatures has a humbling effect. The speaker—a thinking and feeling "I"—is no longer the center of the universe. In another sonnet, the speaker sees himself through the eyes of a praying mantis: "she seemed to view me with deep feeling, as if I were / St. Sebastian bound to a Corinthian column / instead of just Henri lying around reading" (32). These lines mark a clear departure from *The Visible Man*. Written during Cole's stay in Rome, *The Visible Man* draws its imagery from Italian art. While "St. Sebastian" recalls the diction of this earlier book, such lofty language is then critiqued, mocked, and replaced by a simpler description of "Henri lying around reading." There is a touch of humility, a lack of self-aggrandizement through poetic language. Seeing himself through the eyes of the insect, the speaker comes back to a humble reality where he lies on the futon and reads. The praying mantis even mocks the speaker's tendency to dramatize his loneliness: "then she started / mimicking me, lifting her arms in an attitude / of a scholar thinking or romantic suffering" (32).

Cole's ability to acknowledge the presence of others—to see himself through the eyes of animals and insects rather than using them as part of his own psychological landscape—is something I cherish about *Middle Earth*. Not only does Cole avoid objectifying animals as mere symbols;

he responds to them with the kind of affection one directs to friends and lovers. Cole has cited Elizabeth Bishop as an influence on his poetry—another poet who was drawn to animals—but these sonnets in *Middle Earth* also show differences from Bishop's poems. In both poets' works, animals are physically present and seem real rather than imagined. But in Bishop's work, these animals rarely confront the speaker in a way they do in Cole's work. Think of any of the famous Bishop poems. "The Fish" is full of visual details, but it is hard to tell whether the speaker is actually touching the caught fish. In "At the Fishhouses," a seal emerges from the ocean to give the observer a "shrug"—a kind of mocking gesture you might expect in Cole's work—but from a distance. In "The Moose," the animal appears on the road while the speaker admires it from the bus. Unlike Bishop, Cole relates to animals through touch: "Holding him firmly / against my chest, kissing his long white ears, / tasting earth on his fur and breath" ("The Hare" 6). It is difficult to find such extremely close, tactile relationships to animals in Bishop's poems.

In *Middle Earth*, such physical encounters represent interpersonal relationships that depart from the kind described in *The Visible Man*, which takes a hard look at feelings of shame, self-hatred, lust, bitterness, cruelty and also explores the violence people inflict on one another. Moreover, one of the book's themes is the inability to love, to relate to others: "Because I was not loved, / I cannot love. Sometimes I think I am not alive / but frozen like debris in molten glass" (62). In *Middle Earth*, the mood changes; the speaker becomes more forgiving toward himself, toward others whom he has loved. The opening poem of *Middle Earth* strikes a new tone of sincerity and appreciation—"Thank you, / Mother and Father, for creating me"—announcing a departure from what Cole described as his "most astringent book" ("The Art of Poetry" 149). Similarly, he writes in "My Tea Ceremony": "I don't want to hate anymore. I want love / to trample through my arms again" (39).

This renewed sense of love stems in part from the way the speaker interacts with animals. In their presence, it becomes much easier to be emotionally vulnerable. To show affection to another person always involves the risk of rejection, betrayal, and disappointment. But one can show love to animals and insects without worrying about whether love will be reciprocated; one can be mocked without feeling humiliated. The pain of human relationships, through these nonhuman characters, is purged for a moment; as a result, *Middle Earth* has a greater degree of tenderness than his previous book. The speaker is willing to be vulnerable as he comes into contact with these animals that bear no malice and make no judgment, that do no real physical harm to the speaker.

The sonnet "Original Face" illustrates this recuperative process. The speaker describes how psychological tug-of-war with other humans has hardened him: "The real characters and events would hurt me. / The real lying, shame and envy would turn / even a pleasure-loving man into a stone" (lines 6–8). But at the volta, his "plain human flesh wakes up" and sees "real sparrows skimming the luminous / wet rooftops" (lines 9–11), and all the negative feelings that plague human relationships are washed away. In the final couplet, the speaker lets himself be vulnerable again, exposing his "original face" to be touched by morning light: "the ivory hands of morning touching / the real face in the real mirror on my bureau" (lines 13–14). The image of "hands" suggests that the speaker might still discover intimacy with another human being, just as he was able to take simple pleasure in the immediate presence of the sparrows.

Such physical others do not fit easily within the conventional definition of lyric poetry. This definition holds that lyric is about a self in solitude, a speech overheard, words said when there is no one else in the room. In that sense, the sonnet is a quintessential lyric form as it enacts a solitary mind in action, its twists and turns highlighted by the structure of octave, volta, and sestet. But while gazing into himself so deeply, Cole never forgets that he is part of a larger world, constantly thinking of himself in relation to other beings, even inviting them to come closer, letting them touch him. In his hands, the sonnet becomes an all-inclusive yet intimate form, a seemingly tiny room one can share with others.

Works Cited

Cole, Henri. "The Art of Poetry No. 98." Interview by Sasha Weiss. *The Paris Review*, vol. 56, no. 209, Summer 2014, pp. 146–82.

———. *Middle Earth*. Farrar, Straus and Giroux, 2003.

———. *The Visible Man*. Farrar, Straus and Giroux, 1998.

Vendler, Helen. *The Art of Shakespeare's Sonnets*. Belknap Press of Harvard UP, 1997.

Acknowledgments

We thank the poets, scholars, and sonnet enthusiasts who showed up to the Sonnets from the American Symposium to discuss sonnets in a pandemic year. The symposium was entirely free and open to the public thanks to the sponsorship of the Writing Seminars at Johns Hopkins University and *The Hopkins Review*. This project has received additional support from the Department of English at Johns Hopkins University and the English Language and Literature Department at Stevenson University.

Index

Abu-Deeb, Kamal, 143
Abushanab, Chad, 294–95
Adams, John Quincy, 151–52
Adorno, Theodor, 143, 188
Alexander, Elizabeth, 222, 224, 227; "When," 98, 350–54
Ali, Agha Shahid, 88, 134
Alighieri, Dante, 142, 253, 268, 304, 322
Alleau, Rene, 337
Alvarez, Julia, 89
American Sign Language poetry, 242
"Americanness" of American sonnets, 3, 32, 133–38, 233; domestic desolation, 314–18; formal radicalism, 154–55, 158, 161–67, 231, 273, 291–92, 304; Ginsberg on "an American sentence," 204; nationalism in early American sonnets, 146–52
Anarchiad, The (mock epic), 147
Anderson, Maggie, 229, 230; "Sonnet for Her Labor," 86, 232–33
Appalachia: Affrilachian sonnet, 229–31; stereotypes of, 229
Asad, Talal, 142
Ashbery, John, 155, 189n3, 285
Atsitty, Tacey M., 123
Atwood, Mary Anne, 337–38

Bakhtin, Mikhail, 135
Baldwin, James, 98
Baraka, Amiri, 98, 283
Baudelaire, Charles, 172–74
Bell, Catherine, 141
Bellay, Joachim du, 149
Benét, Stephen Vincent, 216–17, 219
Benjamin, Walter, 302n2
Bennett, Gwendolyn, 333
Bergengruen, Werner, 137
Bernstein, Charles, 107; "Questionnaire," 90–91, 201–11
Berrigan, Ted, 286; "Sonnet XXXIV," 70
Berryman, John, 204, 305
Bervin, Jen, 85, 107–08
Bingham, Kate, 313
Bishop, Elizabeth, 263, 357; "Sonnet," 48–49, 273–75, 276; "Sonnet of Intimacy," 48–49
Black Arts Movement, 78, 221, 222, 225, 352
Black diaspora, 21, 197, 215
Blackmur, R. P., 185, 210
Blake, William, 33
Bloom, Harold, 135
blues form, 43–44, 100, 113, 223, 288
Blunk, Jonathan, 66
Bogan, Louise, 38, 41
Boland, Eaven, 271
Booth, Mark W., 139
Botha, Marc, 300

Bromwich, David, 260, 261, 266
Bronson, Ruth Muskrat, 40
Brooks, Gwendolyn, 155, 223, 224–25, 326–32, 333–38, 340–42; alchemy in, 335, 337–38; *The Anniad*, 328, 329; "the children of the poor," 340–41, 342; "kitchenette building," 54, 326, 328–30; "A Lovely Love," 55, 333–38; "my dreams, my works, must wait until after hell," 328, 330–32; "the rites for Cousin Vit," 54, 140–43, 269; "the sonnet-ballad," 288, 294, 328, 329–30; "The Womanhood," 141, 340–42
Brown, Jericho, 155, 235–40; "Duplex," 112, 239; "The Tradition," 113, 237–38
Brown, Mike, 113, 237
Brown, Sterling, 216, 224
Browning, Elizabeth Barrett, 40, 49, 313, 333
Bryant, William Cullen, 146–47; "Sonnet—To an American Painter Departing for Europe," 11, 151–52; translation by, 2, 172
Burke, Edmund, 300
Burns, Robert, 285
Burt, Stephanie, 139, 288

Catullus, 79, 269–70, 315
Caws, Mary Ann, 281, 283
Chang, Jennifer, 204
chant, 288–89
Charleston, Cortney Lamar, 293
Chase, Lewis B., 263
Chesnutt, Charles, 251–52
Churchill, Winston, 223
Clifton, Lucille, 38, 133; "the death of fred clifton," 72; Lorde and, 227n6
Cole, Henri, 95, 142, 355–58
Coleman, Wanda, 3, 82–83, 106, 138, 155
Coleridge, Samuel T., 33, 301
Collier, Mary, 156
Collins, Billy, 134, 155
colonialism, 191, 194, 197; decolonization, 176
concrete poetry, 57
Cornell, Joseph, 278–84
Crane, Hart, 188
Cullen, Countee, 171, 175–76, 203, 223–24, 346; Baudelaire translations by, 172–74; "From the Dark Tower," 45

Culler, Jonathan, 140–41, 145, 281–82
Cummings, E. E., 161–67, 207, 210, 224, 225; "next to of course god america i," 39, 163–66

Damon, S. Foster, 187
Darwish, Mahmoud, 143
Davis, Doris, 300
Day, Meg, 84, 242–46; "Boy Corona," 124–25, 245; "Deafing," 125
dialect poetry, 249–53
Diaz, Natalie, 115–16
Dick, Bruce, 230
Dickinson, Emily, 256
disability poetics, 242–46
Donne, John, 85, 139, 178, 188, 261, 301; Day on, 245–46; on sonnets, 313
Douglass, Frederick, 51, 253
Dove, Rita, 136–38, 140, 170, 304
Dryden, John, 327
DuBois, W. E. B., 194
Duck, Stephen, 156
Dunbar, Paul Laurence, 223, 249–53, 288; in Jess, 305, 308; "Slow through the Dark," 22
Dunbar-Nelson, Alice Moore, 29
Duncan, Robert, 283
Dwight, Timothy, 147

Easthope, Antony, 291
Edwards, Brent Hayes, 177, 179
elegies, 77, 100, 121, 141, 142, 232, 256, 269
Eliot, T. S., 159n2, 177, 187, 201, 223, 263
Eller, Ronald, 229
Ellison, Ralph, 336
Emerson, Ralph Waldo, 255; "Woods: A Prose Sonnet," 12, 153–54, 158, 159n1
Espaillat, Rhina P., 68, 89
Euripides, 172, 316

Faizullah, Tarfia, 84, 117–21
Faraday, Michael, 211
feminism, 1–2, 3, 50, 69, 86, 102, 221–22, 226, 230
Finch, Annie, 292, 298
Finkin, Jordan, 32, 347
Finney, Nikky, 230
Fisher, Mark, 299, 301–02
Floyd, George, 192, 193, 196

Ford, Karen, 224
Francini, Antonella, 304
free-verse sonnets, 13, 39, 75, 155, 158, 162, 184, 201, 232, 319, 355
Freeman, John, 302
Freneau, Philip, 146
Frost, Robert, 207, 209–10, 255, 257, 294, 300, 315; "Acquainted with the Night," 203–04, 262, 315; "Design," 262, 264, 265, 300; "Hyla Brook," 28, 265; Shakespeare and, 260–64; "The Silken Tent," 261–62; Wordsworth and, 263–66
Fussell, Paul, 202, 204–05, 267

Garner, Eric, 113, 196, 237
Gates, Henry Louis, 288
ghazal form, 88, 113, 239, 305
Ginsberg, Allen, 204, 242
Goll, Claire, 173
Gravendyk, Hillary, 246
greathouse, torrin a., 125, 207; "Ars Poetica," 128, 211
Greene, Roland, 140
Griffin, Barbara Jackson, 192
Guillén, Nicolás, 44, 175–76

Hacker, Marilyn, 76
Hahn, Kimiko, 128
Hall, Manly P., 337–38
Hammer, Langdon, 297
Harlem Renaissance, 44, 45, 170–76, 197, 304, 319, 333; Lorde and, 222, 223–24
Hass, Robert, 13, 155
Hayden, Robert, 29, 51, 333
Hayes, Terrance, 133, 136, 143, 144n10, 155, 203; *American Sonnets for My Past and Future Assassin*, 105–06, 138–40, 168n4, 271, 327; "Sonnet," 236, 288–89
Healy, Margaret, 334, 335
Heaney, Seamus, 265, 266
Hecht, Anthony, 59–61
Hejinian, Lyn, 74–75, 91, 204
Hellerstein, Kathryn, 34
Herbert, George, 142, 204, 268–69
Hill, Leslie Pinckney, 31
Hirsch, Edward, 243, 244, 271
Hong, Anna Maria, 102, 293–94
Hong, Cathy Park, 204
Hopkins, Gerald Manley, 203
Hoppenthaler, John, 232

Housman, A. E., 185
Howarth, Peter, 209, 223, 225
Hughes, Langston, 171, 222, 223–24, 291; "Seven Moments of Love," 43–44, 175–76, 288
Humphreys, David, 146–52; "Sonnet III," 9, 149–50
Huntingdon, Selina Hastings, Countess of, 159n8

iambic pentameter: tradition of, 141, 201, 236, 267, 291
Iceland, Reuben, 345
immigration, 89, 193, 194, 323, 346–47
Iowa Writers' Workshop, 214, 219n1

Jackson, Helen Hunt, 16
Jackson, Lawrence, 216
Jackson, Virginia, 281
Jefferson, Thomas, 159n7, 235–36
Jess, Tyehimba, 304–08; "Millie and Christine McKoy," 99, 305–06
Johnson, Helene, 319–25, 333; "A Missionary Brings a Young Native to America," 46, 319–22, 324; "Sonnet to a Negro in Harlem," 46, 319, 320, 322–24
Johnson, James Weldon, 171–72; "Plácido's Farewell to His Mother," 21, 172–73, 176
Jordan, June, 71, 76, 82

Kane, Daniel, 286
Kearney, Douglas, 110
Keats, John, 33, 111, 244, 261; "Bright Star," 329; "Endymion," 173; "If by Dull Rhymes Our English Must Be Chain'd," 140; negative capability of, 258; "On First Looking into Chapman's Homer," 135
Keller, Lynn, 1–2, 76
Kenney, Richard, 87
King, Martin Luther Jr., 336
Komunyakaa, Yusef, 233, 304

Language Poetry, 75, 91, 159n2
Larkin, Joan, 73
Lazarus, Emma, 89; "Assurance," 17–18; "The New Colossus," 17–18
Lentini, Giacomo da, 143, 244
lesbian poetry, 18, 67, 73, 76, 222, 227

Levertov, Denise, 233
Levin, Phillis, 139, 267, 270
Lewis, C. S., 140
Leyb, Mani, 32, 345–48
Longenbach, James, 263
Longfellow, Henry Wadsworth, 146–47, 252
Lorde, Audre, 38, 72, 221–27, 242
Lowell, Amy, 25
Lowell, Robert, 314, 315–16; "History," 53
lynching, 31, 84, 139, 194–95, 304, 338. *See also* McKay, Claude: "The Lynching"
lyric poetry, 139–41, 143, 163, 188, 224, 231, 275, 281–82, 355

Mackey, Nathaniel, 283
MacLeish, Archibald, 139
Magnusson, Lynne, 192
Mariani, Paul, 53
Marshall, Nate, 127, 289
Mason, David, 299
Masters, Edgar Lee, 166
Maxson, H. A., 265
Mayer, Bernadette, 285; "Sonnet (You jerk you didn't call me up)," 79, 269–71
Mayne, Seymour, 276
McClellan, George Marion, 20
McDougall, Brandy Nālani, 114
McGurl, Mark, 214, 219n1
McKay, Claude, 155–56, 170, 177–81, 191–97, 203, 346; "America," 35, 134–36, 143, 155, 191, 192, 195–96; "If We Must Die," 35, 223, 231, 350–54; "The Lynching," 191, 192, 193–94
McSweeney, Joyelle, 84, 111, 135, 143
Mei-en, Lo Kwa, 84, 126
Melville, Herman, 83
Meredith, George, 203, 317
Merrill, James, 62–65, 314, 316–18
Metres, Philip, 104
Meyer, Leonard, 287, 288
Michaels-Dillon, Athena Lynn, 207
Mikics, David, 139
Millay, Edna St. Vincent, 72, 221, 223, 291; "Sonnets from an Ungrafted Tree," 37–38, 314–15
Millhauser, Steven, 296
Milton, John, 148–49, 159n5, 163, 242, 264, 266

minimalism, 41, 58, 276n1
Moore, Alice, 249, 251, 252, 253
Moraes, Vinicius de, 48
Moretti, Franco, 135
Morton, David, 162–63
Muench, Simone, and Jackie K. White, 97, 343–44
Müller, Timo, 134, 136, 215, 276n3

Native Americans, 16, 40, 150
Naydus, Leyb, 346
Nelson, Marilyn, 84, 133
Neruda, Pablo, 122
Nerval, Gérard de, 279
New Formalism, 68
New Lyric Studies, 281–82, 283
Nielsen, Aldon Lynn, 288–89
Nurhussein, Nadia, 253

Obama, Barack, 195
O'Hara, Frank, 278, 280–81, 283
Oppenheimer, Paul, 139, 153
Orage, A. R., 333, 335–36

Padgett, Ron, 270–71, 286–88
Perez, Craig Santos, 122
Petrarch, Francesco, 2, 25, 140, 178, 257, 322
Petrosino, Kiki, 133
Phillips, Carl: "Givingly," 96; on sonnets, 201–06
Plácido, 2, 21, 172
Plath, Sylvia, 314, 316; "Sonnet: To Eva," 69, 342–43, 344
Plato, 179
Poovey, Mary, 281
Pope, Alexander, 156, 159n5
Posey, Alexander, 23, 29
Pound, Ezra, 159n2, 283, 301
Prima, Diane di, 222
Prins, Yopie, 281
prose poems, 66, 308; Emerson's prose sonnet, 12, 153–54
protest in poetry, 192–93, 343, 350–52
Prynne, J. H., 299
Pugh, Christina, 268

queerness, 185, 201–02, 225–27, 242, 245, 273–74, 276, 353–54; neuroqueerness, 91, 109, 207–12

racial violence, 35, 191, 237, 350–54. *See also* lynching
radio: poetry on, 182–83, 187–88
Redling, Erik, 251
Reed, Ishmael, 225
Reese, Lizette Woodworth, 19
Regan, Stephen, 139–40, 147
repeated-line sonnets, 285–89; Brown and, 235–36
Reynolds, Barbara, 268
Rich, Adrienne, 38, 71, 76, 133, 201, 203, 216, 226; "Twenty-One Love Poems," 67
Ridge, Lola, 24
Robbins, Hollis, 140, 215
Robinson, Edwin Arlington, 163, 166, 314
Ronsard, Pierre de, 244
Rosenblitt, J. Allison, 210
Rosenfeld, Alvin H., 187
Rosenthal, M. L., 53
Rosetti, Dante Gabriel, 140
Rosier, J. Howard, 289
Rukeyser, Muriel, 50
Rush, Sam, 245
Ryan, Kay, 296–302; "New Rooms," 80, 296, 298–99, 301; "Say Uncle," 80, 297

Said, Edward, 143
Saintsbury, George, 302
Sassen, Saskia, 178, 273
Schwartz, Lloyd, 273–74
Scott, Rebecca, 229
Scott, Winfield Townley, 183
self-reflexivity (and self-metaphorization), 134–35, 138–39, 140, 143, 285, 313; "metasonnetry," 162
Senghor, Léopold Sédar, 98, 352
Seuss, Diane, 94, 204
Shakespeare, William, 13, 45, 135, 138, 141, 178, 192, 202, 203, 223, 252, 269, 327; Brooks and, 334–37; Frost and, 260–64; Leyb and, 346; plays: *Hamlet*, 282, 335, 337; *Romeo and Juliet*, 335; sonnets: #8, 85, 138; #18, 261; #22, 107; #23, 140; #66, 285; #68, 108; #102, 138; #116, 260, 261, 262; #126, 334; #127, 334; #130, 139, 334; Taylor and, 282
Shapiro, Karl, 136
Shelley, Percy Bysshe, 33, 134, 155, 192, 196

Shenstone, William, 159n5
short-lined sonnets, 72, 273–76, 297, 298
Shtok, Fradel, 32, 34, 346
Shurin, Aaron, 85, 108
Sidney, Philip, 164–65, 178, 266
Siegel, Linda S., 210
Simic, Charles, 280, 281, 283
singleton, giovanni, 103
Skeltonics, 297
Smith, Barbara Herrnstein, 287
Smith, Charlotte, 256, 257
Smith, Elizabeth Oakes, 2
Smith, Patricia, 203, 291; "Salutations in Search Of," 92–93
Solt, Mary Ellen, 57
sonnet: as box, 278–84, 298, 299; etymology of, 136, 139–40, 320; formal features of, 2, 22, 65, 66, 136, 139–40, 147, 163, 204–06, 215, 236, 244, 256, 267, 285, 313–14, 320; history of, 1–2, 58, 134, 136–37, 143, 146–52, 162, 170, 304, 313, 327; Italian vs. English, 202, 204–05, 267; marginalized appeal of, 201–04, 206, 229; political uses of, 148–49, 164–66, 215–17, 264; portraiture in, 163, 166; rebellious appeal of, 201, 204–06; ritual qualities of, 140–43; song and, 319–24; translation of, 170–76. *See also* free-verse sonnets; repeated-line sonnets; short-lined sonnets; *tenzone*; voltas
sonnet crowns, 84, 111, 121, 133, 177–78
Soyinka, Wole, 98, 352
Spenser, Edmund, 178, 203, 298
Spiegelman, Willard, 300, 301
Spoon, Nathan: "Kiddo," 109, 209; on neuroqueerness, 207–12
Stavros, George, 326, 331
Stein, Gertrude, 287–88; "Sonnets That Please," 26–27
Stern, Gerald, 155
Sterner, Lewis G., 146
Stevens, Wallace, 137
Stewart, Susan, 179
Su, Adrienne, 101, 273, 274–76
sublime, the, 300

Tate, James, 285
Taylor, Ken, 278–84
tenzone (sonnets as dialogue), 97

Terence, 157
Thomas, Dylan, 140
Thomas, Lorenzo, 78, 216
Thompson, Dunstan, 56
Thompson, Virgil, 27
Thomson, Rosemarie Garland, 307
Thoreau, Henry David, 256
Thorsson, Courtney, 327
Thurman, Wallace, 252
Till, Emmett, 84, 133
Tolson, Melvin, 224, 333
translation issues. *See* sonnet: translation of
transnationalism, 3, 49, 135, 137, 142, 176, 232; Black transnationalism, 21, 36, 170–73, 176
Trethewey, Natasha, 44, 100
Tuckerman, Frederick Goddard, 255–59, 314; "Sometimes I walk where the deep water dips," 14–15, 256–57, 258; "That boy, the farmer said, with hazel wand," 14, 255
Turner, Darwin T., 252
Turner, Victor, 142
Tyler, Meg, 139

Untermeyer, Louis, 3, 264

van der Noot, Jan, 149
Van Duyn, Mona, 58
Vendler, Helen, 355
Very, Jones, 255
Voigt, Ellen Bryant, 77, 270
voltas, 267–71, 273, 321; in Anderson, 222; in Bishop, 274; in Brooks, 141, 269, 334; in Cummings, 164, 167; in Emerson, 153; in Frost, 263, 264; in Hayes, 105, 138–40, 271; in Herbert, 268–69; in Johnson, 321; in Lorde, 225; in Mayer, 269–70, 271; in McKay, 134; in Padgett, 270–71; in Ryan, 298; in Smith, 256; in Wordsworth, 269

W1XAL (radio station), 182–83, 187
Wakoski, Diane, 233
Walker, Frank X, 229–31, 233
Walker, Margaret, 214–19, 333; "The Struggle Staggers Us," 52, 217
Walker, Nick, 207
Wall, Cheryl, 223
Wang, Dorothy, 275
Warhol, Andy, 286
Watkins, Lucian B., 2, 30
Weiman-Kelman, Zohar, 18
Wheatley, Phillis, 156–58, 350; Jefferson on, 159n7; "To the King's Most Excellent Majesty," 156
Wheelright, John, 182–89; "Phallus," 42, 185–86
white supremacism, 170, 191, 195, 196
White-Johnson, Jennifer, 209
Whitman, Walt, 13
Williams, Candace, 235
Williams, William Carlos, 138, 253, 348
Wilson, August, 231
Woodson, Jon, 224
Wordsworth, William, 137, 139, 163, 179, 192–93, 256, 257; Frost and, 263–66; "Nuns Fret Not at Their Convent's Narrow Room," 264, 265, 276n3, 298, 313, 338; volta in, 269
working class, 4, 192, 216, 232, 282
World War I, 62, 317
World War II, 56, 223, 341
Wright, James, 66
Wroth, Mary, 178
Wyatt, Thomas, 204, 327
Wylie, Elinor, 33

Yerby, Frank, 333, 336
Yergeau, M. Remi, 207
Yerman, Forrest, 230
Yiddish sonnet tradition, 346–47